MEMORIES

Anecdotes of a Modern-day Saint

VOLUME 1

MEMORIES
Anecdotes of a Modern-Day Saint

VOLUME 1

Transcriptions from video interviews
conducted and compiled
by Siddhanta das

For more information, contact the Publisher:

MONSOON MEDIA
P. O. Box 1015, Culver City, CA 90232-3415, USA
www.monsoonmedia.org

To inquire about books by His Divine Grace
A.C. Bhaktivedanta Swami Prabhupada, call:1-800-927-4152.

To order more volumes of *Memories: Anecdotes of a Modern-Day Saint*
or *Memories: The Video Series*, please contact:
www.monsoonmedia.org or **www.prabhupada.tv**

Dedicated to

His Divine Grace
A. C. Bhaktivedanta Swami Prabhupada

I offer my respectful obeisances
unto His Divine Grace A.C. Bhaktivedanta Swami
Srila Prabhupada, who is very dear to Lord Krishna
having taken shelter at His lotus feet.

Our respectful obeisances are unto you,
O spiritual master and servant of Sarasvati Goswami.
You are very kindly teaching the message
of Lord Chaitanya Mahaprabhu
to the western countries which are filled
with impersonalism and voidism.

CONTENTS

FOREWORD

WITH THE PUBLICATION in video and print of *Memories of Srila Prabhupada*, Siddhanta has made a contribution of monumental and historical proportions to our understanding of Srila Prabhupada, the modern Gaudiya Vaishnav movement, and human religiosity in general. All too often, the contemporary followers of a great religious leader have failed to adequately record his or her life and teachings, resulting in long centuries of frequently futile debate and conflict among historians and religionists alike.

Thus Siddhanta's documentation in both video and print of the testimonies of Srila Prabhupada's disciples about their master provides an invaluable, irreplaceable, and unique treasure of information to all those who desire today, or seek in the future, an accurate, reliable, true picture of Srila Prabhupada, the founder-*acharya* of the International Society for Krishna Consciousness.

Siddhanta's patient, creative, and professional work will surely be seen by future generations as one of our generation's greatest contributions to the human family. Thus it is with the soundest of reasons that I acknowledge here my deep personal gratitude to Siddhanta, congratulate him on his outstanding achievement, and urge all those seriously interested, for whatever reason, in Krishna, Srila Prabhupada, ISKCON, and spirituality itself, to stock the favorite shelves of their library with the singular treasures of the *Memories* series.

With best wishes,
Hridayananda das Goswami

PREFACE

MY FIRST CONTACT with the Hare Krishna movement came in the summer of 1969 when I saw its members chanting on the streets of Hollywood. My initial reaction to the shaven heads, saffron-colored robes and seemingly strange activity was one of bewilderment and, to some degree, comic relief. It was not until a year later that I was able to appreciate the sound philosophy which stems from one of the world's oldest religious traditions, as explained in their *Back to Godhead* magazine. I soon realized that there was a tremendous wealth of knowledge and logic behind the activities of the International Society for Krishna Consciousness, and that it was far from being a new "hippie" cult. In fact, the information contained in that first magazine concisely answered all the questions I ever had regarding life, its purpose and more.

The next year in Dallas, Texas, it was my good fortune to actually come in personal contact with the author of that *Back to Godhead* magazine, the founder of the Hare Krishna movement, His Divine Grace A.C. Bhaktivedanta Swami Srila Prabhupada. I greeted him along with the other devotees at the airport and then followed the procession back to the temple where Prabhupada gave a Sunday Feast lecture. What struck me most about that lecture more than anything was one question that was asked of him by a member of the audience. Srila Prabhupada had been stressing the importance of chanting the Hare Krishna *maha*-mantra: Hare Krishna Hare Krishna, Krishna Krishna Hare Hare, Hare Rama Hare Rama, Rama Rama Hare Hare, and the guest asked what Srila Prabhupada personally felt when he chanted this mantra. Without hesitation, Srila Prabhupada answered, "I feel no fear." Because his response was so immediate and filled with such conviction, I sensed that not only what he said was true, but I felt an urgency to try the same mantra-meditation process myself.

Over time, it became apparent to many who observed him firsthand that Srila Prabhupada was steadily situated in a higher state of consciousness, beyond anything that was part of our common experience. But that was not all. After a further study of the teachings in his books and observing his interactions with others, I realized that here was a person who was not materially motivated. He was not interested in mundane acquisition, exploitation or adoration. He was also in complete control of his senses, the very foundation of all yoga practice. By his own example, he was a perfect teacher of the divine process of devotional service, or *bhakti-yoga*. And by means of his unconditional love and devotion, he was in touch with and connected to the Supreme Being. His mission appeared to be for all of our best interests by making me and everyone else who cared to listen, spiritually happy by engaging our mind, body, and soul in serving God, Krishna. Srila Prabhupada taught that as a fish out of water cannot be happy out of its constitutional element, water, similarly, we as spiritual beings cannot be happy simply engaging in activities meant to satisfy our material senses.

Years later, after accepting Srila Prabhupada as a pure representative of God and having taken spiritual initiation from him in Denver, Colorado, I had the opportunity to be with him again. Previously I had been convinced on an intellectual level that Prabhupada was in direct contact with the Absolute Truth, but not until I offered flowers at his feet and looked at him as I offered my obeisances did I understand on an emotional level the depth of my guru. When Srila Prabhupada looked at me, he looked right through the external me, touching the internal me, the soul. I felt naked in front of him, feeling as though he could not only read my mind, but my heart as well. It was the most humbling experience of my life.

That morning during Srila Prabhupada's daily walk, he was talking about *prasadam*, food offered to God before it is personally consumed. Prabhupada said *prasadam* is so spiritually potent that if a human being simply eats *prasadam* once, in his next life, he will take birth in a family of devotees. He then stated that if an animal eats *prasadam,* in its next life it will immediately take birth in the human form of life, jumping over all other species of life that a soul would normally have to pass through before obtaining a human birth.

After this discussion, I was contemplating asking him about something that had been bothering me for some time. I had become affected by so many people I met when distributing Srila Prabhupada's books who would say that we as devotees should get jobs and not take from society by asking for donations. I said to Srila Prabhupada, "People think we are just trying to escape material life by joining this *sankirtan* movement." Srila Prabhupada turned to me, smiled and asked, "A rich man, does he work? We are rich men. We don't work. Any rich man, he is not working. Is he escaping? He is engaging everyone in the factory but he is not working. So is that escaping? We are rich men. We are Krishna's sons." He said the problems we have are eating, sleeping, and mating, and we can arrange for these things very easily. Prabhupada taught the philosophy of "Simple Living, High Thinking." One can till the ground anywhere and get some food. He said, "I keep some cows and I have got land. My whole economic question is solved." He asked, "Why shall I make big, big arrangements for these things?" He continued, "You may do it, but why should you forget your real business? That is the defect, that you are so foolish that only for maintaining this body, you have forgotten your real business—self-realization." Prabhupada then said, "In the spiritual world there is no question of working. You get everything. So why not endeavor to go there?"

Prabhupada then looked around the beautiful park that we were walking in, surrounded by trees, lakes, and swans. He noted how there was no one else in the park and how we were the only ones who were taking advantage of the park and all its beauty. He said, "They worked so hard, yet they are sleeping. We are taking advantage." He then told the story of the mouse and the snake. The mouse builds a nice home for himself underground and lives comfortably. Then the snake comes and eats the mouse and lives comfortably in the home the mouse has built. He finished by telling me and the others that accompanied him on his morning walk that we can tell people that actually, "Yes, we are escaping this horrible condition of life—meat-eating, drinking, and intoxication. We are escaping these things, but not happiness."

In his kindness, Prabhupada dispelled my doubt about distributing books rather than living to fulfill the expectations of the public by having a 9-to-5 job. I had been affected by the negative feedback I received from the people I met, but Prabhupada, who was unaffected by them, reminded me that the point of life is self-realization and our role in the *varnashram* scheme of things was to remind others about that fact.

Later on I realized that if I had this small glimpse of truth from being with Srila Prabhupada for such a brief period of time, there must be many more realizations from other devotees who had as much or more association with His Divine Grace. It was obvious that each devotee's encounter would be unique and would reveal other aspects of Srila Prabhupada's personality and boundless wisdom that were not necessarily contained in his books which could help me and others in our daily lives. It is with that belief that I ventured out to acquire the stories contained in this book. These stories are not only informative but also entertaining in the way the devotees express themselves, seemingly going into a regression-type trance as they recall those times spent with Srila Prabhupada. From an historical standpoint, it seemed important to record these personal instructions thinking that if someone had been able to record the recollections of the disciples of Jesus Christ, that these memories would be meaningful today. So starting in 1991, the process of obtaining the oral histories of Srila Prabhupada's disciples began through videotaped sessions and subsequently transcribed to be presented in this book form.

There are no hard and fast rules in reading this collection of memories as they are not recorded in any chronological order or by subject matter. The memories are simply a stream of consciousness by each devotee, and therefore, can be read in a non-linear fashion. This book is meant to be, as Srila Prabhupada stated once about his books, readable in such a way that one can start in the middle and still derive sweetness, as biting into candy anywhere will result in the same sweet taste. As there were some 5,000 initiated disciples, this process has just begun, and we hope that there will be more volumes to come in the future.

We must thank Nitai das, Kartika, Kishore das, Raghunath das, Vikram das, Jalandhar das, and Kalpalatika dasi for their hard work in the transcription process; Kapila das and Ram Prasad das for their proofreading; Sri Kanta for his proofreading and assembly of the Glossary; Visakha dasi for her tremendous work in refining the transcriptions; and Bhojadev das for his assistance with the Introduction. This publication would not be in its present form without the hard work and patience of two members of the *Back to Godhead* staff: Yamaraja das who formatted the book and also beautifully designed the cover, and Nagaraja das who contributed valuable assistance and suggestions. We want to acknowledge Bhakta Jack Stephens, Dr. N. D. Desai, and Ambarish das for their encouraging words and financial support in bringing Srila Prabhupada's message to the world. I also want to acknowledge my wife, Ajita devi, and daughters Kartika and Renukah for their emotional and spiritual support in this ongoing project. We of course would be remiss not to give our heartfelt appreciation to all the devotees who shared their memories of Srila Prabhupada, and we pray that we have delivered their stories accurately.

Siddhanta das

INTRODUCTION

sadhu-sanga, sadhu-sanga—sarva-sastre kaya
lava-matra sadhu-sange sarva-siddhi haya

"The verdict of all revealed scriptures is that by
even a moment's association with a pure devotee, one can attain all success." (Cc 22.54)

THIS BOOK OF ORAL HISTORIES is a word-for-word transcription of
the video series, *Memories of Srila Prabhupada,* which are interviews
of those fortunate souls who had that all-important association with
a pure devotee in the person of His Divine Grace A.C. Bhaktivedanta
Swami Srila Prabhupada. The founder-*acharya* of the International
Society for Krishna Consciousness, His Divine Grace has been well
recognized by scholars, religionists, and lay persons alike, as one
of the most prominent ambassadors of India's spiritual culture in
modern times.

The recollections presented herein are testimony to the transcendental character of Srila Prabhupada, whose purity, compassion, knowledge, humor, humility, strength, and determination
seemed to be almost effortlessly exhibited on a daily basis. To get a
complete picture of Krishna consciousness, it is essential to not only
have the written teachings contained within Srila Prabhupada's
books, but also how he acted in so many circumstances so that we
may follow in his footsteps, as he is a true *acharya,* one who teaches
by example.

Many times Srila Prabhupada did mention that everything he
wanted to tell us was in his books. Yet oral tradition is part of every
society and culture, and we can only offer as a disclaimer that the
interviews documented here have been accepted at face value, with

the onus of veracity left to the integrity of the interviewed party. On our part, we feel all of the accounts are genuine, as many of these events / interactions were witnessed by more than one person.

In his *Prabhupada Nectar* books, His Holiness Satsvarupa das Goswami has chronicled numerous anecdotes in which Srila Prabhupada's transcendental perspective is gloriously revealed through his interaction with his disciples and well-wishers. As mentioned in the Preface to *Prabhupada Nectar*, the glories and pastimes of the Lord's pure servants are seen to be as sweet and instructive as the Lord's own unlimited pastimes.

In the same mood of appreciation for Srila Prabhupada's transcendental glories and instructions, we hope this volume will be of some value for initiates and novices alike who are thirsting for new or revisited facets of the spiritual jewel that is Prabhupada-*sanga*. As the disciples in this book are guaranteed spiritual benefit from the direct contact they had with their spiritual master, it is our hope and prayer that anyone who hears or reads of this relationship with the pure devotee will also receive that same benediction for success in life.

TAPE 1

Hridayananda das Goswami
Hari Sauri das
Atma Tattva das

 **Hridayananda Goswami:** Srila Prabhupada brought me to Krishna consciousness in 1969. I had seen the devotees on the street in Berkeley, and I'd seen the Hare Krishna festival in the Berkeley Hills. I'd given donations, bought magazines, taken *prasadam*, and so on, but it was when I heard Prabhupada give a lecture in the International House at the University of California at Berkeley that I really became fixed on Krishna consciousness.

For a Sociology / Religion class I had to go and observe different religious performances and ceremonies. I had gone to see a so-called swami who seemed like he wasn't saying anything practical or substantial but only telling people how to relax. Just as Prabhupada said that he was reluctant to see his spiritual master because he had seen so many so-called *sadhus,* so in a little way there is some similarity.

As soon as Prabhupada entered the auditorium, I could see that this person was very different—his gravity, his power, his demeanor. He came in practically like a military commander, not in the sense of a violent person but in the sense of his authority. I could see that here was a person who was filled with authority and yet serene at the same time. The program started, the devotees began to chant, and Prabhupada got off the *vyasasana* and

1

began dancing and jumping in ecstasy. To see this holy person, so filled with authority, over 70 years old, dancing in ecstasy, was overwhelming.

 **Hari Sauri:** As Srila Prabhupada's servant, the first instruction he gave me was, "Now your only business is to be with me twenty-four hours a day." I took that quite literally except, of course, when I was asleep. When we were in Vrindavan for ten days, I was able to live in his quarters, and I was with him day in and day out. I got a chance to observe everything that he did, everything that he spoke, and every little action that he made. One of the first things that struck me very strongly was that Prabhupada was like a living, breathing *Srimad-Bhagavatam*.

In the *Bhagavatam* and in volumes and volumes of other books, there's a full description of what it means to be Krishna conscious, and if you read them it might seem as if it's going to take a long time to realize such a vast subject as Krishna consciousness. But it was all there in Srila Prabhupada at every moment. I understood that, and I resolved to take advantage of the opportunity to see him as much as possible. By observing how he did everything, how he managed things, how he spoke, how he walked, how he relaxed, how he dealt individually with different people showed me the best example of Krishna consciousness.

 **Atma Tattva:** Everybody was singing *Sri Guru Charana Padma* while Prabhupada was on the *vyasasana* with his eyes closed, playing the *kartals* and singing. I asked Lokanath Swami, "Isn't this song glorifying Prabhupada?" He said, "Yes." I said, "How come he is singing?" He said, "He's singing it to his spiritual master." The day before Lokanath Swami had asked me to put my name in for initiation. I said, "I am not ready yet." After I heard this explanation from Lokanath Swami I said, "You include my name for initiation."

He said, "Why now, all of a sudden? You always said, 'Wait, wait, wait,' and now you are ready?" I said, "Yes, I can see that he will be my spiritual master because when he is glorified, he glorifies his spiritual master. Now I know that this is actually part of the disciplic succession. Put my name down for initiation." My name was added, Swami Atmananda. I heard from other godbrothers that when Prabhupada was looking at the names for initiation he said, "*Bhakta* this, *bhakta* this, *bhakta* that," and then he said, "Swami? Who is this swami?" Someone told him "It's a new bhakta." Prabhupada said, "New *bhakta,* a swami? All right, what's his name, Atmananda?" Then Prabhupada said, "*apasyatam atma tattvam griheshu grihamedinam.* His name will be Atma Tattva."

Hridayananda Goswami: When I was initiated in Los Angeles, I got a little piece of paper with my name on it, "Hridayananda." For some reason I thought that someone had left out the "a" and that my name was actually "Haridayananda." When people said, "What's your name?" I said, "Haridayananda". It sounded like a perfectly good, Krishna conscious name. No one ever questioned me. No one ever said, "That doesn't sound like a bonafide name." For the first several months after I was initiated, I was Haridayananda. In fact, there's an old *Back to Godhead* article by Haridayananda das Brahmachari. Anyway, I wrote Prabhupada a letter about a year after my initiation, and I signed it "Haridayananda." Prabhupada wrote back saying, "Dear Hridayananda, please accept my blessings. By the way, your name is Hridayananda." I thought, "How in the world would Prabhupada remember who I am?" I had no real importance within the structure of ISKCON, as I was just a young member. I was amazed that Prabhupada remembered who I was.

Hari Sauri: It was Srila Prabhupada's qualities of warmth and kindness that touched me the most. From being with Prabhupada you could immediately understand that he had a genuine concern for your welfare. He was serving us. He was putting himself out in so many different ways just to give us the opportunity for spiritual life. It made you want to reciprocate by offering whatever service you could to Srila Prabhupada. There was nice reciprocation going on.

I always felt very comfortable in Prabhupada's presence. Of course, there was the formal guru-disciple relationship, and one had to be careful not to transgress that, but at the same time, Prabhupada was very accommodating. He was wonderfully warm and humble. He always made you feel wanted. He always made you feel significant in some way. He knew what you were doing, and he was happy with it. He would encourage you. He would also chastise you at different times if you did things wrong, but that chastisement had the same effect as his praise—it made you Krishna conscious. You understood that it was for your own benefit. It was never materially motivated.

Srila Prabhupada was very happy to be with us. He appreciated the fact that young men had given up the best part of their lives for spreading the Krishna consciousness movement, and he always showed that appreciation.

Atma Tattva: For about two weeks before my initiation on Radha-stami Day in Delhi, I had some infection inside my mouth, so I couldn't brush my teeth properly. I was just gargling with hot water and salt. The temple room was small and had a big lotus *vyasasana.* Prabhupada sat at the tip of the *vyasasana,* and I was close to him when I got my beads. He asked, "What are the four regulative principles?" I said, "No meat eating . . ." My mouth was close to his nose, and Prabhupada opened his eyes, looked at me, and said, "Why are you not cleaning your teeth properly?" I said, "Infection." He said, "Infection?" and he turned around and took the *japa* beads from Gopal Krishna and gave them to me, "Chant sixteen rounds." It was as if "infection" was the observation and "chant sixteen rounds" was the prescription. Then he said, "Your name is Atma Tattva das." The devotees banged the *mridunga,* "Haribol!" and I sat down. I was not there. I was thinking, "I got initiated, I have beads, I have a guru," and I was completely emotional.

That evening on the lawn in front of the temple, Prabhupada had an evening *darshan*. I took the *chamara* and fanned him so that I could be close to him. Most probably I was doing a big number on the *chamara*, swinging it very fancifully. Prabhupada was cold. He looked at me, and then I fanned so slowly that flies were sitting on his face. Again he looked at me while he was singing *Jaya Radha Madhava*, and I was scared. I didn't know whether to fan fast or slow. But still I did not want to give up fanning him. He said the "Jaya Om" prayers and then, "Thank you very much." Then he looked at me and said, "Material life is an infection." He lifted his *kurta* and said, "You scratch . . . then you feel satisfied. You scratch more, you feel some satisfaction, and you scratch more. Then you stop. Not because you are satisfied but because blood comes." I didn't hear the rest. I only remember those lines. I was going through my whole life and realizing that this person has gone into me and taken an x-ray and given it to me. He'd caught me exactly, and it was very moving for me. I have heard many disciples say the same thing, that "Prabhupada saw through me." I had faith that it happened, but when it happens to you, it's totally different because it's you, and not somebody else. I was very happy.

Hridayananda Goswami: Karandhar and I were in Prabhupada's room in the early seventies. It was a beautiful afternoon, a breeze was blowing, the sun was setting and golden rays were shining on Prabhupada. It was a sublime atmosphere. Prabhupada began to talk about India at the turn of the century. He explained how people used to work, the relationships between the householders and their servants, and how people used to cook. He took us back to his early childhood when he was having Ratha-yatra and worshipping Radha-Govinda. Then he looked at us very strongly and said, "Whatever I am doing now I was doing then. Do you understand?" We were speechless. Prabhupada said, "Never was there a time when I did not know Krishna. Do you understand?" He said it in such a way that it was clearly the case. That was a very powerful experience.

Hari Sauri: Whenever Prabhupada talked about anything, somehow he would link it to Krishna consciousness and make a spiritual point. For instance, when we were in India he would sometimes talk about how the British ruled and managed India. He would always use that as an example of how we should manage things. Sometimes he would talk about recent Indian history and point out if a person were acting in a spiritual or mundane way. He would relate that to the degradation of Vedic culture.

Prabhupada had a unique ability to see Krishna in everything and to explain things so that we could also see Him. He was teaching us at every moment. He had no private life, for his was the life of an acharya. That meant that he taught by his example at every moment of every day.

He was remarkably consistent, absolutely regular. It always amazed me. We traveled all around the world, and he would keep the same schedule. He would do the same things day in and day out and be completely steady and undisturbed. He would be up in the middle of the night translating his books. He would go out for his morning walk. He would take his massages. He would have his meals at the same time, no matter what. It didn't matter where we were going. I suffered from jetlag as we traveled around. Prabhupada seemed completely impervious to it. It just didn't seem to affect him. He would go right on. As soon as we arrived in the new place, he would immediately resume his schedule. He never showed any sign of fatigue or disturbance.

Atma Tattva: One big businessman said, "Swamiji, I have a factory here in Delhi, and I have a factory in Jaipur. . . ." He listed his things and said, "I have all this, but I can't sleep." Prabhupada said, "You can't sleep because you have so many things. Give them to me, then you can sleep peacefully," and he turned to somebody and said,

"Take his address." The man said, "No Swamiji, I can come any time." "You can come any time, but we should also be able to go to you any time. Take his address." "No, No Swamiji." Prabhupada said, "If you give some of your things to Krishna, you will be peaceful. We will relieve you of your problem." The man was smashed right there, and he gave his address. He had to.

Hridayananda Goswami: We brought Miss Mexico to see Srila Prabhupada. In those days we were young and brought any celebrity to Prabhupada. Miss Mexico spent her years doing events, smiling, saying a few nice words and getting her picture taken. She was more or less in that mood. She sat in front of Prabhupada and made her customary spiel, saying in Spanish that it was very nice being Miss Mexico and fluttering her eyelashes. I was translating. She said, "I am very glad to be here. I have enjoyed the program very much and I hope to come again sometime." Prabhupada said to her, "Why do you want to come again?" He was not at all concerned with the glamour of it. He was very sober. She couldn't really answer. No one asks questions like that to Miss Mexico. He asked her very seriously, "Why do you want to come? Have you read my books?" She said, "No." He said, "Then why do you want to come? Why do you say you want to come again?" So she was caught without an answer, and at that point she stopped being Miss Mexico and just started being a soul.

Hari Sauri: On the Disappearance Day of Srila Bhaktisiddhanta Saraswati we were in Bombay, and in the afternoon a lady came for *darshan*. She was a follower of a well-known Mayavadi guru. During the conversation there was some discussion on the philosophy of the *Bhagavad-gita*, and she espoused her guru's interpretation of Krishna's words. In Sanskrit the word "Krishna" means "dark." So this so-called guru had written that Krishna means dark. Dark means unknown, and so the absolute is the unknowable, unmanifested supreme. Prabhupada quickly fired back, "Well, if dark means unknown, and if Krishna is unknowable, then he does not know Krishna. So why is he commenting on Krishna's words, the *Bhagavad-gita?*" He said, "Krishna says that His devotee can know Him. Because this man is not a devotee, he cannot know Krishna. Only devotees can comment on *Bhagavad-gita.*"

Prabhupada was very expert. He could pick up the basis of anybody's argument immediately. In India there were always a lot of different interpretations, false ideas, and misconstruing of *Bhagavad-gita.* Prabhupada was expert at keeping a person focused on Krishna, the Supreme Personality of Godhead.

Hridayananda Goswami: At the end of July in 1971, Prabhupada came to Gainesville. He sat on the *vyasasana* that we had made for him, gave a beautiful lecture, and then took questions. There was a young girl there, and in a somewhat challenging tone she said to Prabhupada, "I see that you have mostly young people here. Why is that?" Prabhupada immediately shot back, "Why do you have mostly young people in your University?" She was so caught off guard that she dropped her pencil. She stuttered and said, "Well, that's the age for education." He said, "Yes, therefore that is the age for Krishna consciousness."

A few days before I took *sannyas,* a reporter was interviewing Prabhupada in his quarters in L.A. This reporter knew something about Hinduism. He said, "Well, isn't it old people that take *sannyas* in India? Why are you giving *sannyas* to young people?" Prabhupada shot back, "What does it mean to be old?" The man had no answer. Prabhupada said, "Old means about to die. Can you say that I am older than you? Can you say that you are not going to die before me?" He couldn't answer that. Prabhupada said, "Therefore, we are giving them *sannyas.*"

Atma Tattva: I was cleaning the temple room in Delhi, and a sixty-year-old gentleman came in and paid his obeisances to the Deities. We started talking, and he found out that I was initiated by Prabhupada. He said, "I want to become a disciple of Swami Prabhupada. I've asked before, but they told me that I have to serve in the temple for six months." Then he showed me that his leg was swollen. He said, "I have a big problem with my leg, and I cannot serve in the temple. Can you please ask Prabhupada to accept me as his disciple anyway? I said, "You can go to Prabhupada and ask him. He sees people every evening. You come tomorrow and be the first person to see him." I told him to bring an offering for Prabhupada. He said, "Yes, yes, I will do." The next day he came with a big plate covered by a cloth. He was the first person there for the *darshan,* and I went with him. He put the plate on Prabhupada's desk. Prabhupada looked at him and said, "Yes?" Emotionally, he said, "Prabhupada, I want to chant *Hare Krishna.*" Prabhupada smiled and said, "Who is stopping you? Do you know how to chant *Hare Krishna?*" The man said, "I know the mantra, *Hare Krishna, Hare Krishna, Krishna Krishna, Hare Hare / Hare Rama, Hare Rama, Rama Rama, Hare Hare.*" Prabhupada said, "Yes," and he took the man's beads and demonstrated, "You start like this and on every bead you chant the whole mantra, '*Hare Krishna, Hare Krishna, Krishna Krishna . . .*' " And Prabhupada went to the next bead and then to the next bead. He chanted a whole round and finally said, "Now you chant." I was so blissful. I thought that this man was initiated.

After traveling for awhile I met this man again. He was still chanting, and he had a big picture of Prabhupada in his room. The second time I went to meet him, he had passed away. I heard that they could not take the beads from his hand. In the last two to three weeks of his life he didn't do anything but chant. In the last week he sat in one place, looked at Prabhupada's picture, and chanted. When he left the last thing they heard was his chanting.

Hridayananda Goswami: Often I would enter Prabhupada's room in a serious mood, and he would sometimes joke with me. Once I went into his room with that serious mood, and he looked at me with mock seriousness, "Yes, what is your message?" Another time I was on a college preaching tour, and I went into his room in New York when he was finishing his breakfast. He was in a jolly mood. He said, "Oh! Hridayananda Maharaja, you are traveling and preaching. I am just here eating."

He was pleased with the college preaching tour, and we talked about it for a while. He gave me a little attention, so I was feeling very happy. "Prabhupada likes my program." But the next day I went into Prabhupada's room thinking, "Well here I am, the college preacher." I sat in front of Prabhupada, and he didn't speak to me. He was doing his business. But there was an innocent young *brahmacharini* there who was changing Prabhupada's flower vases with devotion. Prabhupada was very pleased with her. He was smiling like a loving grandfather. He said, "Thank you very much. What is your name?" So that day Prabhupada didn't have a word for me, but he was very pleased with the devotion of this young girl. I was a *sannyasi*, and she was just some innocent girl. But she's the one that pleased Prabhupada, because I was thinking, "I am a *sannyasi*," and she was an innocent girl serving with great devotion. I never forgot that lesson.

Hari Sauri: Prabhupada liked to eat fairly simply. His standard fare for breakfast was cut fruits, freshly fried cashew nuts, and, in India, sometimes a bowl of puffed rice and a small *sandesh*. It was a light breakfast. For lunch, he would have the standard rice, *dahl,* and *chapatis,* a wet *subji,* a dry *subji,* and maybe a small sweet. If the cook was good, he or she could add to that, but those things had to be there. Prabhupada liked the *chapatis* to be fresh off the stove. He had a little bell on his table. When you first brought the plate in, there would be one hot *chapati* on it, and as he finished that one he would ring the bell, and we would immediately puff up another one and run in with it.

Atma Tattva: The day we inaugurated the bullock cart party, I was asked to bring some *prasadam* to offer to Prabhupada and give to all the devotees. So, being a stupid South Indian, I brought coconut and *gur*. That's what *prasadam* is in South India. But the coconuts I brought were not soft—they were very hard. And the *gur* was also not first class. So I had a big plate of pieces of coconut and *gur*. It was brought in front of Prabhupada. Prabhupada looked at it, "What is this?" Lokanath Swami said, "This is *prasadam,* because they are starting the bullock cart. . . ." "Oh! Bullock cart, oh," and he took a small piece of coconut and *gur,* put it in his mouth and was talking about the bullock cart party. As he talked, he moved the *gur* from one side of his mouth to the other, back and forth, and in that way he kept it until it melted and he could eat it. I thought, "I should have asked Lokanath Swami what *prasadam* to bring. It should have been *sandesh*." But even though the *prasadam* was unfit for him, he accepted it. He showed that, "Because you have given it with love, I have taken it."

Hari Sauri: From Australia we went to New Zealand, but there was nobody who knew how to cook there. So for the first time I had to do the whole thing. I put the cooker on the flame, finished the massage, came back to the cooker, and everything was totally ruined. I had left the flame on too high. All the *dahl* had dried up at the bottom. The rice was like sludge. It had disintegrated. The vegetables were so soft they fell apart. There was nothing else to cook, and there was nobody else there to do a quick job of cooking either. So I had to serve what I had. When Prabhupada saw it, he was really disappointed. He said, "What is this?" I said, "I must have had the flame too high." Prabhupada said, "You are too dull—you cannot cook." My first attempt was a disaster. I felt really bad. Prabhupada's digestive system was delicate, and it was important that he had a consistent diet. Otherwise he could have all kinds of physical problems.

Once Palika cooked in Calcutta and was about ten minutes late bringing Prabhupada his *prasadam*. He got angry about it and chastised her strongly. I hadn't seen him chastise one of his women disciples as strongly as that. He explained, "When the appetite comes, it must be fed. Otherwise disease comes."

When I was with him I regulated the time for serving his lunch *prasadam* to 1:30, regardless of when the massage ended. By 1:30 he expected his *prasadam* to be there. That meant that the thought of eating made the digestive juices in the stomach flow, and then you have to feed it. Otherwise there is disease. It was a science, and Prabhupada was aware of that. Apart from that, Prabhupada had problems digesting food anyway. It was important to give him a high standard of *prasadam* regularly. Unfortunately, I wasn't very good at cooking it.

Hridayananda Goswami: A young *sannyasi* is in a precarious position. He has to be very serious about Krishna consciousness. So I was trying very hard to be a good *sannyasi*, to be Krishna conscious. Then I realized that I was not really Krishna conscious enough, that Prabhupada deserved to be served much better than I felt I was serving him. I was in that mood, a little unhappy, a few months after I had taken *sannyas*. I thought, "I better eat less." So I was trying to eat very little for a few days.

Every day in New Dwaraka Prabhupada would walk down the stairs on his way to his garden, stop by the little *sannyas* room, peek in the door, walk in, look around, walk out, and keep going. That was the signal, and I would immediately jump up, offer obeisances, and run after him. I was trying not to impose on Prabhupada, but every day he would come and get me in that way. So one day we were coming back from the garden, and near the stairway to his quarters, on top of a radiator, there was a paper plate with a big mound of leftover potato or rice *prasadam*. Prabhupada stopped, put his cane down, looked at it, turned to me, and said, "Eat that." (So much for my austerities.) I immediately offered obeisances, took the plate, and ate the *prasadam*.

I was in Prabhupada's room once when Jadurani came in. Her health was not good, and she told Prabhupada that she wanted to fast. Prabhupada told her, "Don't fast completely. It's not good to fast completely. At least take fruit."

Hari Sauri: Prabhupada explained that one of his strategies for making people Krishna conscious was to distribute profuse amounts of *prasadam*. He said that people are almost like animals in the way they live. They don't know anything other than their bodies. "At least let them eat *prasadam*, for that's also Krishna," he said. "Our program is to help people gradually become Krishna conscious. Simply by eating *prasadam* they'll gradually develop an attraction to Krishna, and when that develops, they'll be able to understand the philosophy simply by eating *prasadam*." *Prasadam* distribution was one definite way that people could make some advancement.

Hridayananda Goswami: Prabhupada said that you should eat what you can digest. He told me, "If you eat what you like, it will be good for you."

Hari Sauri: I was with Prabhupada in London when my parents went to the Manor, so I went to meet them. I hadn't seen them for about five years, and they had never seen me as a devotee. During the course of the afternoon, I looked for some *prasadam* for them, but there was none. I was told, "We have an early Sunday feast here, and there is nothing left." I wasn't able to give them *prasadam*, but I took them around the Manor, and I explained the philosophy to them. Prabhupada came from London just as we were saying goodbye, so they got a glimpse of him. That was all. After they had gone, I went to see Srila Prabhupada, and he asked me, "How did it go with your parents?" I said, "It was nice. They were very favorable. I showed them the Deities, and I explained a bit of the philosophy." Prabhupada said, "Did they get *prasadam*?" I said, "Oh, well, I was told that there wasn't any." Prabhupada said, "Oh." It was almost like, "What was the use? If they didn't get *prasadam* then your service was basically a failure." He emphasized *prasadam*. It was a practical way for a person to make advancement in Krishna consciousness.

Hridayananda Goswami: My mother was never favorable to the Movement, but she was polite and respectful to me and always thinking, "How to get him out of this thing?" I told her to see Srila Prabhupada. When she sat down in front of Prabhupada she transformed. She became like a young girl. Prabhupada told her how fortunate she was to have a son who was a devotee of Krishna. She nodded in agreement. Ever since I had joined she was unfavorable, but in Prabhupada's presence she was overwhelmed and gladly nodded in agreement. After a few minutes she went downstairs and for the first time she opened her purse and said, "Can I give you something for your Movement?"

Atma Tattva: The next day Prabhupada walked around the yard and saw the bullock cart. It had a semicircular banner saying BHAKTIVEDANTA BULLOCK CART TRAVELING SANKIRTAN PARTY. Prabhupada read the sign and said, "*Jaya.*" Then he fed the bulls some grass, patted them on the cheeks, and said, "These bulls are carrying Gaura-Nitai for preaching. They will go back home, back to Godhead. They won't have another life."

Hridayananda Goswami: We were desperately trying to get the first Spanish *Bhagavatam,* which was being printed in America, to Caracas in time to give to Prabhupada while he was there. There were a few glitches, and the book was late. We were disappointed. Finally, by frantic negotiations with the printer, we arranged for the book to be rushed by air-freight to Caracas. It arrived the same morning Prabhupada was leaving. Some of the leaders in Venezuela were desperately trying to get it out of customs, but South America is not the easiest place to do such things.

Meanwhile, Prabhupada went to the airport, and we checked him in. To my great dismay the book hadn't come. Prabhupada went through the immigration check, passport check, and left for the "Passengers Only" waiting lounge. We paid our obeisances, and suddenly the book came. I became inspired to give this first Spanish *Bhagavatam* to Prabhupada. I went running through the airport. You can't run through the police check in any country, and certainly not in a South American country. But I was inspired. Somehow Krishna arranged everything. I ran right past the passport check. No one said a word to me despite my shaved head and *danda*. I ran right past all the checkpoints where you have to show this and show that, and no one said a word to me. I ran right into the international waiting lounge, offered obeisances, and Prabhupada had me sit next to him. I gave him the *Bhagavatam*. Prabhupada was very pleased. He looked at it, and then he wanted to check if it was bonafide. He said, "Can you translate?" "Yes, Prabhupada," I said. He said, "All right," opened it to the preface and said, "Read this in English." I read it in English and Prabhupada saw that it was correct. It was bona fide. He was very happy. Then they called him for his flight. He walked off holding the *Bhagavatam*.

Atma Tattva: When the bullock cart traveling party arrived in Mayapur, we went to the temple and had a big *kirtan* for forty-five minutes. By then it was 11:00. Maharaj said, "Let's see Prabhupada." We were going upstairs when Hari Sauri stopped us and said, "What is all this noise? Keep quiet. Go back. Prabhupada is tired and sick." Prabhupada was opening his bathroom door to go into his room. He turned and saw us. He said, "Oh! The bullock cart party! Come. Come." Hari Sauri was still trying to stop some of us, but everyone went in. Prabhupada sat down and said, "So? Lokanath Swami, how are you?" Prabhupada looked tired, but he was becoming stronger. He opened a bottle of *burfi* and gave everyone one piece. He asked, "Where were you last night?" Lokanath Swami said, "At a Gaudiya Math in Navadvip, where they charged us two *rupees* per head to sleep in a *kirtan mandap* which had no roof." Prabhupada laughed and said, "That is nothing. They used to use the Shaligram *shila* for cracking betel nuts. This is what has happened to the *brahmans*." Then he was asking, "Did you go to this village? Did you meet this man there?" He said, "Did you go to Fatehpur? Did you see that

Gaura-Nitai Bhavan? Those nice Deities, did you visit that?" He said, "You know how I know these places? I have gone there for preaching. I stayed in the Gaura-Nitai Bhavan." He said, "How did you do the Bihar side? How did you do the Bengal side? Were you in Bardwan?" And the last thing he said was, "Now that you have come to Mayapur you should go to Jagannath Puri."

Hridayananda Goswami: We were flying to Los Angeles to see Prabhupada and give him the first Portuguese *Bhagavatam*, but we arrived at the airport late. The flight had already boarded. We were determined, "How to get this *Bhagavatam* to Prabhupada?" The airline people said, "I am sorry, the flight is closed." Mahavira grabbed the walkie-talkie from the lady at the counter and said, "Hold that flight." They held the flight, and we ran on.

When Prabhupada arrived the next morning in Los Angeles, we met him. I was eager to give him this Portuguese *Bhagavatam* because it pleased him so much. It would always please him to receive these books. I couldn't wait until he went to his room. I handed him the *Bhagavatam* as he got off the *vyasasana*. Finally, when we went to his room, he looked at me and said, "This is your most important service: Printing and distributing books." When he said those words it went deep into my heart. It was a very important moment. I was the GBC of all of Latin American. We had so many projects going on and yet, when I would see Prabhupada, his first question would always be, "So, how is *sankirtan*? How many books are being distributed?"

TAPE 2

Jayapataka Swami
Govinda dasi
Badrinarayan das

 **Jayapataka Swami:** Prabhupada's presence was so powerful that when you came in his presence, you felt as if you were no longer part of the material world. You felt that you were in some kind of a spiritual, transcendental environment. I didn't know about Vrindavan then, but now we would say that Prabhupada brought Vrindavan with him. We felt the Vrindavan mood whenever we came in Prabhupada's presence. He was carrying Krishna in his heart. I didn't understand that but I felt it. Just being with Srila Prabhupada I could feel myself change. I could see that he was a genuine spiritual master, and that he practiced what he preached. Other people that I visited had books and teachings, but they didn't practice those things.

Seeing this helped build my faith and Prabhupada was very merciful to me. He immediately engaged me in service by having me assist his secretary, either Govinda dasi or Gaurasundar. When they went shopping during Prabhupada's afternoon nap, I sat outside in case Prabhupada woke up and wanted something. Sometimes Prabhupada would call me in and ask me different things. He told me, "If I get a flower every day it will increase my longevity," and he asked, "Can you bring me a flower; a rose?" I was very excited. My spiritual master was asking me to bring him a rose daily. I said, "Yes."

I went back to the temple and told the temple president that I

17

was going to get a rose for Srila Prabhupada. He said, "What are you doing? You're in *maya*. You can't do that." I said, "Why? Prabhupada told me to get him a rose." I thought, "I do everything else you say, but Prabhupada asked me to bring him a rose and I am going to bring him a rose." I phoned a florist and was going to go pick up a rose. The temple president got angry and said I couldn't do that, that I should do something else. So I became a little angry because he was yelling at me. I walked off with the vibrations ringing in my ear, and I came to a dead end. Nearby there was a florist shop. I walked in and the salesperson said, "I've been waiting for you. Here is the rose." It was the shop that I had called, but I had forgotten the address. I offered Prabhupada the rose, and he said, "Thank you very much."

 **Govinda:** After Srila Prabhupada got out of the hospital I spent three weeks with him. Those three weeks changed my life and I wanted to continue serving him in that way. So, during the six months Prabhupada was in India, every day I prayed to Lord Jagannath, "If he comes back, please let me be his servant. Let me cook for him. Let me clean his room. Let me do anything, just let me serve and be near him. This is my strong desire."

One of the first letters Prabhupada ever sent me was when he was in India, and the last statement in the letter was, "I know your mind."

 **Badrinarayan:** When Prabhupada walked through the gorgeous building in Detroit, in the front lobby there was a painting of naked women bathing, and all the *sannyasis* were trying to be proper about things. Prabhupada looked at the painting, turned to them and said, "Very nicely done." Then they came to a big polar bear rug that had the polar bear's head and teeth. Srila Prabhupada looked at it, gingerly put the tip of his cane in its mouth, lifted it up, looked at the teeth, and, wide-eyed like a child, turned to Jagadish Maharaj

and asked, "They eat men?" Jagadish Maharaj said, "Sometimes, Srila Prabhupada." Prabhupada put it down and made a wide berth to walk around it. It was sublime.

The man was asking close to a million dollars for the building. Prabhupada said, "Every room is worth a million dollars. Krishna engaged a rich person to build this building for us, and it's simply been waiting for us to pick it up." Prabhupada walked through the whole thing as if he could pull the money out of his bead bag. Price wasn't an issue when Prabhupada was talking about this and that, but actually he had no money for this project.

Outside there was a sunken garden, and Prabhupada and the man, who was very greedy, were peacefully sitting in the sun in the grotto area. Srila Prabhupada loved the building, and in his sublime, aristocratic way, Prabhupada said, "This building is perfect for our purposes. Every room is exquisite. It's exactly what we want. It's a very aristocratic building." The man could taste the money. Prabhupada said to him, "But we are not aristocrats, we are professional beggars. Therefore you should give it to us." I thought the man was going to have a cardiac arrest. Prabhupada toyed with him back and forth, and ultimately Prabhupada got the building. Ambarish gave half the money and Lekhasravanti gave the other half of the money. In this way, although Prabhupada had nothing but his desire, Krishna arranged the building, and Prabhupada picked it up. No one could believe the price that Prabhupada got it for. In fact, after the papers were signed, a neighbor called to say that the man was stripping the building. He was taking the mirrors off the walls, the doorknobs, the light fixtures, because everything was very opulent. We stopped him and said, "How can you do this?" He said, "I can't help it. Your Swami cheated me." Later on we told Prabhupada the story and Prabhupada said, "Yes, I am a Calcutta boy." That man met his match in Srila Prabhupada.

Jayapataka Swami: Once Srila Prabhupada was giving a lecture about how we have to be cent percent Krishna conscious. He was ramming home the point that we have to surrender to Krishna one hundred percent. At the end of the class the devotees were serious. They were looking down thinking, "Who can come up to the standard of complete surrender?" As if he could read their minds, Prabhupada relaxed his mood a little bit and said, "If you can be ninety percent Krishna conscious, then you can also go back to Godhead." He was on a large, high *vyasasana*, four feet in the air, and had to go down some steps to get off the *vyasasana*. As he started down he said, "Even if you are eighty percent surrendered, Krishna will still take you." Then he got off the *vyasasana* and started walking away. His *chaddar* was flowing behind him, dragging on the ground. He stopped, looked at the devotees and said, "Even if you are seventy percent Krishna conscious, still Krishna will take you." He threw his *chaddar* over his shoulder and walked off with his head high.

Govinda: Several times when I brought Prabhupada's lunch plate in with *subji*, rice, *dahl*, and *chapatis*, he said, "When I was in India, everyone told me, 'Oh Swamiji, don't go to America. In America there will be no food for you. You will starve. They only eat meat in America.'" Back then there wasn't much interchange between India and America. Prabhupada said, "I simply told them, 'What is that? I shall live on bread and potatoes.' I thought I would be living on bread and potatoes, but now I see that Krishna has sent everything; *dahl*, rice, *chapatis*, *subjis*." He was amazed and happy about that.

Badrinarayan: Karandhar told me that once Prabhupada was walking in Cheviot Hills, Los Angeles, when they went past a big house. Prabhupada said, "Someday we will have a big house like this for Krishna." The devotees said, "*Jaya*, Prabhupada!" Prabhupada walked a little further, and there was a big circular driveway with a big stretch limo. Prabhupada said, "Someday we will have a big car like this for Krishna." The devotees said, "*Jaya*, Prabhupada!" They walked past another house, and out of nowhere a dog came running down the driveway. Prabhupada said, "Someday we will have a big dog like this for Krishna." The devotees said, "*Jaya*, Prabhupada!" Prabhupada said, "You fools, what do you want a big dog for?"

Govinda: The night he had a stroke was very traumatic. He was weak and the boys, Satsvarupa, Brahmananda or whoever was there, would take turns sitting him up, opening the *Srimad-Bhagavatam* and listening as he continued teaching and reading the story of Prahlad Maharaj. Even though he was apparently suffering and at a very critical time, hovering between life and death, he didn't care. He only cared about teaching us. I was deeply affected at that moment and realized a lot of things. I saw how much he loved us. I had never seen such selfless, pure love. And I realized that he wouldn't be with us very long. I made a vow that I would do everything I could to take care of him, help him, and do whatever I could to make things easier for him.

Jayapataka Swami: A devotee told me, "You should ask a good question every time Prabhupada gives class." So at the end of every class I would always ask a question about something that related to the class. Once I asked about Radharani. Prabhupada said, "Who are you to ask about Radharani?" I asked questions every day, and Prabhupada would respond in a different way every day.

At that time we worked outside to maintain the Montreal temple. There was no other source of income. So I could only attend the morning class and had to miss the evening class. But the next day I would listen to the tape of the evening class. Once I was listening to the tape, and at the end of class Prabhupada asked if anyone had any questions. Nobody had any, and he said, "That Jay, he has nice questions." Hearing that was a big thing for me because normally Prabhupada didn't praise disciples to their face. He was very grave with his disciples. But sometimes he would comment to other devotees, and you'd hear it through the grapevine. That time I heard it on the tape.

Badrinarayan: An Indian professor said that it was all one. Prabhupada explained that it is not all one, that there are differences. Prabhupada said, "If I say cotton ball or cotton shirt, is there a difference?" The man said, "Ah, cotton ball, cotton shirt. . . ." Prabhupada said, "If I say cotton ball or cotton shirt, is there a difference?" The man said, "Ah, cotton is . . ." Prabhupada said it three or four times. He was sitting behind a low table, and the man was sitting on the other side. Prabhupada reached over, grabbed the man by the shirt, shook him and said, "If I say cotton ball or cotton shirt, is there a difference?" The man got it. He didn't just get it to be polite, but Prabhupada, while still friendly, managed to shake through his buffalo brain. The man understood that there was a difference between a cotton ball and a cotton shirt. However, after the man left, Prabhupada pointed out, "This is the special sanction of old men and little children. They can go anywhere, and they can say anything. You cannot imitate."

Jayapataka Swami: I was on a morning walk with Srila Prabhupada when he stopped near a church. He looked at it and said that in the future our ISKCON temples were going to be something like the churches in that there would be some devotees living in the temples and many devotees living around the temples who would come on the weekends and for festivals. At that time, 1970, there weren't many temples, and the whole mood was making temples, joining the temple, and becoming a temple devotee. But Prabhupada was saying that in the future the temples would be a center with big communities of devotees around them. Now I am coordinating congregation programs, and that instruction has a lot of importance to me, although at the time I really didn't know what to think of it. It was a prediction.

Govinda: When we were in New Jersey all of us used to sit and eat together. Prabhupada sat on the sofa and ate on a little table in front of the sofa, while we sat and ate on the floor. We would talk about different things during the meal. Once we were talking about brown rice, white rice, long grain rice, this rice, that rice, and Prabhupada said he once had a servant who didn't like long grain, fine rice. That servant preferred lesser quality rice. Then Prabhupada said that brown rice was for animals. I said, "Wow! I must be an animal because I like brown rice." He laughed and laughed and laughed. I said it in the mood of simplicity, but he thought it was funny.

Badrinarayan: Beyond the park there were museums and a quiet, forested area. I had walked in the park many times, but I had never seen this area. When Prabhupada walked there, deer came on both sides of the walkway and walked with us. They'd run twenty yards ahead and then wait. Prabhupada would catch up, and then they'd run ahead and wait again. Twice when Srila Prabhupada was there they followed us all the way down and all the way up. One of the devotees quoted the "*atmarama*" verse; that even dull animals can appreciate a Krishna conscious person. We were thinking, "What is the status of Srila Prabhupada? Is he like Chaitanya Mahaprabhu?" We weren't *sahajiya*-like, but we saw that the deer sensed Prabhupada's purity.

Jayapataka Swami: In Montreal we would walk to McGill University or walk around the block, and Prabhupada would make observations. Once he said that if you see a big, healthy person, you can ask him where he does his grocery shopping because, since he's healthy, he must have a good source. It happened that a taxi drove up and the taxi driver was very big. Prabhupada said, "Yes, ask him where he does his shopping." Prabhupada was spontaneous in that way. A devotee asked the taxi driver where he did his shopping, and the taxi driver was bewildered. Why would someone ask him such a question?

Govinda: In New York before he got ill, he had us drawing the story of Prahlad Maharaj and Hiranyakashipu. He was keen on having the story as a slide show for children, which we eventually did. Prabhupada told us about the poses and demonstrated them. He posed for Hiranyakashipu, standing on one leg. He loved to pose for Lord Nrsimhadev. At least once a day he would come in, do a roar, and describe how Lord Nrsimhadev came out of the column, "*rrrrrr-hhhhhh!*" His eyes would get big, and you could see the white up above. "*Rrrrrrhhhhhhh!*" This was his delight and he enjoyed it very much.

Once Jadurani had him pose like Krishna. He wrapped up in a white *dhoti* so that we could see how the pleats fell from a three-fold bending posture. He was right there watching us, seeing what and how we were doing.

Jayapataka Swami: One day they found a cockroach in the Montreal temple. Prabhupada took the cockroach in his hand, opened the window, and told the cockroach, "Here, I am giving you the whole world. Now enjoy it." Then he threw the cockroach out the window and closed it.

Badrinarayan: Every morning in Los Angeles Prabhupada taught us the Sanskrit for *Sri Isopanisad,* "*Om purnam adah purnam idam.*" He would wait for us to say it, and we would stumble. Only a couple of devotees were learning it. After a week or so Prabhupada said, "These books I am writing are not just for selling, they are also for you. You should learn them." He said we should know his books like a lawyer knows the law books.

Another time Prabhupada was reading from Krishna Book and sometimes adding things that weren't in the text. He described how Narada Muni warned Kamsa that any son could be the eighth son of Devaki. Kamsa was waiting for the eighth son to be born and was letting the other sons go. Narada Muni, however, wanted to speed up Krishna's appearance, so Prabhupada said that Narada Muni showed Kamsa how to count in such a way that Kamsa became bewildered and therefore wanted to kill all of Devaki's children.

Govinda: There was a picture of Prahlad Maharaj sitting in boiling oil, and I had to come up with some demons for the picture. I didn't know what demons looked like, but somehow I drew demons. I asked Prabhupada if they were okay. He said, "Yes, this is very good. There are such demons. They are like this. Yes. Even on this planet there are such demons." I said, "Oh, really? I didn't know that." He looked at me and said, "There are a lot of things you do not know."

Jayapataka Swami: Somehow we contacted a doctor who had just built a new house that he was going to make into a clinic. No one had moved in it yet. The doctor thought, "I will give it to you for six months. It will be auspicious for some *sadhus* to come and stay in my new house." Then we had a place to invite Prabhupada. In the meantime Prabhupada had left America and gone to Japan. We sent him a message that we had a separate place for him. Prabhupada said, "I am coming," and we arranged for a big reception at the Calcutta airport. The media was there, and a whole truckload of Gaudiya Vaishnav devotees came to receive Prabhupada with *kirtan*.

We invited all of Prabhupada's godbrothers. We said, "Who would like to come and receive him?" because he was a conquering Gaudiya Vaishnav missionary who had successfully spread Krishna consciousness in places where no one had even ventured before, and now he was returning. One godbrother, Puri Maharaj, said, "Oh yes. I would like to go." At that time I didn't know much about the internal workings between the different Gaudiya Math people. But a *grihastha* devotee came up and said to Puri Maharaj, "Maharaj, how can you go? You are an older godbrother. You took initiation before Bhaktivedanta Swami did. You took *sannyas* before he did. You cannot go to him, he should come to you." I said, "What does it matter if you were initiated earlier or later? Someone has done wonderful preaching."

In the end none of Prabhupada's godbrothers came to the airport to meet him, but some disciples of his godbrothers came.

Prabhupada noted that and was not very happy that none of his godbrothers had come. Then one of his godbrother's disciples said, "Your godbrother is waiting for you at his temple. He has a feast for you there. He wants you to go from the airport to his temple." Prabhupada became very grave and said, "Let us go in the car." Before that we had had a big reception, a press conference, and an *arati* in the VIP lounge. Prabhupada didn't have to go through any customs or immigration, he went straight to the VIP lounge and then came out and went to the car. We had a big American car from a Life Member for him, and Prabhupada got in it and said, "Take me to the house. I will not go to my godbrother's temple. You can go later and bring the *prasadam* that they've made to the house. We will go straight to our house."

Govinda: When we were in Montreal, Achyutananda was in India with a young *brahmachari* named Hrishikesh. Somehow or other Hrishikesh had gone to Bon Maharaj's *ashram* and been reinitiated by Bon Maharaj. Prabhupada was extremely upset by this. I didn't understand why, and he explained, "This boy is American. He does not know anything, so it's not his fault. He's a foolish youth. But Bon Maharaj is responsible. He knows that by doing this is he is saying that I am not a bonafide spiritual master." I had never seen Prabhupada that upset. He was dealing with a kind of Vaishnav etiquette that I didn't understand.

Badrinarayan: Tejiyas told me that when Prabhupada came to Delhi they took his *vyasasana* to the airport and had a reception and *arati* there. The mayor and some big Life Members attended. Everyone had gathered, and Tejiyas was about to garland Srila Prabhupada when Prabhupada said, "Stop." He said, "What was the collection last month?" Tejiyas said some number. "How much did you send to my book fund?" Tejiyas gave a number that was fifty percent. Prabhupada said, "Begin the *arati*." The first thing Prabhupada wanted to know was that fifty percent was going to his book fund.

Jayapataka Swami: We were invited to a *Bhagavad-gita* conference in Maharastra sponsored by Vinoda Bhave, a disciple of Gandhiji. Vinoda Bhave was one of the most famous saints in the Gandhi tradition, and big political leaders used to meet with him. One of his last campaigns was for cow protection. Somehow he was holding a big conference on the *Bhagavad-gita,* and he invited Prabhupada and many other *sadhus* to come. I was there for that conference. Vinoda Bhave's many women disciples chanted chapters of the *Bhagavad-gita* and Vinoda Bhave spoke. Then Prabhupada had us, his men and women disciples from all over the world, chant Hare Krishna in a big *kirtan.* Everybody got into the *kirtan,* laughing and clapping, and then Prabhupada delivered a very nice lecture. A Mayavadi *sannyasi* was upset at Prabhupada's *kirtan* and the positive effect it had on the crowd. Normally this Mayavadi would have just given a *Bhagavad-gita* class, but now he wanted to do a *kirtan* also. He told the people, "You should all chant with me. We will have a *kirtan.*" It seemed as if he made up some unusual mantra right on the spot. Nobody was inspired by it. In the middle Prabhupada said to the devotees, "Chant Hare Krishna again," and the devotees jumped up with *kartals* and *mridanga* and started chanting. Everyone was relieved because the Mayavadi's chanting was so strange.

Badrinarayan: There was a professor from Cal Tech who had studied Vedanta and who appreciated what he saw as Prabhupada's simplistic presentation, appropriate for the neophytes in the West. This professor thought that as one went further into Vedanta, one understood how the form becomes formless, and he quoted Sanskrit slokas to support his viewpoint. Prabhupada didn't even look at him. Prabhupada looked at the Deities of Radha and Krishna and chanted *Hare Krishna Hare Krishna, Krishna Krishna Hare Hare* . . . while the professor went on speaking. Finally the professor ran out of steam. Prabhupada said, "Are you finished?" and then Prabhupada started quoting from the *Puranas,* the *Vedas,* the *Vedanta Sutra,* the *Upanisads,* the *Samhitas,* as if he were hammering a nail into the ground. For this man it was like body blows. Everyone was sitting on a big rug, but this man was standing. As Prabhupada spoke in his lionlike way the professor stooped a little bit, then he was on his knees, then he could have melted into the floor. Prabhupada, with his noble bearing and his hand in his bead bag, made point after point. It came to a crescendo. Prabhupada finished and said, "Do you have any further questions?" The professor said, "Swami, can we have *kirtan?*" His complaint had been that we just chanted and danced like sentimentalists. The devotees said "*Jaya!*" The professor had seen the light, so to speak.

Govinda: I would open Prabhupada's mail and read it to him. Once Harsharani sent Prabhupada a poem she had written. I thought it was bizarre. She wrote, "I offer my humble obeisances to my spiritual master, who is continuously running here and there playing hide-and-go-seek and leap frog with Krishna and the cowherd boys," and she described many transcendental pastimes. Prabhupada said, "Ah, she has become advanced. Publish this poem in *Back to Godhead.*" And it was printed in *Back to Godhead.*

Jayapataka Swami: I was there with some other devotees when Srila Prabhupada went to meet Indira Gandhi. Prabhupada had a list of things he wanted to discuss with Indira Gandhi, but at that time she was very upset because the President of Bangladesh, Muziba Raman, had just been assassinated. Still she made time for Prabhupada to see her on a Thursday afternoon. Prabhupada didn't consult with astrologers much, but he didn't want to have an important meeting on a Thursday afternoon. He said that it was not an auspicious time. That was about the only astrological thing he observed. He said, "Either in the morning or the evening, but not in the afternoon." So they changed the time, and we all went together. But the devotees with Prabhupada only got as far as the door. Indira Gandhi came and met Prabhupada, and he went on alone to talk with her. Later he said that she was very respectful to him. She actually asked him, "How do you know that your followers are not CIA agents?" He explained, "I went to the West and preached. These people have sacrificed everything. They gave up their bad habits. They are getting up at four in the morning, attending *mangal arati*. If they were CIA, they would live in five star hotels and have a whole different lifestyle. They wouldn't be vegetarians and give up all these habits." She was convinced and said, "All right, I will give your devotees long-term visas." After that meeting she passed some order, and the devotees who needed long-term visas got them.

Badrinarayan: Durlab, the temple President in Laguna Beach, was trying to save money and therefore used peanut oil for all the cooking. But the devotees wanted ghee and went on a nonviolent, noncooperation strike. We said, "No more peanut oil." Durlab said, "I am going to ask Srila Prabhupada." He said, "Prabhupada, can we cook in peanut oil?" Prabhupada said, "This is not first class." Later on in the conversation Durlab asked again, "What about cooking in peanut oil?" Prabhupada said, "Peanut oil is fifth class." Finally he asked a third time. Prabhupada said, "Cook in anything you like." Durlab thought, "Oh! Great! We can cook in anything I like." As he was leaving Prabhupada said, "But I know one man who ate too many *pakoras* cooked in peanut oil." A devotee said, "What happened to him?" Prabhupada said, "He died the next morning." That was Prabhupada's purport on peanut oil and that was the end of peanut oil.

Jayapataka Swami: Sometimes when we walked through the fields in Mayapur, Prabhupada would ask me to lead the way because there were narrow paths between the rice paddies. He said, "These are like little highways in the fields." One winter day we were walking, and he said that he wanted to go to the Ganges. The river was low and clear, with a little saffron color. The flow had reduced so much that we could see the bottom. It was rare to see the Ganges like that. Prabhupada said that we must take bath. His secretary said,

"Prabhupada, we don't have any *gamshas* or towels. We just came for a walk." Prabhupada looked around and said, "There are no women here. We can go in our *kopins* and then wear the top piece. He took off his top piece and with all the *brahmacharis* and *sannyasis* went into the Ganges. Then Prabhupada did something I never saw anyone do before. When he was dipping under, he closed all the holes in his head. He put two fingers over his mouth, two over his nostrils, two over his eyes, and his thumbs over his ears. He took three dips and then came out. It was an ecstatic, spontaneous bath with Srila Prabhupada.

Badrinarayan: Everybody told Prabhupada not to go to Kumbha Mela, but at the last minute Prabhupada made his own decision. He was determined to go. The problem was that there was no way to get into the Kumbha Mela because twenty million people were there. No train or bus reservations were available. People were getting there by lying on top and stacking against the walls of trains. Flying in wasn't an option because Prabhupada's doctor said that he shouldn't fly. But, miraculously, a sweet Indian gentleman named Mr. Gupta, who had joined about two months prior, happened to be the Chief Engineer of the Indian Railway System. He added a first class car and a second class car to the train bound for Kumbha Mela. This was totally unheard of in India. Mr. Gupta also arranged for Prabhupada's car to be freshly painted, to have garlands hanging in it, and he arranged for his personal servant to drive with Prabhupada into the Mela. We stopped outside Allahabad in the dark, got off the train, and drove into the Mela. While we were there, Prabhupada wanted milk. There was no way to get milk. I talked to Mr. Gupta, and he arranged for a cow to be brought to our compound in the Mela so that Prabhupada could have fresh milk. Mr. Gupta was wonderful. He also arranged for a train to pick up Prabhupada when he was ready to leave the Mela. In India, making all these arrangements successfully would be considered a miracle.

Jayapataka Swami: Once Prabhupada was sitting in his room in Calcutta when a Life Member businessman said, "Can you show us some miracle?" Prabhupada said, "Some yogis show a miracle by creating some *rasgula*. I went to America with forty rupees, and in a short span we now have temples all over the world worth more than 400 million rupees. Isn't that a miracle?" The businessman thought for a minute and said, "That's a miracle."

Badrinarayan: We were walking by big houses in Letcho Park in Chicago when an enormous dog came running toward us. Three or four devotees hid behind cars, and a couple of devotees hid behind Brahmananda. Everyone was overwhelmed by the bodily concept of life and the thought of self-preservation. Prabhupada was left out to confront his appointment. Everyone else was stunned and didn't know what to do. With transcendental bravery Srila Prabhupada stepped forward and threw his *chaddar* over his shoulder. It was like Krishna tying His belt before He fights with a demon. Prabhupada took his cane and went "*Huttt!*" and that huge dog turned and went back. The devotees dusted themselves off and regrouped, a little embarrassed. A little further down the road another dog came out. Some *sannyasi* tried "*Huttt!*" but the dog became madder. Prabhupada laughed and said, "You have to know the science."

Jayapataka Swami: We were walking near the river Jalangi one day when a villager came by with a big basket of vegetables on his head. Srila Prabhupada asked, "Are you going to sell those in the market?" He said, "Yes." Prabhupada said, "How much will you sell them for? Sell us the whole basket." Prabhupada had been telling the devotees how he liked fresh garden vegetables, how we should offer our vegetables to the Deity, and how you can save money if you buy wholesale. Prabhupada started bargaining with the villager. He told him, "If you go to the market, you will spend the whole day sitting there with the basket. I will buy it from you right now. You can do something else. You won't have to walk two miles to the market and sell your goods." He bargained him down to six rupees for the basket. Then he said, "Go to the temple and they will pay you." The man went off with the basket, entered the temple and sold those vegetables. The devotees cooked them for the Deities and Prabhupada had them as well.

Govinda: We were sitting in the garden in New Jersey one day when we saw a slug crawling right next to Prabhupada. A slug is an ugly thing, like a snail without a shell. I said, "Ooo! Look." I was a kid. Prabhupada got a look of tremendous compassion on his face and said, "Chant to the poor creature." He had me sitting there chanting to this slug. I still chant to slugs or little insects or whatever, because I remember Prabhupada telling me to chant to that slug, and I take it as one of Prabhupada's instructions. We're given this human form of life, we can chant and they can't. But the soul can hear. The tree can hear, the bird can hear. Prabhupada would sit outdoors and talk this way.

Once he was talking about two butterflies that were flying together, and he said, "Just see, there is also family life in the butterfly's world." We were on the beach in New Jersey, and there were little ants on the beach, and he said, "They say there is no life on the moon, but here on the beach we see there is life. There is life in every part of God's creation." He was constantly viewing the world through the vision of Krishna-*bhakti*. There was never any time that he wasn't seeing in that way.

Jayapataka Swami: Once a Maharaj was cooking hot puris, and we were taking hot *puris* with date *gur,* date molasses. Prabhupada looked through the window and saw the *sannyasis* and *brahmacharis* taking hot *puris* with date *gur* one after another. He said, "This is not very good for *sannyas* life."

Badrinarayan: There was a big statue of an American eagle to commemorate World War II soldiers. Prabhupada went out of his way to look at it. He said that there is a type of bird that flies from one planet to another that is so big that it could pick up an elephant and then drop it to kill it. Then this bird would eat the elephant. Prabhupada mentioned that because he saw the eagle statue.

Govinda: Prabhupada described how the abominable snowman is a big demon that lives in the mountains and how he has big footprints. He explained how there are various entities deep in the ocean, up in the mountains, and in the dark jungles of Africa.

When you are fresh out of school you think that everything has already been discovered and taught. But Prabhupada made it very clear that that's not so, that there are a lot of things that we don't know about. We accepted his view of the world. It was interesting to hear the things that he came up with.

Badrinarayan: Prabhupada was sitting on the lawn in New Vrindavan when some simple neighbor, who had heard that Prabhupada was there, came in his pickup truck. He walked up to Srila Prabhupada, said "Got something for you, Swami," and plopped a grocery bag on Prabhupada's lap.

On one hand Prabhupada was very large. He had a presence that could fill a whole room. But in reality Prabhupada was not very tall, and he was delicate. Prabhupada was sitting there with this big grocery bag full of vegetables on his lap. He reached inside, pulled out a zucchini, and showed it to everybody. He said, "When someone brings you something from their garden, that is love."

Govinda: A devotee sculptor came to visit Prabhupada in Hawaii. This devotee had helped me make some Deities, and at this time Prabhupada wanted him to make some Panchatattva Deities. Prabhupada explained at great length how he wanted the Deities made. After the conversation, this devotee asked Prabhupada if it was okay for his wife to kill silkworms to make silk. After he left Prabhupada said, "These Western boys are so creative. Next they will be asking me if they can kill cows to make *mridangas*."

Jayapataka Swami: One time Tarun Kanti Ghosh, the Home Minister (the number two person in the state government in charge of the police), came to see Srila Prabhupada. He comes from a family of Vaishnavas. His grandfather said that Bhaktivinode Thakur was the seventh Goswami and wrote a book about Chaitanya Mahaprabhu. Now Tarun, his grandson, was a big politician and the editor of a major newspaper. When he came to see Srila Prabhupada, he went behind Prabhupada's desk and tried to grab Srila Prabhupada's feet. Brahmananda was about to jump on Tarun Kanti Ghosh. Prabhupada said, "No, no. It's all right." Tarun Kanti Ghosh grabbed Prabhupada's feet and put them on his head.

Badrinarayan: In the afternoon and evening Prabhupada sat in his garden and read with *sannyasis* and temple presidents. At that time a whole gallery of devotees would look out the temple windows into the garden to see and hear Srila Prabhupada. Gargamuni looked up at us and said, "Get out, get out." He got heavy with us for looking, because he thought we were bothering Srila Prabhupada. The next day, when no one was there looking, Prabhupada looked up and said, "Where are the devotees?" Someone said, "Gargamuni said that they shouldn't be there." Prabhupada said, "Go get them." Then, with Prabhupada's permission, we all sat and looked out the windows at Srila Prabhupada in the garden. Prabhupada liked the devotees there.

Once he was looking through the newspaper about the moon shot. The headline stated, "One small step for man, one great step for mankind." Prabhupada flicked through and got to the fourth or fifth page where there was an article about how taxes were going up to pay for the space program. Prabhupada said, "This is their real business. They have made some scam to squeeze money out of the innocent public. The moon expedition is just a side show."

Govinda: One of my most persistent memories is the sand crab story. This took place in Hawaii when we were walking on the beach. Prabhupada was talking about sand crabs, those little white crabs that run sideways and hide in their holes as one walks along. Prabhupada spoke for some time about the sand crabs, and it finally dawned on me that he was saying that there is no such word in Sanskrit as "instinct."

Prabhupada asked, "Why is the sand crab running?" Scientists would say, "The sand crab is running away due to instinct. His instinct is to go to his hole." But Prabhupada said that there is no such thing as instinct. Instinct is a word that's been coined by the scientists to cover up the fact that there is Supersoul, there is God and there is past experience. He explained this in detail, and it finally dawned on me that, "I have been taught Darwinism in school all my life, and even though I had been a devotee for seven years, I was raised to think that the birds and beasts are operating by instinct." Day after day Prabhupada blasted this philosophy in great detail.

Prabhupada said, "Suppose you know where the privy [bathroom] is, and twenty years from now you return to the same house. Because you were here twenty years ago, you still know where the privy is. Similarly, you have been in the body for many lifetimes, so you know to look for the mother's breast. The baby animal is nudging for the mother's breast. It's past experience, the past lifetime, and it's the Supersoul within the heart that guides the living entity. It's not instinct. There is no such thing as instinct. Instinct makes no sense. What does instinct mean? If you stop to think about it and analyze it, you will see that it means absolutely nothing. Yet the scientists have convinced everyone that the whole of nature is moving by instinct. But the whole of nature is not moving by instinct. It's moving by Supersoul." Prabhupada gave another example, "You can throw food outside, and within twenty minutes the birds will be eating it. They all say it's instinct, but it's actually the Supersoul guiding them, 'Oh! There is food.'" This is the kind of talk that he would get into.

Jayapataka Swami: Once he was strongly chastising me and giving me some instruction. The next time I came to see him he had changed his mood. He said, "I am sorry. Maybe I dealt with you too harshly. I am a very hard person to tolerate. I deal very harshly." I couldn't believe Prabhupada said such a thing to me. I said, "No Srila Prabhupada, I was offensive. There was no wrong on your part."

Govinda: When we were living in Los Angeles, I would usually read *Caitanya-caritamrta* when Prabhupada took his nap. It was a seven-volume edition that Gaurasundar had gotten, translated by some scholar. Krishna das was also reading it. Prabhupada would come in and say, "Oh! What are you reading?" We would say, "This is *Caitanya-caritamrta.*" Prabhupada saw that we were really interested, and he decided to make a good translation of it. He engaged Gaurasundar in the transliteration work, and I started transcribing the tapes for *Caitanya-caritamrta.* He wanted to give us that because he could see that we were very eager for it.

Badrinarayan: A devotee was telling Srila Prabhupada that he was selling *prasadam,* Bengali sweets, at a stand in front of UC Berkeley. He was going on and on about this. Prabhupada stopped him and asked Tripurari, "How many books did you sell?" Tripurari told him some amazing figure. Prabhupada said, "This is the real Bengali sweet, *Caitanya-caritamrta.*"

Jayapataka Swami: Prabhupada came to Mayapur all of a sudden. The new building wasn't ready, but Prabhupada stayed there, on the third floor, anyway. Since the piping hadn't been connected the toilets didn't flush, and our service was to empty the refuse.

One day Prabhupada started calling out, "Jayapataka! Jayapataka!" I ran to the bathroom. Prabhupada was holding the door semishut. A venomous serpent was stuck in the door and was trying to bite Srila Prabhupada. It was leaping out and just missing him. By the pressure of the door that Prabhupada held, the snake was slightly crushed and couldn't get loose.

I hit the snake with a stick and got Prabhupada out. This was a very unusual circumstance and an urgent situation, but Prabhupada never lost his composure. He was calling out, but he was cool and calm under the circumstance. Later he said, "If there is one, there must be two, because snakes always go in pairs." But the other one disappeared down the hall. We could never find it.

Govinda: Once Prabhupada was sitting on the rooftop of the Honolulu temple getting massaged by Srutakirti. The rooftop of the Honolulu temple faces the back of Nuuanu Valley, which is very beautiful. It usually has a rain cloud the color of Krishna and a rainbow or two. That day there was a rainbow. Prabhupada became very poetic and started talking about how the rainbow has the three colors of material nature. The red for *raja guna,* the mode of passion, yellow is for *sattva guna,* the mode of goodness, and blue for *tama guna,* the mode of ignorance. He explained how all the modes of nature came from these three. Just as all colors are made from a mixture of the primary colors, red, yellow, and blue, so the living entities come from various mixtures of the three *gunas—raja, sattva,* and *tama.* It was very poetic and beautiful.

Jayapataka Swami: Prabhupada was walking down the stairway in Calcutta. Many devotees were there. Prabhupada slipped a little bit, and it looked like he was going to fall down. One of the senior devotees said, "Watch out, Srila Prabhupada." Prabhupada stopped and said, "It is your responsibility to watch out. You have to take care of the body of the spiritual master. The spiritual master looks out for your spiritual well-being, but as far as whether I fall or not, that you have to guard against."

Badrinarayan: Prabhupada turned to Ekendra, Rupanuga's son, who was seven or eight years old. He said, "Ekendra, lead *kirtan.*" Little Ekendra sang *"Namah om,"* *"Shri Krishna Chaitanya,"* and

"*Hare Krishna.*" When he was done, Prabhupada called him over and gave him a ten dollar bill. He said, "Buy yourself a red fire engine." Then Prabhupada said, "Children like the color red."

Govinda: I have a color photograph at home showing Prabhupada sitting and holding a globe. He was saying, "Brahmananda will go here, Gargamuni will go here." He was turning the globe and indicating different countries. We were a handful of teenagers who couldn't get it together, who practically didn't know how to brush our teeth, but he had it in mind to send us all over the world to open centers. He was extremely interested in Russia. He always talked about Russia. He wanted the Russian people to receive the mercy of Lord Chaitanya.

Jayapataka Swami: We were on a morning walk with Srila Prabhupada in north Calcutta. Srila Prabhupada said, "Oh, here is a Life Member's home." For some reason Prabhupada wanted to stop in at the house of a wealthy Life Member. He went in and told the servant, "Tell your master that Bhaktivedanta Swami is here." After a while the servant came out and said, "The master is worshiping his Deity. He will be here after some time." Prabhupada commented, "Krishna is more pleased when the devotee is served than when He is served. If this person was more advanced he would have appreciated, 'A spiritual master has come,' and left his Deity worship to receive the devotee of Krishna. But because he thinks that his Deity worship is more important than receiving the devotee of Krishna, that shows that he is a neophyte, or *kanistha adhikari.*"

Govinda: Once in Los Angeles the Jehovah's Witnesses came to visit us and Prabhupada said, "Let them in." I let them in, and they preached their philosophy. Apparently they believe that within this body you become liberated and that this body is eternal. Prabhupada kept asking them, "With this body?" He was incredulous that they could believe that this body was eternal. But he was polite and nice with them. He didn't preach to them, he just wanted know what they were teaching. They gave him some literature, and as they left he had me give them a little brochure about chanting Hare Krishna. It had a drawing of the universal form that I had made and a picture of Lord Vishnu with all His arms. The next morning when he went on his walk, he saw that this brochure had been thrown on the street and run over by a car. He was disturbed that the Lord's picture had been run over. He said, "We should not give out such things freely."

Jayapataka Swami: There was a con artist who dressed like a *sannyasi* and collected money in the name of ISKCON. He gave himself the name "Achyutananda" and was known amongst the devotees as "Achyutananda Number Two." He was based in Rajastan and collected near Jaipur. He made a big construction plan for building a temple and somehow copied receipts, rubber stamps and everything else one needed to collect money.

Some of the people who donated money to this Achyutananda appeared in Bombay and said, "We were made a Life Member by Achyutananda in Jaipur." Achyutananda Number One was in Hyderabad so we sent a few devotees to find out who this Achyutananda was, and they discovered that he was a thief. Somehow they got him to see Prabhupada in Mayapur. Prabhupada had called the CID, the equivalent of the FBI in India, and the Superintendent of Police. In the meantime Prabhupada talked with Achyutananda Number Two, who said to him, "You are a great spiritual master, a saint, and I feel changed after talking with you. I want to surrender at your lotus feet. I am going to surrender my life to you and do whatever you say. I am giving up all my bad ways."

Prabhupada called in the big police officers who had come to take this person away (a case had already been registered) and said, "I have to give this person asylum because he has surrendered to me. As a spiritual master, if someone surrenders to me, I have to give him shelter." The police were ready to dive in on him and take him away, but they said, "Guruji, what can we say? But we don't believe this person. He is a thief." Prabhupada said, "What can I do? If he surrenders then I have to accept." Prabhupada told Achyutananda Number Two, "If you follow, you are safe. But if you leave, I am going to turn you over to the police." To keep him engaged Prabhupada had Achyutananda do some writing for him, but after about ten days some devotees spotted him during *mangal arati* trying to leave the front gate with a bag. They grabbed him and brought him to Srila Prabhupada. Prabhupada said, "You said you were surrendering, and I gave you a chance. But now you have revealed that you are not sincere." He called the police and gave Achyutananda over to them.

Badrinarayan: A devotee said, "Prabhupada, when I joined I was only eighteen and it was easy for me to follow the principles. Now, so many years later, my life has changed." He was going on and on. Prabhupada slammed his hand down and said, "Then why did you promise? Only an animal can't keep his promise." Prabhupada was so heavy.

Govinda: Srila Prabhupada said, "The problem is that the Western boys and girls often go to the other side." I asked, "What do you mean by 'the other side?' Do you mean that they go back to the way they were before they became devotees?" In other words, the tendency is that when devotees stop devotional service, they return to their previous lifestyle. He said, "Yes. They go as they were before. Therefore many of them will have to take birth in India to finish their Krishna consciousness."

Jayapataka Swami: When we moved from the grass hut to the lotus building, the first multistory temple guest house where Prabhupada's quarters were, we had a big feast and invited many villagers to come. After the feast was over, all the leaf plates were thrown behind the temple, and Prabhupada went upstairs to his room. I was sitting with Srila Prabhupada in the room when we heard a dog barking in the back. Prabhupada got up and walked all the way to the veranda, looked over, and saw the big pile of banana leaf plates. So many people had taken *prasadam* that there was a big pile of leaves (using a leaf as a plate is the organic way that one eats in India). There were some very poor young children with torn clothes and sticks in their hands who were beating off the dogs to get the remnants of food that people had left on their plates. When Prabhupada saw how children had to fight dogs to eat throwaways, he started to cry. Tears were coming down. He said, "How hungry they must be." Who would stoop to that situation, to fight off dogs to eat things that other people had thrown away? Prabhupada was so moved by these hungry children that he said, "We have to organize in such a way that nobody within a ten mile radius of the temple is hungry. Everyone should have food to eat." That's when they organized "ISKCON Food Relief," which later became "Food for Life." Prabhupada wanted a regular program of *prasadam* distribution, and we were distributing seven days a week. Five days for children and pregnant and nursing mothers, and seven days for anybody without discrimination—Hindus, Muslims, and Christians, men, women, young and old. Prabhupada was so moved when he saw that the people were hungry.

Govinda: When Srila Prabhupada spoke about something, you would experience it. It was like a transmission. Before going back to Hawaii, he began to speak about compassion. His eyes were closed and there were tears running down his cheeks. He said, "People are suffering in this world." He was expressing divine compassion for all the souls suffering in this world without Krishna consciousness. He said, "Please go and teach them. Tell them about Krishna. Give them this knowledge because they are suffering. They don't know they are suffering but they are suffering." He was in such a compassionate mood that tears were coming down his cheeks. He was showing how much love he had for all the *jivas* in this world who don't know about Krishna.

TAPE 3

Brahmananda das
Nara Narayan das
Gurudas das

Brahmananda: I went up to the Swami's apartment and knocked on the door. The Swami opened the door. "Yes?" he said. I said, "I would like to speak with you." "Oh, yes. Come in." We went together into the sitting room. Prabhupada sat down behind a little metal box, and we started talking. It was very quaint. He asked me my name. I told him, "Bruce." Then Prabhupada told me that in India during the Raj period there was a "Lord Bruce." I started telling the Swami about myself, and I found myself saying, "I want to become your full time student." I had just finished taking a special training course for teaching, and I was employed by The New York City Board Of Education to teach Remedial Reading, a special program for culturally deprived children in the ghettos. I told the Swami, "I have just finished my training." My assignment was beginning the next day. I said, "I have a job beginning tomorrow, but I just want to be your student." Prabhupada said, "That's fine, but you have a job." I said, "Yes." He said, "What is the salary?" Prabhupada explained *Bhagavad-gita* to me in a nutshell. He explained how Krishna told Arjuna to do his duty, to do devotional service, to work for Him, but not to partake in the fruits of the activity. He explained how one should give all the fruits of one's activity to Krishna. Then Prabhupada gave me a practical instruction. It was my first instruc-

43

tion. He said, "You can be my student, and you can also do your job. You can give the fruits of your job to Krishna." So my first service was to work and give my salary to Prabhupada.

Nara Narayan: Some friends of mine had a place at 518 Frederick Street in Haight-Ashbury, San Francisco, that they were about to give me for a sculpting studio. Before I could move in, Prabhupada somehow moved into my studio. I was rather shocked and upset. My studio! I thought, "What's going on here? I had this great studio, and now it's gone." But then my heart softened, and I thought, "Well, he is a yogi and he is doing good, so I guess it's okay." I forgave fate, little realizing what an amazing turnaround was going to take place.

Gurudas: Prabhupada, Swamiji at the time, didn't tell us about the *vyasasana*. He didn't make us cut our hair. He didn't say anything about bowing down. He just accepted things as they were. He accepted us. Krishna had sent us, enthusiastic, young and believing we could do anything. We were adventurous and not too staid in any lifestyle. We were able to go along with and do anything, and that's what happened.

A New York contingent slowly came to San Francisco. Among them there was an artist, Haridas, Harvey Comb, who came in an old Cadillac. We called it the "Krishnalac." For some reason Haridas put a totem pole with noses, rings, masks, and moons right by the temple altar in Frederick Street. Prabhupada just accepted it, along with eclectic pictures, pictures of Lord Jesus, and so on. Prabhupada didn't tell us to do too much, but he did teach Yamuna, Harsharani, and Govinda dasi how to cook. Once, when Prabhupada was sick, the doctors told Govinda dasi to give Prabhupada a special diet. Prabhupada called them the "starvation committee." He wanted his standard diet instead.

Brahmananda: I had been home to visit my mother, and she knew we were strict vegetarians. We wouldn't eat the food that she cooked because the pots were contaminated, and she was contaminated. The whole house was contaminated. She said, "Hey, what's happening here?" and one evening just before the *kirtan* she went to visit Prabhupada to see what we were getting into.

Prabhupada had a folding metal chair in his room, which was meant for VIPs who couldn't sit on the floor. My mother sat on this chair. Everyone else, including Prabhupada sat on the floor. She asked Prabhupada, "What are you doing with my boys?" After explaining and preaching, Prabhupada told her, "I am taking care of your sons," because by that time Gargamuni and I had moved into the storefront. "I am feeding them, looking after them, and providing. Actually, we have no income here. Maybe you would like to give some donation?" My mother looked at us, looked at Prabhupada, and said, "Donation? I have already given a donation. I have donated my sons." Prabhupada said, "Oh, yes, very good." By her saying that, it was as if she gave us to Prabhupada.

Nara Narayan: On Hippie Hill in Golden Gate Park, 1966 or '67, Prabhupada led a *kirtan* while Hayagriva played the trumpet, others played drums, gongs, and cymbals, and incense burned. One of the things I used to do for pleasure was to look at people when they weren't looking at me and make them turn around. I thought I would try that on Swamiji. I stared and stared and stared, and nothing happened. Then I looked at a bunch of other people that were standing around in the crowd, and they turned around very fast just as if a little bee had landed on their neck. But when I stared at Prabhupada nothing happened. I was alarmed and became very determined "I am not going to leave this place until the Swami turns around." It was a control issue. I went on and on staring. I was sweating and still nothing happened. Swamiji was simply chanting, looking ethereal, totally unaffected. Finally I began to plead and actually beg. The minute I sincerely begged, his eyes floated around to the side and he looked at me. I froze. That moment seemed like an eternity. He neither beckoned nor rejected, just observed. My whole system collapsed from the inside out. I said, "Oh my God." All sorts of confusing emotions ran through me. I thought, "I must straighten myself out and think things through. I am not ready to become his disciple yet." My first impulse was to become his disciple.

Gurudas: Haridas decided to paint the Panchatattva Deities, but he thought They were women and he painted Them with breasts. When the new painting was unveiled over the new altar, Prabhupada said, "*Ahhhh,*" and told Haridas, "Those are men, not women. Please change it." Haridas changed it. It's amazing how Prabhupada was so patient. He introduced things very slowly.

Brahmananda: When the Swami walked into the storefront to give class, everyone bowed down, and I started bowing down too. Gargamuni was the only one who wouldn't. He would just sit there. This went on for some time, and Gargamuni felt a little self-conscious about it. After class, Prabhupada would always ask for questions, and on one occasion Gargamuni said, "When you come into the room, everyone bows down, but I don't feel like bowing down, so I am not going to do it because it would be artificial. I am asking if this is all right." Prabhupada said, "You should bow down. By bowing down the feeling will come." This was a very nice instruction, and when Gargamuni started doing that, it worked.

Nara Narayan: In the early days we were used to Prabhupada's personal association, and his association was galvanizing. He was like a magnet, and everything else was like iron filings. All things fell into place. It was simple to be a devotee, to be spiritual. If Prabhupada said, "This is how to cook *dahl,*" suddenly you became empowered to cook *dahl.* If he said, "This is how you chant," suddenly you became empowered to chant. If he said, "Get this building," suddenly you got that building. All you had to do was to suspend disbelief long enough to do it. By Prabhupada's direct, kinetic, personal presence, it happened.

If Prabhupada told people to work together on something, never mind they were enemies ten minutes before, they could work together perfectly just as the lion got along with the deer when Lord Chaitanya went through the Jarikhanda Forest. Prabhupada took away the ego barriers that made it impossible to see the higher self and to see one another's relationship with Krishna. Since Prabhupada was continuously channeling Supersoul, he was channeling the source of everyone's well being. He had all the information. When Prabhupada went to another temple, everyone tried and tried to maintain the standard, but being what we were, it would gradually sink down. When Prabhupada came back, all of a sudden there was excitement and everything worked again. In those days we imagined that Prabhupada would always go from temple to temple to temple keeping us revived.

Gurudas: I would take lots of photographs, and sometimes Prabhupada would tease me, saying, "Why you are photographing me so much? Photograph something important like people chanting." Once in San Francisco when I was photographing he said, "There is a superstition in India that if someone is photographed, it will shorten his life. What do you think?" I stopped. I said, "I think how long one lives depends on how one lives." He said, "Yes. That other idea is just a superstition."

Brahmananda: Prabhupada told me to invite my parents to the initiation. My father wouldn't come, but my mother came. Again she sat on the folding chair. We had the fire sacrifice, and at the end Prabhupada gave me my beads and I bowed down to him. Then Prabhupada said, "Now bow down to your mother." So I turned and bowed down. Of course, I said the mantra of obeisances to Prabhupada. My mother felt quite uncomfortable having her son bowing at her feet. Prabhupada instructed me, "Whenever you see your

mother, offer your obeisances," and I did that. My family lived in
Connecticut, and once I went there to distribute books to them and
to friends. I rang the doorbell, my mother opened the door, and
there was nobody there because I was on the ground offering obeisances. She didn't like it, but it was Prabhupada's instruction, and
by doing it we felt closer to Prabhupada, and our family attachment dissipated. It made the relationship more formal. It was a nice
instruction.

Gurudas: Yamuna and I knew a number of people who could have
married us, but we said, "We would really like the Swami to do it."
So we asked him, "Would you marry us?" He said, "First you must
become initiated." I said, "When do you want us to become initiated?" He said, "Tomorrow." Tomorrow came, and I was still with
my old jazz friends, uncertain whether to go ahead with it or not. My
friends said, "Don't get initiated. Stay with us." Some Christian said,
"This Krishna consciousness is paganism." I was swayed, and right
up to the last minute I was calling the temple saying, "I am coming,"
and then hanging up the phone and saying, "I don't want to do it."
No one, including me, was sure if I was going to show or not, but
finally I did.

Four of us got initiated that day. I was afraid. I knew that it
meant that I would have to surrender even though there was no
great Movement at the time, just twelve, fourteen, sixteen people
around who ate and chanted. There was no bowing down nor shav-
en heads. It was just a lot of fun. Prabhupada was like our father
sitting in our midst.

In the early morning *kirtan,* people were still coming off all-
night LSD trips. It was part of the whole scene. They would come
to the temple to chant and have breakfast. At my initiation there
were all sorts of freaks. The temple was smoking like anything
because Janaki brought compressed wood instead of real wood.
We also used margarine instead of butter, so the flame sputtered
and smoked. Prabhupada said to me, "You will be Gurudas das,"

but I was so frightened at the time that I didn't hear my name. Afterwards I said to Prabhupada, "When would you like to marry us?" He said, "Tomorrow." He didn't want to give me too much time to think.

Nara Narayan: I joined a few weeks before Srila Prabhupada arrived. I had been fixing up the temple, fixing up *sankirtan* vans, and doing all sorts of other work. When Srila Prabhupada was due to arrive, the devotees rented an apartment for him on Ashbury Street, and they told me, "Quick Nathan, you have to build an altar for Srila Prabhupada." So I made a simple wooden altar for Srila Prabhupada and decorated it. When Srila Prabhupada came, he asked, "Who has made this altar?" They said, "Nathan." He said, "Bring him here." So I came, and he approved. Before that I had written a letter to Srila Prabhupada saying that I wanted to serve Krishna in every way possible. He wrote back and said, "My dear Nathan, this is a very rare manifestation. I think you were a devotee in your previous life. To begin your service, wanting to serve Krishna in every way possible means you have done devotional service before." He said, "Please continue. Chant your rounds. Engage in devotional service. Carve Deities." He gave me his blessings through that first letter, which in and of itself was enough to keep me going for a lifetime.

Gurudas: Rabindra Svarup was a sensitive, thoughtful, poetic, and ascetic-looking person who obviously loved Prabhupada. He didn't speak too much, but sometimes said things honestly and abruptly. He said what he thought. Prabhupada loved him very much.

In the middle of a *kirtan,* Rabindra Svarup said, "I've got to reach God directly. I cannot do it through anybody else" and he started to cry. This was his conflict. He didn't want to do it with any priest, or intermediary. He loved Prabhupada, but he said, "I've got to do it on my own." Prabhupada said, "Come here, my boy." Rabindra Svarup came right up on the *vyasasana* and put his head on Prabhupada's lap. Prabhupada said, "Dear boy, I just want you to be happy. I just want you to be happy." Rabindra Svarup looked into Prabhupada's face and cried. Prabhupada looked at him very compassionately. Then Rabindra Svarup bolted up off the *vyasasana* and out the front door. He didn't sneak out in the middle of the night. We were all there. We saw him run out, and we were all shaken by it because we were a family. His girlfriend Haladapi was there, and she didn't know whether she would ever see him again. He just left, slamming the door behind him. Prabhupada said, "Now let us chant," and he led with sizzling *kartals*. Prabhupada didn't say anything about the incident. We all chanted and cried.

Brahmananda: On Memorial Day weekend in '67 Prabhupada had a stroke. After that he couldn't type. He was partially paralyzed on one side. Gargamuni had seen office dictaphones in a store window, and when he told Prabhupada, Prabhupada said, "Yes. Bring that." Gargamuni bought one, a German Grundig, and had the salesman show him how to operate it. It took Gargamuni an hour to learn. He brought the dictaphone to Prabhupada and offered to show Prabhupada how to use it. Prabhupada said, "No, no. That's all right. You just leave it here. I will see to it." Prabhupada was able to operate it without anyone showing him how to do it.

Then Prabhupada dictated tapes, and we transcribed them. Everyone took a try at transcribing. We all found it tedious, and we weren't making much progress on it. Prabhupada was doing more and more tapes, and this became a problem. Hayagriva was the best typist, but he was going to teach in the University. Then one day Neil from Antioch College walked in the storefront. At Antioch College, you can work at a job and get college credit for that job if it has something to do with your study. Neil came to New York wanting to work for the Hare Krishna organization for a semester. He didn't know what we were doing. I asked him, "What do you do?" He said, "I am a typist and a transcriber." I said, "Okay." It was like the answer to a prayer. There were many little miracles. Everything with

Prabhupada was always accompanied by little miracles one after the other.

Neil raced through those tapes transcribing. He finished *Bhagavad-gita, The Nectar of Devotion, Teachings of Lord Caitanya,* and the *Sri Isopanisad.* When his semester ended, he left and we never saw him again. But he had done so much, and it was just what was required.

Nara Narayan: The first experience I had alone with Srila Prabhupada was in Seattle. We had rented a gorgeous place for Prabhupada, a garden apartment overlooking beautiful lawns with flowers. Prabhupada loved it. Harsharani and Govinda dasi were his servants. I came over, and Srila Prabhupada spoke to me about going to New Vrindavan to build dioramas. He wanted to start a F.A.T.E.-museum-type-thing in New Vrindavan. At some point Prabhupada and I were alone in the room. Srila Prabhupada was sitting on a cushion on the floor behind his low desk showing me how he would save paper by writing the first draft of a letter on the back of a used envelope, which he opened up with a letter opener. When he had it down the way he wanted it, he would draft it out again onto a letterhead.

Somehow he had asked me to do something, and in the end I was behind his desk and he was on the other side. I was on my toes and alarmed by the experience of being alone with Prabhupada. "Oh my God, what do I got to do now? I have no instruction. I don't even know what to say." I was just initiated and was still psychadelicizing a little, having recently been part of the Haight-Ashbury. I was mortified, wringing my hands, squirming my toes, not wanting to leave, but not knowing what to do if I stayed.

Srila Prabhupada said, "We should always be considering, 'What is my duty?'" I thought, "Duty. Okay." I was hearing impaired since I was young, and between Prabhupada's accent, my inability to hear, and the psychedelics residually floating in my brain cells, I was having a hard time understanding. Prabhupada pointed to his coffee table and said, "Do you see this ant?" I looked carefully. I knew that Srila Prabhupada was the external representative of the Supersoul, and if he said that there was an ant, then there was an ant. But there was no ant.

I didn't want to say "No" and appear stupid to not see the spiritual or whatever ant that was there, and I didn't want to say "Yes" and be proven a liar because I couldn't see the ant. Srila Prabhupada looked at me intensely, as though the ant issue was now solved. He wanted to get on to real business. He said, "My job is to understand, 'What is my duty to this ant?'" Not only was there an ant that I couldn't see, but now I had a duty to it. Prabhupada looked at me almost beseechingly, "Somehow I have to help this ant. Maybe I can chant Hare Krishna to it or feed it a little *prasadam*. If we can help one ant become Krishna conscious, then our whole movement is a glorious success."

I realized that it was a pure metaphor. I had a duty to feed and chant to this invisible ant, and if I did so, and if we all did our respective Krishna conscious duties, our whole movement would be successful.

Gurudas: Prabhupada liked how Saraswati, Malati, and Shyama-sundar's four-year-old daughter, helped encourage everyone to chant during *kirtan*. Later on he gave her a small Deity of Krishna. Saraswati became quite attached to her Deity, and one day Prabhupada hid her Deity behind his back. Saraswati was looking, "Where is Krishna?" Prabhupada also encouraged her, "Where is Krishna?" Saraswati became anxious, "Where is Krishna? Where is He?" When Prabhupada returned the Deity to her he pointed out how separation from Krishna can increase our awareness of Him and love for Him.

Brahmananda: Prabhupada was determined to publish *Bhagavad-gita As It Is*, but we didn't have enough money to print it ourselves. Allen Ginsberg, who wasn't a devotee but who was very sympathetic and enthusiastic, tried to help. Allen had been to India and liked chanting. Prabhupada had instructed him to chant Hare Krishna before he read poetry, and Allen used to do that. He gave Prabhupada a harmonium, which he had brought from India. He also gave donations, and he was helping with Prabhupada's immigration papers. Allen sent Prabhupada's *Bhagavad-gita* manuscript to his publishers, but they rejected it. He sent it to some other publishers, and they also rejected it. After about six months of trying, he lost interest.

Prabhupada gave the manuscript to Rayrama, who was the editor of *Back to Godhead* magazine. Rayrama sent it to academic publishers, and again everyone rejected it. He gave up. Then Prabhupada gave the manuscript to me. By that time I could see that this book had no commercial value. Every page was Krishna consciousness. I thought, "If you are not Krishna conscious and you are not interested in Krishna consciousness, you are not going to be interested in this commentary." There was no fancy poetry, no scholarly footnotes, no academics, and no esoteric things. I had no faith, and I didn't know what to do. I went to bookstores and the library to learn how to get a book published.

In the meantime, Prabhupada had recorded the Hare Krishna record, which the Beatles eventually got interested in, and the record was doing well. One alternative radio station, WBAI, played it over and over again for ten hours.

I used to get the mail, bring it to Prabhupada, and he and I would go over it together. He would dictate the answer, and I would take notes. One day an order came for the record from the world-wide publishing company, MacMillan. The order was on MacMillan letterhead, and a check was included. I rushed to Prabhupada and said, "Prabhupada, someone's written from MacMillan!" I didn't know what to do. I was helpless. Prabhupada had to tell us everything. Prabhupada thought for a while and then said, "You personally bring the record tomorrow. Tell the person that you have a *Bhagavad-gita* that you want to publish." I said, "Okay. Should I bring the manuscript with me?" He said, "Just tell them." I said, "Okay. But I have to say something about you as the author. Maybe I should bring some of the books you published in India." He said, "No. Just tell them that you have a *Bhagavad-gita* to publish." I said, "Okay."

The next day I dressed in a suit and tie and went uptown to the MacMillan Company skyscraper. The person who bought the record was an accountant. He added numbers and had nothing to do with publishing. I was thinking, "How am I going to tell him? What am I going to tell him?" We were talking about the record and the mantra and I was bewildered. Then the door opened and all of a sudden the accountant said, "This is James Wade. He is our senior editor." I shook hands with Mr. Wade, looked him right in the face, and said, "I have a *Bhagavad-gita* to publish." He said, "A *Bhagavad-gita*? By a Swami? An Indian Swami? Here in New York? He did this himself?" I said, "Yes." He said, "Complete? The entire *Bhagavad-gita*?" I said, "Yes. Yes." He said, "That's exactly what I am looking for to fill out our religion section. I've got Buddhism, the Koran . . . We have everything, but we don't have a *Bhagavad-gita*. We will publish it."

I couldn't believe what had happened. He agreed to publish it without seeing the manuscript. Everyone else had rejected it for whatever reason, and here he accepted it without even seeing it. I flew back to Prabhupada and told him the news. I was so excited. Prabhupada nodded as if he had expected it.

Nara Narayan: Prabhupada and Allen Ginsberg had a joint program at a university in Columbus, Ohio. Prabhupada led an incredible *kirtan*. Everyone was ecstatic and wanted to dance, but it was an auditorium and there was no place to dance, so they danced on the armrests of the theater seats. Not only devotees danced, but everybody, thousands of students. Ginsberg was excited about Krishna consciousness. Although he never became a devotee, he was enthusiastic about chanting the Hare Krishna mantra. He used to hold *kirtan* all over the place on his own.

There was supposed to be a wire to hold the microphone around the speaker's neck, but it was missing. Allen Ginsberg offered Srila Prabhupada his shoelace as a substitute, but Prabhupada did not want to take Allen Ginsberg's shoelace to hold a microphone. He said to me, "Nara Narayan, give me your sacred thread." He had told me never to take the sacred thread off, but now he gave me a direct instruction to take it off. I felt exalted. I said, "Sure," took it off and handed it to Srila Prabhupada. He said, "Thank you," and put the sacred thread on the microphone.

The whole program went fabulously. Allen Ginsberg chanted, Prabhupada chanted, and it was very exciting. It gave a great boost to the beginning of the Columbus temple.

I was designated to wash Allen Ginsberg's clothes in the laundromat. He and Prabhupada were carrying on great dialogues in the small temple room. All the devotees couldn't fit into the room, so we drilled a hole through the wall of the closet in the next room, and a dozen of us, trying not to cough or sneeze, peered through that closet wall at what was going on in the temple room. During one of those sessions Srila Prabhupada talked to Allen Ginsberg about the nature of Kali-yuga.

Prabhupada described how bad Kali-yuga was going to get, how there would cease to be any foliage, how all the animals would be carnivorous, how people would be cannibals, and how fruits will be big seeds surrounded by skin. There would be nothing to eat, and what few devotees there were would live in caves. He described the Krishna conscious version of the end. Allen Ginsberg said, "And your disciples? They will be in the caves?" Srila Prabhupada said, "My disciples will have gone back to Godhead by then." Ginsberg was very impressed. He said, "Oh, really?" Prabhupada said, "Yes. They are very advanced. They are going to go back very shortly. They are chanting. They are taking part in this process. They are becoming pure devotees in this lifetime." Ginsberg said, "Yes. And what will happen to the rest of us?" Prabhupada leaned over to Ginsberg, and Ginsberg leaned over to Prabhupada. Prabhupada said, "Allen, at the end of Kali-yuga, I will eat you and you will eat me. To avoid this you must go back to Godhead."

Gurudas: Prabhupada had a fast wit. People would say, "Swamiji, you look so nice today." He would say, "Just today?" When he was trying to get permission to immigrate, Nandarani and Dayananda were thinking of sponsoring him. He said, "You can adopt me, but they will say, 'What will you do with such an old child?'" Also for immigration purposes, Allen Ginsberg offered a woman for him to marry. He said, "No, no. I cannot do that." (In the early times there was more than one woman that asked him to marry her not for immigration purposes. One person followed him to Montreal.)

Brahmananda: Prabhupada had a serious stroke on Memorial Day weekend when everyone had left New York City. Prabhupada couldn't function. We didn't want to bring him to a hospital, so I called my family doctor, but he was out of town. I started making random calls, but everyone was out of town for the weekend. Ultimately an old Jewish doctor came to see Prabhupada. The devotees were walking around barefooted, wearing jeans and T-shirts, chanting. We had no furniture, just a carpet. The doctor couldn't figure out what was going on. Meanwhile Prabhupada was very sick.

It took the doctor a long time to understand what was going on, what to speak of examining Prabhupada with the stethoscope and this and that. Afterwards we asked, "What's wrong?" He said, "I think the old man prays too much." We said, "Oh. Yeah. Okay." The doctor said, "He's got to get out. He's got to get some exercise." Prabhupada could hear him from the other room. "In the mornings he should go to the park for a walk." Then the doctor left.

Eventually Prabhupada went to the hospital. When he came out we took him to a rented house by the seashore in New Jersey, where he recovered. One day he announced, "Now I will take a morning walk. That doctor said something valuable." We thought the guy was nuts. Prabhupada said, "No, no. He has given a good instruction. I will take that up." Prabhupada proceeded to take a morning walk, and Prabhupada always took that morning walk, no matter what his condition, what his health.

When Prabhupada was in a hotel in Switzerland it was snowing. Prabhupada couldn't go outside for his morning walk, so he took it in the hotel corridors, walking and chanting just as if he were outside. When Prabhupada and all of us were injured in an automobile accident in Mauritius, we had aches and pains, but the next morning he went on his morning walk. Prabhupada followed that doctor's instruction.

Gurudas: Prabhupada was on a live call-in talk show hosted by a man who had a reputation for being unkind to guests. Jayananda, Mukunda, maybe Hayagriva, and I went along. Gargamuni stayed back to call in some questions.

The host began, "Welcome to the United States, Swamiji," and one of us gave a brief introduction about the philosophy of Krishna consciousness. Then Gargamuni called and asked, "What is the meaning of life, Swamiji?" Prabhupada explained, "The meaning of life is to be a servant of God," for about twenty minutes. The next question was "Why are we on the earth planet?" Again Prabhupada gave a long answer. The host said, "We want questions from people outside of your group." The third question was tremendous, "Why are we here? What is our purpose for being here?" Again Prabhupada took fifteen, twenty minutes to answer. The host was anxious to get another point of view. Finally a woman with a midwest twang asked, "Swamiji, why is your temple in the Haight-Ashbury?" Prabhupada said, "The rents are inexpensive." She said, "Why are you teaching hippies?" Prabhupada said, "They are not hippies. They are happies." She said, "How did you get here from India?" He said, "I received free passage from my friend, Sumati Morarji, on the Scindia Steamship line." She said, "Who paid for it?" He said, "Free passage means there is no paying." She was getting frustrated. She said, "Are you a freeloader?" Prabhupada had never heard the word before, but he said, "Yes." We could hear her practically fall down on the kitchen floor. It sounded like she fainted. The host said, "I don't like her questions. I am going to punch her out." Then he started asking questions like, "What's that mark on your forehead?", and the program ended.

Nara Narayan: In 1969 I was casting the Kartamasha *murtis* and Govinda dasi was painting Them. I made eighteen of Them because that's how many temples we had at the time. I said, "My task is over, Srila Prabhupada. I've made as many Deities as there are temples." Srila Prabhupada said, "No. You must continue." I couldn't continue, because the mold went out, and I couldn't make another casting. I said, "Really? Who will we sell Them to? If we sell Them to karmis, they might put Them out on their lawns as some sort of lawn ornament like flamingos." Srila Prabhupada said, "If one karmi buys one *murti* and puts it on his lawn, our whole movement will be a glorious success." I thought, "Wow! That's different from the general gist of what we had been pursuing." His idea was that any contact with Krishna is a good contact with Krishna.

From that point on he encouraged cottage industries. He said that cottage industry keeps the family together in the house. He was against family members traveling long distances to work, and he mentioned how commuter trains "go fast in one direction simply so that later they can go fast in the other direction," and how the commuters must see less of their family.

People are meant to live and work in the same house together, with their family. He said, "The grandmother, the son, the child, the husband and the wife work. Together they make some product like the paintings of Puri or Rajastan. It's a group effort done by people who know how to do one part expertly. They sell their product and stay together as a family and practice God consciousness."

Gurudas: When Achyutananda was speaking with Prabhupada in

Vrindavan he said, "Gurudas is stationed in Vrindavan, but it would be good if he could come preaching around India." I said to Prabhupada, "I am happy in Vrindavan but I would like to preach too. What should I do?" He said, "Preach to the devotees. They need preaching." And it's true. I saw that after somebody joined, the courtship was over, and we grew complacent, forgetting that they were unique. So I took his instruction to heart and started preaching more. It was great. Everybody appreciated it.

In London when the devotees came back from *sankirtan*, Yamuna would serve them milk, and I would tell them stories or read Krishna Book. The devotees said it was like I was their father and Yamuna was their mother. Prabhupada encouraged us by saying, "Men and women are in this Bury Place temple. There is just one floor difference, but there is no illicit mixing. That is because this is a family. You are like the father, and Yamuna is like the mother. It is not artificial." It was a family type of thing.

When I was to take *sannyas*, I pointed out that my preaching to the devotees would diminish because people treat *sannyasis* differently and because married couples would stop coming for counseling. Prabhupada said, "Yes, that is so. But as a *sannyasi* you can preach more widely to the world."

Nara Narayan: In London in 1970, when I was a householder living like a *brahmachari*, I began to wonder, "How am I going to get anywhere?" Certainly Prabhupada is proof positive that Krishna consciousness is not a fantasy but a practical, normal condition of existence. Normal people are devotees, and there are more of them than there are of us. They are happy, real people that are perfectly fixed in the *atmarama* state of pure, unalloyed love of God. "But what about me? Will I ever get there?" I was chanting *japa* in the small Bury Place temple in London. I had just finished redecorating the whole place, and I was pacing in front of Srila Prabhupada's room when I became overwhelmed by the urge to knock on the door and ask Prabhupada "Am I going to make some progress?"

I knocked on Prabhupada's door and regretted it immediately afterwards. Srila Prabhupada said, "Yes? Come in." I opened the door. I was twice as scared as the first time I described. I crept into his room, and there he was pacing up and down, his *japa* bag in his hand, in the wonderful atmosphere that he had created for himself. Hare Krishna Hare Krishna. . . . I came in saying, "Oh no. I am here. I have to ask a question." I shut the door behind me and crouched in a corner like a mouse. Prabhupada looked at me and said, "Yes?" I said, "Srila Prabhupada, I am chanting. I am following the program. I keep wondering, is it possible that I could ever become a pure devotee? I see that you are a pure devotee, but can I ever become a pure devotee?"

Srila Prabhupada looked at me appraisingly and marched back and forth a few times, all the while muttering, "Hare Krishna Hare Krishna" to himself. I got more and more nervous because I was wondering about the answer. He looked at me and said, "Why not? You are in the process." I was so happy I was melting into a puddle of *ghee*. He chanted a few more times, came around the room, looked at me with a glimmer in his eye and said, "But it may take some time."

Gurudas: Prabhupada and I were walking together. I had begun to go to the India Office Library and the British Museum in London. The British Museum library had some old Gaudiya Math books, and the India Office Library had everything, including Bhaktisiddhanta's works and the poem that Prabhupada wrote to Bhaktisiddhanta Sarasvati in 1935, "Adore, adore ye all the happy day." I had found that in his handwriting and sent it to him, and he was happy to receive it.

In the library I had begun to read Bhaktivinoda Thakur's writing about Puri, and I liked his poetry, imagery and compassion. In my heart I liked Bhaktivinoda Thakur's writings the best. I liked Prabhupada the best, but Prabhupada had a formal side, a public persona. When he lectured he was sometimes stern. His writing is very nice, but sometimes I found it repetitious. I am just being

honest, not blasphemous. I liked Bhaktivinoda Thakur's writings
the most, but on the walk I lied. I said, "I like Bhaktivinode Thakur
as my second favorite author." Prabhupada looked at me and said,
"Second?" Again he read my mind. I said, "Actually, he is my favorite." He said, "Yes. If I were one-tenth of Bhaktivinoda Thakur, I
would be a great devotee."

Brahmananda: Prabhupada didn't specifically order the different
aspects of the movement. He guided us, but we had to find them
out for ourselves, from our enthusiasm and realizations. He never
made any demands, even with initiations. He didn't say "All right.
Now I am going initiate you." No. We had to come to Prabhupada
and ask, "Would you initiate us?" He never said, "Now you wash
my clothes." We had to come to Prabhupada, "Can I wash your
clothes?" That was the way it was done. "Can I learn how to cook?"
And even with *harinam*. . . . when Prabhupada was there, he led
every *kirtan*. He would play the drum. He would say the prayers. No
one even dreamed of leading a *kirtan*. The Swami did it.

When Prabhupada left to go to Vrindavan after his stroke, then
we had to do it ourselves. As a matter of fact, when Prabhupada left
to go to San Francisco and do the Mantra Rock Dance that Mukunda
had arranged, all of a sudden those of us in New York thought,
"Who is going to give the lecture?" Prabhupada had given every
lecture. "Who is going to play the drum?" We were standing around
not knowing what to do. "All right. Why don't you try?" "Okay. I
will give the lecture." We just started doing it.

I wrote a letter to Prabhupada, "We miss you." Prabhupada
wrote back. "It's very nice that you are missing me, and if you like
you can put my photograph on my sitting place." That meant in
Prabhupada's apartment where he would sit. We didn't even have
a photograph. No one had a camera. We didn't even wear watches.
That is where we were coming from. We didn't want things. I
asked the devotees in San Francisco to take a photograph of Prabhupada and send it to us. We had it blown up and framed, and we

put it on Prabhupada's desk.

On Sundays Prabhupada used to take us to the park. We would carry the rug, and Prabhupada would sit under a tree and have a kirtan. But it was Prabhupada having a kirtan. Nobody ever thought, "Well, we will go ourselves," because everything was done by Prabhupada. It's hard to believe, but we were shy and reluctant. Just to do what we were doing at that time was far out, and people didn't know what to think of us. We felt self-conscious.

One summer night in New York we were having kirtan in the storefront, and it was too hot to be in there. Someone said, "Let's go outside." We went outside and started having kirtan. When we had kirtan in the storefront, some people would stop and look in, scratch their heads, and walk by. They thought that it was nuts. Mostly, the people who came in were drunks, Bowery bums. They would lurch in, and then I would lurch them back out. Only young hippie kids would actually walk in and stay.

I will never forget that first outdoor kirtan. We went to the street corner. I thought, "If we chant loudly enough, maybe Prabhupada will hear it in India. Somehow we will call out and connect." Someone played the tom-tom drum, and everyone chanted enthusiastically. A huge crowd formed, hundreds of people, some of them chanting along with us. We had flyers but no books. In the temple at the end of kirtan we used to pass around a collection bowl. Someone put that bowl on the sidewalk, and people started pitching money in. We realized, "Hey, this is a way to spread Krishna consciousness and to also get support." I wrote Prabhupada in India relating what happened. Prabhupada said, "Oh, very good. You continue this. Expand it." Prabhupada always guided us, but from behind.

Gurudas: Street sankirtan started in New York, but for us it began on Lord Chaitanya's Appearance Day. We were told to go to the temple and alternate between kirtan, japa, and reading the scriptures. After about three or four hours, Jayananda, Jivananda, Uddhava, and I thought, "Let's take this outside." Chanting, we went around

the corner to Willard Street where Prabhupada was staying. Prabhupada came to the window and motioned to us. We thought, "Oh, no.
He is telling us to go away," and we started back to the temple. Upendra, Prabhupada's servant, came storming out and said, "No, no.
That's the Indian way of saying 'Come here. Come here.'" We went
upstairs, and Prabhupada said, "Krishna has given you the intelligence to chant in the street. Now I want you to do this every day."
Street *sankirtan, harinam,* started for us as of that day.

Nara Narayan: Prabhupada's level of compassion was amazing.
While we were beginning to think that only "important" service was
important, that only "big" devotees were big, that monkeys were
good for building roads to Lanka but spiders weren't, Prabhupada
was taking a totally different approach. That approach was based on
true compassion. He had natural concern for people.

Just after Shyama dasi married Hayagriva in 1968, she got an
infection in one of her fingers. Prabhupada wrote five letters in
which he expressed concern about Shyama dasi's finger. In those
days we thought, "Oh, it's just your body. It's just made of stool,
worms, blood, puss, and all those nice things. Who cares about your
body? Chop off the finger and continue to serve Krishna." But
Prabhupada didn't think like that.

In those days we would copy Prabhupada's letters and distribute them to all the temples. Every temple had a book of Prabhupada
letters, probably a hundred or two hundred of them. When new
devotees came we would say, "Do you want to hear what a letter from
Prabhupada is like?" "A letter from Prabhupada" was like a buzz-
word. It must be like what ants feel like when they get their grain of
sugar. Once I was in the Detroit temple going through the letters
from Prabhupada and noticing how much compassion he was
directing towards one and all.

Gurudas: Srila Prabhupada had all the qualities of a great devotee.
Just by seeing him, one would think of Krishna. But the quality that

I remember most was his compassion. Prabhupada, although non-compromising and strict at times, was also open-minded. He did what the situation called for, whether tying up a microphone with a *brahman's* thread or understanding our complaints. With a compassionate look he once said to me, "If I don't forgive you, then Krishna will forgive you. And if Krishna does not, Radharani will."

Brahmananda: In the final days we were with Prabhupada in Vrindavan taking turns to softly chant with little cymbals in a vigil *kirtan*. At a certain point I got sick. I collapsed in my room with a fever, and it took me about a week to recover. Then I was able to again go and see Prabhupada. When I came into his room Prabhupada was lying on his bed conversing with his servants. Sometimes he would ask who was leading the *kirtan*. That particular day he mentioned my name. Prabhupada said, "Oh, Brahmananda?" I came forward. He said, "You were ill? You were not feeling well?" Here is Prabhupada completely shriveled up from fasting, but he was concerned that I was not feeling well. I just had a little fever, and here is Prabhupada on his departure bed saying, "Oh, you are not feeling well?" with such concern and love. I was totally affected by that, how Prabhupada could be thinking that I wasn't feeling well.

The thing that affected me most was how much Prabhupada loved us although we are not very lovable as we all had defects. Why did Prabhupada love us? He loved us because he saw us as servants of Krishna. He said that we were sent by his Guru Maharaj to help him in his mission. Prabhupada saw us as Krishna's servants, and Prabhupada's mission was to spread Krishna consciousness. Whatever we could do to assist in this cause of Krishna consciousness, Prabhupada very much appreciated. I think that is the essence of Srila Prabhupada. He can see us as servants of Krishna. So let us just try to be that. That's all.

TAPE 4

Madhudvisa das
Lokanath Swami
Srutakirti das
Nara Narayan das

 **Madhudvisa:** I had strung my own beads, but I didn't have *tulasi* beads. Gargamuni, who ran the store, ran out of *tulasi* beads because so many people were getting initiated. I had other beads, dark, blackish-red wood beads, which I had very proudly strung on an orange cord. They were very nice beads, I thought. On my initiation night, the moment of truth came when I gave Prabhupada my beads. In those days it was a very personal thing. Prabhupada would be sitting before the fire as you gave him the beads, and he would chant a whole round in front of you. So I came up and I gave Prabhupada my beads. He looked at the beads and said, "Oh. Rudraksha. We don't chant on Rudraksha. Rudraksha is like the Shiva bead. Shaivites chant on such beads." I had the sudden feeling of being rejected, "Oh no, I am right on the brink of becoming his disciple, but my beads are being rejected." I said, "No, no, Prabhupada. They are not Rudraksha." He looked at them more closely and saw that they weren't Rudraksha, and they also weren't *tulasi* beads. He said, "How come you don't have *tulasi* beads?" I said, "Oh, Gargamuni ran out of *tulasi* beads." He said, "Oh, this is all right," and he chanted on them.

Lokanath Swami: About fifteen of us went from Bombay to Mathura on a train and then to the Radha-Damodar temple by *tonga*. It was early morning when we entered Prabhupada's small quarters. I was sitting in front of Prabhupada, and we were all listening as he spoke. Whenever I used to hear someone with attention, I had a tendency to shake my knees, and I was sitting in front of Prabhupada doing that. Prabhupada said, "Stop it." That was my first personal meeting and his first instruction to me.

Srutakirti: We were always anxious to get some mercy from Prabhupada in the form of his belongings. The first opportunity I had to do this was after my *brahman* thread disappeared. I had gotten *brahman* initiation in Los Angeles in 1972, and one month later my original *brahman* thread—the one that Prabhupada had chanted on—was gone. I was very attached to this thread and totally devastated that my link was gone. I thought, "This is definitely a bad omen." Of course, then we didn't have *brahman* threads from India. We just got six strings and tied them in a knot, and that was a *brahman* thread. So that's what I did to continue chanting my *gayatri,* but I was never content. Later, when I had become Prabhupada's servant, for some reason there was no question of asking him, "Would you chant on a thread for me?" But I devised a plan. After being with him for a month he told me that on each Ekadasi he would change his *brahman* thread and at that time I could give him a new one. I thought, "Well now I will get Prabhupada's old *brahman* thread." Prabhupada was bathing, so I set up his table with his *tilak,* mirror, and a new *brahman* thread, as that day was Ekadasi. At this time Prabhupada was staying in the downstairs room at the Radha-Damodar Temple. I was on the veranda outside, just sitting, watching, and waiting. I was happy that I was going to get Prabhupada's *brahman* thread. Prabhupada put his *tilak* on and placed the second thread around his body and began chanting *gayatri*. By this time I was busy in the kitchen helping Yamuna get his lunch together. Prabhupada finished his *gayatri* and walked into the kitchen to take *prasadam*. I raced into his room to find that he had broken all six strands of his *brahman* thread. "Why did he do this?" I thought, "Because I wanted his thread?" I was very stubborn, so I tied each strand in a little knot, all six of them. I thought, "Now I have my *brahman* thread. Despite everything I still have it. Prabhupada has chanted on it so many times. So it is better than my original *brahman* thread." I took the *brahman* thread and put it in my pocket and went to Prabhupada while he was taking *prasadam*. He said, "So, that *brahman* thread that I have left on the table." I said, "Yes, Srila Prabhupada." He said, "You should take that *brahman* thread and dig under *tulasi* devi and bury it. I thought, "No. This is impossible. Is this what they do, or is he just doing this to me?" I said, "OK, Srila Prabhupada." Of course, I didn't obey that order because I was so determined. That was one order that Srila Prabhupada gave me that I just reneged on because I thought that I have to have this *brahman* thread. That was the beginning of many opportunities I had to get *maha-prasadam* from Srila Prabhupada.

 **Nara Narayan:** Once, in the La Cienega temple, on the occasion of his spiritual master's appearance day, Srila Prabhupada cooked a pot of *kichari*. He said that *kichari* was his spiritual master's favorite dish. Prabhupada cooked it using polished *urad dahl*, and it had a creamy consistency. There were thirty of us at that celebration, and there were many other dishes besides *kichari*. Since it was a holiday, everyone was in a jolly mood, talking and chatting, and we all got a dab of Prabhupada's *kichari* on our plates. By this time the *kichari* was cold, and Prabhupada had already gone to his quarters. We popped the *kichari* into our mouths, and all of sudden the conversation died out everywhere. As soon as that *prasadam* touched our tongues we fell silent. We sat there in dead silence tasting grain after grain of it until it was all gone. Then we searched for stray grains on

our plates. Then everybody began crawling towards the pot in the middle of the room where there was still a little bit left. We were taking little pieces out of the pot. No one spoke a word until there was nothing left. Then we all went back and sat down in silence. Something about that *prasadam* was charged with what must have been *gopi bhava*. There was ecstasy involved in that *prasadam*. We were struck by it. Every exquisite feeling that Prabhupada had for his spiritual master was present, and we had a chance to experience that; we realized that Prabhupada had given us an extra special benediction—he had allowed us to open the door a little and peek into what his world was like.

Madhudvisa: He said, "Your name is Madhudvisa das." The way he said it, it became genuine. When he said, "Madhudvisa das," everybody said, "Wow, Madhudvisa das? What does that mean? Who is that? What did he say?" Then I forgot my name right away. Although I heard him say it clearly, I forgot it. Later on I asked Prabhupada what the name meant. He said, "'Dvisa' means to be envious and 'Madhu' is a great demon. So 'Madhudvisa das' means one who is envious of Madhu." I said, "Prabhupada, how can Krishna be envious of anyone?" Prabhupada said, "No. Krishna can be envious too. Madhu was such a great demon that He became envious of him and cut his head off. He annihilated the Madhu demon. Anything is possible for Krishna, any emotion in its perfect form."

Lokanath Swami: One morning we were walking on Juhu beach while birds were flying overhead in perfect formation. These birds would fly in a line or make a u-turn all together. So I asked Prabhupada, "How do these birds fly in a perfect formation? How do they communicate with each other?" And Prabhupada's response was, "They are not less intelligent like you are."

Madhudvisa: The first time Prabhupada gave me a personal assignment was in Los Angeles after we had just moved into the La Cienega temple, which was the first church in the history of ISKCON. Before this, in New York City, Los Angeles, San Francisco, we had always operated out of storefronts. That was the modus operandi of the devotees in those days: "Rent a storefront and open a temple." But on La Cienega Boulevard we had rented a fairly good-sized church. I was the treasurer, and Tamal Krishna Maharaj was the president, and we were at lagerheads with each other; somehow or other we were sometimes pulling in different directions. Srila Prabhupada called Tamal and me in together and said, "Why is there a problem?" Tamal said, "Madhudvisa can do the same things I can do. Sometimes he wants to do them, and sometimes I want do them, so we get into conflicts." Srila Prabhupada said, "Let Madhudvisa go to San Francisco and be the temple president there." I said, "Great. This is a breath of fresh air. I am going to become the temple president in San Francisco—the temple where I originally joined." That was a special responsibility because that's where the Ratha-yatra festival was held. In those days there was no other Ratha-yatra festival on a grand scale. There were some small festivals, but there wasn't even a Ratha-yatra festival in Los Angeles. San Francisco, however, was New Jagannath Puri and had a tradition of grand Ratha-yatras. So the first personal instruction that I received from Srila Prabhupada was to go to San Francisco, and he also said, "Make this Ratha-yatra even grander. Make it like it is in Jagannath Puri in India." I went to San Francisco with a feeling of responsibility.

Srutakirti: I went to New York when I got initiated, and, since I was with Kirtanananda as his servant, I would sit near Srila Prabhupada's *vyasasana*. The New York temple room wasn't very big and was very crowded because devotees from all over—Columbus, Pittsburgh, New Vrindavan, and other places—had come to New York to see Srila Prabhupada. Once, during *kirtan* in the temple room, devotees were crunched together. After we bowed down to pay our obeisances, a devotee behind me, whose head was right at my feet, got up at the same time I did. This devotee pushed me forward so that

I fell across Prabhupada's *vyasasana* and literally onto him. He looked over and said, "What is the difficulty?" Just like a mouse, I said, "It's nothing, Srila Prabhupada" and cowered back into my space. That was the first time I made my presence known to Srila Prabhupada.

Nara Narayan: There was a family named Acharya on our property in Juhu, and Srila Prabhupada was going to stay in their house. When Prabhupada was on a morning walk or traveling, he always had a flying wedge of disciples behind him. He'd be leading, and we would be swept along in his wake. So we came to the Acharya's small house, and the whole family was standing at the top of the stairs beaming and smiling, welcoming Prabhupada. Although we knew it was a small house, we were planning to crowd inside and sit down with Prabhupada because he always said some wonderful things when he came to someone's home. We all wanted to witness those wonderful things. So Prabhupada went up the stairs with his cane, turned in front of the Acharya family, looked grandly over his disciples and said, "Ah, now I am finally taking shelter of the Acharyas."

Madhudvisa: Srila Prabhupada was tremendously pleased with the Ratha-yatra festival. He said, "This is the process of keeping all of the devotees enlivened."

Lokanath Swami: Prabhupada gave instructions about bullock carts in September of '76, around Radhastami, when our Nitai Gaur traveling *sankirtan* party had come to Delhi. At that time we had lost our big buses from Germany. These buses could only stay for so many months in India, and Hamsadutta also had to return to Germany for some business. So I was left in charge of the traveling party. When Prabhupada realized that we had no mode of transportation he called me to his quarters and said, "What about bullock carts? These big machines and vehicles always break down and require so much maintenance." Maybe he knew that I had a simple village background and so came up with this new assignment of traveling from village to village in bullock carts.

Srutakirti: Every afternoon we would have Krishna Book readings, and I, fortunately, was the designated reader. Sometimes Prabhupada would make comments during the readings, sometimes he would just sit very quietly, and sometimes he would laugh. I would always try to find stories about demons because Prabhupada would react to these stories more than others. He would usually laugh when Krishna was killing the demons. One day while I was searching for a story to read, he said, "Just read from anywhere. Krishna is like a sweetball. Wherever you bite, it's sweet." Then I quickly went to the next page and began reading.

Madhudvisa: Prabhupada would stress how Lord Jagannath's going out for a chariot ride was part of our tradition. Prabhupada made it a very personal thing. Whenever Srila Prabhupada talked about Krishna, he made it personal. When we were standing before the Lord we couldn't sense that personal feeling and have that sense of rapport with Him.

When Srila Prabhupada arrived at the temple the day before the festival we were making the chariots right across the street in the lot. Prabhupada went over to the small lot, which was in disarray, and paid his obeisances in front of the chariots. Then he looked at me and said, "The chariots are as good as the Lord." That made it much more personal. Here we were building chariots for the Lord, but the chariots themselves were objects of worship. The whole spectrum of Krishna consciousness was there in the Ratha-yatra festival. The chariots, the garlands, the *prasadam*, the instruments, and the clothes for Deities, were all on that same worshipable level.

Nara Narayan: In Boston, Prabhupada said, "A devotee may come and may go away again tomorrow." We looked at Srila Prabhupada in disbelief and said, "Go away? But why would any devotee want to go away? This is it. This is the perfection. This is where you go to after you've done everything else. Why would anyone ever want to leave?" But Prabhupada said, "Nonetheless, some devotees will go away. Things will happen. Things will change. The words will be altered." "But we all listen to you, Srila Prabhupada. How would anything ever get altered? We will always just repeat what you say, and therefore it can't possibly get altered." Little did we know, but Prabhupada, having knowledge of past, present, and future, was planning for ten thousand years. Not simply planning for this week or this month or this year.

We were having a wonderful time bringing new people to the movement, *Back to Godhead* magazine was beginning to expand, and devotees were distributing more books. Then, years later, book distribution took off, and it became self-evident as to why and how so many books could be distributed. Prabhupada acknowledged that the people getting his books might misuse them and that we might have to absorb a karmic reaction from giving someone a book—maybe forcing it on them—that they later threw in the trash. Prabhupada said, "We have to accept that that might happen, and this is the risk that we were taking."

Madhudvisa: Prabhupada always had a close feeling with Jaya-nanda. Jayananda was the nuts-and-bolts man in San Francisco. When he first became a devotee he drove a taxi, even though he had a degree in Engineering from the University of Ohio. Somehow he was in San Francisco, became a devotee, and felt responsible for providing money for the temple. In the beginning, Jayananda was one of the few devotees who held down a nine-to-five job. Jayananda would always have a personal feeling if something were wrong or broken in the temple, specifically the cars. You could always find him underneath the cars, fixing them. Srila Prabhupada knew this. He knew that Jayananda was behind the scenes making it all work. Once when Prabhupada was lecturing and Jayananda walked in,

Prabhupada said, "Oh, the Goswami has arrived." Another time he said, "Jayananda looks just like Lord Chaitanya, big shoulders, big man." And Jayananda almost blushed his way out of existence. Prabhupada would compliment him like that because Jayananda was naturally so humble.

Srutakirti: Kirtananada said, "I have trained him in cooking. He cooks very nicely, but he doesn't know how to massage yet." Prabhupada said, "Anyone can massage. It's not very difficult." Then Prabhupada said to me, "So, follow me." We went outside, and he said, "Take the *lota*." I grabbed the *lota*. We walked about twenty or thirty paces and he said, "Give me the *lota*." I handed him the *lota,* and he went off into the bushes to pass. After a few minutes he came back and said, "Here. Now wash this." I immediately became aware of my service. As Prabhupada's servant, I did every menial thing, no matter what. I took great pleasure in this. I thought it was great. I was actually going to be taking care of Prabhupada in whatever little need he had.

Lokanath Swami: We went to see Srila Prabhupada the day we started our bullock cart *sankirtan* from Vrindavan to Mayapur. We wanted him to give an inaugural speech and some further instructions. Since it was winter, he told us that we should all have two blankets. He also said our carts should have rubber tires, not wooden ones, and he said that when we go to the village we should park next to the well because "the well is the heart of the village. All the people of the village come to the well to get water. So you need not go to them. They will come to you if you are next to the well." He said, "The well water will help you to be *suci*, to be clean." Those were his instructions. He also explained how Mahatma Gandhi had failed. Mahatma Gandhi had tried to keep people in the villages by stressing village industry and being happy with whatever resources were available in a five-mile radius. He was good, Prabhupada said, but "what was lacking was the spirituality which would satisfy the people's souls and enable them to be happy with the bare minimum facilities." He gave us a task. He said, "Go to the villages and try to increase their attraction for the holy names so that they have a higher taste. Then wherever they are, they will stay there." These were some of his instructions the day we started.

Madhudvisa: Srila Prabhupada used to travel with an entourage of three or four people: a secretary, a cook, a Sanskrit scholar. But when he was going to Nairobi, Africa, it was only for two weeks, and he decided that I would come with him. No cook, no secretary, no Sanskrit scholar would be coming. I was going to be everything rolled into one for those two weeks. I thought, "This is fantastic." I had been in India for a couple of years, and it was a struggle in those days. I was getting a little burned out.

Two or three days before we were to leave, we got a telegram from Brahmananda in Nairobi saying that the Deities which had been shipped from India had broken in transit. One reason why Prabhupada was going to Nairobi was to install Deities in the temple there. According to *shastra,* a broken Deity is not supposed to be installed. At that time we were in Jaipur, where all the Deities are made, and I had to frantically go around in a *riksha* for a couple of days trying to get new Deities for the Nairobi temple. When I finally found Deities, we realized that we couldn't ship Them because They might break. So we personally took these marble, three-and-a-half-foot, heavy Deities from Jaipur to Bombay to Nairobi. I carried each Deity onto the plane and set Them down in front of us. Prabhupada had a Deity in front of him, and I had a Deity in front of me. It was physically strenuous just to get on the plane. I had to go to customs, pick up Radha, walk up the gangplank onto the plane, put Her down, run back, get Krishna, and come back. Finally, we were on the plane, and I was a little tired. Prabhupada said, "Are you ready to fight?" I said, "Fight, Prabhupada? What do you mean?" He said, "We are Vaishnavs, and we must be ready to fight with the Maya-vadis." I said, "Well, yeah, all right." He said, "You be the Mayavadi, and I will be the Vaishnav. We will have a fight." I said, "Oh, Prabhupada, I don't know if I am qualified to debate with you like this." He said, "No. You be the Mayavadi." So as we flew over the Indian Ocean, Prabhupada and I, with the Radha and Krishna Deities in front of us, debated. I was a Mayavadi and, as I am not a very good devotee, I am also not a very good Mayavadi as far as sparring with Prabhupada philosophically. I was soundly defeated. Then he said, "All right, now, I will be the Mayavadi, and you be the Vaishnav. I said, "All right." I thought, "Now I know all the arguments. There is no way he can defeat me." So we started to argue again. And he was so expert that he was able to defeat me both as a Vaishnav and as a Mayavadi. After the defeat, Prabhupada said to me, "This is how expert you must become in your preaching. You must know your opponent's position so thoroughly that you can defeat your own philosophy with his philosophy. That's how expert you must become in this preaching of Krishna consciousness."

Srutakirti: As Prabhupada's servant, massage was the best time for me, as I was in close contact with him and doing nice service. It always made me feel very good. During massage in the morning, Prabhupada's secretary would come in, and Prabhupada would hear his letters and answer them. While he was doing this I was massaging him. I would start on his head and continuously massage his head until he said, "Okay," or gave a gesture with his body, and then I'd go to the next spot. Sometimes, if he was immersed in something, I could massage part of his body for a long time. Massage generally lasted about one hour. But sometimes it would go to two hours or two and a half hours if he was absorbed in his business. It was very nice, but it could also become a little bit tiring.

After being with him for some time, I started to feel that I knew what I was doing quite well. I would massage his head, and when I felt that I had done it sufficiently, I would move on to the next part of his body. I was doing this for probably a week or so. Then one day I was massaging his head, and I went on to massage his back. He didn't say anything. Then I stopped massaging his back and started to move around to the side when he said, "You massage until I tell you to stop, not you tell you to stop." From that time on, massage took a different turn—again I would do whatever Srila Prabhupada wanted.

Madhudvisa: After flying all the way to Nairobi, we finally arrived at the airport, exhausted. Then there was the ordeal of taking the Deities off the plane—first Krishna all the way down to customs, and then back up to the plane to get Radharani, and again all the way down to customs, waiting in line, moving one Deity up and another Deity up. Gradually we got through customs, and finally we were standing outside with the Deities and our luggage, and there were no devotees! There was not one devotee at the airport. A Hindu gentleman came over and said, "Oh, Bhaktivedanta Swami, you were supposed to arrive tomorrow." Prabhupada said, "They've got it wrong again." The gentleman said, "Well, I have a car. I will take you to the temple." We jumped in the car and went to the temple, but the door was locked. We knocked, and Brahmananda opened the door. He had just a little towel on. There is Prabhupada looking right at him. Brahmananda said, "Oh, my God!" and paid his obeisances. It was the day before Prabhupada was expected, so everything was in total disarray. The paint was still wet on the banister, the floors were wet, and construction was going on. Brahmananda fell flat on his face. "Prabhupada, you were supposed to come tomorrow." Prabhupada said, "Where is my room?" "Oh, it's not finished, Prabhupada." "Where is my room?" "Oh, back here." Prabhupada walked to his room, which was just a bare space with nothing in it. While he was sitting there, everybody was frantically running around trying to make his room into a room. Gradually everything came about. His room was completed, and the Deities were installed. Unfortunately though, I got hepatitis as soon as I arrived in Nairobi. So in my shining hour to be the secretary, the Sanskrit man, the cook, the masseur, everything, I was laying on my back. I was useless. Prabhupada came into my room while I was lying down, and I struggled to get out of the bed to pay my obeisances. Prabhupada said, "No, no. Stay there. Stay there." I said, "Prabhupada, I feel so bad. I am supposed to do all these things for you, and I can't do anything." He said, "That's okay. We can manage. You just get your health back." His compassion was there at every step.

Lokanath Swami: One time, while we were on the way to Mayapur with his bullock cart *sankirtan*, I wrote to Prabhupada hinting that we needed financial help to maintain the program. Prabhupada responded by sending me a letter with big *sankirtan* scores showing how many books were being distributed. He said that this is how we maintain our institution, by book distribution, and that I also had to do this. He said that outside help was not healthy. If my program was to be appreciated by the public, their appreciation should be practical. They should help by assisting me. Otherwise it was just lip service. In this way he encouraged us to increase book distribution in our bullock cart *sankirtan* program.

Madhudvisa: At the end of one Ratha-yatra festival, Prabhupada was sitting in his car getting ready to leave. I knelt down beside the open car door and said, "Prabhupada, is everything all right?" Prabhupada put his arm around my head, put my head on his lap, held his hand on top of my head and said, "Everything is first class." That was probably the most affectionate embrace I had ever experienced.

Srutakirti: In Bombay there were two kinds of cars: one looked like an old Plymouth and the other was an Ambassador. Everyone either had a Plymouth-like car or an Ambassador. Shyamasundar had driven Srila Prabhupada, Pradyumna, and me in the Plymouth-like car to go for a morning walk. We parked the car, got out, and had a nice walk. One and a half hours later we returned to the car. Shyamasundar tried to start it for a few minutes and then said,

"The key is not working. The key is not working." Prabhupada said, "What is wrong?" Shyamasundar said, "I don't know. I can't get the key to work in the car." We were sitting there for about five minutes, and all of a sudden two Indian men came up to the car and began talking to Srila Prabhupada in Hindi. Everything was very friendly. Prabhupada said, "He said that this is not our car. This is their car." The men decided that they wanted to take Srila Prabhupada to his quarters. They convinced him that they wanted to do this service because he was a swami. They said, "Swamiji, we will take you to where you are going." Srila Prabhupada and I remained in the back seat, and the two gentlemen got into the front seat of the car, while Shyamasundar and Pradyumna went to find the other car. Srila Prabhupada said, "This is the difference between your country and India. In your country, if we were sitting in someone's car, immediately they would have had us arrested. But here, we sit in their car and they want to take us home."

Madhudvisa: An old social worker, who was a very meticulous gentleman, came to see Srila Prabhupada. He had a well-tailored suit, a starched and cuff-linked shirt, a silk tie, spotless shoes, and neatly combed hair. Everything was just proper. Prabhupada started to talk about sex life and how, if a person just wants sex life, then he is like a dog. This gentleman said, "But I like sex life." Prabhupada said, "But to just want sex life is a doggish mentality. Does that mean you are a dog?" The gentleman said, "I guess so. That's what I like." The conversation went on in that way, and at the end, although the gentleman was soundly defeated, he didn't feel bad. Prabhupada said, "Bring prasadam." The gentleman said, "Oh, no. I am not eating anything right now." Prabhupada said, "No, no. You must take prasadam." Prabhupada knew that although this man was defeated philosophically, it really didn't affect him. Prasadam would enable him to make a little spiritual advancement. So Prabhupada insisted that this man take prasadam. Then a devotee brought a gulabjamun, a big sweet full of juice. The devotee plopped this particularly big *gulab* in the man's hand, a *gulab* that, like a sponge, had soaked in sugar water for a long time. The man had developed a nice, friendly relationship with Prabhupada and was saying some final words, like "Maybe we can see each other again." At the same time he was trying to balance this *gulab* in his hand so that it didn't drip. The juice from the *gulab* started to run down between his fingers. He was trying to tilt his hand up while talking to Prabhupada so that the *gulab* juice didn't drip. But the juice ran down his wrist, over his starched shirtsleeve, and dripped from his cufflink. He didn't know what to do with this *gulab*. Prabhupada said, "Eat it." "No, no. I don't want to eat it. I can take it with me." Prabhupada said, "No, no. You must eat it now." The man thought, "Well, I'll take a little bite of this *gulab*, and it will be all right. It will satisfy Prabhupada." So he took a little bite of the *gulab*, and it ruptured, and a deluge of sweetball juice ran out of the *gulab* and down his tie, on to his patent leather shoes. Juice was all over the place. Prabhupada said, "No, no. Eat it all. Eat it all." By this time the man didn't care. He threw it in his mouth, and the juice started to run down his face. His hand was full of *gulab* juice, his cufflinks, his tie, his pants, his shoes, and it's coming down his face. But he finished the *gulab,* smiled, and said, "That's very good." Prabhupada said, "Yes." Then the man said, "I'd like to have another one of those." Prabhupada said, "Very well." The man then said, "I think it will go well in my rum." Prabhupada said, "Wait a second. This is not to be put in your rum. This is *prasadam,* food offered to the Lord." The man said, "No, no. It tastes sweet. It will go well in my rum. I drink rum every night. I will put this *gulab* in my rum." Prabhupada called for another *gulab* and gave it to the gentleman. The gentleman got up and said, "Thank you very much, Prabhupada. It was nice meeting you" and started to walk out the door, when Prabhupada said, "Now, don't put that in your rum." The gentleman said, "All right. I will just eat it," and went out smiling with *gulab* juice all over him. It was hilarious. We couldn't believe what was going on.

Lokanath Swami: I had been two-and-a-half years in the movement when I asked Prabhupada if I could take *sannyas*. He said, "Wait." I waited for one year and again approached him. This was around the time that Prabhupada had asked Sridhar Swami, my colleague in Bombay, to go to Vrindavan for his *sannyas* initiation. When Prabhupada heard that I wanted to take *sannyas,* his first response was, "You are already a *sannyasi.*" When I was not satisfied, he started to explain the first verse of the sixth chapter of *Bhagavad-gita:* "One who is unattached to the fruits of his work and who works as he is obligated is in the renounced order of life, and he is the true mystic, not he who lights no fire and performs no duty." Prabhupada explained how that verse defines *sannyas.* But I was not budging an inch. I was keeping some pressure on. He said, "So you want to undergo the formality of *sannyas?*" I said, "Yes, Prabhupada." Prabhupada said, "You also go with Sridhar and meet me in Vrindavan." This was in December of '75. So Sridhar and I both jumped on the train. Prabhupada had gone with Ambarish, Hamsadutta, Gopal Krishna, and Harikesh Maharaj to Kuruksetra and when he returned he gave us *sannyas* in the courtyard of the Krishna-Balaram temple.

Madhudvisa: Once I walked into Srila Prabhupada's room, looked over in the corner, and saw Prabhupada in a white *sari.* It was Prabhupada's sister. She looked so much like Prabhupada that I had to do a double take. Then Prabhupada walked into the room. Prabhupada and his sister were both sitting in the room together talking in Bengali until it was time for Prabhupada to rest. His sister rolled over and also started to rest in the room. I said, "Prabhupada, is it all right?" He said, "Yes. She won't go away. She's staying here." So she moved in and started cooking *kachoris* for Prabhupada. Prabhupada liked *kachoris,* and his sister could cook them just the way he liked them. But we weren't used to eating such *kachoris.* The next day no one came to *mangal arati.* Prabhupada called us and asked, "What's the matter? How come no one came to *mangal arati?*"

We said, "Well, your sister cooked these *kachoris* for us yesterday, and we all ate so many that we couldn't get up in the morning." He called his sister and started arguing with her in Bengali. Then he said to Achyutananda, "I am going to drive this woman out of this house. She is killing all my *brahmacharis* with these *kachoris*." Srila Prabhupada and his sister had a relationship that was far above our understanding. That was just one incident.

Srutakirti: Sometimes at breakfast Prabhupada would have *halava*, which was unheard of on a normal basis. At Bhaktivedanta Manor in England, where it was cold, he sometimes requested heavier food, but normally his main meal was at lunch. In the evening he regularly had hot milk and sometimes puffed rice when it was available, especially in India. When I was with him in '72 and '73, he showed me how to make plain *parathas*, and he would have those along with potatoes. This could be at nine or ten in the evening if he had some appetite. Without an appetite Prabhupada never ate. In Los Angeles he sometimes had the popcorn that was served to the *sankirtan* devotees in the evening. But he like puffed rice, which was light. He said that heavy food eaten at night is difficult to digest and makes it hard to get up in the morning. He didn't like to eat heavily in the evening.

Madhudvisa: Another incident that comes to mind was in 1968 or '69. We had a temple on La Cienega Boulevard in Los Angeles. The devotees went to Griffith Park in Los Angeles and chanted and distributed *prasadam*. Vishnujana had little puppets, and we would have puppet shows there and bring people from Griffith Park to the temple. We also went to the meditation room in The Mystic Arts book store in Laguna Beach. They let us have *kirtan* there, and we would bring vanloads of people from Laguna Beach to Los Angeles for the feast. In this way the feast was very well attended. On this particular day the temple was especially full. Srila Prabhupada was going to preside over an initiation and fire *yajna* ceremony. At that time an Italian film crew was filming at the temple. If somebody could get that film, it would be an historical piece of footage.

A lady named Shyama Devi, who was the guru of many Hindus, came into the temple. Her disciples, older Hindu ladies and gentlemen, rolled out a carpet. She sat down on it, and they sat around her while Srila Prabhupada performed the *yajna*. After Srila Prabhupada had finished, he sat on his *vyasasana,* which was on the stage, and led the *kirtan*. Then he told someone else to lead. In those days the *kirtans* were ecstatic, but they weren't uproarious because we did "the swami step". The swami step was a choreographed step in which we were in two, long aisles facing one another as we all danced by putting one foot in front of the other while our arms were upraised. During the course of this *kirtan*, Srila Prabhupada got off his *vyasasana* and did the swami step with us. We were all doing the swami step. Then Srila Prabhupada did something that he had never done before. Nobody had ever experienced this before. Srila Prabhupada stopped doing the swami step and started to jump up and down. We had never done this jumping up and down. We just knew the swami step, and we were all happy doing the swami step. But now Srila Prabhupada was jumping up and down. It was the most amazing thing, because it seemed like the whole universe was rocking when Srila Prabhupada started jumping up and down. We looked at each other and said, "Wow! Prabhupada is jumping up and down. I guess we can jump up and down too." *Kirtan* has never been the same since then. The swami step is still there, but it's only done by very conservative devotees. Everybody likes to jump up and down and get into the uproarious *kirtan*. So Srila Prabhupada was jumping up and down, and all the devotees were jumping up and down, bouncing off the walls. It was fantastic.

Meanwhile one of Shyama Devi's disciples opened a bag and gave her a little *mridanga*. In those days it was usually one *mridanga* per temple, and only devotees who were good *mridanga* players and who wouldn't drop it or put their hand through the end of it could play that *mridanga*. They had to be very concerned that the *mridanga* didn't get damaged, because we didn't have our American-made plastic *mridangas*. If the *mridanga* got broken we had to send it to India for repair, which took a long time. But they pulled out a small clay *mridanga* and gave it to Shyama Devi and she started playing it. We stepped aside, and she moved up to the front. Srila Prabhupada was jumping up and down dancing. All the devotees were dancing, and Shyama Devi, playing this *mridanga*, also started to dance, taking little steps and floating around like a butterfly. She was a very conservative elderly lady, about fifty or sixty, but she danced around with her *sari* over her head while she played the *mridanga* like a *gopi*. All the female devotees thought, "All right, Prabhupada obviously approves of this Vaishnavi who could play the *mridanga* and who was dancing." Then Prabhupada jumped off the stage and joined the devotees, jumping up and down chanting Hare Krishna. Shyama Devi was still playing the *mridanga* and dancing. Then the *kirtan* ended, and Srila Prabhupada said to her, "Now you lead." So she started to lead the *kirtan*. Now the women were really ecstatic. This is another precedent: "We can jump, we can dance, we can play the *mridanga*, and now we can also lead *kirtan*, because here, this lady is doing it. Prabhupada asked her to do it." Everybody was in total euphoria. Shyama Devi led the most melodious *kirtan*. It went on and on. Srila Prabhupada was dancing, and she was dancing, and it built up and was the most fantastic experience that all the devotees could have had.

Before the dust even settled from the *kirtan*, a devotee was on a phone saying, "Prabhupada is jumping!" "What do you mean he is jumping?" "You don't have to do the swami step anymore. Prabhupada is jumping up and down. *Kirtan* was going on. Prabhupada was jumping up and down." And Brahmananda said, "Well, how do you do it? How do you jump?" "You just jump up and down. Just be ecstatic. Put your hands up in the air, and just jump as high as you can." Brahmananda told Boston, Boston called Montreal, and in a matter of hours the whole country was jumping. *Kirtan* has never been the same since.

Lokanath Swami: After the *sannyas* initiation ceremony for Sridhar Maharaj, Prithu Putra from France, and I went into Srila Prabhupada's quarters to check two things: whether our names were going to change and whether we had new assignments. Prabhupada said, "Just add 'Swami' to your name," and he did not change our assignments. Then he talked to us about "*man mana bhava mad bhakto mad yaji mam namaskuru*" (*Bhagavad-gita* 9.34). "Krishna is asking us to do four things: to remember Him, to worship Him, to offer Him our obeisances, and to become His devotee. If you just do these four things without duplicity, then your preaching will be effective, and people will take you very seriously." That was his instruction in the personal meeting he gave us.

Madhudvisa: We had a very intimate Janmastami celebration in Tokyo, Japan. In those days, Dai-Nippon was the printer that was printing our books, and they were hosting Prabhupada in a nice house. We all went to Srila Prabhupada's house on Janmastami day because he wanted us to cook a big feast for midnight and read the Krishna Book during the day. Srila Prabhupada started the tradition of reading as much as you could of the Krishna Book on Janmastami. He said, "Read the whole Krishna Book if you can. Read it constantly throughout the day." So we started. I took a turn reading the Krishna book. Tamal Krishna took a turn, and Kirtanananda took a turn. Then Srila Prabhupada said, "Now it is my turn." He took the Krishna Book and started reading. When a person reads something you can tell by their manner and the feeling that they put into the reading if they are really fascinated with it. Srila Prabhupada was reading very feelingly. Later on I said to Prabhupada, "Prabhupada, you were reading the Krishna Book so feelingly." And Prabhupada said, "Yes. I like to read my Krishna Book. It's very entertaining. It's not that because I wrote it, I don't care about reading it anymore.

These are Krishna's pastimes, and it's very ecstatic to read the pastimes of Krishna." On that Janmastami day we went on and on reading Krishna Book until midnight. We didn't finish the whole Krishna Book, but we read quite a bit of it.

Srutakirti: Once in 1972, Prabhupada blasted me at the Radha-Damodar Temple in Vrindavan during the time he spoke from *The Nectar of Devotion*. He had *The Nectar of Devotion* classes every afternoon in the garden. At this time I was still learning a lot as I had only been his servant for about one month. I was recording his lecture, and there were many flies buzzing about Srila Prabhupada. But everyone was just sitting there paying attention to class. He said, "Get a fan." So I brought a *chamara* fan. As Prabhupada spoke, I was doing an *arati* ceremony to him. Flies were buzzing around, but instead of just chasing flies I was enjoying doing this service. I was turning the whisk around, but the flies were still there. Prabhupada flung his hand to chase the flies, and still I was so enamored by the situation and so dull-headed that I continued turning the whisk. Finally Srila Prabhupada looked at me and said, "Get someone up here with some intelligence." I was devastated. I sat down, and who should grab the *chamara*? A very crazy, peculiar devotee named Kunja-bihari. He started swatting at these flies. I was sitting by the tape recorder trying to occupy myself so that I didn't have to pay attention to what had just happened to me, and Kunja-bihari was swatting at these flies. I looked up at Prabhupada, and Prabhupada looked at me and nodded his head in appreciation, which further devastated me. I had failed. Here I was his servant and a total failure. The class went on, and Kunja-bihari continued to harass the flies so that they didn't bother our spiritual master. Prabhupada was satisfied, Kunja-bihari was in ecstasy, and I was still trying to deal with my false ego.

Madhudvisa: The next day was Vyasa-puja. We were not well seasoned. Kirtanananda was the most senior, as he had been a devotee for two or three years. (Although we still should have known how to celebrate Srila Prabhupada's Vyasa-puja.) Srila Prabhupada arrived at the temple about 11:30, sat on the *vyasasana,* and said, "Where is the *puspa?*" We were thinking, "*Puspa?* What is *puspa?*" Sudama thought, "Oh, he wants *puspa* rice, a fancy kind of rice." There is some kind of rice called *puspa* with nuts and curd balls. Sudama immediately started making this rice, which delayed the process even further. Prabhupada said, "Where is the feast?" But the feast was late. "Where is the garland?" We didn't have any garlands, and there were no flowers to do the *puspanjali.* Srila Prabhupada said, "No *puspanjali.* The feast is not ready. You are not saying the right prayers. There is no garland for the Deities. How is this a Vyasa-puja? This is not a Vyasa-puja. This is a disgrace." To Kirtanananda he said, "You are a senior disciple. Don't you know how to celebrate the spiritual master's appearance day? Don't you have any understanding? This is a disgrace." Then he said, "Tomorrow we will celebrate it properly," and got up and walked out the door. Kirtanananda started to cry, and we were all devastated. The whole temple was full of guests, and everybody felt as if a cold ice pick had been stabbed into their hearts.

Prabhupada called us to his house that same day and said, "I will tell you how to celebrate Vyasa-puja, and you must not forget it for the rest of your lives." He said, "You must have flowers for the *puspanjali.* You must stand and offer the flowers to the spiritual master three times, bow down three times, say the *mangala-caranam* prayers to the spiritual master, and have the offering ready. The offering has to go on one minute before twelve so that it is on the altar at twelve. You must also read homages." We didn't have any homages written either. "You must have the homages written. This is the way you celebrate the appearance of the spiritual master." Srila Prabhupada was very strict with his disciples, and at the same time he was very kind. After you became his disciple, he was still kind, but he wanted you to be trained up in Krishna consciousness for your own spiritual benefit so that you would know the right things to do and not be offensive by your ignorance. The next day, when Prabhupada came back to the temple, we celebrated Vyasa-puja exactly the way he wanted us to do it. He was pleased.

Srutakirti: After Prabhupada took breakfast in his quarters in Los Angeles, I would bring his plates back to the servants' quarters down the hall and clean and transfer all the remaining *prasadam*. Now, the very first piece of *maha-prasadam* I ever had from Srila Prabhupada, back in August of '72, was an orange rind. Then I had eaten the whole rind, because it was *maha-prasadam*. But now that I was Prabhupada's servant, I took the orange rind from his breakfast plate and threw it in the trash can. Then I transferred and distributed the rest of his *prasadam*. Later on in the morning, I was in the servant's quarters, where there was a two-burner gas stove and a little cutting board, cutting vegetables for Prabhupada's lunch. Srila Prabhupada was chanting and walking back and forth in the hallway. He walked by, saw me cutting vegetables, and saw the orange rind in the trash can. That was it. He said, "What is this? This *muchi* thing you have sitting there in the can? You are preparing lunch for the Deities, and you have an eaten orange in the can?" I could not say anything. One thing I never did was to say anything to Srila Prabhupada when he was yelling at me. He said, "Do they do this in the Deity kitchen? They have garbage in the can at the same time they are preparing for the Deity? Do they do that downstairs?" I said, "No, Srila Prabhupada." "But you are doing it up here? You are so *muchi?*" He repeated it. "You are so *muchi*. You are a *mleccha*. How can you do this?" This went on for approximately five minutes. It wasn't at this time but a later time when Prabhupada was arguing with me and he said, "Why do you do this?" And I said, "I am just a fool." He said, "You are no fun to argue with because you never fight back."

Madhudvisa: The devotees were doing a fire *yajna* in the Vrindavan temple, and in the middle of the *yajna* one of Srila Prabhupada's god-brothers leaned over to Prabhupada and said, "Srila Prabhupada, they're doing it all wrong. They're doing it all wrong." Prabhupada leaned back, looked at him very calmly, and said, "That's all right. They're just practicing."

Srutakirti: We were taking a domestic Air India flight, and while everyone was getting seated, Prabhupada and I were already sitting down. They had Indian classical music, sitar and tabla, playing very loudly. Prabhupada said, "Do you like this music?" I looked at him, wondering if that was a trick question. It was nice music but it wasn't Krishna conscious music. It was *maya*. So I didn't say anything. I didn't answer, because I hated to be wrong. I could never answer honestly, because I didn't want to say the wrong thing. Finally Prabhupada said, "This is very nice music." Then of course I said, "Yes, Srila Prabhupada. This is very nice music." But I didn't want to say the wrong thing. That's probably why I didn't say too much while I was with Srila Prabhupada.

Lokanath Swami: We were in Badarikashram in North India when we heard that Prabhupada, in Vrindavan, was getting sicker. So we rushed back to Vrindavan. Soon after our arrival there we were allowed to go into his quarters for *darshan,* and we spent quite some time with him. He was lying on the bed. For months he had been on the bed, but he was very enthused by our *sankirtan* reports. He inquired, "Which book is selling the most? What is your daily collection?" As we had just returned from Badarikashram, in a humorous way I said, "Srila Prabhupada, we presented your *Bhagavad-gita As It Is* to Srila Vyasadev." In Badarikashram there is a cave where Srila Vyasadev still resides, and we had visited that cave. We did not see Vyasadev but carried *Bhagavad-gita* with us, and we imagined that Srila Vyasadev saw it. So I said, "We presented your *Bhagavad-gita* to Srila Vyasadev." Prabhupada smiled.

Srutakirti: On many occasions Prabhupada gave me things. One was very funny. After I was married and had a child, I again became

Prabhupada's servant. I was traveling with Prabhupada when my son, Mayapur Chandra das, was about six months old. We were in Los Angeles,, and Prabhupada called me into his room and said, "Call Nanda Kumar. I want to see him." I went and found Nanda Kumar, and a few minutes later we both went into Prabhupada's room and paid our obeisances. I was about to leave when Prabhupada said, "No, no. Get me my white bag." Prabhupada's white bag was very special. When Prabhupada traveled, he had his white bag where he kept his important effects—bank books for the Bhaktivedanta Book Trust and Mayapur-Vrindavan Trust, the personal items from his desk, like a Gold Crest pen a disciple had given him, his silver *tilak* mirror container, and a little bit of money. So I brought his white bag. He went into this bag, took out a fifty-dollar bill, and gave it to Nanda Kumar. He took out another one and gave it to me. He said, "These are for your children." Nanda Kumar said, "No, Srila Prabhupada. I can't take this from you." Prabhupada said, "It's not for you. It's for your son." That immediately stopped the objection. If Prabhupada wanted to stop an objection from someone, he could stop it very quickly. He was very good at that.

Madhudvisa: One time in Australia there was a five-year-old boy named Janaka who came up to Srila Prabhupada to get a flower. Prabhupada had the flower in his hand and wouldn't let it go. The boy had the flower, and Prabhupada had the flower, and the boy realized that everybody was looking at him, and he didn't know what to do. Should he release his grip and go? He wanted the flower, but he didn't know if he should grab it. Prabhupada knew that, and he was holding it and watching the boy, with a grin on his face. Eventually he gave the boy the flower. It was just a little playful incident.

Srutakirti: I was massaging him at Bhaktivedanta Manor. We would always use mustard oil for his body and sandalwood oil for his head, unless he was ill. If he was ill there was no cold oil applied to his head. Sometimes during massages he would say, "Put the lid back on the mustard oil." This particular day we were alone in the room, and I was sitting behind him, rubbing his head with sandalwood oil. Then I massaged his back with the mustard oil that was in the bottle that I didn't put the lid on. I got up and proceeded to move around to his side, when I knocked the small bottle of mustard oil over onto the floor. Immediately he turned around and said, "Why didn't you have the lid on the mustard oil? You are so foolish. You will be intelligent when you are eighty." Then he said, "Get a cup." I ran into the next room and got a cup. Both Prabhupada and I got the mustard oil on our hands and scraped it into the cup. He said, "Now use that oil on my body." This was another one of his qualities. Srila Prabhupada never ever wasted anything. Whatever you take, you use. Whatever *prasadam* you take, you finish it. That was always his example. Anyway, I did joke with Srila Prabhupada on occasion, but whatever I said to him I would think about once, twice, three, four times before I'd say it. A few minutes went by. I was massaging Prabhupada's arm. He was very quiet, and I was very quiet. Finally I said, "Srila Prabhupada, thank you so much. I thought it would take a lot longer than that to become intelligent." He cracked up, laughing. He found it very amusing. Everything was so funny.

Madhudvisa: Srila Prabhupada's quality of compassion distinguished him from everyone else. He was totally compassionate. The Sanskrit description for a person who is always compassionate to other's suffering is *para duhkha duhkhi*. That's the quality of the greatest devotee.

No one was insignificant to Srila Prabhupada. A devotee once introduced his father to Prabhupada by saying, "Oh, this is my father; he is all right but he is not a devotee." Prabhupada said, "No. A good fruit does not come from a bad seed." In this way, because Prabhupada complimented him so nicely, the man felt good about his son being a disciple of Srila Prabhupada.

In our temple on La Cienega Boulevard, sometimes old ladies

would come from the neighborhood with their old-lady shoes that laced up, and Srila Prabhupada said, "They don't have to take their shoes off. Put some chairs in the back of the temple." He let them sit on chairs while they heard his talk and the *kirtan*. During the *kirtan*, Srila Prabhupada started circumambulating inside the temple with all the devotees. When he came to the back of the temple he would raise his hands in front of those old ladies and say, "Hare Krishna!" The old ladies would jump out of their chairs with their canes and their little old lady shoes and little spectacles, and say, "Hare Krishna! Hare Krishna!" and then they would sit down again. Prabhupada would also make sure that they got *prasadam*. His compassion was there for everybody. He did not say that anybody was insignificant. Everybody was a child of God in Prabhupada's eyes. Everybody had the right to go back to home, back to Godhead, no matter what situation they were in. Some people were closer to getting there, and some people were further away. But comparatively speaking, we were all thousands and millions of miles away.

Srutakirti: On many occasions devotees would say to Prabhupada, "This devotee is doing something wrong," or "This devotee is not chanting his rounds." But Prabhupada would never say, "Then he should be removed." Instead he would always say, "Perhaps he is so busy that he does not have time to chant his rounds." It was interesting, because when Prabhupada would lecture and write, he was always strict: "One must follow the four regulative principles. One must chant sixteen rounds. One must be fully engaged in Krishna's service." That was it. But as soon as he was in his quarters and some difficulty was brought to his attention, then he had nothing but compassion. He would say, "You have done so much service. See how you can take care of this. You just try." And, "Chant your rounds and we will see what we can do." An arrangement could be made. He would never reject someone because of falling down and breaking one of the regulative principles. There was always some way to work it out. Of course, if someone said something about the philosophy, then that was bad. Immediately he was gone. But a fall down was different. "This was to be expected," Prabhupada would say. Once in Los Angeles he said, "If it were not for the chanting of the maha-mantra, you boys and girls could not do anything. In the West you have used so many drugs that you cannot accomplish anything. Chanting Hare Krishna has enabled you to get all these temples and devotees. It's simply Krishna's mercy and the chanting."

Madhudvisa: To our limited vision, Srila Prabhupada's health was deteriorating. He requested that I come to Vrindavan to see him. I had just gotten married, and my wife was pregnant with my first son. We were living in a very remote part of Hawaii, and I couldn't leave at that particular moment. But I promised that as soon as my wife had her baby, then I would come. Time passed. After my son arrived, Srutakirti came over to Maui, and together we flew off to India. At that time I wasn't living at a temple, so I had let my hair grow a little bit longer. When we arrived in Delhi, I thought, "Well, I can't see Srila Prabhupada like this." So I shaved up and had a big, long *sikha*. When I walked in Prabhupada's room there was a very sober mood. It was dark, as everything was subdued, and the devotees were morose and quiet. They said, "Srila Prabhupada, Madhudvisa has arrived." Srila Prabhupada sat up in his bed. I paid my obeisances, and the first thing Prabhupada said was, "Wow! Look at Madhudvisa. He has maintained such a nice *sikha*." He chuckled, knowing that I hadn't maintained such a nice *sikha*. I had just shaved up in the Delhi train station. The second thing he said was, "Where is your wife?" You see, I had left Srila Prabhupada. I was a *sannyasi,* and then I had left and gotten married. That's not the way you should do it. But Srila Prabhupada shrugged that off. It was immaterial to him. He wanted to know where my wife was. Not that, "Why have you gotten married? Why have you done this?" He wanted to know, "Where is she?" He was fully aware that I was married and had a child, and he wanted to see my wife. I said, "Well, Srila Prabhupada, she just had her first baby, and she really doesn't want to travel." He said, "That's right. She shouldn't travel. But is she feeling okay?" And I said, "Yes. She is feeling good." "And you had a son?" I said, "Yes, Prabhupada. I had a son, and I named him Abhay Charan. Is that all right?" And he said, "Yes." Then he went on to explain the famous purport that's in the *Srimad-Bhagavatam* about the elephant and the crocodile. "The elephant is very mighty and strong, but when he enters the water, he becomes victimized by the crocodile because he is not in his proper atmosphere. If he is on land he can crush the crocodile, but because he is in the water, he is at the mercy of the crocodile." He said, "Similarly, we may be situated in the wrong atmosphere for executing Krishna consciousness. We must put ourselves in the right atmosphere, and then we can execute Krishna consciousness with all strength and vigor. You were a *sannyasi,* and now you are a householder. That doesn't make any difference. The proper thing is just to go on with your Krishna consciousness. Execute it. If you can't execute it, if you are becoming weak by artificially embracing the *sannyas* order, then you must take another order to become strong again. That is all right. The most important thing is not to leave the association of devotees and to continue with Krishna consciousness." He made me feel so good. It was very enlivening and personal to be with Srila Prabhupada in those last days.

TAPE 5

Gopavrindapal das
Yasodanandan das
Sudama das
Brahmananda das

Gopavrindapal: The first time I saw Srila Prabhupada was at the Los Angeles airport in 1972. With great anticipation, hundreds of devotees were waiting for him to come around the corner of the concourse. Every other person on the plane exited, and as every new face came around the corner, we thought, "No, that's not him." Finally Prabhupada came. He literally peeked around the corner of the concourse hallway with a playful look, gave a little wave, and then walked out. It may have been his plan to keep us all in antici-pation and to heighten our ecstasy, and it worked quite well. The devotees went wild. From all the anticipation that had built up, I expected a six-foot man with broad shoulders and a great presence. Of course, the presence was there, but it wasn't physical. He was much smaller then I expected, but no less regal. I was half-dazed at that moment, as was everybody.

Yasodanandan: I had read Prabhupada's books and, unlike all the other *Bhagavad-gitas* that I had read from many yogis and swamis, Prabhupada's was very clear and precise. He explained Krishna, the Person-ality of Godhead, and the nature of the soul in a very convincing way. The other versions of *Bhagavad-gita,* even the entire *Rig Veda* by some Sanskrit scholars, were not appealing or convincing. But Prabhupada's book was potent. His words really touched the soul. So when I first saw Srila Prabhupada in New York, it was incredible to link with this person and be in his presence. His spiritual potency was there, and his attraction was magnetic. He was able to channel the slightest spark of sincerity and bring it to Krishna.

 **Sudama:** I moved into the temple the day before Srila Prabhupada arrived. We went to the San Francisco airport, and I saw his airplane coming in, a TWA jet. Immediately I almost fainted as I cried without knowing why. Now I understand that the reason why I was crying was because I hadn't seen him in so many lifetimes. But I wasn't aware of that then.

All of sudden I saw everybody getting on their hands and knees, and I thought to myself, "Oh, my God. What will my family think of this? Here I am on my hands and knees." Then I looked up, and there he was. My life changed from that moment. I was initiated the next day. Tamal said: "Hey, everybody is getting initiated. You've got to get initiated too." I said, "Okay." It was like joining the country club or a fraternity. I didn't know what it meant. He gave me the name Sudama. The next day he called me into his quarters. Govinda dasi was his head secretary and servant, along with Purushotam and Kartikeya, and he asked me what he had named me. I reminded him that my name was Sudama das, and he said, "What do you do, Sudama?" I said, "I am an actor and a dancer from a very famous dancing and acting family." His eyes lit up and he said, "Oh, I played Hamlet once in Calcutta," and he handed me a play that Hayagriva had just written on the life of Lord Chaitanya. It was two inches thick—much too long. He said, "I want your opinion. Come back tomorrow." So I went back the next day and he said, "To communicate through creativity affects the heart of people."

 **Brahmananda:** In Boston, Hamsadutta had just gotten a school bus, the first bus in the movement. One morning Prabhupada called Hamsadutta and said, "Let us go for a ride in your bus." Hamsadutta excitedly said, "Oh yes." But then he realized that they had taken all the seats out of the bus. There was just the floor. Prabhupada couldn't sit like that so I got a chair from the temple and held it down while Prabhupada sat in it. All the devotees piled into the bus. Everyone was very excited. "Where are we going?" I said, "For a ride with Prabhupada." Ramandeva was driving, and Prabhupada was giving directions, "Turn here. Go on this road." Nobody knew where we were going, and no one was bold enough to ask Prabhupada, but Prabhupada knew where he was going. While the devotees chanted on their beads, we got to the downtown area and finally came to the waterfront, the dock area. And then we arrived at Commonwealth Pier. Actually, no devotees had ever even seen it. Prabhupada was always talking about Krishna and didn't tell us so many details about his arrival in America. Even when we got there, we didn't realize where we were, but this was the place where Prabhupada had first entered America. Prabhupada started walking, and we clustered around him on this big pier with big roads, warehouses, and factories surrounding us. Prabhupada preached as he always did on his morning walk. He talked about pure devotional service to Krishna, and he used the word "unalloyed." It's exotic, this "unalloyed" devotional service, because an "alloy" is a metal made of many different kinds of metal. Prabhupada was always saying "unalloyed." That meant just one metal, not many.

At a certain point he said, "Yes. Unalloyed devotional service," and he pointed with his cane. We all followed the cane, and there was a hundred-foot long sign on the entire side of the warehouse that said, UNALLOYED STEEL COMPANY. We all said, "Yes, unalloyed." That sign was one of the first things Prabhupada had seen when he entered America, and he showed it to us to explain unalloyed devotional service; a very simple instruction that he made so graphic. We were like Prabhupada's young students, and Prabhupada was our teacher. As a teacher writes a word on a blackboard and then takes a pointer to show the class, so Prabhupada was showing us.

Gopavrindapal: In Vrindavan there were just a few book distributors who got an audience with Srila Prabhupada to discuss that very topic. I asked about the quality of our preaching and our book distribution, and I suggested that there was a problem. People said that the only time they see us is when we are hunting for their money or trying to give them some of our books. They don't know us other than that. His response was typically inspiring and insightful. There was almost a query on his face, as he said "No, no. They shouldn't think like that. You should tell them, 'You can be with me twenty-four hours a day. You come with me, live where I live, and in that way you can get to know me, and after three days of staying with me, you will become like me.'" He used the pronoun "me." That inspired us all because it suggested to us that our example was just as important as our preaching and book distribution. Our example, how we lived twenty-four hours a day, should be public information.

Yasodanandan: When Prabhupada first introduced the "*namaste narasimhaya*" prayers, he said that they were for the protection of his movement. While he was singing them, some Indian lady in the crowd started to sing *om jaya jagadisha hare*. Prabhupada interrupted the prayer and said, "Who has said this?" He said, "No, no. Not *om jaya jagadisha hare*. It is *jaya jagadisha hare*. Don't concoct." Prabhupada was very specific about that, because various Hindus sing *arati* prayers with the words *om jaya jagadisha hare*. Then Prabhupada chanted the "*namaste narasimhaya*" prayer in a very grave tone, repeating each and every word. It was an ecstatic experience to see and hear Srila Prabhupada introducing this new, potent, transcendental prayer and showing the devotees how to sing it to protect his movement.

Sudama: During the second *darshan*, Srila Prabhupada instructed me to use my talent to preach. I was enamored. I was eighteen or nineteen years old and on my way to India. He said, "Just see. India has come to you. Now you don't have to go so far." In fact, I didn't get there for another six years. I had tickets in my hand to go to Bombay, but Lord Chaitanya had another plan.

We went from San Francisco to Seattle and Govinda dasi noticed my talent for cleaning. I am always impeccable. And my *chapatis* blew up. Kartikeya, on the other hand, was very confused and not reliable. So Govinda dasi was pushing Srila Prabhupada to take me on board. That meant no *brahmachari* ashram, nor austerities in the sense of hanging out with neophyte godbrothers. I jumped at the opportunity and began my short but eternal career of looking after Srila Prabhupada.

Brahmananda: Prabhupada went to Mauritius, where some devotees were preaching, primarily to see the Prime Minister, Ra Gulam. But when Prabhupada arrived, the Prime Minister was busy with some other affair so he gave Prabhupada one of his personal limousines, a Citroen, with an army officer as the driver. Citroens are very special cars made of aluminum instead of steel, with a suspension system like an ambulance. You feel as if you are floating. At that time I went to someone's house to make an international phone call, and while I was there I saw the Prime Minister on TV inaugurating a big chicken processing plant. The TV show showed how the chickens are hung and then come out ready for cooking. It was shocking. When I mentioned to Prabhupada what the Prime Minister was doing, he said, "The Prime Minister is a Hindu? I cannot meet him." Prabhupada decided not to meet him because he had no principles.

There were some days when no programs were scheduled, so on one such day Prabhupada said, "Let us go for a ride." Mauritius is a very scenic, pristine island. Prabhupada was riding in the back seat, I was sitting next to him, and Pusta Krishna was in the front seat. The driver was whizzing along the coastline. It was very pleasant. The sea breezes, the beautiful ocean, the sky, and the sugar cane growing were very nice. Prabhupada had his window down and was sitting crossed-legged on the back seat with his cane beside him. He was enjoying it very much. Then Prabhupada took the cane, put it on the floor, and held it with two hands. Just after that we turned around a bend and immediately . . . *bang!* There was not a second to react. It happened so fast; a head-on collision. A tourist from South Africa was driving on the wrong side of the road. Everyone was in shock. The driver was full of blood. I didn't know what his condition was. Pusta Krishna was wounded and bloody, as I was. My arm was gashed. Prabhupada had blood on his *dhoti* near his knee. My first reaction, which was a little bit inappropriate, was to put my arms around Prabhupada and hold him. Prabhupada didn't say anything. Pusta Krishna was unconscious. I was the only one who could function. Somehow, I got out of the car. The other car was a Volkswagen with a man and a woman in it. The woman was unconscious, and the man was getting out of the car. I realized that I had to get Prabhupada out of there. I didn't know where we were or where our house was. After a while, a car came by. Now, Mauritius is an Indian place, and there are very few white people. But the car that we had hit had white people, and the car that came also had white people. I tried to stop it, but it went right by. Then another car came. This time I stood in the middle of the road. The car stopped. I went up to the people in the car and said, "Please, we need some help. My grandfather is injured, an old man. Please take us to the nearest hospital." They said, "Okay. Okay." The only reason they were taking us was because I forced them. I took Prabhupada out of the car and put him in the other car, and the people started driving. Prabhupada was absolutely silent. Then these people started saying, "We don't know where the hospital is. We are going to our hotel and you can go to the hotel and . . ." I said, "No, no. We want to go to a hospital right now." Prabhupada didn't say anything, so I knew that he was agreeing with what I was doing. But these people didn't even want to find the hospital. They just wanted to go to their hotel. I told them, "All right. Stop the car." They stopped the car, Prabhupada and I got out, and they left. There we were standing in the middle of nowhere, lost. Then another car came along. I stopped that car. This car had three Indian people. They saw Prabhupada and offered respects. I said, "Take us to the nearest hospital." Then Prabhupada said, "No. Take us home. No hospital." They were very happy to take us home immediately. We were on the other side of the island, and it was quite a drive.

The car pulled in to our place. Harikesh Maharaj hadn't come with us as he was doing the transcription, so he was there. He didn't know what was going on, because we left in a limousine and we came back in a junky old car with three Indian boys. Prabhupada got out of the car, and there was blood on his *dhoti*. Harikesh was shocked. Prabhupada did not speak. He went into the house, sat down, and we cleaned and dressed his wound. Then Prabhupada said that he wanted to go back to Bombay. Prabhupada never wanted to leave Bombay anyway. Prabhupada was very concerned with the Bombay project, with getting the land, fighting the government, the municipality, the local politicians, the residents, and the seller. There was a battle there which required his constant supervision. Prabhupada said, "Let us immediately go back to Bombay," and he never spoke about the accident.

Gopavrindapal: In the early '70s we were traveling from temple to temple teaching others how to distribute large books, the *Srimad-Bhagavatams* and the hardbound *Bhagavad-gitas*. At that time we were questioning whether or not we should perform book distribution skits for the devotees. In these skits, one of us acted as a nondevotee receiving a book, and the other acted as a devotee. We would pass each other on the street. The devotee would stop the nondevotee and have an exchange with him, ending up in a book sale. So we asked Prabhupada, "Should we perform these skits as we go around and preach to the devotees?" He said, "No. It's a little unnatural. But you should travel, you should preach, and you should teach the devotees how to be sincere." His point was that sincerity was the essence of book distribution and preaching. He went on to articulate that preaching depends on circumstances. I am paraphrasing, but he said that there is no static or rote way to distribute a book or preach. Each person is different. He said, "By teaching the devotees to be sincere"—and he made one of those gestures, which in my mind was very sweeping—pointed to his heart, and said, "If you teach them to be sincere, the real teacher from within will give them information according to the circumstances. Krishna will teach them how to distribute the books."

Sudama: Gargamuni had obtained an apartment for Prabhupada. It was a dump. Srila Prabhupada walked in with Govinda dasi. Govinda dasi had a very interesting, blessed relationship with Srila Prabhupada. She used to tell him, "This will never do." That was part of the requirement of being a good servant for Srila Prabhupada. You had to be almost parental with him because his health was not good. Sometimes you had to have a heavy hand which, to most people, is not thought of with the guru. Srila Prabhupada, as a pure devotee, was so real that he identified his relationship with each individual devotee, and he expected you to respond. If you were going to debate, then he wanted to debate. If I wanted to cook for him and massage him and make his home clean, he would give me that facility until I didn't want it any longer. Well, he comes into this place, and Govinda dasi said to Gargamuni, "This will never do. We have to find another location. Srila Prabhupada, what do you feel?" Prabhupada's from Calcutta. Govinda dasi says, "No, no, no. I am sorry. I have to put my foot down." So she and Gargamuni went to find another location while I stayed with Srila Prabhupada. As it happened, there was a television in this place. Prabhupada said, "Turn the TV on." I thought, "Turn the TV on?" I had joined just a month before, and I was told when I joined, "Oh, no. We don't do this, we don't that, we don't do drugs." In fact, I remember having my last LSD experience on my way to move into the temple. So I said, "Okay," and turned the television on. We were chanting. Somehow Prabhupada was always chanting. A washing machine commercial came on with stick cartoon characters. Prabhupada was almost on the floor laughing. He said, "Oh, you Western people. You make a box to wash your clothes, then you sell it for a lot of money and you have them assume characters." Well, we watched. I laughed frightfully because I didn't know if I should laugh or not. It wasn't until later on that I understood what my position was in serving him. He was chuckling. He wanted me to change the station. He wanted more commercials. He thought that they were the most interesting, bizarre display of material life that he'd ever seen. That was my first experience with Srila Prabhupada that was not in the mood of awe and reverence.

Gopavrindapal: Prabhupada had a unique innocence about our Western ways and our interpretation of things. Once we were discussing book distribution and *sankirtan,* street preaching. Tripurari said, "In many temples there is no *sankirtan* class," meaning that they weren't teaching each other how to distribute books and inspiring each other about street preaching and *sankirtan* in a class format. That was Tripurari's intent. But Prabhupada took it in an entirely different way. He said, "No? No *sankirtan* class?" And we all in unison said, "No, Prabhupada," because we were expecting him to suggest that, "Oh, this should happen everywhere and you should head it up." We thought we were going to get some new service. He said, "No? No *sankirtan* classes?" We said, "No, Prabhupada. They are not doing that." He asked three times, "No? There should be *sankirtan* in every class; before class and after class, always *sankirtan.*" He was thinking that there was no chanting of the holy names prior to the regular morning and evening *Bhagavatam* and *Gita* classes. But we were thinking that there was no technique class about preaching, which was a foreign concept to him.

Yasodanandan: The next time that I had a chance to meet Srila Prabhupada was in Calcutta in the summer of 1971. I was in his room with Bhavananda, Jayapataka, Revatinandana, and a few others. This was one of the first times I had a chance to ask Srila Prabhupada a question. I said, "Prabhupada, there has been considerable controversy over your statement that materialistic scientists never went to the moon. A lot of people don't understand this. We accept your statement. I am your disciple so I accept it. I firmly believe it. But how do you explain this?" Prabhupada put his hand up in the air and said, "As far as I am concerned, they never went." He elaborated on why they hadn't gone, saying that the moon is a luminous, self-effulgent body, and it is contradictory to say that they had recovered some dark dust and stones from a luminous body. He also said that according to the *Vedas* and the *Bhagavatam,* you cannot go to another planet without a suitable body. You cannot force entry to another planet. For example, he said, you cannot force your entrance into America. You have to go to the immigration department, get a visa, and then you can come in. He gave another example about the days of the week. In all ancient cultures the week starts with Monday, the planet of the moon, which indicates that the moon is first. He said that they did not go to the moon but to Rahu, a planet between the moon and the earth. "They cannot access the moon," he said, "for the moon is far above the sun." When Prabhupada first announced this, Purushotam, one of Prabhupada's servants, brought a TV set into Prabhupada's room to show Prabhupada the entire moon landing. Prabhupada still said, "They cannot go there." Over that incident Purushotam had left Krishna consciousness and gone on to other pursuits. But Prabhupada did not compromise.

Sudama: One afternoon after his nap I was bringing him a little *rasagulla* and some drink. The sun was going down when I started to enter his room, which faced the backyard. The whole room seemed purple and gold. There was a certain energy in the room. Srila Prabhupada was chanting and crying tears of ecstasy. Well, we didn't even have *The Nectar of Devotion* yet. I got alarmed, backed out of the room with the tray, went to Govinda dasi and said, "Govinda, what's happening? Is Prabhupada OK? Is he having a fit?" She said, "No, no. That's just Srila Prabhupada having a relationship with Krishna. That's Krishna consciousness." I said, "Wow!" I went back in five minutes later. Srila Prabhupada was still there, and this time he stopped me from leaving. He said, "Sudama don't leave. I am crying because of the mercy of my Guru Maharaj. By his mercy I am allowed to see Krishna. I see Him right now over those grasses." Oh, man. It was so heavy that I started crying. He said, "Why are you crying?" I said, "Because you are so powerful and merciful. I have never met a soul like you." He said, "That is Krishna's arrangement."

Gopavrindapal: Another time one of the local book distributors asked how, upon his arrival in New York, Srila Prabhupada had such success in distributing the first volumes of the *Srimad-Bhagavatam*. Prabhupada thought for a moment and said, "I do not think it was my success. I think that they saw me as some fancy Indian gentleman, and therefore, they took whatever I asked them to take." He never thought that there was a technique. He thought it was his Indian flair, his Indian gentlemanliness.

Yasodanandan: The first time Prabhupada started the annual Mayapur meetings, there was a little hut near the entrance gate where he stayed and gave *darshan* to the devotees. We stayed with him for hours there, asking questions and hearing his answers. Many of Srila Prabhupada's godbrothers came to see him at that time, because Prabhupada had the idea of engaging his godbrothers. He wanted to make an alliance, a united front, so all the Gaudiya Vaishnavs could preach together. The Mayapur project was his way to unite his godbrothers and have them participate in this plan. Some of Prabhupada's godbrothers criticized him for using the name "Prabhupada." His godbrothers requested us (Gurukripa, Shyamasundar, Rishikumar, Tamal Krishna Maharaj, Prabhasha, and others) to leave the room. We were outside watching what was going on through the bamboo and straw walls. Voices were being raised. Prabhupada rang his bell and asked his servant to get his stationery. He was speaking in Bengali, explaining. The words "Prabhupada" and "Swamiji" were spoken many times. Afterwards, Prabhupada called us into the room and gave the example that, "In the spiritual world Radharani is the topmost *gopi*. She is the favorite of Krishna, and all of the other *gopis* assist Her. There is no envy whatsoever. Everybody is assisting the favorite *gopi* of Krishna, Radharani. In the same way, if one is a true devotee he does not become envious like some of my godbrothers." Prabhupada was not pleased with their materialistic, critical attitude toward him. He said, "I do not call myself Prabhupada. My disciples call me Prabhupada." So, on the one hand, Prabhupada tried to engage his godbrothers, and at the same time he firmly tried to protect his disciples and preach Krishna consciousness.

Brahmananda: In 1971 Prabhupada was having big public programs in India, and one evening an Arya Samajist challenged Prabhupada. He said, "Oh, Swamiji, you have come to India with your western *chelas,* but we know all these things. This is our culture. Better you go to the other places and do your work there. All right, you have been to the West, but what about the Muslim countries? What about Pakistan? You should go to Pakistan and preach there. Make them devotees." This was in a public *pandal* with thousands of people. Prabhupada said, "You are challenging us to go?" The man said, "Yes. I challenge you. You must go to Pakistan." Prabhupada said, "All right. We will go."

Prabhupada wrote a letter to me, "Immediately go to West Pakistan." He also wrote to Gargamuni, "Immediately go to East Pakistan." We got these letters and we left the next day. I didn't have any money. Somebody paid for the bus from Florida to New York. Gargamuni had money so he flew. I had to go by overland to India— hitchhiking, buses, trains, whatever way I could go. At that time a war was starting. Prabhupada found out about the war and the hostilities between Pakistan and India afterwards and then wrote a second letter saying, "I don't advise you to go at this time." But we never got that letter. We had already left. We walked right into a war situation. It was difficult, but we were preaching and trying to do something. I was in Karachi. North of Karachi is the Singh Desert, the hottest place in the world, averaging 125 degrees. It was May, the hottest month, and I was sick with dysentery. I had no books, people were spitting on me on the street, threatening to put a knife in my back. When we had *kirtan,* people would rub off our *tilak* and spit. What a situation! Then a report appeared in the Pakistani and Indian newspapers saying, "Four Hare Krishna Missionaries Shot." In Bombay, Karandhar showed Prabhupada the newspaper report. It didn't give any names. Gargamuni was with Pusta in the east, and I was with Jagannivas in the west. There were four of us. Prabhupada was very disturbed. He thought that we had been shot.

I sent a telegram to Prabhupada saying, "Can I get out of here?" Prabhupada sent a telegram back, "Come immediately, Bhakti-vedanta Swami." Four words. Those were the best four words. To get out of the country was a big thing. Somehow we were able to get out. I came to Bombay and went to the Akash Ganga Building where Prabhupada was staying. When I walked into his room, Prabhupada immediately got up, came over, put his arms around me and hugged me to his chest. He was putting his hands all over me just like a mother would touch her child if she thinks that he has been hurt. The mother wants to see that the child is still intact.

Sudama: At that time Prabhupada told me that he saw Krishna as a cowherd boy. I didn't know anything about cowherd boys. I just knew Prabhupada. He was my life. If he said so, okay. He talked about how beautiful the grass was and how fortunate he was to have the mercy of his Guru Maharaj.

That same week Purushotam, Himavati, Hamsaduta, Tamal, Dayananda, his wife Nandarani, and I entered Srila Prabhupada's room. Again this is in the afternoon. Srila Prabhupada was sitting at his desk chanting while tears flowed down his face. We were not aware of this because we were just aware of ourselves. We paid our obeisances and sat up. There was Srila Prabhupada, crying. Hamsaduta said, "All glories to you, Swamiji," and we all started crying. By the pure devotee's mystic power, neophytes were allowed to experience this. We had no idea why we were crying. We just felt an overwhelming mercy. We fell down again and paid obeisances. Srila Prabhupada said, "Why are you crying? Sit up." We said, "Srila Prabhupada, we are crying because you are so merciful." "No, no," he said. "It's my Guru Maharaj. Without his mercy, I'd be nothing." These were my first lessons in accepting a pure devotee of the Lord.

Gopavrindapal: One night at about 11:00 I was chanting *japa* outside Prabhupada's room on the third floor in the guest building in Mayapur. I had chanted *japa* there previously, and one of the Mayapur temple authorities had told me, "Once this gate is closed, I don't want it opened for anybody. I don't care what they say." I said, "Okay. I am up late chanting my rounds. I will help you with that." So there was a lady downstairs shaking on the gate, the very gate that this temple authority had told me not to open. I just sat there chanting my *japa*. I heard this lady's voice, "Haribol!" and the gate rattling back and forth. I was ignoring this ruckus on the local authority's plea. Finally it got so bad that Prabhupada came out. He was a bit upset. He said, "Why are they banging?" I said, "Well, Prabhupada, so-and-so told me that after these gates were locked, they should just remain that way no matter who wanted to get in." Prabhupada shook his head. He was almost disgusted. He said, "Come on." He and I walked down three flights of stairs and he personally unlatched the gate for the lady, who was a hard-working, sincere cook in Mayapur. She had been in the Mayapur temple for a long time and was the backbone of the kitchen. He let her in, and they chatted for a while. Then he closed and locked the gate behind her. As we were walking up, he looked at me disdainfully, and I was feeling very bad that I hadn't done the needful at the time. He said, "Why didn't you let her in?" I repeated that so-and-so told me not to do this. He laughed and said, "Do not listen to so-and-so swami." From that point on I let anybody in who wanted to come in. I figured that the *sannyasi's* authority had been superseded.

Yasodanandan: Once Prabhupada asked Subal Swami, a scholarly devotee, "Please describe the three kinds of Vishnus." Subal Maharaj quoted from the *Bhagavatam* and gave an elaborate explanation of Maha Vishnu, Garbhodakashayi Vishnu, and Kshirodakashayi Vishnu, as well as Their functions. After that, Prabhupada was speaking in Hindi with his godbrother, Dr. O.B.L. Kapoor, and they were laughing. Dr. O.B.L. Kapoor was shaking because in India when they appreciate something, sometimes they shake their head in a seemingly negative way. Subal was wondering what was going on. Prabhupada was very appreciative of the wonderful explanation. He was pleased that his disciple had explained the philosophy so nicely. He said, "Just see how they have learned." His reciprocation was very sweet.

Sudama: Srila Prabhupada told me, "Sudama, you were Japanese in your previous life." In a year I had learned Japanese fluently and I was thinking and dreaming in Japanese. It was bizarre.

In 1971 Srila Prabhupada arrived at the temple in Tokyo and was not pleased. I had a huge portrait of him in the anteroom where you take your shoes off. "Even you," Prabhupada said, "have become infected." I said, "Srila Prabhupada?" He said, "Yes, I can see it. I see so many discrepancies here." He chastised me for two hours. I was crushed. Then he said, "You have not made devotees." That was my worst nightmare, because that's what I always heard from other GBCs. My peers would say, "Come on, Sudama. What are you doing over there?"

The next day was Vyasa-puja. This was the initial Vyasa-puja that everyone follows in ISKCON today. We were taught this in

Tokyo. Prior to that, we had it all wrong. Srila Prabhupada arrived at the temple. I was just improvising the ceremony. I didn't know. Srila Prabhupada sat on the *vyasasana*. Some guests were there. He was angry with all of us. "How dare you bring me here. How you insult the spiritual master." What could we say? You could have heard a pin drop. I was embarrassed. I left the room and cried. I had displeased him. I went back into the tiny temple room. He said, "All right, tomorrow we will observe Vyasa-puja the correct way. I will instruct you. Now take me home." Sure enough, that evening he told me what I had to get. The next day we did it just the way we have done it for years now. Then Prabhupada lectured on the spiritual master's mercy.

That evening he got a phone call from Harikripa in New Vrindavan, stating that Vishnujana, Subal, Gargamuni, and Brahmananda had upset many devotees by preaching that Srila Prabhupada was the speaker of the *Gita* and that we Westerners were not qualified to worship Radha Krishna because we were *mlecchas*. Little did we know how insidious and power hungry and envious some of Prabhupada's godbrothers were. Srila Prabhupada was relieved. He said, "Finally, the bubble has broken. I knew that my godbrothers were behind this."

Srila Prabhupada was the person who began the fructification of Lord Chaitanya's prediction that in every town and village the Lord's name will be heard. His godbrothers couldn't even do it in London. They had to come back. Prabhupada sent eight white girls and boys to London to chant, and they turned on all of London, and all of Europe for that matter. Anyway, Prabhupada was glad that these devotees had done this, because he wanted them to go and preach. They couldn't stay in temples, couldn't lecture, and had to go preaching. And that's what they did. They split up. Brahmananda and Gargamuni went to south Florida. That was their penance.

Srila Prabhupada got ready to leave Tokyo to go to India. He said, "I have opened the West. Now I will take my dancing white elephants to India."

Gopavrindapal: We were some of the first book distributors to begin wearing pants and a skullcap. Kirtanananda was upset by this nondevotional clothing, while Karandhar thought, "What the heck. It works." They were both approaching Prabhupada by letter in an attempt to influence him to their own view. To encourage me, Karandhar would show me the letters that were coming to him and explain the letters that Prabhupada was sending to Kirtanananda. In the letters to Karandhar, it was quite clear that Prabhupada's mood was "whatever is going to maximize our effect." One of Kirtanananda's arguments was, "They dress like hippies when they go out." Prabhupada responded, "They shouldn't dress like hippies. but that doesn't mean that they can't dress like they are nondevotees." As far as I heard that was the last word. From that point on, we regularly distributed books and approached the public in nondevotional clothing.

Yasodanandan: In the morning, after a *Nectar of Devotion* lecture, Prabhupada was sitting in the courtyard of the Radha Damodar temple near the *samadhi* of Rupa Goswami, when some simple, devoted Brijbasi villagers came. They were very attracted to Prabhupada and had an incredible exchange with him in Hindi. We were thinking, "Who are these people? They are not initiated, they are not even devotees, they are not even in ISKCON, they are not this, they are not that." But Prabhupada spent over an hour talking and laughing with them. He experienced increasing ecstasy over the course of this hour. We couldn't understand what they were saying, but they talked about Krishna, Mother Yasoda, Nanda Maharaj, the *gopas*, the *gopis*, the Yamuna, this and that. Prabhupada was in total bliss. Later Prabhupada said that some of these people were liberated souls, exalted transcendentalists, although they looked like ordinary village people. This was one way Prabhupada taught us to be respectful to the inhabitants of the Dham.

Sudama: My first lesson in making *halava* was at two in the morning when Hayagriva suddenly arrived from New York. Srila Prabhupada said, "Sudama, go make *halava*." I had never made *halava*. Fortunately, I made it correctly, if not too sweet. Prabhupada told me, "Oh, Krishna likes this. I know you have made this very sweet. That is why He is Bala Gopal, because He is the butter thief. He takes from the kitchen. He likes the sweetness." He said, "Sudama, you have a knack for this. You should make more sweets." I said, "Yes, Srila Prabhupada, but I don't have the patience for sweet making." He said, "Yes, we have to preach in this age. Go out and chant Hare Krishna. Never mind *rasagulla* and *rasa malai*. Who has time for this?" Then he looked at me, Hayagriva, and Govinda dasi, and said, "But they are so nectarean. Hurry! Go make it." So we all sat and ate *halava* at two in the morning.

Gopavrindapal: Sometimes he liked to hear about how we approached the public. Once we were talking about the energy crisis which had become a big issue. The approach we used was, "You know this energy crisis that has people backed up for miles at local gas pumps? Well, there isn't any. This book explains the absence of the energy crisis that everyone thinks they feel." Prabhupada liked our creativity in distributing books. He liked to hear the anecdotes that we weaved about his books and how we created a positive impression.

Yasodanandan: Once Prabhupada told Gurudas that when he was staying at the Radha-Damodar Temple he had a chance to look at some of the original manuscripts of Jiva Goswami and Sanatana Goswami. Prabhupada said to Gurudas, "If you knew the contents of these books, you would faint." This was another manifestation of Prabhupada's mercy. He revealed a glimpse of the transcendental potency of the Goswamis' literatures.

Sudama: Prabhupada said, "You should always have food ready when a friend or others come, no matter what time they arrive. If nothing is ready, then you make something." He said, "That is the Vaishnav way."

Gopavrindapal: A rumor went around that Prabhupada had successfully distributed his periodical to folks in tea stalls in India. So I asked him how he had succeeded. He was a bit incensed. He said, "No, not tea stalls," as if that were beneath him, and he suggested that, "My success was with government men. I would meet the government officers in their offices. I would go to downtown Delhi, to the bigger cities, and offer my books to the bigger men, the more reputable men of society, and somehow or other try and preach to the higher class of people." The idea of him approaching folks that were sitting at the roadside tea stalls was not his idea of how he had begun book distribution.

Yasodanandan: In January of 1973, Gurukripa and I went to Bombay, where Prabhupada was residing near the ocean at Kartikeya Mahadevia's house. We told Prabhupada that we had gone to Madurai, South India, where we were given a wonderful facility by a wealthy man. For fifteen days we preached and tried in every conceivable way to make Life Members and raise funds for the Vrindavan temple, but we hardly got anything. We made two Life Members in three weeks. Then we went to the next city, and all we did was have *kirtan,* hear and chant, and within three days we had made twenty-two Life Members. We couldn't understand it. In one place we tried so hard, we worked, we preached, and we couldn't do anything. In the next place we just sat on our bottoms, and all the money came. We related this incident to Prabhupada, and he said, "The problem with you two is that you're too attached to the result. Our business as devotees is to try to please Krishna. If you are very sincere, Krishna will personally make sure that you become successful. You just try. Whether there is success or failure is not up to you, it is up to Krishna." In this way Prabhupada was very encouraging.

Sudama: When we were in Hawaii, Prabhupada told me how Hawaii was conducive for spiritual advancement. Outside of India, Hawaii was the prime place for spiritual advancement. It was always a comfortable 80 to 85 degrees, with trade winds blowing. You could live with no shoes and just a pair of shorts, picking pineapples, bananas, and fresh coconuts. Of course, I never did that but he said that it was a perfect place for that. We talked about the Samoans and different races. He said, "Unfortunately these people must have the worst karma on earth. They eat pigs and look like pigs." We were walking, and a Samoan family walked by us when he said this. I thought, "No, no!" But then I thought, "Wait a minute, I am with a pure devotee. I have God on my side in case they should get offended." But they weren't. Srila Prabhupada talked about what they looked like and how ugly they were and, literally using those terms, preached to them.

Gopavrindapal: Hawaii was one of Prabhupada's favorite places to poke fun at. I think Hawaii was a pet peeve for him. He saw both sides of it. On one hand, he claimed it was a holdover from another era of goodness. On the other hand, he said that the enjoying mood was very strong there. It was in Hawaii that he coined his famous reaction to the surfers, calling them "sufferers." Another time he described how people become very attached to their flat on the tenth or twentieth floor of the high-rise apartment buildings that were coming up like wild in Waikiki. Because of their attachment, he said, they would come back in a subsequent life as a cockroach in that very same flat.

Yasodanandan: At one point Prabhupada started a mock debate. He said, "Let's say that I don't believe in Krishna. I don't accept your *shastras*. You prove to me that there is a God." I was so dumb. I said, "Well, Prabhupada, it says in the *Brahma-samhita* . . ." Prabhupada became a little angry. "No *shastra*." I said, "Everything comes from a cause and . . ." Prabhupada said, "No, no. You don't know." The other devotees tried to answer, and he said to them, "You also don't know. None of you know." He asked me, "Do you have a father?" I said, "Yes." He asked someone else, "Do you have a father," "Yes." Then he asked, "Does your father have a father? Does your grandfather have a father?" Prabhupada argued on this basis, that any intelligent person can see that there is God, the cause of all causes, by looking for the original father. There must be a father from whom everyone originates. Prabhupada was very kind in that way.

Sudama: Srila Prabhupada saw me come in. I paid my obeisances, and he jumped all over me. "What is this? Why you have left? Why you are dressed like that?" He asked me all these questions for twenty minutes. I was sweating, crying, very upset, very confused, very on edge, very on trial in front of my godbrothers, who were really strangers. I had gotten a temple that was too big, and my men had been stolen. It was the old politics game. Srila Prabhupada said, "I want to know one thing before I send you out of here. Do you still love Krishna? Do you believe in Krishna?" I said, "Yes." He said, "All right. You will be okay." Then he turned to everybody in the room and said, "This is disgusting. This is not how Vaishnavs behave. You knew that Sudama needed help. You knew that Sudama was crying out in *maya,* and you ignored him. This is not Vaishnav behavior. A true Vaishnav," he said, "would have taken him by the hand earlier on so that this would never have taken place."

Gopavrindapal: I said something about, "When we distribute your books Prabhupada . . ." He stopped me and said, "Do you know what book distribution means?" I wanted to think of something quickly to save my skin, but I couldn't. So I said, "Actually, no. I don't. I know that there is a lot of depth to it and things about it that I don't understand." He turned to me with a strong glance and said, "Book distribution means distribution of knowledge. Do not forget this." It wasn't a sales thing. He didn't look at the distribution of his books as something that would be done with a sales mentality but rather with the mentality that we were giving knowledge to people who needed it.

Sudama: At one point Prabhupada started to talk about Krishna's intimate childhood pastimes, how He showed Mother Yasoda the Universal Form within His mouth. As Prabhupada described this, he started to cry profusely. Then he described the pastime of Krishna killing Putana, and he explained that even though Krishna was a baby, He was able to kill such a gigantic demon, and how that is the transcendental potency of the Supreme Personality of Godhead, Krishna. Prabhupada was crying. This was the first time that my understanding crystallized. It became a bit more like a realization. We knew that Prabhupada was a very exalted, saintly person and a great preacher. But this time I felt that Prabhupada was actually experiencing these pastimes with Krishna. We read them and think, "This is very nice and very sweet." But Prabhupada was actually experiencing the transcendental pastimes of Krishna in his heart. And although he was always enjoying these sweet realizations of Krishna, he was preaching Krishna consciousness in a practical way. That was Prabhupada's mercy.

Sudama: I didn't want to discuss death, although ninety-nine percent of our process is chanting Hare Krishna and preparing for the moment of death so that we can become liberated. In Berkeley, Prabhupada talked to me about his leaving, and I didn't deal with it well. I didn't want to hear it. As far as I was concerned, he was living forever, which he does. But he was talking about the position of the *siksha* and *diksha* guru. I was totally confused. I said, "Srila Prabhupada, all I know is you. Now you are saying there is another kind of guru. What is this?" "Wait, wait," he said. He chuckled and told me, "When you do not see me here physically, always listen for me. I will instruct you through the bodies of others from time to time. Always listen for me." I said, "What does that mean, Srila Prabhupada—if a dog barks?" He said, "Just what I said—anyone, it can be anyone."

Yasodanandan: After the 1976 Mayapur festival, the GBC decided to send Rupanuga Maharaj and me to Australia. When I came to Vrindavan in the summer of '76, I told Prabhupada that I was on my way to Australia. I had already made arrangements for a visa and a plane ticket. My body was in India, but my mind was already in Australia. Prabhupada said, "What is this Australia?" So I described to Prabhupada, "Well, the GBC decided to send me. They wanted somebody to go and preach there." Prabhupada said, "I will write them a letter." He also said, "If you want, you can still stay here. That is okay." For about a day and a half Prabhupada played with me like a father would play with his son. He told me, "If you want to stay, you can stay. It's very nice. If you want to go, you can also go. It's very nice." After some time I thought, "What is this? Prabhupada is telling me, 'you can do this or you can do that.'" I went to Prabhupada one afternoon and said, "Prabhupada, you have told me that I could go there if I want and I could stay here if I want. That is confusing. Please tell me what you want me to do." Prabhupada pointed at me and raised his voice, "Yes, that is what I want to see from you. This is the attitude I want from all my disciples. You just do what I tell you to do." I took it as Prabhupada's mercy. He wanted me to stay in India to work in the *gurukula* and preach.

Sudama: On a morning walk Srila Prabhupada told me, "If you think that you have become spiritually advanced and you start acting a role, you will become mad."

He instructed other people to read his books because he is in his books. I know that he is. I was just never a big reader. In Hawaii I went to him in tears. I said, "They all criticize me because I don't chant enough Sanskrit. I don't quote *slokas*." Srila Prabhupada laughed. He said, "They sound like my godbrothers. Sudama, you speak from your heart. That's all that counts. Krishna doesn't care if you can't quote *slokas*. You are a darn good preacher. You bring many people because of your heart." I said, "I have only read *The Nectar of Devotion* twice, *Bhagavad-gita* ten times, and that's it. I can't

even finish the First Canto of *Srimad-Bhagavatam*." He said, "So?
You cook *samosas*. You chant beautifully, you have love for Krishna.
What else is needed? Don't make things so complicated. It's very
simple."

Yasodanandan: At night he would frequently talk about how he
wanted his *gurukula* system to work, how he wanted the children to
be fed, how they should be taught, what he wanted them to do, and
the outline of a *varnashram* society. He wanted our society to have
a place for the children who may not be inclined to be *brahmans*.

At one point he mentioned masonry, carpentry, organic gar-
dening, and taking care of cows. He said, "We should have a wide
variety of engagements, a multileveled arrangement so that all of
these children can stay within the Krishna conscious movement."
Prabhupada's vision for his *gurukula* program was something very
precise and detailed. At one point he told me, "This *gurukula* program is the most important program in this movement." I said,
"Prabhupada, didn't you say that distributing books and so many
things are important?" He said, "Books are very important. We distribute books to make devotees. But these children are already
devotees. You have to train them." He attached special importance
to training our devotees' children. He also commented, "The children of these children will be real devotees." So he attached great
importance to the *gurukula* project and to giving Krishna conscious
children special training and care.

Gopavrindapal: Another thing that I liked was his attempt to rec-
oncile with the Gaudiya Math. Although many times Prabhupada
tried to steer his disciples clear of involvement with Gaudiya Math
issues and Gaudiya Math representatives, his personal approach to
the Gaudiya Math was always one of reciprocation and reconciliation. In one letter he said, "We have been involved in fratricidal
warfare; we don't see the same philosophically. Nevertheless, there
is no reason why we can't unite for the higher cause, preaching the

mission of Sri Chaitanya Mahaprabhu and Srila Bhaktisiddhanta Sarasvati Thakur." While he wanted to compartmentalize our understanding and keep our fledgling outlook on the philosophy pristine and free of external input, his personal approach to the Gaudiya Math was always one of reconciliation. When he was dealing with his godbrothers individually, either through letters or personal interaction, he was always seeing the higher purpose of uniting for the preaching cause of the *sankirtan* movement.

TAPE 6

Sridhar Swami
Baradraj das
Harivilas das
Gurudas

Sridhar Swami: After Ratha-yatra I went to Los Angeles for my initiation ceremony. I was always very nervous in Prabhupada's association because I felt he could understand my thoughts and see my heart. When it was time for me to get my beads, I walked to the *vyasasana* and began to offer my obeisances. Prabhupada said, "So? You are *brahmachari?*" I was so nervous that I didn't know what to do, so I continued to offer my obeisances. Someone was telling me, "Prabhupada's talking to you," but I just kept offering obeisances. I wanted to avoid him. To me Prabhupada was like God. He had come to save me. It relieved me of a huge burden. In the material world I was in such anxiety, and Prabhupada had relieved my burden. He was so beautiful and I was very shy. But afterwards it struck me, "Maybe he is blessing me as a *brahmachari.*" By Krishna's grace I never got married. Here I am struggling.

Baradraj: It was very important to me to have a good Sanskrit name. I liked the names of the initiated devotees, but I was worried that I would get a name that didn't sound right, that didn't mean very much. I knew that I had to accept it because Prabhupada knew

121

my spiritual name and he was going to call me by that name. But I was struggling inside on a completely superficial platform. My mind was distracting me. I was attracted to a particular name, "Madan Mohan." I kept saying, "Madan Mohan. That's a good name. I hope I get that name."

I had been in the temple for six months in Montreal, and I was using some ready-made beads, so I brought them with me to the initiation *yajna*. It was a beautiful scene and a wonderful experience. I had never witnessed so much grandeur and so much effortless grace. During the ceremony, Prabhupada took one's beads, chanted on them, and then returned them. When my turn came I handed him my beads. He took them. They were not overly small, but they were on the small side. He looked at them with disapproval and said, "You couldn't have gotten bigger beads?" At that moment I was thinking, "Beads?" I was already being demolished. I had no leg to stand on. I didn't know what to say, so I was quiet. I may have shrugged. He was chanting on my beads, and I was thinking, "Madan Mohan, Madan Mohan." The mind was going on as if it were on hold; waiting, waiting. Finally he stopped chanting. He handed me the beads. Before I took them, he said, "Is there already someone named Madan Mohan?" The devotees said, "Oh, yes, Prabhupada. There he is." And with that: "Your name is Baradraj das."

 **Harivilas:** I was invited to his room to receive the *brahminical* initiation, the Gayatri mantra. I was really excited. I walked into the room and offered my obeisances. Prabhupada motioned to me and said, "Come closer." I went as close as I thought I should be. He said, "Come closer." He made me sit right next to him, and then he gave me a piece of paper with the Gayatri mantra on it. He said, "Come a little closer," and he began to repeat the words of the mantra close to my ear. It was very intimate. We were alone in the room. He began to speak to me, saying, "So, you are leaving?" I said, "Yes, Prabhupada." I was going to leave the next morning. He said,

"So you are going by Cale?" I was wondering, "Why is he saying this? How does he even know about Cale?" Cale is a port on the French coast, the North Sea coast. I was going from Dover to Bologne. I said, "No, Prabhupada, not Cale. The Hovercraft doesn't go from Dover to Cale." He said, "You are sure?" I said, "Yes, Prabhupada. You are wrong." Then I realized what I was saying. I was telling Prabhupada that he was wrong. I felt that I shouldn't say that. He looked at me and smiled. "That's all right." I said, "Thank you very much," and offered my obeisances. He said, "Thank you very much. You continue pursuing the work in Paris." So I went. I kept thinking, "Why did I say 'no' to Prabhupada? I should not have said anything." When I got to Dover there was an announcement: "Ladies and gentlemen, due to rough seas today, the Hovercraft will not be going to Bologne." I was a little bit surprised. "The Hovercraft will be going to Cale today." I said, "Oh, no! What a fool I am." Prabhupada had asked me, "Are you sure?" And I kept insisting, "Yes, I am sure." I remember that very vividly.

 **Gurudas:** We'd been apprised of the rules and regulations. Prabhupada didn't go through them at our initiation. He just said, "Chant sixteen rounds, and Krishna consciousness means happiness," which he had said many other times over the years and which was a very strong statement. Prabhupada sometimes gave nice, short instructions. Once we were in Nandagram looking at the beautiful paintings. He turned to me and said, "Art means full belly." He said, "If someone is hungry, they cannot think about making or looking at art. They are thinking about filling their belly." Very pointed, very short, very sweet, and a bit of philosophy. So, Krishna consciousness means happiness. It was powerful.

Sridhar Swami: Prabhupada was in Los Angeles, and we were doing well distributing books. We thought we would go and tell Prabhupada about it. I had the idea that we should memorize a verse in Sanskrit. Not many people were into Sanskrit at that time. I thought we should offer a prayer to Srila Prabhupada. We came in to see him about lunchtime and we offered him this prayer:

> tvam nah sandarsito dhatra
> dustaram nistitirsatam
> kalim sattva-haram pumsam
> karna-dhara ivarnavam

"We think that we have met Your Goodness by the will of providence, just so that we may accept you as captain of the ship for those who desire to cross the difficult ocean of Kali, which deteriorates all the good qualities of a human being." (*Srimad-Bhagavatam* 1.1.22)

Prabhupada asked us to take lunch with him. I thought, "No. We want to get back out and distribute more books, Prabhupada." It was funny, but I curse myself now. We missed another opportunity.

Baradraj: My parents were horrified by the idea that I was going to marry in the movement and they opposed my marriage. They refused to come. The day before the marriage, my mother wrote an angry telegram to Prabhupada saying that I had a history of mental illness. It was totally untrue. Well, maybe true, but not to my knowledge. I didn't see the telegram, but I heard about it. Prabhupada called me in right away and said, "I received a telegram from your mother. She says you are crazy. Is this true?" I thought about it and said, "I don't think so, Srila Prabhupada, but I suspect that she might be," which was not a proper thing to say about one's mother in front of Prabhupada. Prabhupada generally did not tolerate disrespect to one's parents. Once he made Brahmananda bow down to his mother. But I showed a kind of independence in front of Prabhupada. I wanted him to know that my mind was set. The whole process was a way of cutting the bonds of worldly family influence, bonds that were stopping me from doing that which I should wholeheartedly do, guided by his wisdom and kindness. When I said, "But I think she might be," he laughed. He said, "That's all right."

Harivilas: Before the press conference, Prabhupada spoke to the devotees. There were about thirty people there who were very young, seventeen or eighteen years old. I arrived after everything had started. When I walked in, I had the illusion that I had organized this thing. I made everyone move out of the way, and I went right up to the front. The devotee I came with, Ghanashyam, sat near the entrance very humbly, quietly. I went right up and sat down next to Prabhupada. Lochanananda was introducing everyone. He said, "This is Harivilas das, president of the temple." Prabhupada didn't look at me. I thought, "Why didn't he look at me? My name was mentioned, but Prabhupada didn't say anything. He didn't even nod." I realized that I must have done something wrong, and I was feeling bad that I had pushed everyone out of the way to sit up front. Then Lochanananda said, "And that's Ghanashyam in the back. He translates your books." Prabhupada said, "Oh? Where is he? Let him stand up." Ghanashyam stood up, and Prabhupada said, "Thank you very much."

I realized that I must have been puffed up, otherwise why wouldn't Prabhupada acknowledge me as he had acknowledged Ghanashyam? Prabhupada thanked the devotees for participating in Krishna consciousness, and finally it was announced that we had just gotten a new temple. This was a major accomplishment. Prabhupada said, "Where is it?" Lochanananda said that it was a little bit out of town. Prabhupada looked at me for the first time. His look was very weighty. I could barely look at him. He had already put me down in a sense, and I was contrite about it. He said, "How far is the temple from Paris?" That question took me off balance. I said, "Well, it's not very far, Prabhupada." He said, "Oh? How far is it by car?" I said, "It's about forty-five minutes." He asked, "And by train?" I was thinking, "Wow! Why is he asking me these questions?" I was confused. I said, "It's over an hour." He said, "Oh. So it's very far." I said, "Yes, Prabhupada, it's very far." Then I realized that my guru is correcting my imperfect intelligence and my illusions about myself. I realized that I had accepted him as my spiritual master because he was able to point these things out in a precise way. I needed that. I was very humbled but very happy at the same time.

Gurudas: We were on a train and Prabhupada said, "Just as rain falls everywhere, on the land as well as on the ocean, so Krishna loves all His devotees equally. But if someone steps toward Krishna, He reciprocates. He shows His love for that person." Similarly, Prabhupada did not love any devotee more than any other, but he showed his love to the devotees who were doing something.

At the first Kumbhamela we attended, Prabhupada was in a large, grand tent that looked like a nomadic bedroom. All the so-called "big guns" gathered. Again, it wasn't because he loved us more. It was because we were doing something and he was reciprocating with us. He asked us, "How do you know Krishna is God?" Somebody said, "Because it says so in the *Bhagavad-gita.*" Prabhupada said, "Someone can say that that is just a book." I said, "Because you say so, Prabhupada." He said, "Someone will say, 'What does he know? He is an old man.'" So we didn't know. Prabhupada said, "The answer is because you feel ecstasy. You feel blissful. You feel the nectar. The proof of the pudding is in the eating." I thought, "What a great answer," because many times I had felt ecstatic. That's what kept me going, along with Prabhupada. I was scholarly but from the very beginning my Krishna consciousness was interacting with Prabhupada.

Baradraj: Prabhupada said, "Can you draw a picture of Lord Chaitanya?" He wanted to see. A few days later, after the marriage, my wife Rukmini brought in her painting, and other paintings were there. Jadurani was there. Prabhupada looked at everything. I had done a drawing of Lord Chaitanya that was not finished. The figure of Lord Chaitanya was there, but everything else was just barely sketched in. I had put everything I had into Lord Chaitanya's face, His expression and attitude. Whatever I understood to be right I put into the picture. Prabhupada looked at the other pieces of art. He looked at Rukmini's painting and appreciated it. Then he noticed that there was a rolled up paper on the desk. He said, "What is this?" Someone said, "A drawing by Baradraj." Prabhupada took it, and as he unrolled it from the top, the first thing he saw was Lord Chaitanya's face. Prabhupada's eyes got really big. His eyes were big to start with, but whenever he got excited about something they really expanded. He unrolled the whole picture. He had the biggest grin on his face. His teeth were showing. It was as if his whole face became the sun. He said, "Ah, the husband is better."

Harivilas: After the press conference, I ordered a taxi for Prabhupada, Aravinda, Shyamasundar, and myself. I was sitting on the left side in the back seat, Prabhupada was sitting in the middle, and Aravinda was sitting on the right. We started driving through the center of Paris. We went to crossroads called the Concord, which is a very prestigious place in Paris. I was always reading *Bhagavad-gita,* and I was always writing down questions, thinking that if ever I met Prabhupada, I would ask him. We were stuck in the traffic, and I asked Prabhupada, "What does this verse mean?" The verse was, *Ya nisa sarva-bhutanam,* what is night for all beings is the time of awakening for the self-controlled; and the time of awakening for all beings is night for the introspective sage" (*Bhagavad-gita* 2.69). There was noise so he said, "What is that?" Aravinda said, "What does this verse mean?" And Prabhupada said, "Oh, yes." He heard, "time of awakening. What does this verse mean?" Prabhupada said, "Yes, 4:00. All of our devotees wake up at 4:00 and take shower and go to *mangal arati.*" Aravinda smiled and said, "No, Prabhupada. What does this verse mean—*Ya nisa sarva-bhutanam*"? Prabhupada started smiling and said, "Yes. This means that when we see the karmis, we laugh. And when the karmis see us, they laugh. But our laugh is better. We know that they are wrong. They see us, and they think that we are wasting our time chanting Hare Krishna. We see them, and we know that they are wasting their time in material life. Our laugh is best."

Baradraj: The first exhibits in Mayapur were completed miraculously. This was the first year that devotees came out in droves for the Gaura-Purnima festival. It was a wonderful year. Prabhupada came, and lo and behold, we had actually completed a series of exhibits which were arranged in a horseshoe shape in front of the incomplete Mayapur temple. The exhibits were in bamboo shacks. Everything was barely kept together with some cow dung and arrowroot twine. But to this day, I think that those were the most wonderful exhibits. They had such a vibrant, raw energy.

I missed the beginning of Prabhupada's first tour because I was getting things ready. All the devotees were there, and I was running to catch up. They started at the wrong end and were going backwards from the end to the beginning. The beginning exhibit was my work, and one of the last exhibits was Rukmini's work. Her piece was of Lord Chaitanya fainting in ecstasy in front of Jagannath, Subhadra, and Balaram. Lord Chaitanya was like a stick in His transcendental, ecstatic condition. Prabhupada looked at it and was drinking its nectar. He was very affected and said, "Who has made this?" By that time I had caught up and I said, "Rukmini, my wife, has made this." Prabhupada said, "Very, very good." Then slowly he moved down to the next thing, came round, and finally came to the last exhibit, which was mine. It was of Nrisimhadev tearing Hiranyakashipu with Prahlad standing nearby offering prayers. Prabhupada looked at it and said, "Who has made this?" I said, "This is my work, Srila Prabhupada." "You still have some learning to do. This is not yet perfect. The wife is better, I think."

Gurudas: So, in the tent at Kumbhamela Prabhupada had said, "You know Krishna is God by your ecstasy. The proof of the pudding is in the eating." Seven or eight years later we were on a morning walk in Philadelphia when Prabhupada said, "Stop." Everybody stopped. "How do you know Krishna is God?" I let a few people say this and that. Nobody knew. I said, "Because you feel the ecstasy. You feel the nectar. The proof of the pudding is in the eating." He said, "No, because the *Bhagavad-gita* says it." I said, "But Prabhupada, you said . . ." By that time he was walking on. This was one of those seeming contradictions that aren't actually contradictions, because they're transcendental.

Sridhar Swami: Somehow I never got sick in India. Everybody else would go fat and come back skinny, but I went skinny and came back fat. At one stage at Hare Krishna Land in Bombay, there was a lot of work to do, but we literally had no manpower. There were very few devotees. Tamal Krishna was the GBC, and he was discussing the problem with Prabhupada. I was a *brahmachari,* an insignificant *brahmachari.* I was doing a little preaching, making Life Members. For some reason or other, Prabhupada called me into his room when Tamal was there and asked me, "Sridhar, what should we do? What can we do? There is a problem." I was flabbergasted. I thought, "Well, I'll try to work harder." I didn't know what to say. It was bewildering.

Harivilas: When Prabhupada walked into the temple I was very tense. I didn't know what was going to happen, if he would approve. He immediately wanted to have *darshan.* We had a simple Guru-Gauranga altar with a picture of the Panchatattva. He looked and said, "Oh, my Guru Maharaj is here," and he offered his *dandavats.* That really impressed me. This was in 1970, but still, such a great personality gave his *dandavats* to our very humble altar. That was wonderful.

Baradraj: He said, "An artist worships Krishna by his intelligence." By thinking of Krishna and intelligently making decisions on how to portray Krishna, one engages one's intelligence in worshipping Him. And by doing so, Krishna reveals Himself.

Gurudas: At our *pandal* program in Calcutta we had some seats for Life Members, a *rupee* each. Some communists came and said, "This is a distinction. Those seats are for a *rupee,* and some people might want to sit on those seats but can't pay a *rupee.*" I said, "If there is a distinction and you like the seats, go sit in the seats." They did and were satisfied, but previously they had sent a piece of paper to Prabhupada on the stage that said, "Quit India or die." Prabhupada started the program with beautiful *Brahma-samhita* prayers. It soothed everybody.

Harivilas: Prabhupada was sitting on a wonderful, impressive *vyas-asana* that was built for him. There were two thousand people present, along with a large group of young anarchist and communist hecklers. We were worried. When Prabhupada began to speak, the hecklers said, "On the floor! On the floor! On the floor!" Prabhupada asked the translator, Jyotirmayi, "What are they saying?" She said, "Prabhupada, they are saying that you should sit on the floor." There was a moment of silence. Prabhupada looked at the hecklers and said, "If someone is qualified they can sit on the seat. This seat does not belong to me. It is the seat of Vyas. The person who is qualified to speak the *Bhagavat* philosophy can sit here. But if you can hear me better, I will sit on the floor." When that was translated the weight of that statement was enough to stop them. They remained quiet, and they respectfully listened to Prabhupada. It was the way he said, "If you can hear me better, I will sit on the floor."

Sridhar Swami: In India I had an opportunity to see how Prabhupada encouraged Indians and expected a lot from them. The type of Indians he attracted were very high class, big industrialists with money, as well as people who had principles. Dr. Patel, for example, had amazing association with Srila Prabhupada. On many occasions

Prabhupada was very intimate with Dr. Patel, almost like a friend. Prabhupada let him get away with virtual murder in terms of Dr. Patel's challenging attitude and joking.

I saw that if Indians would take up Krishna consciousness and pursue it the way Prabhupada was, it would be a great addition to Lord Chaitanya's *sankirtan* movement. Prabhupada really wanted Indians to get involved. He was very charming, very respectful towards them, and at the same time he wouldn't let them speak nonsense. So much respect and love was involved that they appreciated being chastised by Prabhupada. And he often said to us, his disciples, "I can do. You cannot."

Gurudas: Prabhupada started out with the *Brahma-samhita* prayers. They were beautiful. It soothed everybody. Then Prabhupada was about to lecture when we heard a lot of noise. Pishima was coming on the stage with her following of mostly Bengali ladies. They were talking, and some men were saying, "Shut up. Shut up," which made the ladies make more noise. Prabhupada called me over and said, "What's going on?" I said, "Pishima is trying to get your attention." He looked at me as if to say, "We've got a program to do here, so what is going on?" I said, "Some disciples and well-wishers of Pishima are making noise." He said, "Get them to stop." As nicely as I could I said to them, "You've got to stop." It subsided in three or four minutes. I went to Prabhupada and said, "Okay." He said, "I used to beat her up, and I still shall."

Baradraj: Prabhupada was talking about how hard it is to judge a man's qualifications. It is almost a gift to be able to judge another man's qualities. It isn't just a matter of comparing one man to another or of going by some socio-economic standard. Prabhupada said, "My grandmother was expert at this. She was a simple woman, not educated, but everyone respected her talent." He said that a number of boys applied for the honor of his sister's hand, but it had to go through his grandmother. She decided who was worthy and who was not worthy. So, a well educated, wealthy young man from a good family was there, and she was drilling him. He was in his early twenties and a gem of a person. The grandmother said, "Can you ride a bicycle?" He said, "No." She didn't say anything. Afterward they came and asked, "Well, what do you think?" She said, "He is worthless." Everyone was in shock. She said, "He has no drive. Any young boy has an opportunity to learn to ride a bicycle. He will get one even if it's his friend's. Anyone who has any kind of drive will learn. He has no drive. He is worthless."

Harivilas: About 12:00 at night we went to get a taxi because we were so poor that we didn't have a car. While we were waiting near an outdoor café, I asked Prabhupada, "I know you are tired. Would you like to sit down here?" He looked at the chair and at the place. He said, "What is this place?" I said, "Prabhupada this is an outdoor café." He said, "Café? They are drinking and smoking here?" I said, "Yes, Prabhupada." He said, "Guru cannot sit in such a place." I felt, "Wow! This is amazing. Every time I talk to Prabhupada, he instructs me about Krishna consciousness." It was wonderful. I said, "Okay, Prabhupada. I'm sorry. I thought you were tired." He said, "That's all right. Guru cannot sit in such a place." The taxi came, and on the way back I said, "It's 12:00. Should we get up for *mangal arati?*" He said, "Well, devotees should sleep six hours. So you sleep six hours and then get up. Is that all right?" "Yes. That's okay." With that understanding we took rest.

At 4:35 in the morning, someone pounds my arms, "Get up, you nonsense. Get up." I woke up thinking, "Is this a bad dream? What's the matter?" He said, "You nonsense. Prabhupada is so angry." I said, "Why? What happened?" He said, "Because there is no *mangal arati.* The devotees aren't up." I said, "Oh, my God." I was really confused. I ran downstairs, and some devotees had just started doing a *kirtan.* Everyone was giving me dirty looks. "Why did you let this happen?" I tried to explain, but then I kept quiet. Someone grabbed me and said, "Come on. Hurry up." "What's the matter?"

We had just started *mangal arati*. "Prabhupada wants you to come on the morning walk." I went outside and there was Prabhupada, waiting. We started walking. That was wonderful. All of a sudden we were in the fresh air. It was about 6:00 in the morning on a nice spring day, and Prabhupada said, "Shyamasundar, why are all the *grihasthas* in *maya?*" Shyamasundar didn't say anything. Prabhupada stopped, looked at him, smiled and said, "Because that is their position."

Gurudas: Sometimes he described what it was like coming to the United States. It wasn't easy for him. He was sick, he had to cook for himself, and he felt out of place. At first he had some doubts about staying in America. The way he counteracted the doubts was to go to the shipping line and find out when the ships would be returning to India. The customs man said, "Swamiji, you have been coming here for a year looking at the times, but when are you going?"

Harivilas: He said, "When I first came to America, my plan was to make *sannyasis*." He looked at us. We were quiet. Then he said, "But that was not possible, so I thought, 'Let them get married. The husband will give his wife one child, she will go to Vrindavan, and then the husband will take *sannyas*.'" He looked at us and said, "That is also not possible. But that's all right. You can chant Hare Krishna." We were all in a state of shock. We kept walking. Prabhupada stopped and looked at a house and said, "This house is first class. In India, only the best gentlemen have a house like this." He said, "Look at the garden, it's perfect. Look at the house, it's perfect. It's too perfect." It shocked me. He said, "It's too perfect. The gentleman in this house cannot leave this situation. When he dies, he will take birth here again as a dog or a bug to continue his attachment." He said, *Ato griha kshetra sutapta vittair janasya moho 'yam aham mameti* [*Srimad-Bhagavatam* 5.5.8]. It's too nice, and he will continue his attachment. This is the flaw of material life."

Baradraj: Prabhupada and I discussed many things. I had just arrived in India, and I had a head full of ideas as I was charged with a dozen projects. I was totally overwhelmed. I walked out of Prabhupada's room, and the first person I saw was Devananda Swami, who I knew from America and who I hadn't seen for a long time. We offered obeisances and hugged each other. I was standing on the steps for about a minute talking with him, when all of a sudden, Satsvarupa, who was Prabhupada's personal attendant at the time, came running towards me with a sense of alarm. He said, "Baradraj, please come. There is something Prabhupada wants to tell you. Please come back." I told Devananda, "Please excuse me. I have to go. Prabhupada is calling me. We will talk later." I had spoken with him for literally a minute. I ran back into Prabhupada's quarters at the end of a long hallway, entered the room, and paid my obeisances. I looked up, and Prabhupada was looking at me very strangely. He said, "We have discussed so many things. You have so much to do. I don't think you have time to stand around and talk."

Sridhar Swami: Prabhupada wanted Indians to get involved in every way. He didn't see them only as people who could give money, although a lot of the gentlemen he was dealing with were businessmen; but many *sadhus,* very religious people, principled people, came to him also. Before he took up the life of a *sadhu,* Prabhupada himself was an aristocratic gentleman and moved in that circle.

One Mr. Brijratan Motek was a very big industrialist and the husband of Birla's daughter, which was the biggest family in India at that time. This man would regularly sit and listen to Prabhupada. He would chant *japa,* and he would give Prabhupada advice. Prabhupada listened very carefully to his advice, because he was a good businessman.

Throughout the construction of the Bombay temple we spent a lot of money, and we made a few mistakes here and there and got cheated. At the end, when it was time to pay all the final bills and deal with all the contractors, we had to go over the contract to see if there was any cheating involved. To our amazement, Prabhupada turned everything over to Mr. Motek. He gave him the final authority on who to pay, how much to pay, and how much to cut. And he saved us a lot of money. There were many examples like that. In his writings, Prabhupada talked about the construction of the Bombay temple. He wrote a letter to Giriraj about Sumati Morarji and told him to form a committee and put the Life Members in charge of building the temple. He said, "Our business is preaching. We should not be entangled in these mundane business affairs. Members have invested in us, and we are investing our preaching in them, so give them responsibility."

Harivilas: Prabhupada seemed to be very fond of George and philosophically interested in John. They had many philosophical exchanges. George, like Prabhupada, is a very down-to-earth person, not a self-conscious person. Prabhupada was able to surmise that. George was also friendly and respectful to Prabhupada. They were talking about addiction. "As someone may be addicted to drugs, we are addicted to Krishna," Prabhupada said. At the time, John and Yoko were addicted to heroin. Sometimes, if you are just speaking the eternal truth, it will cover a situation. But Prabhupada seemed to be able to read minds. After that, basically, it was about developing a taste, a love, for chanting, for this philosophy. It was quite nice the way Prabhupada was doing it. He wasn't judging them or asking too much about them. He was talking like artists talk when they get "in the zone." It's actually a trance state, a state of meditation. At that time you become so involved in what you are doing that everything else disappears. That's what Krishna consciousness is. It's that taste for chanting. That's what Prabhupada was preaching.

Baradraj: He said, "Aravinda's disciples were so enamored of his greatness that when Aravinda died, they didn't know what to do with him. They were in a fog. They thought he was in *samadhi*.

They let him sit there until he began to smell. Aravinda didn't have intelligent disciples. His disciples didn't know the difference between a living man and a dead man. What is the use of disciples like that? That is less intelligent. It is not your position to criticize other teachers, but it is okay to criticize their disciples. You can tell if they are less intelligent."

Harivilas: We used to go out on morning walks in the suburbs of Paris. One morning we were walking, and I came down with a serious blood infection from a cut on my foot. I hadn't taken care of it. Prabhupada noticed that I was a little cold. It was chilly in the morning, and I only had a thin *kurta* on. Prabhupada asked, "How is your health?" I said, "It's okay, Prabhupada." He saw that I was limping, and he said, "Are you cold?" I said, "Well, not really." He said, "If you want, I will give you some clothing." That was very considerate of him. He was so concerned about my health and the health of the other devotees too. Then I came down with such a serious infection that I had to go to the hospital. Right before I went to the hospital, we had a big program at the School of Architecture. During that program, Prabhupada gave a speech about *varnashram-dharma* and how people who didn't follow it were like dogs. When the question and answer period came, one gentleman stood up and said with a French accent, "Yes, Swami. I want to ask you a question. What is wrong with being a dog?" Prabhupada said, "If you think it is good then I give you my blessings. You can take birth as a dog in your next life." When he said that, all the devotees gasped for breath because they realized that a pure devotee gave this person the benediction to become a dog in his next life. That was quite an event.

Gurudas: Prabhupada asked me to arrange a meeting with the United States Ambassador to India. Some devotees and I had already met the Ambassador, Kenneth Keating. He liked me. He knew me from the Food for Peace program, and through him I was able to get tons of food for distribution. In two days the Ambassador was leaving Delhi, but I arranged a meeting for the next day, which turned out to be quite friendly. The Ambassador asked if we'd like tea. Prabhupada said that we don't take tea, so he gave us warm milk in gold-rimmed, American Eagle cups and saucers.

Prabhupada explained that there are many designations but these are not very important. "You may think you are American, and you may think that I am Indian or Hindu, but in Krishna consciousness we rise above these bodily distinctions. These distinctions can change." Prabhupada explained that, "We can change our name, we can change our passport, we can change the country we live in. These things are temporary, and we should not think of each other in these ways because it only separates us. I don't call you Mr. Striped Suit, and you don't call me Mr. Orange Robe. We know each other for something greater than that. Our clothes don't stop us from being friendly towards one another."

He went on to make some other points, and to demonstrate one of them, he said, "Just as I don't drink this milk with my elbow," and we all laughed uproariously. Kenneth Keating was enthralled, but his secretary came in and said, "Mr. Ambassador, you have another appointment now." Finally Mr. Keating said, "We have to bring this meeting from the sublime to the mundane. I have to go." Prabhupada immediately said, "I have to bring this meeting from the sublime to the mundane. I want to meet your President," who was Nixon at the time. Kenneth Keating said that he had gotten that request before and that Mr. Nixon was not interested in meeting anybody from India, but he would try.

Baradraj: I had a predicament, an enigma, "What do I know about Krishna? How do I paint Krishna?" I had this struggle. "What's my qualification? How is it possible? How can I look at what I am doing as a divine representation? And if I can't, then what would it be to somebody else?" So I was sitting in front of Prabhupada in his room in San Francisco along with Muralidhar, a newcomer who had just started to paint. There were many different pictures of Krishna, posters and so on, in the room. Muralidhar was bewildered. He asked Prabhupada, "There are so many pictures of Krishna here. But they are all different. Can you tell me which one is most like Krishna?" Prabhupada looked at him as if he was totally crazy and said, "They are all Krishna. Each one of them is exactly like Krishna."

Harivilas: I said, "Prabhupada, I think that our temple can be maintained by doing a little business." Immediately he said, "You should not do." I said, "Why not?" He said, "Because your business is preaching. You are a *brahmachari*. If there is *grihastha* . . ." I said, "Yes, Lochanananda." He said, "Yes. Lochanananda can do. He is a *grihastha*. He can do business. But you are *brahmachari*. Your business is preaching." Prabhupada was very firm on that point, and he gave me an important instruction that I followed. Lochanananda started the business, and it helped the temple a lot.

Gurudas: He told us how his Guru Maharaj had gotten somebody to buy cigarettes for a visiting scholar from Germany. His Guru Maharaj would do such a thing for preaching. Similarly, when I was in Russia there was a scarcity of food, and Prabhupada told me, "You can even eat meat if you have to, to keep this preaching going on." I didn't have to, but the principle was there. On one Ekadasi Prabhupada said, "On Ekadasi my Guru Maharaj fed everybody." Based on that example, Prabhupada had us observe Ekadasi and at the same time cook and distribute regular *prasadam*. In other words, he didn't want us to discontinue the *prasadam* distribution program.

Baradraj: One time in Vrindavan he was recovering from a long illness, apparently. When he began to take his morning walks again the devotees were overjoyed. They turned out in great numbers to walk with him. Prabhupada was feeling very inspired. He would talk and was very animated, arguing strongly. He enjoyed the morning walk, but when he came back he was practically exhausted. He would lie down for the rest of the day. One morning he was thinking out loud. He said, "How is this? Now I am feeling strong, talking and walking, but then when I get back, I have no strength. Almost cannot move. What is that?" Brahmananda said, "It's transcendental, Srila Prabhupada." Prabhupada looked at him for a moment and said, "Yes."

Harivilas: After we had secured a new temple in Paris, the Deities were going to be installed. For the installation I purchased small quantities of many precious oils, like jasmine, which is ten to twelve thousand dollars a kilogram. When Radharani was being bathed, Prabhupada applied some perfume on Her face and body. Then he suddenly stopped and asked for yogurt because the perfume had reacted with Her skin and created a slight blemish on Her cheek. Prabhupada bathed Radharani's cheek with yogurt. I felt very bad since I had purchased that oil. Prabhupada kept looking at Her cheek. He was very attentive. All the devotees noticed. He just kept putting yogurt there and looking at Her and putting on more yogurt.

Gurudas: We were invited to Gaurachandra Goswami's house for lunch, and Prabhupada asked me, "What do you think of Gaurachandra Goswami?" I said, "He is a rascal, but I think that he loves you." Prabhupada said, "That is how I feel. He has invited us to have lunch *prasadam*. We should go." So we were there, and Prabhupada was sliding his own bitten-from *chapatis, puris,* and *subji* onto my plate. He kept feeding me like that, which I thought was great. Then I would slide his *prasadam* onto somebody else's plate so that they could share the nectar.

At the end of the meal Gaurachandra Goswami, who was almost blind, wanted to have a *bidi.* He tried to go behind the door to have his smoke, but he wasn't actually behind the door. He was in front of the door and acting sneaky. We had a good laugh, because he was so obvious. He was trying to sneak out and smoke.

Sridhar Swami: I saw how he freely gave his time to the Indian people and listened to their problems. He would talk about petty things and then encourage them to come to the temple more often. For example, one time when Dr. Patel was sick for a few days and missed the morning walks, Prabhupada got very concerned, "Where is Dr. Patel? Somebody please call him and find out what's happening."

I was in Bombay for many years, and then I became the president of the Calcutta temple. There I also had many opportunities to be trained by Prabhupada. When I saw him working with the Indian people it gave a whole new perspective to my understanding of how big Prabhupada's plan was for Krishna consciousness. It was not some kind of cult. He had an idea of a nation—an international society—of Krishna conscious people.

Gurudas: I said to Prabhupada, "Gaurachandra Goswami is in a *goswami* family, but he doesn't want his son to eat *prasadam* with us." Prabhupada said, "Yes. You can find out how they really feel about us in Vrindavan by inviting them to *prasadam*. If they come, they are for us. If they don't, they are not."

Baradraj: After finding out that I spoke another language, Prabhupada said, "You can do this artistic, creative service no matter what language you speak. The image of Krishna speaks to anyone, anywhere in the world. It brings Krishna directly into their minds. This is not unimportant. This is great service. You should be convinced of this." The artists were always anxious that they were not good enough. There was pressure on them to stop painting and go distribute books. "These people can only sit and paint; second rate citizens." But Prabhupada said, "No. This is very important. Sometimes I think of it as even a more important service because it is not restricted. We have to translate our books into so many languages. It may or may not be a good translation. But the paintings are direct preaching."

Gurudas: The book distributors were recognized for their service more than the dancers and actors. These performers wanted to be more accepted, and they asked me what to do. I said, "Let's have a performance for Srila Prabhupada when he comes to New Dvaraka." When Prabhupada came I said to him, "The dancers and theater people would like to do a performance for you. When would you like it?" He said, "Tomorrow." So they did it in the temple. Prajapati played Baladev, and somebody else played the Pralamba demon. Prabhupada was laughing. The next morning we were in the BBT warehouse, and Ramesvara was talking about the books. I guess this is one of the times Prabhupada was reading minds. He said, "Where is Prajapati?" Somebody ran to get him. When Prajapati came, Prabhupada said, "Let us have these Krishna conscious performances in every town and village just like we distribute books in every town and village." This was an affirmation for the performers. After that it was more understood that even if you weren't inclined to distribute books, you could still be valuable.

Baradraj: There was a devotee named Patita-udharan, tall and lanky and very unconventional in many ways. He danced in his own way, he sang in his own way, and he talked in his own way. He obviously didn't fit into the narrow category of a book distributor. After a nice, big *kirtan* in the temple, Prabhupada lectured and then suddenly said, "Are there any questions?" Out of the blue Patita-udharan said, "Srila Prabhupada, we are all eager to hear what will please you the most. There are so many different types of service that are dear to you. Will you tell us clearly what service is most dear to you?" Prabhupada said, "Chant Hare Krishna and become simply wonderful. Eat simply wonderfuls and become simply wonderful. That is all. Hare Krishna."

Sridhar Swami: In Calcutta, Prabhupada would meet his disciples in his office. Since I was the president, theoretically I should have been sitting at his feet in the center of everything, hearing all the nectar. But I was shy, and I thought, "Let me go out and make more Life Members. Prabhupada is here. I should make an extra effort." From my position in the background, I could see how Prabhupada was giving out Mayapur-Vrindavan fund money to leaders such as Jayapataka Maharaj, Bhavananda, Tamal Krishna Goswami, Giriraj, and Gurudas, who were all coming to Calcutta. Prabhupada didn't favor a project. He wanted to see how enthusiastic the devotee was about his project and if he was prepared to organize and manage it well. On that basis he would allot funds. It really depended upon the individual's enthusiasm for a particular project. In the "World of Hare Krishna" video, Tom Hopkins noted how Prabhupada once told a devotee, "Go out and start a magazine." The devotee didn't know anything about starting a magazine, but Prabhupada said, "Krishna will help you." I saw that also. He would look for enthusiasm, for a spirit of depending on Krishna, and he would respond to that.

Gurudas: Prabhupada saw Krishna in everything. He said that if Govinda slaps, we accept it as mercy. During the Pakistan-India war we were in Delhi, and some people were saying, "Now we have black-outs, and you are not putting the lights out. Aren't you afraid?" Prabhupada said, "We are not controlling. You cannot even control your toothache, your stomachache." They would say "But if a bomb should come?" Prabhupada said, "If the bomb comes, I will see it as Krishna."

Harivilas: Another time we were in a car going to the temple from the airport when I told Prabhupada that we were thinking about renting a store and calling it "Krishna Shop." Prabhupada said, "No. Call it 'Hare Krishna Shop.' Let them say 'Hare Krishna' once in their life." Then he told a story from the *Puranas* about a man who was charged by a wild boar. When the boar injured him he screamed "*Haram, haram,*" which means "untouchable dirty thing," and then he died. Prabhupada said, "He went back to Godhead because he said, 'ha-ram.'" Now, *haram* means "untouchable" in Urdu. But because it approximates the name of God, the man went back to Godhead. Prabhupada said, "This is the power of the holy name. Therefore call it 'Hare Krishna Shop.' Let them at least walk by and see the names of 'Hare' and 'Krishna.'" I was very pleased to hear that, and when we did open something, we called it "Hare Krishna Shop."

Gurudas: Most of the time people did not tell Prabhupada the full story. When they did, Prabhupada always wanted to rectify it right away. He didn't want to let it fester. For instance, Siddhasvarup-ananda's people from Hawaii, who weren't initiated at the time, bought a few hundred dollars worth of books from me in London. The next day, someone told Prabhupada that I had sold those books to the people of Hawaii. So Prabhupada got all the parties together. Bhavananda looked at me and said, "You have sold a few hundred dollars worth of books to the people in Hawaii." Prabhupada said, "They are reading my books? And they are chanting the holy name?" Bhavananda wanted to crawl under the cushion.

What I liked very much about Prabhupada was that every time, rather than backbiting, he would get all the parties together and bring the issue out in the open.

Baradraj: Unknown to me, Prabhupada was in the last few days of his life. I kept thinking that Prabhupada was going to blow us away by all of sudden saying, "Okay, enough of that. Now I am back to full life."

The day before, he had stopped my harmonium playing. I didn't know whether I should play it again, because I didn't know why he had stopped it. Perhaps the sound itself was somehow irritating. I chanted without a harmonium. But on one particular morning I ventured once more to play the harmonium. This time I played a tune that I hadn't played for a long time. That tune is very special for me. It was one of the first unusual tunes that Prabhupada had recorded a long time before in Boston or New York. It was Prabhupada's own spontaneous, unusual sound coming from his heart. It was early in the morning, and I began by playing that tune. I don't recall Prabhupada stirring at all. There were days when he was completely motionless. We couldn't tell if he was awake, asleep, or what. He'd been fasting for months, living on a little water and pomegranate juice. Yet every day he would set aside some time for dictation, even if he couldn't sit up. They would hold the microphone to his mouth, and Prabhupada would continue dictating the translations and purports of the *Srimad-Bhagavatam*. He just kept on going. That morning he was motionless. Suddenly when I looked up I noticed he had motioned to Nanda Kumar, one of his attendants, that he wanted to sit up. He sat up. As I was chanting, he began clapping his hands. It was in slow motion, but it was very definite. He was nodding his head in approval. It was such a reward, such a wonderful thing. It was the best reward I could have asked for.

TAPE 7

Pusta Krishna das
Yamuna dasi
Keshava das
Gauridas Pandit das

Pusta Krishna: Srila Prabhupada had just taken his bath and was putting on *tilak* when Gargamuni Maharaj and I went into his room. He didn't have his shirt on. When he saw us, he was very happy. I offered my *dandavats*, and Gargamuni Maharaj introduced me to Srila Prabhupada, saying, "He has given up going to medical school to become a devotee." He told Srila Prabhupada that we had just come from the East Bengal war zone. Srila Prabhupada was very grateful. He said, "You've risked your life for me and for Lord Chaitanya." He asked me, "Do you like our books?" I said, "Yes, Srila Prabhupada." He said, "Which book do you like the best?" I said, "*Bhagavad-gita.*" He said, "Oh, very good." As time went by, I went out of the room, and Srila Prabhupada said to Gargamuni Maharaj "I will make that boy a *sannyasi*." I was 21 years old and had met Prabhupada for the first time.

Yamuna: The first time I met Srila Prabhupada was in his room at a lunch that he had cooked for his first twelve initiated disciples, minus one. Kirtanananda was not present at that time. My sister, Janaki, was the first female disciple. Mukunda warned me, "When you meet Swamiji, you can say 'Hare Krishna' and fold your hands."

145

I walked into Srila Prabhupada's quarters. He didn't have his shirt on and was sitting in a corner in a shaft of light underneath the window, dishing out *prasadam*. I said, "Hare Krishna, Swamiji." He said, "What is your name?" I said, "Joan." He said, "When will the other family members come?" I said, "I am the only one. No one else is coming." He said, "Oh. Generally in India the bride side of the family makes a big celebration. Never mind. We will celebrate."

That day I respected *prasadam* for the first time, and it was a very memorable lunch for a number of reasons. I was a macrobiotic afficionado at that time, and Srila Prabhupada's *prasadam* was power-packed not only due to its taste, but also because his hand had touched it. The way he served the *prasadam* was like no meal I'd ever been served. There was so much affection manifested through Srila Prabhupada's distribution. Each one of the men ate up to twelve *chapatis* at that lunch, which means that Srila Prabhupada made and served a minimum of a hundred and twenty *chapatis* and also served them whatever else they wanted. That was my first meeting with Srila Prabhupada.

 **Keshava:** My first direct conversation with Prabhupada was in his quarters on Formosa before we had the big temple on Watseka Avenue. This was the day that Neil Armstrong was in the moon shot. Kartikeya was making hot *chapatis,* and he told me how much Prabhupada liked *chapatis.* Even though he was a small man, he could eat a dozen *chapatis.* When I went into Prabhupada's room he looked directly at me and said, "According to your knowledge, what is God or who is God?" Having been brought up as a Catholic, I said, "The greatest Person." He said, "God, Krishna, is the Person who no one is equal to or greater than. If you went everywhere throughout the universes, that would be your experience." I left thinking, "Today I found out who God really is. He's the Person who no one is equal to or greater than." That was my first conversation with Prabhupada.

**Gauridas Pandit:** The first time I saw Srila Prabhupada he looked serene, sitting with one leg up behind a coffee-table-type desk. I was so nervous that my hand was shaking. I gave him the rose I had, lay down on the floor like the other devotees, and said my prayers in English. There were twelve of us, and when we all sat up Prabhupada said, "You are all very fortunate to come to Lord Chaitanya's movement, and now that you are fortunate, you should make others fortunate. Preach this message of Lord Chaitanya all over the world." He went on speaking for twenty minutes. He also said that if we served Vishnujana and Tamal nicely, he would be happy.

Pusta Krishna: For Mahaprabhu's Appearance Day, I wrote a poem about surrender to Lord Chaitanya. I gave it to Srila Prabhupada's servant to put on his desk for Mahaprabhu's Appearance Day. Srila Prabhupada read it and liked it very much. Since it was unsigned, he asked who had written it. He called me into the room and very sweetly said, "You have written this poem?" I said, "Yes, Srila Prabhupada." He said, "That's very good. To be poetic is one of the qualities of a Vaishnav," He said, "Get a piece of paper and a pencil." He had written *Six Verses of Surrender,* which I wrote down one after another as he recited them. They were along the line of Rupa Goswami's teachings. I still have them on our altar at home.

During that meeting with Srila Prabhupada, I spoke with him alone and revealed some of the things that were on my mind and in my heart. I said to Srila Prabhupada, "Krishna revealed Himself to me and that's why I have come to you." He said, "Now you must tell them that God is not dead." I said, "Srila Prabhupada, you are the only person I trust in this world." Srila Prabhupada looked at me very kindly and said, "Don't trust me, I will let you down. Trust Krishna. He will never let you down."

Yamuna: In those days we were inefficient in everything that we did and incapable of knowing the significance of initiation. At the fire *yajna* for our marriage, we didn't have enough money to buy butter, so we used margarine. When Srila Prabhupada tried to start the fire, he dipped a piece of wood into the margarine. Prabhupada's hands were magnificent, with long fingers. He held the wood over the flame, but it wouldn't light. He dipped it and held it over the flame. Again, no action. He looked up gravely and said, "Oh, this marriage will have a very slow start." I was mortified. I thought, "Oh, Oh. What have I gotten into now?"

Srila Prabhupada first gave me the name "Kalindi," which is another name of Yamuna dasi, but within ten or twelve seconds he said, "No. It is Yamuna devi dasi." I said, "What does that mean?" He said, "The river that Krishna sports in, in Vrindavan, is Yamuna.

Keshava: I was a *sankirtan* leader, but because others did not have a driver's license, I was also selected to be Prabhupada's chauffeur. My first opportunity to have a lot of private association with Srila Prabhupada was when I drove him to go on his morning walks. In those days the *sankirtan* party, led by Vishnujana Maharaj, came back at midnight or 1:00 AM, and even later on the weekends, and everyone would get up late too. But I got up at 5:00 and, at ten minutes to 6:00, picked up Prabhupada in the temple's little white Maverick. For several months I took Prabhupada alone on his walks because no one else got up early. Only Prabhupada was getting up early in those days, and Muralidhar, the artist, got up early because he didn't go out on night *sankirtan*. He painted. I was the first person to see Prabhupada in the morning, and we would go out. Every day Prabhupada had something to talk about.

Gauridas Pandit: Prabhupada was sitting behind a coffee table giving *darshan* in a small room packed with people. Tamal Krishna Maharaj asked me to give sweets to guests as they left. So, while

Prabhupada spoke, I sat at the door with a box of sweets. Then Prabhupada noticed someone outside the room and asked me to let him in. When I opened the door to let him in, another person went out the door at the same time. They crossed each other, and I didn't give the person who left *prasadam*. Prabhupada asked me, "Did you give him *prasadam?*" I said, "No, Prabhupada." Prabhupada said, "This boy is incompetent." Tamal said, "All right, Gauridas, go downstairs and I will talk to you later." I thought I was finished. That was it. After giving my whole life to Prabhupada, I had displeased him. I thought, "I am going to be sent to Africa or Bombay." Prabhupada's house was on the bank of the Ganges, and I went and sat on a rock in the river, remembering Vishnujana Swami and thinking that I should drown myself. I was crying. About twenty minutes later, Tamal Krishna Maharaj came. He laughed and said, "Gauridas, don't take it so seriously. Go and clean Prabhupada's room." I was surprised because I thought that he was going to send me somewhere else. He had the authority to do that. I washed my face, straightened my *dhoti,* and went into Prabhupada's room. Prabhupada was still sitting there. Upendra gave me a broom and said, "Sweep the floor here." I started sweeping, feeling ashamed that I was such a fool. It seemed that Prabhupada was looking at me, so I looked at him. He was smiling like anything. All my anxiety went away. "*Jaya*, Prabhupada!" I started sweeping really fast.

Pusta Krishna: Srila Prabhupada performed the initiation fire sacrifice for Tusta Krishna and me. Tusta Krishna had come from Hawaii and was with Siddhasvarup at the time. When Prabhupada gave us our names he said, "Tusta Krishna means 'one who is satisfied with Krishna,'" and he said to me, "You are 'Pusta Krishna das.' 'Pusta' means 'strength', one who gets strength from Krishna." He was amused by the names Tusta Krishna and Pusta Krishna. On the morning walk the next day he was jubilant. He looked at me and said, "Pusta Krishna das." I said, "Thank you for giving me a name." Then he became grave. At that time I understood that Srila

Prabhupada could be a little unpredictable and that one had to be grave in his presence. And I always tried to be.

Yamuna: In that early San Francisco period, Srila Prabhupada allowed us to spend time with him all day and into the night, but morning walks were one of the most relishable, glorious times with him. I generally wanted to be on the morning walk. One of the other devotees and I used to get up at two in the morning, pick flowers in Golden Gate Park, make garlands for Srila Prabhupada, present them to him, and go on the morning walk. Those moments in the park were always very special for us, walking next to our spiritual master, trying to chant Hare Krishna just as he chanted Hare Krishna. The morning walks were *japa* walks, and he walked briskly, chanting Hare Krishna with his hand in his bead bag. He walked like a young man of twenty-five. The first day I went I was wearing wooden yogi shoes, and my feet bled because Prabhupada was walking on and on very fast.

Keshava: We usually drove down Venice Boulevard to Santa Monica Beach. Once I told Srila Prabhupada about the La Brea tar pits, and we went there for a walk. One morning about 6:00, there was not much traffic, and a biker with a shaved head on a Harley chopper was driving down Venice Boulevard. He looked in our car, saw that Prabhupada and I both had shaved heads, and started following us, signaling and trying to communicate with us. I was concerned. He followed us all the way to the beach, parked behind us, and asked if he could walk with us. Prabhupada said, "Yes." There were many provoking or intimidating situations like this one, but Prabhupada always remained in control. I was thinking, "Oh, what's this guy going to do?" But Prabhupada's mood was, "Yes, you may walk with us. Please come."

When Prabhupada walked by the ocean, we had deep philosophical talks, stimulated by the elements, by the gigantic ocean. It was like being near Maha Vishnu, Kshirodakashayi Vishnu. The ocean walks brought out some of the best discussions. Prabhupada would walk holding his cane, occasionally stopping to look directly into your eyes when he made a point. On this particular morning Prabhupada explained how material civilization had sprung up and how the ocean had always been there. Barring some earthquake or disturbance, the ocean always came to about the same point on the beach, and civilization came to another point nearby. Prabhupada walked along explaining this to the biker and me, and it was incredible. About half way through the walk the guy turned around and left. Prabhupada just kept going.

Gauridas Pandit: On a morning walk on Magic Island in Hawaii, Srila Prabhupada looked at the surfers and said, "They are sea sufferers. They are preparing to take shark and dolphin bodies." Another day he said of them, "They have mystic power. They are walking on water. I cannot do that."

Once he walked to the *prasadam* room and saw a grain of rice on the floor. He said, "Whoever had spilled that rice will have to suffer. That's Krishna. *Prasadam* should not be wasted." Another time Sukadev caught a bug and asked Prabhupada, "Prabhupada, what should I do with this bug?" Prabhupada said, "Put him out the window." Sukadev said, "Who else can you ask, 'What should I do with this bug?' Anyone else would think that you were crazy. But you can ask Prabhupada anything." Once, someone asked Prabhupada if they could get rid of the cockroaches in the temple by spraying them. Prabhupada said, "No. The cockroaches are there because you are too lazy to clean. Instead of cleaning, you leave the place dirty and kill the cockroaches." Unless it was an extreme emergency, he didn't want us to kill pests.

In Bombay I had just become Prabhupada's servant, when Tamal asked Prabhupada, "Can we kill mosquitoes?" Prabhupada said, "If they are biting you, you can kill them, but otherwise you shouldn't."

Pusta Krishna: We were flying from Singapore to Australia. Prabhupada and Hari Sauri, his servant, were seated in the first class section, and I was in the coach section. The plane hit an air pocket and quickly dropped five or ten thousand feet as if it were going down a huge roller coaster. My stomach was in my head, and I was pretty shaken, although I was chanting through it all. As soon as the drop was over, I got up, walked to the front and asked Srila Prabhupada, "Are you okay?" Srila Prabhupada said, "Yes. We can die at any-time." He looked as if nothing at all had happened.

Yamuna: The first time that I assisted Srila Prabhupada in the kitchen was in New York on the occasion of my sister's wedding. Srila Prabhupada cooked in his apartment in a small galley kitchen with counters on both sides. He gave me the singular task of making a very difficult preparation called *alu kachori*. It's one of the most complex pastries to cook properly because it has to cook for a long time without becoming greasy, which is almost impossible. For nearly eight hours I made *alu kachoris* while Srila Prabhupada single-handedly cooked a fourteen-course wedding feast in his small kitchen.

In the course of cooking for that feast, I made many mistakes. It was my very first day, and the first mistake I made was to wear a short skirt and a little T-shirt. Sitting crossed-legged I said, "Swamiji, may I have a cigarette?" He popped his head out of the corner and said, "Go wash your hands." I washed my hands. Then he explained the four prohibitions in Krishna consciousness: no meat eating, no gambling, no illicit sex life, and no intoxicants. A short time later I said, "Swamiji, may I have a glass of water?" He said, "Go wash your hands." Then he explained that the first and foremost principle in cooking was to engage our senses in the service of the Lord. He said that we should cook for Krishna with love and devotion and not think about our senses, our tongue, our sense of smell or our belly, because we were cooking for Krishna's pleasure. A short time later I said, "Swamiji, it's very hot in here." I was fighting perspiration.

"Go wash your hands." In this way he introduced me to the simplest, most rudimentary principle of external cleanliness. He also explained a simple touch of internal cleanliness and said, "We can serve Krishna through the art of cooking when we are externally and internally clean."

Gauridas Pandit: I was a fancy *chamara* fanner. In fact, I thought I was the best. So, in his garden for two to three hours every morning I would fan Prabhupada with the *chamara*. Prabhupada had three sets of *japa* beads, a little one, medium one, and a big one. They were all by his *vyasasana,* and he would pick whatever one he wanted that day. He was chanting with his eyes shut, and a fly landed right above his lip. I thought, "What am I going to do?" Without touching Prabhupada I tried to get the fly off him with my finger. But the fly kept walking around. He wouldn't leave. After a minute, Prabhupada opened one eye and looked at me. I jumped back a little because I was so close to him. He said, "You are fanning around the world, but you can't get the fly off my face. Give me that *chamara.*" He took the *chamara* and said, "Do this!" And he fanned the fly off his face. A few minutes later another fly landed on his face. I was a bit hesitant but I brushed his face with the *chamara.* He nodded and said, "Yes, very nice."

Pusta Krishna: We were flying from Mauritius to Durban on Quantas Airlines out of Perth, Australia. I was seated beside Srila Prabhupada wearing my little British hat, shirt, coat, and pants. At that time a rugby match had taken place between the South African and New Zealand teams, and there were a lot of rugby types on the plane. We had a seat on the nonsmoking section, but people were smoking there, and I was disturbed. I was also concerned for Srila Prabhupada's welfare. So I asked a stewardess to please ask them not to smoke in the nonsmoking section. She told the rugby-type guys, who were drinking quite a bit as well, to stop smoking. But they didn't stop. I was about to ask the stewardess, "Please ask them again," when Prabhupada stopped me. He said, "What is the difference between us and them if we cannot tolerate these sorts of things? Don't be an ordinary, common, foolish man."

Yamuna: As early as 1967, I wanted to go to Vrindavan. I always had an attraction to Vrindavan. One morning I was walking right next to Srila Prabhupada when he stopped, put his cane out to lean on, and said, "You have received a letter from Achyutananada? He wants some men to join his party in Lucknow." I immediately popped up and said, "I'd like to go, Srila Prabhupada. May Gurudas and I go?" He said, "Yes. We can arrange that. We will start an American House in Lucknow." Then he walked a little further and said, "No. You should not go now." He turned around and said, "Someday I will take you to India, and I will show you India on foot." From that moment I was waiting for that day, and three years later, on October 4, 1970, Srila Prabhupada's party of American and European devotees landed in Bombay. Our party had arrived in Calcutta via Tokyo just a few days earlier. From October 4 to the time Srila Prabhupada left India in the spring of '71, he showed us many places on foot, literally walking through the streets with us.

Keshava: Every night some other devotees sold *Back to Godhead* magazines, while I would invariably sell several of Prabhupada's books. Although later on book distributors disguised themselves with western clothes and sometimes wigs, in those days we never thought about doing that.

Prabhupada stayed up late, and sometimes when we came back at 11:30 Gargamuni would say to me, "Prabhupada wants to talk to you." I would run to his room, and he would ask me, "How many books did you sell?" Or, "How did it go?" "Who were the people?" "What did you say to sell them the books?" He wanted to know precisely what I was telling people and how it was that I was able to move those books. He wanted to see if my technique lacked substance. I explained to him that I told people exactly what I had heard in the lectures, that these books were the Bible from India and they explained your past lives and true goals. I explained that I listened to the classes in the morning and repeated the things I heard. Prabhupada approved. He was a very specific, detailed person. Nothing escaped him.

Gauridas Pandit: The temple room was full of devotees, and one of the big book distributors asked, "Prabhupada, what pleases you the most?" Prabhupada said, "If you develop your love for Krishna that will please me the most." It was really nice to hear that, and all the devotees said, "*Jaya*, Srila Prabhupada!"

Pusta Krishna: Buddhimanta was tall, big, bright-faced, and appeared somewhat crazed. He was an imposing figure begging for money on the streets, and he was collecting a lot of it in a way that devotees had never done before. I had some difference of opinion about how money should be collected, and I made it known that I thought a monk shouldn't act in the way Buddhimanta was acting. This was a point of contention between Bali Mardan and me. Bali Mardan called Srila Prabhupada and talked to Shyamasundar, objecting to my objecting to the way that they were collecting money. In response Srila Prabhupada wrote a very instructive letter. He didn't criticize either of us. He didn't say, "You are right," and "You are wrong." That wasn't his concern at all, which tells something of his character. His concern was that we work together as a family. He wanted all of us to get along despite our different ideas about engaging in devotional service. Srila Prabhupada's simple desire for us to work harmoniously is something that's taken me a long time to understand.

Yamuna: The first San Francisco temple had certain similarities to the first New York temple, as well as quite a few dissimilarities. One dissimilarity was that in New York there were very few women, whereas in San Francisco there was almost an equal balance of men and women. So the chemistry of the temple was different. But in both places we were like Srila Prabhupada's children. He called us "boys and girls," and we were. Most of us were between twenty-five and thirty. I think the *rasa* of our being like his children was foremost, although when one studies the letters of this period, one will find that sometimes Srila Prabhupada referred to us as his "sons and daughters" and sometimes as "mothers and fathers." He would let the roles reverse for intimacy. I think there isn't a devotee from these early days who did not feel that every moment with Srila Prabhupada was intimate. Srila Prabhupada had such a way of showing love and affection through distributing Krishna consciousness that immediately we felt how much he cared about us. I would have never known what love was unless I met Srila Prabhupada, and I think that was true for all of us. Through Srila Prabhupada we learned to love each other. With Srila Prabhupada as our father, we had very deep, wonderful, transcendental relationships between each other as godbrothers and godsisters.

Gauridas Pandit: In the morning Prabhupada would sit in the garden for two or three hours, from about 6:30 to 9:30, to chant, listen to *kirtan*, or to have letters read to him by Tamal and to dictate his answers. Tamal would type out Prabhupada's response, read it to Prabhupada the next day, and Prabhupada would sign it. My duty in the garden was fanning Prabhupada with the *chamara*. Prabhupada was fond of the fountain and the sound it made, so the fountain was always running.

One day when Tamal left the garden, Prabhupada noticed that his keys were on the ground. He told me, "Give me those keys." I gave him the keys. He put them under his *dhoti* and told me to get Tamal. I ran out and told Tamal, "Prabhupada wants to see you." He came. Prabhupada said, "I want my sapphire ring out of the safe." Tamal said, "Yes, Prabhupada," and left. About five minutes later Prabhupada said, "Go get Tamal again." Tamal was tearing up his office, looking for the keys. He said, "Gauridas, have you seen my keys?" I didn't want to lie to a *sannyasi* so I threw my hands up and looked dumb. I said, "Prabhupada wants to see you now." He said, "Run to the bathroom and see if I have left the keys up there." I said, "I can't leave Prabhupada alone for that long. I have to go back to the garden." Tamal came out, and Prabhupada said, "Where is my ring?" Tamal said, "I am just now getting it, Prabhupada. I will be right back," and left again. Prabhupada shook his head, looked at me and smiled. He waited a few minutes and said, "Go get Tamal again." This was the third time. Again Prabhupada said, "Where is my ring?" Tamal started to make another excuse. Prabhupada pulled out his keys, dangled them, and said, "Here, you rascal. If anything is stolen, it is your fault for giving the thief a chance."

Prabhupada was very conscious of security. Everything valuable had to be locked in the safe. He once said, "I have millions of dollars, but I don't waste one farthing of Krishna's money."

Another time Prabhupada was sick and had mucus in his eyes, so he sent Upendra to the store to get an eye rinse and a little glass to wash his eyes. When Upendra got back, Prabhupada asked him, "How much did you pay for the eye wash?" Upendra said, "Four *rupees*." (At the time the exchange rate was sixteen *rupees* to a dollar, so it was about twenty-five cents.) Prabhupada said, "Four *rupees*? It's only worth one *rupee*, maybe two, but you have spent four *rupees*. It's a waste of Krishna's money." Prabhupada didn't want to see any money wasted. To instruct us, he would chastise us, but the next minute he would smile at us. He didn't hold a grudge. He chastised his disciples for their benefit, and even then he only did it when they could take it in the proper way.

Pusta Krishna: I was Prabhupada's secretary when the first copies of the Fifth Canto of the *Srimad-Bhagavatam*, which had just been printed, were sent by air express to Prabhupada in Johannesburg, South Africa. Bhargava was also with us, photographing Srila Prabhupada, and when Prabhupada received this box of books, Bhargava did his job, taking picture after picture after picture. Snap,

snap, snap. Srila Prabhupada was happily relishing the books, but then, in an angry way, he said to Bhargava, "Why are you always taking so many pictures?" Bhargava prabhu was saddened and sheepish about the comment. He walked out of the room and out of the temple. As it happened, that night we had a big program in Peoria, and all Prabhupada could think about was, "Where is Bhargava?" Where is Bhargava? Why has he gone?" It was such a sweet thing, the way he was so concerned. Finally, about midnight, a call came from Bhargava. He felt terrible that he had angered Srila Prabhupada by taking so many pictures. I said, "Stay right where you are. I will come pick you up. Srila Prabhupada is anxious to see you." We picked up Bhargava prabhu and brought him to Srila Prabhupada, and Srila Prabhupada, like a loving father, had a beautiful interaction with Bhargava. He said, "I don't want you to feel saddened. I just don't want you to always take pictures of me. What is the need of so many pictures? Here are my books." Srila Prabhupada didn't want a cult centered around himself. Of course, he is the spiritual master, but he is also the most humble servant of the Lord. He plays the role of a spiritual master to serve his spiritual master, and as the spiritual master, his desire was to magnify Krishna for everybody.

Keshava: There was a devotee in the Berkeley temple named Chandanacharya who was a householder, although almost everyone else in the temple was single. Chandanacharya could imitate Prabhupada's voice so well that you thought you were talking to Prabhupada. On one occasion Shyamasundar called me from London to say that George Harrison had agreed to purchase a temple in England and to pay for publishing the Krishna Books. I was to immediately give the news to Srila Prabhupada. I was in San Francisco, and Prabhupada was in Berkeley, as was Chandanacharya. I called the Berkeley temple and said that I needed to talk to Prabhupada. Usually it would take a while for Prabhupada to come to the phone because the phone was downstairs and Prabhupada's room was on the top floor. Immediately someone picked up the phone and said, "Yes. What is it?" I said, "Chandan, please! I am calling to talk to Prabhupada. Just get off the phone!" Prabhupada said, "What? What are you talking about?" I said, "Chandan, come on. This is serious." Then Prabhupada got mad and yelled at me, "This is Prabhupada. This is A. C. Bhaktivedanta. What do you want to say?" I said, "Oh, excuse me, Prabhupada." I told him the message and he said, "Oh, very good. That is very good." I felt relieved, but, oh, like such an idiot.

Yamuna: Prabhupada was lecturing on the *Caitanya-caritamrta*, and one of the devotees asked, "Who is Lord Chaitanya?" Prabhupada said, "Oh, such a nice, intelligent question. You are so intelligent for asking this question," although this had been the subject of his lectures for several days. He was so patient with us. Whether we fell asleep or cried, somehow or another, we began to feel a little conscious of Krishna. Most of us tasted Krishna consciousness through chanting and dancing and feasting. That was how we engaged our senses best.

Gauridas Pandit: Yasodanandan asked, "Prabhupada, you know what's in your books, so why is it that you like to hear us read them to you?" Prabhupada said, "I didn't write these books, Krishna wrote them."

One day Yasodanandan was reading *Sri Isopanisad* when Prabhupada asked him to reread one paragraph. After he'd heard it for the second time, Prabhupada said, "These are not my words. They are changing my words." He turned to Tamal and said, "My English is not good?" Tamal said, "Your English is perfect, Prabhupada." Prabhupada said, "Then why are they changing?" He said, "Do not become like a leap frog and try to jump over your spiritual master. This is the worst thing a disciple can do. Write them immediately and tell them not to change my books." I never saw Prabhupada angrier than he was at that time. He wanted only spelling errors and grammatical errors changed, nothing else.

In Vrindavan in 1977, the Gurukula was being built, and we carried Prabhupada in his rocking chair to take a tour of it. As we went through the different areas, one devotee said, "This is my room, Prabhupada," then another one said, "This is my room, Prabhupada." Prabhupada was upset and said, "You are all concerned about your own rooms. I built this school for the children. Fill it up with students. This building is for the students." As we carried him back to his quarters, the devotees in the temple saw Prabhupada passing by and chanted, "*Jaya*, Prabhupada, *Jaya*, Prabhupada!" Prabhupada said, "What are they chanting?" We said, "They are chanting, '*Jaya*, Prabhupada!'" He said, "I do not like this. Tell them to chant 'Hare Krishna.'" He didn't want the "*Jaya*, Prabhupadas" to go on and on.

I wrote Prabhupada a letter saying that I was going to get married. He gave me his blessings and wrote, "But above all, continue to follow the four regulative principles and chant sixteen rounds of Hare Krishna mantra every day. That will protect you. My only request is that you don't become an ordinary karmi, a foolish man." He wasn't concerned with one's ashram, whether *sannyas* or *grihastha*. He wrote, "Even Chaitanya Mahaprabhu considered these things external." Prabhupada wanted us to become and remain high-minded Vaishnavs.

Yamuna: In simple ways Srila Prabhupada tried to teach us cooking technique, procedure, quality, cleanliness, and purity, not with a lot of words, but by his example. The preparations that he taught us were generally fatty and juicy, sweet, succulent, and very sumptuous. That was the era of sumptuous *prasadam*. The tongue has two functions, vibrating sounds and respecting *prasadam,* and Prabhupada felt that if he could catch us through those two functions, then we would begin to taste Krishna consciousness more and more. So the food was sumptuous and rich.

As for Srila Prabhupada's *prasadam* preferences, while he had personal favorites, he liked anything that was well prepared. By this time Srila Prabhupada had a little tummy and was eating immense quantities of rice. Sometimes he would finish off most of a very large thali, only leaving a little *maha* for all.

Pusta Krishna: When Prabhupada came to Ratha-yatra, I wanted to cook something very nice for him. His servant told me that he liked okra. A few of us, Bhutatma, Krishna das, some others and I started cooking. We made some special preparations. I made macadamia nut *halava* with cream, as well as a fancy rice with edible gold leaf on it, and, of course, okra. All the devotees were saying, "Wow! We can't wait 'till we get *maha* from this." But Prabhupada's plate came down empty. Prabhupada had really liked the preparations and had eaten everything. That was the apex of my life. I cooked, and it was good.

Gauridas Pandit: In Hawaii, devotees would bring Prabhupada lots of tropical fruits like *liliquio* and passionfruits, but his favorite was mango. There are forty varieties of mango in Hawaii, so one devotee asked Prabhupada, "We have so many kinds of mangos here, which kind would you prefer?" Prabhupada said, "The ones from the eastern side of the tree." He didn't really care about the kind of mango, but he wanted those that grew on the eastern side of the tree because they got the morning sun, which gives *prana* (life energy) and made the best fruit.

Pusta Krishna: Srila Prabhupada was invited to come to Geneva where Guru Gauranga had arranged for a program in a hall with a so-called sophisticated Swiss audience. One person asked, "Why are you vegetarians?" Srila Prabhupada replied, "Why don't you eat your sister?" Prabhupada went on to explain that human life, eating included, involved discrimination. His example was very extreme and very instructive, although some of the devotees didn't know how to take it at the time. Sometimes Srila Prabhupada would shock us to make a point. We could never predict how Srila Prabhupada was going to answer a question. Because of circumstances, he could answer the same question differently at different times. We may never understand why he said a certain thing, but we can appreciate Srila Prabhupada's character and intent.

Yamuna: One day I made Bengali meals and arranged them on the *thalis* in a Bengali fashion. Srila Prabhupada sat behind his desk, and Pishima sat on the floor directly opposite Srila Prabhupada. As soon as I brought the *thalis* in and set them down, Srila Prabhupada started making little comical, teasing remarks about his sister. He said, "You know, she says that it is water. I say it is fat." I thought, "My goodness. He is talking about her weight. What's going on?" Since Prabhupada's voice was light-hearted, Pishima started chuckling. He said, "All this," he was flapping his arms back and forth, "is fat but she calls it water." He started talking about the days in their childhood when they flew kites, and he said, "I always used to beat her at kites." He spoke very brother-sisterly about his little sister, and she was laughing, although she didn't understand a word. In the course of all this jesting, I was bringing in *chapatis*. When Srila Prabhupada finished his meal, he piled every *katori* (the little round bowls that all of the moist preparations are in when serving a *thali*) one on top of the other from the largest to the smallest, nearly twelve inches high. When I walked into the room, Prabhupada knocked down the whole stack with his finger and said, "Yamuna dasi mayi *ki jaya!*" I said, "Srila Prabhupada *ki jaya!*" Pishima said, "Gaura *Nitai ki jaya!*" Then I said, "Oh, Srila Prabhupada. You ate everything." Srila Prabhupada said, "Excellent!"

This was my first meeting with Pishima, and Prabhupada's mood was light, sweet, jovial, and humorous. Although she didn't understand a word of what was going on, Pishima truly loved it. She was very fond of Srila Prabhupada. From the day I met her until the very last day I saw her with Srila Prabhupada in 1976 in Vrindavan,

I saw that she worshipped her brother, and that he was obviously very fond of her.

Gauridas Pandit: Everyday Upendra and sometimes Bhakti Caru would spend three hours in the kitchen cooking a big lunch for Prabhupada, but when Upendra brought the plate, Prabhupada would wave it off, saying, "Distribute, distribute." Once I was distributing Prabhupada's lunch *prasadam* when he noticed the devotees picking and choosing, "I want this, I want that." Prabhupada said, "Mix it all together. They should not discriminate." So I mushed it all together so that the sweets, vegetables, and rice became a big mishmash. Then the devotees were making faces. Prabhupada said, "You shouldn't discriminate."

Prabhupada hardly ate for a whole month. Then Nirjala Ekadasi came, and even though it was 110 degrees, Upendra and I fasted all day. In the evening I felt, "How can I continue this?" but somehow or other, I did it. The next morning I was extremely weak. At lunchtime Upendra brought Prabhupada his plate, and Prabhupada waved it off again. Upendra couldn't believe it. He said, "Prabhupada, how is it that although we are young boys, when we fast for one day we can hardly move, yet here you are fasting for thirty days? How do you do it?" Prabhupada said, "I am living proof that the soul is not dependent on the body for sustenance, but rather the body is dependent on the soul." We were overwhelmed. Prabhupada was getting ready to leave the planet and was completely Krishna conscious and free from bodily identification.

Pusta Krishna: During Prabhupada's lecture, he stressed studying the philosophy. He was concerned that we thoroughly understand the philosophy of Krishna consciousness. He said to me, "Do as I am doing. Sometimes I am managing, sometimes I am preaching, sometimes I am cooking, and sometimes I am cleaning. In that way, whatever needs to be done you do. That's *sannyas*." In this way he was teaching *yukta vairagya*, that real renunciation is to do whatever is required for the service of Krishna. It is not remaining aloof and maintaining some false posture of being only a preacher.

Yamuna: With *kirtan* came the joy of watching Srila Prabhupada pray to Krishna. In the evening on Mondays, Wednesdays, and Fridays, he sang *Mangalacharanam* alone, sitting on his *vyasasana,* and we were all the rhythm section behind his singing. He almost always had his eyes closed and went very deeply into prayer. Simply observing him pray to Krishna, we got an idea of the depth of prayer even in these early days. When he opened his eyes and looked at you, very often you felt as if Srila Prabhupada was looking right through you seeing everything, seeing Krishna.

The San Francisco temple was a very musical place. We had many instruments. Everyone played something, and *kirtan* established a very reciprocal relationship with Srila Prabhupada. They were simply rock-out sessions. If one person stood, everyone stood. If one person danced, you danced, because we were all packed in together. They were very joyous, beautiful, warm, sweet *kirtans.*

Gauridas Pandit: Of all the service I did for Prabhupada, it was the simplest thing that made him the happiest. I was sitting in front of his desk, waiting for him to come, and reading *Srimad-Bhagavatam,* Fourth Canto, Part Four. That night he came a little earlier than I expected, and as soon as I saw him, I put the book on his desk and paid my obeisances. Prabhupada asked me, "What are you reading?" I said, "It's your *Srimad-Bhagavatam,* Srila Prabhupada." He smiled like anything and said to Tamal Krishna, "This is very good. He is reading in his spare time. This is very good." I thought, "Wow!" Out there in the 110-degree sun, spraying the windows, and he didn't say anything, but when he saw me reading, he was very pleased.

Pusta Krishna: One day around Janmastami time in New Vrindavan in 1972, Prabhupada's personal servant was unable to massage Prabhupada. At that time I was a fresh *sannyasi*. Prabhupada said to me, "Pusta Krishna, you can give a massage." I had never massaged anybody. I said, "How do you do it?" He said, "Well, you start on the head with sandalwood oil, and then you do the body with mustard oil. So we sat outside the house Srila Prabhupada was staying in. I went behind him, offered my obeisances, took some sandalwood oil on my hand, and started to very gently massage his head. I didn't know what I was doing. Srila Prabhupada said, "What is this?" I said, "Well, Srila Prabhupada. I am trying to give you a massage." He said, "Massage means hard." So I started rubbing his head hard, and he was pleased. Then I worked on his back with mustard oil. It was a sweet experience to massage Srila Prabhupada because, apart from the personal service, Srila Prabhupada would sometimes talk about Krishna consciousness or business related to Krishna consciousness. He would sometimes be amused by the way that we would massage. You would continue massaging until he said, "Go to the next part." Someone had told me that Srila Prabhupada liked his toes cracked, so I massaged his toes very hard, trying to crack them. Sometimes he used to laugh and say, "That's enough." He was a humorous, kind-hearted person, and those times were very sweet.

Keshava: I was always amazed at how Prabhupada tuned right in and related to you and whoever was with you. I was a *brahmachari* for many years, but my real propensity wasn't to be a *brahmachari*. That kind of advancement and detachment was wishful thinking for me. But in those days, if you expressed the idea that, "Maybe I should be married," then you had someone talking you out of it. When I went to see Prabhupada, more than once he said, "Oh Keshavaji, where is your wife?" I said, "Prabhupada, I don't have a wife." He could see that I wasn't a first class *brahmachari*. He was saying to me, "You'd better think about things a little bit."

Yamuna: Generally, Prabhupada would reveal what he thought we needed to know. Some people's nature is to ask endless questions, but I always felt like a fool asking more than Srila Prabhupada revealed. Sometimes, if we didn't hear properly, then we would have to ask Srila Prabhupada questions, and he would have to repeat himself. But very often I found the same things that he taught in 1967 were revealed again in 1976, so many years later. Prabhupada kept Krishna consciousness very simple, and my relationship with him was to simply hear and follow his instructions.

Gauridas Pandit: Svarup Damodar Maharaj came to the garden in the morning. There were only a couple of people there. He sat a distance away, and Prabhupada asked, "Who is that?" I said, "That is Svarup Damodar Maharaj." He said, "Call him over here." So Svarupa Damodar Maharaj sat right by Prabhupada and began telling Prabhupada about a program in Bombay that he had just held to preach Krishna consciousness to scientists. On hearing this report Prabhupada beamed and then commented, "I appeared in this world for two reasons, to establish Krishna as the Supreme Personality of Godhead and to defeat these rascal scientists. You are doing this. I am very pleased." He went on for a couple of hours talking about this. He wanted it very much.

Pusta Krishna: We were in the country driving from Durban, South Africa, and there were some big, long, white buildings some distance from the highway. Srila Prabhupada asked, "What are those buildings?" I responded, "They are chicken coops that belong to a large chicken farm. They use them as slaughterhouses." Srila Prabhupada said, "Why do they buy chicken? Let them make a chicken. Let them take some egg, put some liquid in it, incubate it, and hatch a chicken. But those rascals can't because they don't understand that life is not the egg but the spirit soul." He carried on in an animated way talking about that.

Keshava: Prabhupada had a flight to catch, and the devotees figured out when to leave the temple to get Prabhupada to the airport on time, but Prabhupada insisted on leaving much earlier. The devotees wondered if something was wrong with Prabhupada because it was only twenty minutes to the airport, and Prabhupada was pushing Brahmananda out the door two hours before they even needed to be at the airport. Sure enough, there had been some bad accidents, and there was a big traffic problem on the road. Everyone was stuck. Prabhupada got to his flight in the nick of time. If he had left the temple even a few minutes later, he would have missed his flight, what to speak of if he had left at the normal time. Devotees realized that Prabhupada knew they had to go early, but how did he know?

Pusta Krishna: Vishnujana Maharaj was a very dear devotee. He was a great friend to many of those who were introduced to Krishna consciousness by his beautiful, angelic, heart-piercing *kirtans* and his traveling *sankirtan* party. Once we were a quarter of a mile away from the main temple building in Mayapur, heading back from a morning walk, when Vishnujana Maharaj asked Srila Prabhupada, "If someone falls down from the *sannyas* position, do they have to do what Chota Haridas did in order to keep Chaitanya Mahaprabhu's mercy?" Srila Prabhupada said, "Yes." Following that, Vishnujana Maharaj disappeared, and we have never seen him again.

Gauridas Pandit: Tamal mentioned to Prabhupada that devotees had been investigating Vishnujana's whereabouts. They had his passport. He couldn't have left India without it, and he didn't apply for a new one. Some *brahmans* came to the Delhi temple and said that a white *sannyasi* in Prayag, the place where Chota Haridas committed suicide, had paid them to take him on a boat and to chant mantras so that he wouldn't take a ghost body. They said that this person had tied rocks to himself and jumped off the boat. When the devotees put all the pieces together, they realized that that must have been Vishnujana. Tamal said, "We think that he committed suicide." Prabhupada began to cry. He said, "Vishnujana didn't have to do that." Tamal asked, "Prabhupada, do you know where Vishnujana is?" Prabhupada said, "He is very advanced. He is still chanting Hare Krishna." About two weeks later, Prabhupada woke up one morning and said that Vishnujana had been chanting to him. Similarly, after Chota Haridas committed suicide, Lord Chaitanya had heard Chota Haridas chanting.

Yamuna: When we arrived in London in 1968, Prabhupada wanted us to make a splash, and our small party decided that the best way to become known would be to reach the Beatles, because they were luminaries of the time. So we made apple *prasadam* dishes and brought them to Apple Records every day to catch someone's attention. The *prasadam* went from the lower floors to the upper floors, and ultimately everyone tasted *prasadam* and became a little addicted to it. The first person to strike a serious friendship with George was Shyamasundar. He and George Harrison just clicked like brothers and became close friends. When George heard that we were into transcendental chanting, he really wanted to hear us. Almost right away we started having *kirtans* with him in his house. He said, "I want to record this," so we recorded the Hare Krishna mantra on a forty-five with "Sri Krishna" on the back. That song became number one in Czechoslovakia, was the top of the pops in England, and led to the *Govindam* album. Srila Prabhupada was very pleased with the connection that we had with the Beatles.

Pusta Krishna: In New Zealand, after Prabhupada had given a lecture, he asked if there were any questions. One after another, fathers and mothers came forward and said, "Srila Prabhupada, please give my child a name." Prabhupada gave one name, then another, and it went on and on until finally when someone said, "Please name my daughter," Prabhupada said, "Rose." His patience had been tested at that point.

Gauridas Pandit: One morning I noticed that there was a little bush in his garden with four white flowers. They looked like small gardenias and smelled wonderful. I picked them and put them on the pillow of Prabhupada's *vyasasana*. When he came, Prabhupada picked them up, started smelling them, and held them the whole two hours that he was there. The next morning he put his hand out to me and I thought, "He wants flowers, but that little bush won't have any more flowers because I picked them all yesterday." To my surprise there were eight flowers on that tiny plant. I picked all eight and gave them to Prabhupada. He smelled them and said, "Smelling this type of flower regulates your life airs." Every day after that this little bush would produce a bunch of flowers that I offered to Prabhupada. Mystically, Krishna was directly protecting Prabhupada and providing for him.

Pusta Krishna: Directed by Srila Prabhupada, in March or April of 1976, I picked up Srila Sridhar Maharaj in Navadvip and brought him to meet with Srila Prabhupada at the ISKCON *mandir* in Mayapur. It was a glorious time, and many devotees were attending the festival. We made the long drive to the Sri Chaitanya Saraswat Math in Navadvip, and I went upstairs where Srila Sridhar Maharaj, an old gentleman, was sitting chanting *japa*. I offered my obeisances, invited him into the car, and took him to meet Srila Prabhupada in Srila Prabhupada's room in the Mayapur temple. There was no doubt that he and Srila Prabhupada were very close, dear friends.

Yamuna: We were behind the closed curtains, adjusting the Deities, when someone inadvertently knocked one of the columns with their elbow, and it fell over. With the speed of lightning, Srila Prabhupada moved the *arati* paraphernalia off the bottom granite step with his right hand and stepped on the first step with his right foot. With his left foot on the second step, he grabbed one huge column (it was six to eight inches in diameter) with his right hand,

and Radharani's hand with his left hand. Little beads of perspiration were on his brow. This was the first time I ever saw him perspire.

Srila Prabhupada showed such chivalry in protecting Radharani that I understood what the *rasa* of chivalry was. This was one example of Srila Prabhupada exhibiting a very personal *rasa* with Krishna, actually saving Radharani from disaster and exhibiting superhuman strength. The movement of the mind couldn't have been faster than Srila Prabhupada's movements that day.

Pusta Krishna: In Australia there were some ISKCON devotees who were displeased with Siddhasvarupananda Maharaj's successful preaching in Hawaii. They noted how not all his followers were coming to Srila Prabhupada, although they used Srila Prabhupada's books and chanted the holy names. When I mentioned this to Srila Prabhupada, he raised his eyebrows and said, "That is Vaishnav *aparad*," meaning it was Vaishnav *aparad* against Siddhasvarupananda Maharaj. With all humility, Prabhupada said that there were many branches of the tree of Lord Chaitanya Mahaprabhu, that ISKCON was not the only branch. He said that we need to develop tolerance for the other branches of Mahaprabhu's tree.

Keshava: Prabhupada had a special love for disciples and didn't show favorites. Prabhupada got much satisfaction from a little child who brought a flower or the devotee that was humble and not in the front lines. I knew that his affection, his benediction, his blessings were evenly distributed.

Gauridas Pandit: At about 7:00 AM, Prabhupada's car pulled up in front of the temple. He got out of the car and into a rocking chair we had ready because by this time he was too weak to walk. He said, "Take me to see the Deities." So we carried him in front of Gaura-Nitai. Prabhupada stood up and paid his respects. Tears began to come down his cheeks. He started to sit down but somebody had taken the chair away and he almost fell. Tamal Krishna and another devotee had to support him. All the devotees were looking at each other thinking, "Wow, Prabhupada is sick." Then he went to Krishna-Balaram's altar and stood up again, but this time the chair was held there. Again, tears came down his cheeks. Finally he went to Radha Shyamasundar, Lalita, and Visakha, and gazed at Them for a while. Then he turned and said, "I want to see all the devotees in my room." We carried him to his room, where he sat behind his desk as all the devotees packed into the room. There wasn't enough room for everyone, so devotees were looking in the doors and windows. There were devotees everywhere. Prabhupada said, "I have come here to leave my body, but you should not lament because I have given you everything in my books. If you simply read my books and cooperate with your godbrothers, everything will go on nicely." Some of the devotees began to cry, "Oh, no, Prabhupada, you can't leave us." Prabhupada said the same thing over, "I am in my books; read my books and cooperate."

TAPE 8

Revatinandan das
Malati dasi
Citsukananda das
Yadubara das

 **Revatinandan:** The *kirtan* ended, and Prabhupada put his spectacles on. This was in early '68, and he was using his own *Srimad-Bhagavatam* that was in front of him. He read from it and then spoke much of the time with his eyes closed. He wasn't advertising himself or trying to appear as a holy man, as other so-called gurus did. He was just speaking the teachings from the book and then explaining them. I recall him remarking, "Now they say that everyone is God. You are God, I am God, there are so many gods loitering in the street. If you think of God in that way, then God does not mean very much to you." He also said, "G-O-D, D-O-G. What is the difference? You say you are God. I say you are dog. If we are all God, and gods are loitering in the street, then what is the difference between God and dog?" It immediately struck me that he was right. How could God be in such a bad situation?

 **Malati:** The first thing he said that struck me was a few straightforward words, spoken without condemnation or opinion, but as a simple fact. If it was raining now, for example, and I said, "Oh, it's raining outside," it would be a simple fact. You may or may not

like the rain, but the fact is that it's raining. In the same way he said to us, "There is no love in this material world." We were all from the hippie generation, and the thrust of the hippie movement, particularly in San Francisco, was love. Every living entity is searching for love. Even little animals can't go without love. If you have an animal in your house and you ignore it, that animal becomes despondent. Every living creature in this world needs love and innately desires to seek and find love through relationship, through creating a loving situation with others. But all of us have been disappointed. We have all been in love, or almost been in love, or thought we had been in love, only to find that the love was gone, the love was lost. The person we loved went away. That propensity to love brought sorrow, yet that wasn't what love should be or was supposed to be. We hadn't found love. So when he said, "There is no love in this material world," it was such a simple and yet profound statement. It brought great relief to my heart. I didn't have to look anymore. I didn't have to think about it anymore. It wasn't there. And it wasn't a negative statement, because he went on to explain that the reason we were not finding love was because we didn't understand what love was. He told us that real love was found in our relationship with Krishna. That was my first strong memory.

Chitsukhananda: About five weeks after I had been in the Montreal temple, I wanted to go to Buffalo to get initiated. Nanda Kishor also wanted to go, to get his second initiation. We had no money. We were living in Canada impoverished. Somehow we easily hitchhiked all the way to Toronto and from there took a bus to Buffalo. The Buffalo temple was in a little house. When we arrived I felt great excitement and anticipation, as well as fear. I was afraid that when I looked into the eyes of this great personality, I would get scared and I would say, "I better get back to work." I was deathly afraid. Finally a car pulled up, and there for the first time I saw Srila Prabhupada. Nanda Kishor and I fell at his feet as he crossed the street. He put his hand on my head and on Nanda Kishor's head, and he walked into the temple.

 **Yadubara:** During the two-month period when I lived with the devotees in India, in different ways Prabhupada encouraged me to become more of a devotee. Once I was a bit reluctant to bow down. I was taking pictures all the time and used that as an excuse. He sent one of his disciples to ask me to pay my obeisances when he came in. I didn't have any hesitation doing that, as I had great respect and love for Prabhupada. Another time I shaved off my mustache. When I came in front of him, he said, "Oh, that is very nice. You look very good." In this way, with small exchanges, he encouraged me.

Revatinandan: One day I was cooking in the temple kitchen with Aniruddha. Aniruddha came back in from seeing Prabhupada and said, "Prabhupada just told me that we are not supposed to cook with mustard seeds or mustard oil or fenugreek anymore." Prabhupada wanted us to use simple spices, cumin seeds, chiles, asafoetida, as well as simple techniques. He specifically mentioned not using mustard seed and mustard oil, as well as fenugreek. In India later on, he once remarked, "My godbrothers generally prefer mustard oil, but I like *ghee*."

Malati: We didn't know very much about Vaishnav etiquette, and we had to get a fire ceremony together, although we had never seen one before. We were told what to get. The first thing was *ghee*. I found out that it was butter, and that it was going to be put into the fire. I thought, "My God, what a waste." The whole thing seemed bizarre. But we got the various items together, and Prabhupada performed the *yajna*. He gave the four of us bananas. We looked at each other, "What do you do with the banana? Well, you peel it." Somebody came up hurriedly and told us, "No. You put it in the fire." Okay. We put it in the fire. The next thing you know he said,

"Bow down. Bow down," but his accent was thick. There you are, you have just gotten a new name, you've just gotten your neck beads on, the fire is crackling, and "Bow down. Bow down." We were looking at each other again, "What to do? What to do?" Then Haridas figured it out. He got on his hands and knees and we all got on our hands and knees and started blowing the fire right on Srila Prabhupada's face. Srila Prabhupada's eyes could become saucer-like, humongous, and at this time they got very large. He picked up his *kartals* and started a *kirtan*. Of course he was asking us to bow down. But we had no concept or instruction on Vaishnav etiquette. This was the third fire ceremony, and we were confused souls exhibiting our confusion through this completely astounding behavior.

Chitsukhananda: After that we were ecstatic, and all my fears seemed to be dissipating. Prabhupada's presence wasn't at all what I had imagined. He was very sweet, gentle, kind, and very strong. Of course, there were also other aspects to his personality, like his sternness, his severity, his austerity, his dedication to Krishna, and his heaviness as a guru. But I wasn't afraid anymore.

The initiation was scheduled for that Saturday, the 19th of April, 1969. They told me, "You can go see Srila Prabhupada. He is in his apartment." He was staying in Rupanuga's apartment. Nanda Kishor and I went, and Nanda Kishor introduced me to Prabhupada. "This is Charles." He said, "Oh very nice. Do you like this Movement?" I said, "Yes, I like it very much." He said, "You are happy?" I said, "Yes. I am very happy that I met this movement. Thank you, Prabhupada. And I am very happy to meet you." He said, "Oh, thank you." He was very humble, sweet, and kind. He was like an old, lost relative, a grandfather or grandsire from the ages. I didn't feel strange in his presence. I felt very comfortable. All my fears disappeared completely. I sat with him, and I felt happy and peaceful. I had a guitar with me, and he asked me if I would sing, so I chanted Hare Krishna. Throughout the years, even when we opened a temple in Mexico, we would play guitars in *kirtan* in Prabhupada's presence. He would say, "Yes, yes, more. This is what's making people dance and chant. Use it for Krishna." It's nice to hear the sitar and tambura, but it's also nice for people to play the instruments of their own nation to worship God, and Srila Prabhupada was open-minded about that. There are no hard and fast rules for chanting. He tried to accommodate everyone.

Yadubara: In 1973 in New York City, we started making the *Hare Krishna People* film, and at the Mayapur Festival in 1974, we premiered it. We showed it in Prabhupada's room to Prabhupada and all the GBC members. He very much appreciated it. In fact, due to the Indian voltage, it was playing very slowly and all the voices were slow. That was traumatic for me, but Prabhupada and the devotees loved it.

Revatinandan: Srila Prabhupada gave a Sunday feast lecture about *kirtan,* and he said things that I never heard him say at other times, particularly not during a lecture. He remarked that melodic instruments, including the harmonium, are not meant for *kirtan,* and he explained why. He said that the ear will automatically follow musical strains, and then our attention will be diverted from the mantra. He said that rhythm instruments are good for *kirtan* because they make one more inclined to dance, and dancing, in turn, unlocks devotion. He liked graceful dancing. He used to mention that Jayatirtha was a graceful dancer. He said, "See how he dances. This is very good. This will help one feel more devotion." Another time he told Vishnujana that he did not like melodies that had long, extended notes in them. He liked the melody to be filled with the mantra.

    During the lecture he gave that day he also said, "Don't harmonize during the response." The leader may sing little variations, but the group should sing a steady response. One person shouldn't be singing one melody and another doing another melody during the response. "These things," he said, "will help one pay more attention to the mantra as one is chanting and dancing. That way one will get the maximum benefit, and the *kirtan* will also become more ecstatic." He also said that the dancing should be graceful and gentlemanly. Then, during the second *kirtan,* he got off the *vyasasana* and danced in the middle of the *kirtan* party. He danced back and forth very gracefully in what we called the "swami step." After a while he put his hands up and started leaping up in the air straight up and down. He wasn't shaking his body around. His hands were up, and he was leaping in the air. He kept leaping and leaping and leaping for a long time, and we were doing it with him. I got tired. I stopped and started to dance back and forth at one point. I was twenty-two years old at the time, and he was over seventy. Yet Prabhupada went right on leaping. He seemed to have no physical exhaustion at all. I was impressed because I thought, "I play basketball and here this guy can jump more then I can." I shouldn't say "guy," but those are the kind of thoughts that were going through my mind. It was the first time I had ever seen him dance, and I was amazed.

Malati: In the beginning we were curious about how to chant. What do you do when you chant, and what do you think? Srila Prabhupada said, "Two things. You don't do anything, and you don't think anything. You simply hear." To this day my endeavor is to somehow or other hear this chanting.

Revatinandan: One morning in India I was very sick, but I went to the *pandal* program anyway. Prabhupada was lecturing about Ajamil and about *prayaschitta,* or atonement for sins. Sometimes I thought he was giving those Ajamil lectures for me because Ajamil's fate might also be my fate. Anyway, in the lecture that day, Prabhupada said that the problem is that you atone but you do not remove the seed of sinful desire from your heart, and therefore you sin again. Thus you go through sinning and atoning again and again. So atonement is not the solution. One has to purify the heart.

He talked about how chanting purifies the heart and eventually cleanses even the seed of sinful desire from the heart, and then he said something that I'll never forget. He said, "But do not be impatient. After all, it took me thirty years to chant in this way."

Some people hypothesize that Prabhupada was this or that in his past life. Once in Calcutta he said, "In my previous life I was a doctor, and I lived sinlessly. Therefore, I was able to take up devotional service seriously in this life." But in the *pandal* lecture that day, he said it took him thirty years to chant with the devotion and purity that he chanted with, which was obviously with pure ecstatic love.

Chitsukhananda: When I was in Vancouver I wrote to Prabhupada, "After living as a *brahmachari* for so many months, I think that it's best if I get married." In his reply Srila Prabhupada instructed me. He wrote, "It's nice that you have taken to Krishna consciousness. You want to get married? I am not against that. We want to have nice devotee marriages and devotee children. It's wonderful. But one thing is that you must marry a girl from our Society. Make sure she is a devotee. Otherwise, if you marry someone who is not a devotee, your life will not be happy, because nondevotees don't understand. When you come to Ratha-yatra, we will discuss this personally." Even though I thought Srila Prabhupada had not remembered me from Buffalo, in fact he had never forgotten me.

Yadubara: Every time I filmed Prabhupada, he was totally himself. He wasn't like a person who is usually in front of a camera, but he was completely natural. He never made any errors, and I never had to do a retake. In other words, I never had to stop Prabhupada and tell him to do this or that. Of course, that would have been the wrong thing to do anyway.

Once we were filming in Bhaktivedanta Manor in England, and the tape recorder wasn't working properly. We had to ask Prabhupada to stop speaking, and he didn't like that at all. Finally we explained to him what the problem was, and he turned to Bhargava, who was operating the tape recorder, and said, "The tape recorder is useless, and you are useless."

Chitsukhananda: I thought Prabhupada had forgotten me because he didn't mention anything at Ratha-yatra. In the back of my mind I also thought that there were more important things to think about at Ratha-yatra than one's own arrangements. Later, I went to Los Angeles, and one day, when the whole temple was filled with devotees enjoying the Sunday feast, all of a sudden someone came in and said, "Chitsukhananda?" "Yes?" "Prabhupada wants to see you." I said, "Me?" All the devotees were stunned, "Who is this little, new devotee that Prabhupada has invited?"

I washed my hands and mouth and ran into his room. I said, "Yes, Srila Prabhupada?" He said, "Oh, remember you wrote me a letter discussing marriage? I have found one girl for you." I said, "Oh?" He said, "But there will be many obstacles for you. It will be difficult. You must learn to tolerate." I said, "Who is this girl, Srila Prabhupada?" He said, "Chandravali." I had heard about her and had seen a little bit of her. Prabhupada saw my eyes roll. I said, "Oh, Oh." Tamal Krishna was sitting next to Prabhupada, and they began to laugh, and I got more bewildered as they laughed harder. I didn't know what was going on. I knew that Chandravali was rebellious. She used to go into Prabhupada's room and discuss with him how women should be given more attention, which I am also in favor of. We want rights for everyone. That's what this Movement's all about. Anyway, Prabhupada said, "Yes, call her and I will marry you here." I said, "Yes, Prabhupada, I accept." Enthusiastically I called her on the phone and said, "Hello. Is Chandravali there?" She said, "Yes, who is this?" I said, "This is Chitsukhananda. I am a *sankirtan* devotee from Berkeley. Srila Prabhupada wants us to get married, and he will make the arrangements." She said, "Yuk! Marry you?" I said, "What? Prabhupada—" I never heard of anyone saying no to

Prabhupada. She said, "Oh, no." I heard the phone hang up, and I thought, "Oh, my goodness." I was too embarrassed to go back to Prabhupada, but I told his servant, "She doesn't want to marry me." Prabhupada heard about it, and he said, "Hmm . . . that's okay."

Malati: Anything from India was exotic and attractive to us. If it came from India, we thought, it must have something to do with Srila Prabhupada, because he was from India too. This was a whole new realm of mysticism.

One day an aerogram came, and Janaki took it to Prabhupada, but we were just dying to know what it said, because it was from India. After a while we both went in, and we saw that it had been opened. We were waiting for him to tell us what it said. Why wouldn't he want to tell us about this aerogram from India? But he didn't say anything. Finally Janaki said, "Swamiji, you got a letter from India?" He said, "Yes." "Was it good news?" He said, "Yes." "What was it?" we asked. He said, "My sister has died. She was a pure devotee. She was a Vaishnav." We were stunned. Suddenly we realized that Prabhupada's connection with Krishna was on the absolute level. We got a glimpse of eternity, a glimpse of being part of an eternal connection. And we got a glimpse that there was no loss.

Revatinandan: In Calcutta Prabhupada once said that when a pure devotee leaves his body he takes another birth on the planet where Krishna is appearing. Then, when Krishna leaves that planet, the devotee goes with Him back to the spiritual sky for good. So there is one more birth after one becomes a pure devotee, but it's not a material birth, because it is a birth with Krishna where He is appearing and having His pastimes, and after that one goes to Goloka with Him.

Another time in his room in Calcutta I asked him, "Because you are a devotee of Radha and Krishna, does that mean all of us are in-herently devotees of Radha and Krishna?" He said, "Not necessarily." I said, "So we might be devotees of say, Lakshmi-Narayan or Sita-Rama?" He said, "Yes." I said, "Am I to understand that by doing this process our relationship with Krishna, in whatever form, will be uncovered?" He said, "Yes," again. Ultimately not every devotee would become attached to Radha and Krishna.

I was thinking of the story of Murari Gupta in the *Caitanya-caritamrta,* to whom Lord Chaitanya said, "You are a pure devotee of Lord Ramachandra. You are Hanuman." In other words, there are some devotees who are constitutionally attached to other forms of the Lord. But Radha and Krishna contain all the other forms within Them, and by purification we would find our ultimate relationship. At least that's what he told me in Calcutta.

Chitsukhananda: Hakoblo Sabludoski, a nice Jewish man, was Mexico's number one emcee newscaster and respected throughout the world. I had been on his show, and I had explained, "Our mission is to bring happiness to the Mexican people. They are very joyful people, but we have come to give them even more happiness by the grace of my spiritual master." I showed a picture of Srila Prabhupada, and before I left, I asked Mr. Sabludoski, "When my spiritual master comes to Mexico, please let him come on the show." He said, "Fair enough. He can come."

I arrived in Mexico June 2, 1970, and Prabhupada arrived June 1, 1971. He had planned to stay five or six days, and I had programs and a whole itinerary of activities scheduled for those days. The first engagement was at the Masonic temple in Mexico City. Prabhupada was cordial, beautiful, and as kind as ever. People wanted his autograph or were melting away in his presence. Everywhere we went it was like that. One night around 9:30 or 10:00, I asked Srila Prabhupada, "Are you very tired?" He said, "No." I said, "You have been preaching all day and fasting. Basically you just took a little fruit today. Srila Prabhupada, I don't want to take advantage of you and your presence here, but there is an opportunity to go to the television station tonight with Mr. Sabludoski. He has a very important program that millions and millions—" He said, "Millions watch? How many millions?" I said, "Many millions, Prabhupada. Twenty million, thirty . . . I don't know. Many millions." He said, "Oh, then we must go." "Prabhupada, it is very late. I feel bad even to have mentioned it. I am taking advantage of your health." He didn't care for his health. He came to give everything. I said, "Srila Prabhupada, it's very late at night." He said, "So what? We work tonight and sleep tomorrow." He said it just like that, "Work tonight, and sleep tomorrow." "Okay, let's go."

Sure enough, after we had waited a little while they presented Srila Prabhupada on the show. We got a bit too ecstatic and brought his big, marble *vyasasana* and put it on the stage. They are accustomed to popes and bishops, so why not Swami Prabhupada on the beautiful chair? We sat around him. Hakoblo asked, "You have come to our country, what is your message?" Prabhupada said, "Mine is a message of joy for all countries. Everybody should be peaceful and happy, and not be misled." Hakoblo said, "How can they do that?" He said, "The main thing is to be in harmony with God. By chanting you will find that harmony." He gave many nice instructions and then we chanted. Afterwards I went to thank Mr. Sabludoski, but his head was in his hands and he was noticeably shaken by Prabhupada's association. I said, "Thank you very much." His mood was sober and quiet. He said, "No. Thank *you*," and we left.

Yadubara: In Los Angeles I filmed Prabhupada's daily activities for about a month, and then he traveled to Denver. I didn't tell him that I was coming, but I also flew there to continue filming. I wanted to film Srila Prabhupada as much as I could. I set up lights in front of the *vyasasana*, and when he saw the lights he was disturbed. They were too bright. Brahmananda, his secretary, was asking, "Why did he come?" Prabhupada called me and said, "Whether I am sitting here or in Los Angeles, what is the difference? What is the need for more filming?" He cut me off at that point, but he was very concerned about what service I would have if I went back to Los Angeles. We did have another project, a film on New Vrindavan later called *The Spiritual Frontier*. But I was impressed that Prabhupada was concerned about what I would do next. He was always concerned in that way for his devotees.

Revatinandan: The room wasn't very big, and there were forty or forty-five of us in it, along with Prabhupada and a couple of guests. During the evening *Bhagavad-gita* classes he would sit in a chair at one end of the room, and the rest of us packed in. One night Prabhupada was looking around and everybody was there but Jayananda. Prabhupada said, "Where is Jayananda?" We said, "He is still out parking the van, Srila Prabhupada." Prabhupada waited, and when Jayananda walked in, Prabhupada looked at him, smiled, and said, "Oh, Jayananda looks just like Lord Chaitanya." Jayananda blushed purple. He blushed and blushed because he was a homespun, shy, humble devotee.

Malati: When we first arrived in Mayapur, it was the days of the huts with the thatched roofs, the water pump, and the mud everywhere. Srila Prabhupada was staying in the brick hut. My husband, Shyamasundar, was his secretary, and I was his cook. I had always wanted to be his cook, and Krishna had rewarded me. But in Mayapur I was faced with not only service of guru, but service of husband, service of daughter, and trying to maintain my sanity in the situation. Materially it was impossible. There was no facility. I was living in a tent. I had two buckets of water to cook with and the servant would come every day and grab one of the buckets before the meal ended to heat water for Prabhupada's bath. Each day I had to confront the treasurer, whose duty it was to not give money, and I would usually have a royal argument with him concerning funds for Srila Prabhupada's *bhoga*. Then, while going to buy the *bhoga,* I would have an argument concerning money with the *ricksha-wala,* with the boatman, with the vegetable *walas,* because they all expected ten times the proper amount from a white person. I had to fight with everybody I dealt with.

To double my anxiety, which was already at peak level, Prabhupada's servant would come and take away the stove just before lunch. On top of that, every day I was thinking, "How can I please Srila Prabhupada?" I really wanted to cook perfectly for him. I would think about it all day. Even when I wasn't cooking, I would be planning for the next day, "How can I do it perfectly?" And it seemed as if every single day he told me something that I was doing imperfectly. One day there was too much salt. The next day there was too little. I started thinking, "What am I doing? I can't do it right. Everything I do is wrong. Maybe I shouldn't be cooking. Yeah, someone else should be cooking. I will tell Prabhupada to get someone else, or I will get someone else who can do it better." I started feeling relieved. All I had to do was tell Prabhupada, and that was it. The next day I went into his room full of this idea. His godbrothers were coming for lunch that day. Another source of my anxiety was that Prabhupada's godbrothers were criticizing Prabhupada for many things, and one of them was that Prabhupada had a female cook. I was the cook, and therefore I felt badly about that too.

Since his godbrothers were coming for lunch I thought, "He certainly won't have me cook today. I will tell him tomorrow." But he called me into the room and started telling me what he wanted for lunch. So, I went to make the lunch, and I brought it in. He was sitting at the end of the room like a royal king, and on each side of him were old, stately Vaishnavs with *dandas*. It was an impressive sight. I felt completely intimidated, but I had to go in. I entirely covered my head and hands with my *sari*, and I got down on the floor on my hands and knees. I curled in with the plate, put it down, offered obeisances, and started slithering back out. Then I heard Srila Prabhupada say, "Yes, she cooks for me, and all I do is criticize her. But she would slit her throat for me, and I would do the same for her." When he said that, I completely disintegrated. By the time I got to the other door, my *sari* was wet with tears. I realized how mundane my consciousness had been and how my anxiety had been based upon a misunderstanding of the relationship between the guru and the disciple. Every day I had been thinking, "How can I do it perfectly? What would he want?" and he was telling me. He wasn't criticizing me. I was just taking it in a mundane way. But because I wanted to know how it could be more pleasing to him, he told me. I was in illusion as to the position of a disciple and what the relationship of servitude meant. It is not, "You pat me on my back." That was my misconception.

When I heard Srila Prabhupada say that, I realized that it was absolutely true. There was no doubt about it. My mood was that I would have done anything for him. But it had never occurred to me how Prabhupada would also do anything for us. Then I realized that he was already doing everything for us. My insignificance at that point was immense, along with my gratitude and love for him. The potential for love was certainly revealed to me.

Yadubara: I had gotten quite sick in India and, after returning to America, had gone on a special diet to try to regain my health. But the diet hadn't worked. I had lost a lot of weight and was still sick. On a morning walk in Denver, Tamal Krishna Goswami began telling Prabhupada that, "Some devotees are involved in special diets. Yadubara has just tried one." There was a discussion about such diets for a little while, and at one point I said, "Yes, Prabhupada these diets are useless." All of a sudden Prabhupada stopped walking. Everybody else also stopped and got close to him to listen. Prabhupada looked at me and said, "The diet is useless or you are useless!"

We create the diet and we embrace it. So we are the useless persons. We cannot blame the diet.

Revatinandan: He went into his room and called for Jayapataka. We were standing outside on the covered balcony at 3 Albert Road in Calcutta. Prabhupada practically roared at him, "Why is your complexion greenish?" Jayapataka stammered something. Prabhupada said, "If you do not eat better, you will die. The devotees are looking weak. All of you are not eating properly." He said, "Every day go to the place where the sweet merchants buy the freshly made curd that's delivered from the countryside, and buy curd for each devotee. Fry it with a little salt and asafoetida, and give it to the devotees along with other, more substantial food." We were having a lot of puffies as well as *dahl* and *chapatis,* but it wasn't enough for us. When Prabhupada came he immediately saved us. He saw that the devotees in the temple at that time were suffering from malnourishment.

Chitsukhananda: Wherever Prabhupada went, I would also go along and stay near him. He would look at me and say, "There is my little puppy," but he didn't seem to mind me being there. Once I was eating mangoes with Shyamasundar, and I was in ecstasy watching Prabhupada eat fruit. He said, "If we just eat fruit, we can never overeat." So we were eating our mangoes, but I was inexperienced in the way in which mangoes should be eaten. They shouldn't be eaten over your *dhoti* so that the juice drips all over you. Shyamasundar said, "Chitsukhananda, look at you. You are getting the mango all over you." Prabhupada immediately corrected him. He said, "He is simply enjoying. Let him enjoy. Just let him enjoy." I said, "Thank you." And I got juice all over my face and *dhoti,* but I enjoyed it.

Malati: During the early days when we were trying to understand and follow the initial principles, Shyamasundar was carving the first Jagannath Deities. To see how the work was going, Prabhupada surprised us by visiting us in our apartment. He was looking at this Deity, that Deity, and the other Deity. All three of Them. On top of Balaram's head was a package of Pall Malls. Prabhupada said, "What is that?" Shyamasundar said, "Oh." Prabhupada said, "That is all right. It is very difficult to give up smoking. But why not smoke one less cigarette every day?" He said, "Don't let such a small thing as a little cigarette stand between you and Krishna." It was a loving, gentle instruction, and it was very clear. Shyamasundar followed that instruction. Prabhupada was tolerant, but at the same time he didn't say, "Yes, go on smoking." He explained how to stop smoking. It was a positive way of prohibiting smoking.

Chitsukhananda: The next morning we got up around quarter to six, just before sunrise, and Prabhupada came into the little temple room in that rustic house. When Srila Prabhupada realized that we had arisen late he was very serious, almost angry. He began the class without revealing his mind, but we could tell that something was wrong. Shyamasundar made some mistakes reading the Sanskrit, and Prabhupada said, "You are traveling with me for so many months, and you do not know these verses?"

Towards the end of the lecture Prabhupada said, "Why are you getting up late? I know you are traveling and that you are tired. But you must be up in the morning no matter what. You can rest later but you must be up in the morning." Then he said, "Chitsukhananda, is this getting up at six in the morning going on in your temple?" I said, "No. Srila Prabhupada." He said, "Hmm. You must be very careful. You may travel, but you must rise and chant no matter what." We all felt bad, especially me since I was the primary host in these places. I thought, "We have had five days of ecstasy, but now we are getting the nectar of a little chastisement." Then I thought, "Oh, my God. Now that he is unhappy and has seen how fallen we are, maybe I have ruined his trip."

After the class he went outside to go to his quarters, and I ran behind him. As I went I picked some jasmine flowers to offer to him. I said, "Srila Prabhupada, please take these flowers." He turned to me and said, "Thank you," and smiled brightly. I said, "Srila Prabhupada, your appearance like an angry lion has gone." He said, "I am never angry with any of you." This was after we had felt his thunderbolts for an hour. He said, "When you fall from the path, my duty is to put you back on. That's all. Otherwise there is no anger." I said, "Thank you, Prabhupada." His anger is displayed only for the care of the child, just as a parent may say, "Don't do that," so Prabhupada was the same way with us. We were his young children.

Yadubara: One time I was with Prabhupada when he arrived in Pittsburgh. I was walking backwards filming him as he came down the aisle. A devotee had paid his obeisances right behind me and I tripped and fell. The film shows what my camera did. Prabhupada walked by while I was on the ground, and he looked at me, unfazed. I was very fazed.

Revatinandan: Prabhupada spoke from the *vyasasana* saying, "On one side there is a blazing fire," and he pointed towards the street end of the building because Calcutta is Calcutta, "and on the other side there is Radha and Krishna. People do not know that there is an alternative. We have to give them the alternative."

In the Calcutta temple, it was refreshing to see the nice Radha-Krishna Deities, who were wonderfully worshiped by Yamuna, Kaushalya, Chitralekha, and Devananda Swami. The Deities were decorated with lots of little, white jasmine flowers as well as *champak* garlands, so They looked pretty and smelled heavenly. There was a window behind Them allowing light to come in, and black bees would also sometimes come in, fly around the Deities, land on a flower or two, and then go out again. Prabhupada said, "When those black bees come, it is a sign that Krishna is pleased with the Deity worship."

Malati: On the Vrindavan *parikram,* Prabhupada and all the devotees stopped at a *dharmshala* near Govardhan Hill. Prabhupada went into a room to have his massage while I cooked for him on the veranda. The system was that as soon as Prabhupada finished his massage, we would have his lunch ready. I only had so much fuel and so much *chapati* dough, and it was a tight schedule. Anyway, I had it ready, and we all sat down, the *brahmacharis* and *sannyasis* on one side and the *grihasthas* on the other. Just as we started to eat, two dogs began to bark, "*Woof, woof, woof.*" Some *sannyasis* and a couple of *brahmacharis* got up to save us from these dogs. Prabhupada said, "No, stop," and he took his *chapati,* tore it in half, and gave one half to one dog and the other half to the other. Then he said, "*Hut!*" and they walked away. He turned to us and said, "You never know who they are, these dogs in Vrindavan." It was intense because we suddenly had a glimpse of the fact that we were in the holy *dham* and, while we were seeing dogs, Prabhupada was seeing spirit souls, and we didn't know who they were.

Prabhupada didn't discriminate. He didn't play with dogs, he didn't have them in his house, but he didn't kick them either. He didn't treat anybody in a mean way. One time in Mayapur Prabhhupada learned that the devotees were beating dogs, and he said, "The devotees who were doing that should be beaten." Meanwhile, in their ignorance, the devotees had been proud of their dog beating activity. Prabhupada always had genuine concern. His concern was not a superficial pat on the head. He wasn't ever falsely sympathetic or sentimentally sympathetic.

Chitsukhananda: In tropical places like Mexico, it rains very beautifully and hard in the afternoons, and then the sun sets. Srila Prabhupada was on a plateau watching the sunset, and I was sitting next to him like a little puppy. Mosquitoes were starting to buzz around a bit. I thought, "Oh, no. They are going to bite Prabhupada." I said, "Srila Prabhupada, are the mosquitoes biting you?" He looked at me and said, "No." I thought of something very wise to say. "Srila Prabhupada, it must be because you are a pure devotee and therefore they respect you. I am impure so they are biting me. They know the difference." He said, "But in Calcutta they make no distinction."

Gurudas told me the other part of the story. One evening in the Calcutta temple, Prabhupada had begun to lecture from his *vyas-asana,* when all of a sudden mosquitoes started flying and buzzing and creating a commotion. Prabhupada was so bothered that he got off the *vyasasana* and sat with the devotees. He said, "Just see, they have dethroned me." So the Calcutta mosquitoes were renegades, and the Mexican mosquitoes were respectful. They didn't bite him.

Yadubara: I was with Prabhupada in 1973 when George Harrison visited him in his room at Bhaktivedanta Manor. George had recorded a song called "Krishna, Where Are You?" that he played for Prabhupada. It had a very nice melody and words. Prabhupada appreciated it. He said, "Yes. Searching for Krishna is the proper mood." As he heard the song he sat back and tapped his leg in time. He and George had a very nice relationship. They often would tell stories and laugh together in Prabhupada's room.

Revatinandan: One day we were going to a Gaudiya Math in Calcutta. This particular Math had a bookstore with all kinds of old Gaudiya Math publications, some of which were quite rare. Prabhupada and I were standing in the doorway of the ISKCON temple on Albert Road, and I asked, "Srila Prabhupada, I understand that your books are all that we need, but there will be books for sale at the Math. Once you told Bali Mardan that if he read the *Brahma-samhita* he would become a good preacher. I was wondering if it would be all right if I bought the *Brahma-samhita* and some other books, since we are going to this place."

Prabhupada answered my question in three parts. He said, "For one thing, I do not think you will be able to understand those books very well. My Guru Maharaj was not pleased with the sincerity of most of his disciples, and he wrote his books in a difficult language so that almost none of his disciples could understand them." Then he said, "Actually, my Guru Maharaj wrote those books for me. Only I could understand them." Another thing he said was, "We shouldn't read anything published by the Gaudiya Math after 1932, because by that time politics were entering into the editions that were being printed." I said, "Didn't your Guru Maharaj pass

away in 1936?" He said, "Yes, but in the last four years he was infirm
and was not directly supervising the editing."

The final thing he said was, "Besides that, for an intelligent
disciple, what his spiritual master provides is sufficient."

Chitsukhananda: When I went to Trinidad to help reopen the temple, I sometimes gave lectures to groups of Hindus. One morning I
gave a small talk at a Hindu society, Sanatan Dharma Mahasabha.
Afterwards a Mr. Riki said to me, "Your guru is A.C. Bhaktivedanta
Swami?" I said, "Yes. Do you know him?" He said, "He was writing
to me some time ago," and he showed me a letter Prabhupada
had written to him in 1964 or '65, before Prabhupada came to
America. Prabhupada had written about going to Trinidad since it
had many Hindus, and Mr. Riki had responded on behalf of his
Hindu society.

The next time I went to Los Angeles, I spent some time with
Prabhupada, and I said, "Srila Prabhupada, when I went to Trinidad,
I saw a letter you wrote before you came to America. Were you going
to go to Trinidad first?" Prabhupada smiled and said, "Yes. I was
ready to go there but the people in the Sanatan Dharma Mahasabha
society were telling me what I would have to do, how I would have
to preach, how I would have to do this, and how I would have to do
that. So, that I could not do." They were trying to control him. He
said, "No, no. I will not let them run my life. I will preach the way
I want to preach and serve Krishna the way I see fit."

Malati: Prabhupada was personally instructing Yamuna in Deity
worship. One night Yamuna was doing the *arati* to Prabhupada's
little Deities. She offered the flower to the Deities and then gave it to
Srila Prabhupada. At that time my daughter Sarasvati started to leave
the room, and Prabhupada threw the flower at her, hitting her on the
back of her head. She picked it up, marched over to him and popped
the flower in his mouth. Prabhupada smiled at her. Purushotam was
also there and later mentioned that this incident was one of many

reasons why he left Prabhupada's service. He thought that his spiritual master shouldn't behave frivolously with a female during *arati*.

Saraswati went to Calcutta when she was four and a half, and Prabhupada would sometimes tease her, "I am going to put a stamp on your forehead and send you to the *gurukula*." She would say, "No. No." "Yes. I will put a stamp on your forehead and you will go to *gurukula*." Eventually she did go to *gurukula*, but her father took her. A year later she came to visit me in India, and when Srila Prabhupada saw her he said, "Oh, you have come back from *gurukula*. Recite something." She recited the first verse from the First Canto of the *Bhagavatam*." He was pleased with her. "Yes, very good. You must always speak like that." Then he handed me twenty *rupees* and said, "Here, buy her a dress." I said, "No. I can't take this money from you, Srila Prabhupada." "No. You must buy her a new dress."

Yadubara: I had a number of memorable incidents when I filmed Srila Prabhupada. One was on the roof of the apartments on our land in Juhu before the temple was built. Prabhupada would speak there in the twilight hours. One time the local eight-, nine-, and ten-year-old girls got dressed up and went to the roof to garland Prabhupada and do a dance for him. I filmed both the garlanding and the dancing. Later, when I was editing that film, I noticed that Prabhupada didn't look at the girls. He had his hand in his bead bag, and he would look down and over and up but never at the girls. In this way he showed the example of an ideal *sannyasi*.

Revatinandan: In the spring of 1975, Gurudas took *sannyas* at the Stewart Street temple in Berkeley. Prabhupada gave a very nice lecture that day. He spoke just as highly, if not more highly, of Yamuna, Gurudas' former wife, than he did of Gurudas. At one point he said, "His wife is practically a *sannyasini*." When the program was over and Prabhupada was walking back to his room, I asked him if it was

conceivable that women in our movement might formally take
sannyas. Prabhupada looked at me, made a very disgusted expression and said, "Never!" It was an emphatic answer. From his point
of view, that would never be possible.

Chitsukhananda: I was in India when Srila Prabhupada was collecting money for the Vrindavan and Mayapur projects. At that time
I was not doing much preaching, and I thought, "I'm going to get a
little money together and start a farm with my family, and maybe
it will become successful." Prabhupada told me, "You really want
to start a farm? Very nice. You can take this *sannyasi*, Chavana, with
you. He can work under you." Prabhupada never thought that,
"This is a *grihastha* and a *sannyasi* cannot work under him." No. He
would always make arrangements according to time, place, and
circumstance.

    I wanted to help, and since at that time I couldn't help by mak-
ing devotees or opening temples, I could send some money. I said,
"Prabhupada, when I make money from my project, I am going to
send it to you." He said, "No. You keep the money. I don't want your
money. I want you to have your money. I know you will employ it
for Krishna's service." Not that, "I want you to employ it." He said,
"I know wherever you go, you will try to employ this money for
Krishna."

Revatinandan: One day had been especially difficult for me. I had
been on the street collecting for a long time, I was tired, and I had
just fought with another devotee. I felt that I couldn't go on, that it
was time for me to disappear and leave.

    That night, after another eight-hour day of street *sankirtan*
and magazine selling, we were driven over to the bungalow where
Prabhupada was speaking. I didn't get into chanting during the first
kirtan because I didn't want to get carried away again. Every time I
felt like leaving, it was either one of Prabhupada's lectures or a feast
that would wind up changing my mind to stay. *Maya* was really

tugging at me.

When Srila Prabhupada started to lecture that night, I had my head down. Prabhupada said, "When one is engaged in devotional service he will become joyful. If one is morose, that means he is not Krishna conscious. If one is Krishna conscious, he cannot be morose." That hit me hard. I looked at him, and his eyes were right on me. He was speaking to me at that moment, but I was so psychologically fragile, if he had singled me out I would have probably run from the room or broken into tears or gotten very agitated, even angry, and left. Instead he did it in a lecture. I knew that he had seen exactly what I was feeling, and he said it for me. And I knew he was right, because all day I had refused to engage myself and, therefore I had been miserable. My legs hurt, I was tired, I was this, and I was that. Otherwise, I would have been absorbed, time would have passed, and little by little I would be getting stronger.

Periodically other devotees had experiences similar to mine. Prabhupada was very good at reading faces. He once said that the face was the index of the mind, and he had that art down by training or intuition or both. He knew what to say at a particular time to keep us from faltering or to encourage us in different ways.

Malati: Another mystical experience I had with Srila Prabhupada was after Shyamasundar and I were released from prison. We couldn't believe what had happened, but we had been sentenced to five years and we had to go. Totally inexplicably, after twenty-four days we were released. Even the parole officer did not know why we were getting out. I was hesitating to sign the paper, because I didn't know what it was, and she said, "It's your release." I signed it fast, and she said, "I don't know why you're being released, because I wouldn't have approved. It went over my head."

We immediately went to San Francisco. Prabhupada had arrived from India while we were in prison, and the devotees told us, "Hurry up. Prabhupada is here." We ran home, got changed, and went to see him on Carl Street. I knocked on his door, and he said, "Oh, Malati. Come in. Just last night I was thinking that five years was too much." He said to Upendra or Kartikeya, "Bring that." It was his case. He pulled out a *sari* and gave it to me, a white Bengali *sari* with a green and red border. It was amazing.

Yadubara: In Mayapur in '74 or '75, Prabhupada's godbrother Sridhar Maharaj came to visit Prabhupada at the ISKCON Chandrodaya Mandir. When Prabhupada heard that Sridhar Maharaj had arrived, he immediately left his room and went down three flights of stairs to greet him. Sridhar Maharaj was old and weak and had to be carried upstairs. In Prabhupada's room, the two of them had an affectionate, close, intimate discussion. Then out of ecstasy, Sridhar Swami started leading a *kirtan*, singing, "Haribol," wonderfully. He jumped out of his chair, and as he got up, everybody got up and started dancing. In an old *Vyasa-Puja* book there is a black-and-white picture from that time, showing Srila Prabhupada and the devotees dancing in Prabhupada's room. Their meeting was very wonderful.

Revatinandan: In the mid-seventies, Nitai das, a devotee Sanskrit scholar, started hearing from a Brijbasi Goswami and left ISKCON as a result. Nitai claimed that Prabhupada had not given us all the information we needed. He criticized Prabhupada for not telling his disciples about their eternal *rasa* with Krishna. So, in Berkeley in 1976, I asked Prabhupada, "Are there any matters concerning the nature of our devotional service and our relationship with Krishna that you have not explained to us? In the future will it be necessary for us to find someone else for more instructions? Or, if we follow your prescription for *sadhana, sankirtan,* preaching, and chanting, will our hearts be purified so that Krishna will reveal subsequent things to us from within?" When I said the latter part, Prabhupada smiled and said, "Yes, that is the way. You will not have to go anywhere else. If you simply follow my instructions, everything will be revealed to you from within." He had a pleased look. It was clear to me that there was no need for information about our *rasa*, because everything is revealed to a pure-hearted devotee.

Chitsukhananda: I arrived twelve days before Prabhupada left the planet. When I came into his room the devotees said, "Chitsukhananda is here." Prabhupada smiled and said, "Oh. Thank you for coming." Even then he was totally attentive. I was able to be with him during his last few days. It was very wonderful. I hated to see him in that condition, but he was so clean and pure. His mind was centered on Krishna and clear. There was never any question of senility, of being an old person, or of being very ill. It was not because I was his disciple that I saw this, but because it's the truth. Anyone, who reads what he wrote and hears what he spoke at that time will also see that his mind was perfectly clear.

Yadubara: Once, during Srila Prabhupada's last days in Vrindavan, I had the opportunity to massage him, and I was concerned that I didn't give him pain. I asked Prabhupada, "Are you feeling pain?" Prabhupada looked at me as if to say, "What kind of a question is that?" and said, "No." I could see that he was completely aloof from his bodily condition. His last purports, the third volume of the Tenth Canto, some of which I filmed him dictating, are lucid and clear. Although Prabhupada's physical condition had deteriorated, his consciousness was perfectly clear, perfectly centered on Krishna.

Malati: The special quality Srila Prabhupada had, that set him apart from all others, was his loving exchanges. We had contacted other teachers who were purporting some form of so-called spirituality but who were actually "chewing the chewed," to use Prabhupada's phrase. There was no spiritual taste from these people.

Srila Prabhupada gave us spiritual life. He didn't come to exploit, but he genuinely cared and was concerned for everyone who came to him. We definitely felt that. Never before, from anyone else in our lives, not even our own parents, had we felt the love and care and concern that Srila Prabhupada had for us. Krishna consciousness was a process of falling in love with Srila Prabhupada. We were responding to the warm, deep, great love that he offered us.

TAPE 9

Dhananjaya das
Tribhuvanath das
Sakshi Gopal das
Kaliyapani das
Bhajahari das
Dhruvanath das

Dhananjaya: I could detect a slight Scottish accent in some of Prabhupada's words. Later on, while I was massaging him, Srila Prabhupada asked me where I came from. I said "Scotland," and he started reminiscing about his education at Scottish Churches College in Calcutta and how all his teachers were Scottish. He studied the Bible there and learned the catechism. He asked me if I knew any Scottish Lords. I said, "I don't know any Scottish Lords personally." He said, "Oh, one Lord Zetland came to our college in Calcutta." He asked me if I studied British history, and I said, "Oh yes," and then he tested me. "When was the battle of Trafalgar?" I said, "1805," "When was the battle of Waterloo?" "1815." He said, "You know British history just like I know British history." He also asked, "How far is Scotland and Glasgow from London?" and I told him, "Approximately 400 miles," "How long did it take to go there by train?" "Approximately eight hours." He put me at ease in that way, because I really didn't know how to start a conversation with Srila Prabhupada when I was in the process of massaging him. That's the way he won over my heart too, because he related to me in a way I could appreciate and respond to. It wasn't a philosophical discussion on the first meeting.

After we arrived at John Lennon's estate, Prabhupada led a *kirtan* and gave a very philosophical class, but all I was thinking about was when I could get initiated. At the end of class Prabhupada asked for questions. I raised my hand, and he said, "Yes." "When can I take initiation?" My question had nothing to do with the class. Srila Prabhupada said, "That is another thing; that we will see." About a week later Prabhupada initiated me.

 **Tribhuvanath:** When Prabhupada came through the doors of the lounge, his smile was oceanic. He was beaming. I was supposed to put a garland on him, but I froze. I thought, "This person is not in this dimension." I was only 18, but I could tell that he was not of this world. Other devotees were garlanding him, but I didn't even pay my obeisances. Prabhupada walked straight past me as I was standing there looking at him and holding a big garland. Then I ran up to him and slipped the garland on him. It was funny because I was obviously the reception committee, but I was motionless. Prabhupada's smile had knocked me out. The other devotees were practically crying, and that made me more amazed at this person's potency, that he could walk through a door and cause everyone to cry. It was fascinating.

 **Sakshi Gopal:** I was struck by Srila Prabhupada's seriousness. In the temple in Manchester there was a black-and-white poster of Prabhupada sitting on his bed in Bury Place. I used to think, "Why does he look so serious? Why isn't he laughing like other gurus do?" Then it suddenly hit me that life itself is serious. At that point Prabhupada's gravity and the depth of his compassion came across in that picture.

 **Kaliyapani:** He was in a car leaving for the airport, and I was sitting in the driver's seat of a van, waiting to follow him. I had my hands folded, and as he very slowly passed right by me, he looked up at me and returned my gesture, which astounded me. Then our eyes met for one or two seconds. That glance is probably the most memorable experience of my life, because it seemed as if time stopped. I felt that Prabhupada saw thousands of my nonsense births and still completely accepted me in spite of everything. It was an experience that was timeless, that was in another dimension. Then he was gone. But he had created an incredible link with me which I've never forgotten and which I can never forget.

 **Bhajahari:** The first time I ever spoke to His Divine Grace was on a morning walk. At that time it was the American devotees who were interacting with Prabhupada. The Welsh and English devotees were younger and felt somewhat intimidated and nervous. I was afraid to speak. I thought only Americans could speak to him, and I also thought, "Well, what's there to say?" He's speaking, and I'm listening. But one particular morning I felt inclined to ask my first question. Prabhupada had walked past some young hippies sleeping on the benches in St. James Park and had commented, "By good fortune all these people can come to Krishna consciousness." As he carried on walking, the words "good fortune" kept going around in my mind. "Does this mean that there is some kind of luck involved, that somebody gets Krishna consciousness and somebody else doesn't by some throw of the dice?" In my neophyte state I was trying to understand, "What did Prabhupada mean by good fortune?" So, after a few hundred yards I plucked up enough courage to nervously ask, "Srila Prabhupada, can you please explain what you mean by "good fortune," because I understand from reading your literature and hearing you speak that nothing happens by chance." He continued to walk for a bit and then all of a sudden

stopped dead in his tracks. He frightened me, because he turned straight to me as we were twelve inches apart, pointed his cane at me, and said, "We are their good fortune." I meditated on that for years and years and years. In his humility, Prabhupada never said, "I am their good fortune," but, "We are their good fortune." Gradually I began to understand the importance of spreading Krishna consciousness.

 **Dhruvanath:** I'd come back from India as a hippie in '69 or '70, and I was attempting to write a book based on the hallucinogenic drug experiences I'd had there. At that time the devotees had a big hit record, *The Hare Krishna Maha Mantra,* and I thought it would be a great idea to have a chapter of interviews with the devotees. When I finally found the temple, I met Kulashekar prabhu, and he said, "Our spiritual master is upstairs, why don't you talk to him?" I said, "Great, why not?" We went to Prabhupada's room on the first floor in Bury Place. Before we entered, Kulashekar told me that Prabhupada was a great personality and we should offer our respects to him. I said, "Fair enough."

Prabhupada was sitting on a cushion behind a low desk on the far side of the room with his back to the window. He was writing something and had his glasses down his nose. He peered up and said, "Hare Krishna," and somehow I felt overwhelmed to be in his presence. I automatically fell to the floor like a stick as I had seen devotees do in the temple downstairs. I simply lay there frozen, thinking: "What do I do now? When do I get up?" A few moments passed and Kulashekar motioned, "Okay, you can get up now." I had preconceived questions I was going to ask, because at that time LSD was my method for achieving self-realization. But when I sat there directly facing Srila Prabhupada, I went blank. I was speechless. Somehow or other I had read *The Nectar of Devotion,* and I remembered that the pure devotees' eyes are anointed with the salve of love. Looking at Prabhupada's eyes I could see this, and I could see that he was unlike anyone I had ever met in my life. After we had exchanged pleasantries, some moments passed, and then Prabhupada broke the ice by saying something that showed he knew what I was thinking. He said, "How unfortunate it is that the youth of today are trying to become self-realized through the use of hallucinogenic drugs." I was totally taken aback because this was exactly what I was going to challenge Prabhupada on. All my thoughts of writing a book went out the window. After that I plucked up some courage and asked a question, "What are the characteristics of a pure devotee?" Prabhupada expounded for about twenty minutes just on that question.

I was with Prabhupada for about an hour, and Kulashekar was the only other devotee in the room at the time. Before I left, Prabhupada looked at me straight in the eyes and said, "Man is the architect of his own fortune, so you make your fortune now. Whatever is done is done. Now start a new chapter in your life, and in the next life go back home, back to Godhead." Those words are still ringing in my ears to this day.

Dhananjaya: He said, "Do you know what the four principles are?" I said, "Yes." "And you are chanting a minimum of sixteen rounds?" I said, "Yes." On that premise he accepted me, and then he said, "Your name is Dhananjaya das, a name for Arjuna which means 'conqueror of wealth.' You will have no difficulty in acquiring wealth. Actually there is so much wealth everywhere, money is flying in all directions," and he put his hands up in the air, "you simply have to learn the art of catching it."

Tribhuvanath: At the initiation Prabhupada was very grave when he chanted on the beads. I was sitting just below the *vyasasana* when a boy came up and Prabhupada said to him, "What are the four regulative principles?" The boy said, "No intoxication, no gambling, no meat eating, no illicit sex." Prabhupada shot back, "So, which one do you like the best?" The boy went bright red. I thought it was funny, because Prabhupada had been so grave. It was a serious occasion, yet he talked like that.

Sakshi Gopal: He asked me what the four principles were and said, "Do you vow to chant sixteen rounds a day?" With all sincerity I said, "Yes, Prabhu." Prabhupada said, "Yes, good." I think that Prabhupada saw past my lack of etiquette to perhaps a little sincerity. I was very serious when I said it. He should have chastised me then, but he didn't.

Bhajahari: Prabhupada talked about ugra-karma and how people had difficult lives, how they worked hard with no result. Revatinandan Swami began to speak about how he used to work in a hellish canning factory in California before he became a devotee. I felt shy and nervous, but I began to talk about how, when I was twenty, I worked in a steel factory for a month. I described it in some detail, the huge hydraulic press and all of our activities. Prabhupada listened carefully. I said, "Well, Prabhupada, they invited me to make extra money by working the night shift. I thought they had asked me because I was a good worker, but actually nobody else wanted to do it. After one or two weeks of night shift, I nearly had a nervous breakdown from the strain." Prabhupada said, "Actually that's because in your last life you were all brahmans. Otherwise how could you come to the platform of Krishna consciousness so quickly?" He thought for a moment, leaning back on his cushions in a relaxed mood with his hand behind his head, and then said, "Actually my Guru Maharaj has ordered all of you to take birth to help me spread this mission." There were about ten of us in the room, and everyone was very attentive at that point. Prabhupada looked at each person and finished on me. He said, "Now we are all together again," and beamed. Everybody went "Jaya, Prabhupada." Some devotees began to cry.

Dhruvanath: Shyamasundar was eager to have Bury Place transformed into a proper temple, so the building became a construction site. He mentioned to George (Harrison) that it was difficult for us to live there because there was so much dust and noise from the work. George said, "I'll speak to John Lennon. He's just acquired a big property, and he might be able to put you up." As it happened, John agreed. In fact, he was incredibly favorable and offered us five acres of land on his seventy-six-acre estate. Srila Prabhupada said that we should utilize that land for growing fresh vegetables and fruits, and if we grew more than we needed, we should take the extra by bullock cart to the local market in London and sell it. I said, "But Prabhupada, the lorries will get there before the bullock-cart." We were at least twenty-five miles outside of London. Prabhupada said, "No, the bullock-cart should leave the night before. We'll walk all night and reach the market before the lorries arrive." So, in 1969, this was Prabhupada's vision. He wanted us to train up animals, hitch them to a cart, and take fresh market produce into central London. He also said that we should hold a big Ratha-yatra festival starting from John Lennon's estate all the way to central London, stopping at different towns and villages on the way.

Tribhuvanath: In St. James Park Prabhupada would constantly point out different things. Once he saw some bird droppings and asked, "What is this?" Everyone was looking at the bird droppings and thinking, "Maybe Prabhupada reads tea leaf formations and sees it esoterically." Prabhupada said "What does this tell you?" Everyone was bewildered. "This tells you that the same bird is sleeping on the same branch every night. Even the bird becomes attached to his residence. So be careful."

Dhananjaya: John and Yoko had made a record album called *John and Yoko Forever*, because Yoko's desire was to somehow or other live with John for eternity. When Yoko asked Prabhupada if this were possible, Prabhupada said that it was not, that at death you are immediately separated. At that point Yoko lost all interest.

John and his wife were regularly taking heroin while we were there and were having withdrawal symptoms coming off it. They were searching for their identity through the drug culture and through spirituality as well, which is why we were there. One evening, just after his twenty-ninth birthday, John invited Prabhupada to listen to a song that he had just recorded called "Cold Turkey".

Trivikram and I knew about this invitation, and without Prabhupada or John Lennon knowing, we peeked into the room to watch. Prabhupada came in and was invited to sit on a very large, comfortable sofa along with Purushotam. Yoko was sitting in a chair next to Prabhupada. John said, "I made this recording, and I would like you to hear it," and he started playing around with the dials on his equipment, but he couldn't get it to work—there was no sound. After a minute or so Prabhupada realized that he was having difficulty and said, "It seems you are having trouble, but I've also done some recording, and I've got my tape recorder." It was a little portable one. Prabhupada had been recording some *bhajans* accompanied by harmonium and tambora. He told Purushotam to start the recorder. So instead of Prabhupada having to hear John's horrific song, he was able to play his music to John. John retired from his equipment, sat near Yoko, and listened. After it was over and after a few minutes of conversation, Prabhupada said, "Now I have to go back, I have some translating work to do," and he left the room. As he was coming around we jumped out of the bushes and paid our obeisances. Prabhupada rubbed us on our backs and said "*Jaya!* So, you saw?"

Sakshi Gopal: On one morning walk at Bhaktivendanta Manor there were about five of us with Srila Prabhupada. For the first third of the walk Prabhupada chanted *japa* and didn't speak. When we reached the top of the road Prabhupada started explaining how the living entities reflect Krishna's mystic power. Krishna has complete mystic power, and the living entity has partial mystic power. "Just like a frog," Prabhupada said, "the frog has yogic powers. If you bury him in the ground he will still live." I said, "But Prabhupada, the frog breathes through his skin." Prabhupada said, "No, he has yogic powers." Since then I've learned of frogs and toads coming out alive after being buried in solid stone for tens of thousands of years. So they do have that mystic power.

Bhajahari: I organized the Janmastami festival, and for the first time arranged to make some extra *prasadam,* like pizza and chips. People who didn't want to take the free rice, *chapati,* and *subji* would pay for this special *prasadam.* Later on I was in Prabhupada's room, and Prabhupada said, "Are there any questions?" One Indian gentleman, who came regularly but complained often, began to criticize, "Why are you selling *prasadam? Prasadam* is *prasadam.* It should be given away." My heart started pounding. I panicked. Prabhupada looked around and then said to him, "If we don't charge you then you will never give anything." I felt completely vindicated. It is okay to sell *prasadam.* The gentleman was quiet after that.

Tribhuvanath: One time we were driving past Buckingham Palace in a taxi with Prabhupada, feeling proud that one boy who was part of the Queen's guard, those soldiers who wear the big furry hats, had become a devotee. We said, "Prabhupada, one of the Queen's personal guards has joined." Prabhupada said, "Oh, so how about the Queen?"

Dhananjaya: George asked if he should move into the temple and shave up. Prabhupada said, "No. What you are doing through your music is much more important. You are already a devotee of Krishna. So continue." George had written a song for Lakshmi Shankar, Ravi Shankar's sister-in-law, called, "Krishna, Where Are You?" Prabhupada listened to that recording in George's presence and said, "This is the correct Gaudiya Vaishnav mood. We should be crying out, 'Krishna, where are You?' We should not think that we have captured Krishna, that we know Krishna." He said, "This is how you can serve our Society best."

Another time we went to George Harrison's house after a program at Redding. Shyamasundar could not find George, but he knew where we should wait for him, so we went inside. As we waited, it got dark. Finally George arrived with a big bouquet of flowers and a basket of fruit. He would never come empty-handed but would always bring an offering for Srila Prabhupada. When he presented these he paid full *dandavats*. Srila Prabhupada said, "The purpose of the human form of life is to leave this world of darkness and go back to the world of light." As he was saying this, the room was getting darker and darker because there was no light on. Prabhupada emphasized this point. He was expert at using any situation that he would find himself in. "This is the world of darkness. This world requires illumination. The only illumination we have is from the sun and the moon. Without the sunshine, there would be no light and no life. When the sun sets, we must call upon artificial illumination, electricity or fire. But in the world of light there is no need for any kind of artificiality." He said: "This is where we all wish to live, in the world of light, not in the world of darkness." George appreciated his words very much.

Sakshi Gopal: Srila Prabhupada said, "What living entity eats through his feet? Krishna can eat through any part of His body. Any one of His senses can perform the function of any other. There is a living entity that eats through his feet. Who?" We were scratching our heads. None of us could figure it out. Prabhupada stopped and pointed to a tree. "The tree eats through his feet." It was a sweet little discussion.

Tribhuvanath: On morning walks Prabhupada would regularly comment about the state of society. He noticed people sleeping in the park in their sleeping bags or on a newspaper and explained, "Karma is so stringent that even though these people live in such an advanced society, they still cannot avoid their karma." Prabhupada said, "Even though they are living in a very civilized country, they are still suffering, sleeping in an abominable condition." Once we asked Prabhupada about advancement, and he very determinedly stopped walking. He took one step forward, pointed to his leg, and said, "When one leg is firmly fixed, then one moves the next leg. In that way one can make advancement. But if one runs, one will simply fall."

Dhananjaya: Once we were walking and saw a patch of yellow grass. In his famous way Prabhupada stopped, pointed to this patch of yellow grass, and said, "Why is this grass yellow when all the other grass is green?" Gurudas offered some practical reasons, "Because of the nature of the soil, because of too much rain," and so forth. Prabhupada said, "No. This grass is yellow because it is detached from the root. All plants get their nourishment from their roots. As soon as they are detached from their roots, there is difficulty. Similarly, we are in difficulty in this material world because we have become detached from Krishna. As soon as we are attached to Krishna, our lives will become successful."

Bhajahari: There were two important instructions I absorbed from the morning walks. One was in 1974, in relation to book distribution. At that time we were collecting money by distributing records. Prabhupada made it very clear that it was okay to use paraphernalia to collect funds, but a book must be given also. He was not in favor of just collecting. He said, "I am not a beggar. I never begged anything. Whenever I took a donation, I gave some literature." That was very strong.

Another morning while we walked through the village and around the fields, we talked about cleanliness. Prabhupada said that if you are not clean, rats and mice will come. One devotee piped up, saying that in the Edinburgh temple the devotees had exterminated the rats and mice. Prabhupada turned on him strongly and said, "You should be killed." Prabhupada was angry that they exterminated vermin. His idea was that the temple should be so spotless that there was nothing for them to eat. That would keep them away.

Tribhuvanath: Once Prabhupada was so weak and ill that late one night he called out to Shyamasundar, who rushed into Prabhupada's room in time to catch him as he fell. Shyamasundar said Prabhupada was incredibly light. That morning we stayed in bed because we did not want to disturb Prabhupada. When we finally got up, we had a 24-hour *kirtan* in the temple. About three days later, Prabhupada suddenly got well and went on a morning walk. One devotee asked, "Srila Prabhupada, how is it that a pure devotee gets sick?" Prabhupada stopped and became emotional. His eyes got really big, and he said in a loving way, "It is just like lovers. Sometimes lovers fight." The devotee said, "Oh! A love fight, Prabhupada." Prabhupada said, "Yes. Similarly, Krishna has His love fights. Sometimes He fights the devotee." Then he smiled. It was very deep and ecstatic.

Dhananjaya: I asked Prabhupada about Lord Shiva's position. Prabhupada answered strongly, almost in anger, because this was a regular question that drug-taking hippies in New York and San Francisco asked. They would smoke and say, "This is Shiva *prasadam*." So Prabhupada strongly replied, "Shiva is not God. He is like the chief of police. He is a designated authority, not the Supreme Authority. Krishna is the Supreme Authority."

Another time we were walking across a field where there were some donkeys and horses. Kulashekar started loudly shouting, "Hare Krishna, Hare Krishna!" to draw the attention of the animals. Prabhupada said: "They don't have the ears to hear. They cannot appreciate you chanting at the top of your voice." Kulashekar said, "But Lord Chaitanya went through the Jarakhanda forest and chanted to all the animals." Prabhupada smiled and said, "Well, maybe if you chant loud enough, then they will hear something."

Sakshi Gopal: Prabhupada was walking around the lake at Bhakti-vedanta Manor when he saw a big mound of brambles, metals, and weeds. Prabhupada said, "This should be cleared." Over the next week it was cleared, and under it we found a stage. Later that summer, after it had been repaired, Srila Prabhupada sat there by the lakeside, looking at the lake. He said, "We should build an island and have a temple of Maha-Vishnu in the middle of the lake." He reminisced about his childhood and described some temples that he had seen which were surrounded by water. In the *ghats* they would have *kirtan* from boats. He said "You should also have *kirtan* in the boats around the lake temple." Of course, with the council being as restrictive as it is, we couldn't even get permission to put a fountain in the middle of the lake, what to speak of a temple.

Tribhuvanath: Once Prabhupada was taking *prasadam* in his room. Yamuna had cooked for him, and Malati was running up and down with fresh *puris*. I heard her shuffling up and down the stairs, and I was fascinated, so I popped my head around the corner, and there was Malati saying, "Prabhupada, how many *puris* can you eat?" She had brought a lot of puris while Prabhupada was respecting *prasadam*. Prabhupada's eyes got big, and he said, "More than you can make," and laughed. He seemed ecstatic.

Dhananjaya: After we left George Harrison's estate, we went to Mr. Prajapati's house. Prabhupada was supposed to take some milk and maybe some *halava* and *puri* there and then go back to Bury Place. When we got to Mr. Prajapati's house, many devotees were already there. Mr. Prajapati and his wife were very expert in serving *prasadam*. He asked Srila Prabhupada, "What would you like?" Prabhupada said, "A little milk." Mr. Prajapati said, "Would you like something with the milk?" Prabhupada said, "Have you prepared something?" He said, "Yes, *subji, puri,* and *halava*." Prabhupada said, "All right." Prabhupada liked to take *halava* and *puris* with his milk in the U.K. As Prabhupada was being served, they brought in other preparations as well. Prabhupada said, "What is this? This looks nice." He took a little bit and then someone else came with something else. Then someone else came with something else. All of a sudden there were fifteen or twenty different preparations in front of Prabhupada. Prabhupada said, "Oh! You have tricked me." Mr. Prajapati said, "Yes! What could we do? We felt so honored that you were coming to our house that we cooked a huge feast." Prabhupada said, "But, what about everyone else here?" Mr. Prajapati said, "We have cooked enough for everybody." Prabhupada said: "All right. Everybody else should eat too." At 11:00 at night we had a massive feast. The next morning we had to be up at 4:00 because Prabhupada wanted to have *darshan* of Radha-London Ishvara. After staying up late and eating so much it was difficult for us to get up.

Bhajahari: The next time Prabhupada visited, many devotees were going to the airport to meet him. I decided to stay at the temple to make sure that everything was nice for his arrival and to make a fruit offering for him. When Prabhupada arrived, he and all the devotees greeted the Deities and then went to his room. I came in quickly with a nice silver plate covered with different fruits. I offered the *prasadam*, the *bhoga* at that time, and paid my obeisances. As I was on the floor, Malati piped up, "Srila Prabhupada, Bhajahari has taken a wife since you were here last." I had been struggling for two years to remain a *brahmachari,* and I felt I had fallen down by getting married. I thought that getting married was a step backwards in spiritual life. So I was thinking, "Oh, give me a break, Malati." But she had said it with so much enthusiasm and joy that everyone said, "*Jaya!*" As I looked up, embarrassed, Srila Prabhupada was looking at me and smiling. He said, "That's all right; one wife, that is *brahmachari* life." Prabhupada was always encouraging.

Dhananjaya: I tried to concentrate on massaging Prabhupada's head, but Purushotam was coming in and out. Prabhupada was asking, "What is this? What is happening to Purushotam?" Purushotam was in charge of the television and was giving a running commentary of the moon landing. When the men were coming out of the spacecraft, Prabhupada asked Purushotam, "What do you see?" Purushotam said, "They have landed on the moon, and it looks like an arid and dusty area." Prabhupada said: "Oh! There are no buildings? There are no people? There are no gardens?" Purushotam said, "No Prabhupada. This is the moon." He was a little disturbed that Prabhupada didn't know what the moon looked like. Prabhupada concluded, "This is not the moon. According to Vedic astronomy the moon is an upper heavenly planet, with an advanced civilization, buildings, parks, and lakes. It's a beautiful place with many varieties of life. From what you are saying, my conclusion is that they have not landed on the moon." Purushotam took the side of the scientists and got into a heated discussion. At that moment Prabhupada asked me to come and sit in front of him, and he demonstrated to me how I should massage his head by massaging my head. Then I continued massaging, but Srila Prabhupada said, "You are still not getting it right." I said, "Srila Prabhupada, I promise I am not looking at the television. I am concentrating." Prabhupada chuckled and said, "That is all right." Also at that same moment Prabhupada looked through the crack in the door and saw that Malati had just put dirty milk bottles on the table with the offering for Prabhupada's Deities. She was putting something *muchi* (dirty) with something *suchi* (clean). So he was looking through the door, he was looking at the television, he was talking to Purushotam and he was concerned about my consciousness. He called Malati in an angry mood. Malati flew in through the door and paid her obeisances, "What has happened, Srila Prabhupada?" He said, "Can't you learn what I have taught you?" She was confused. She didn't know what she had done. When Prabhupada explained, she started to cry and then took the bottles away.

Tribhuvanath: Prabhupada greeted the Deities when he first arrived and said, "Be very careful. Do not become proud. You are dealing with Radha and Krishna. If you become proud, everything will be spoiled." Another time one guest asked Prabhupada, "Why does Krishna wear a peacock feather?" I thought that Prabhupada was going to give an esoteric reason, but in a simple way he said, "Because He likes to," On another occasion when he was sitting on the *vyasasana*, he said, "Krishna consciousness is so simple that you will miss it." I remember that because it is so simple and yet so deep.

Sakshi Gopal: Shyamasundar had arranged for a few clergymen to meet Srila Prabhupada. It was a sunny afternoon, so everyone went on the lawn, and Prabhupada sat on the grass. The clergymen were not accustomed to sit cross-legged, so they sat in chairs. A few nuns arrived, and when they joined the group they respectfully said to Prabhupada, "So you are the spiritual master of the Hare Krishna movement?" Prabhupada quietly replied, "No. I am a spiritual servant." He said it so softly that I don't know if they heard him. Prabhupada's vision of himself was very humble.

Dhananjaya: An Anglican nun wearing a nun's habit came to meet Srila Prabhupada. She kept her rosary just like a Catholic nun. Prabhupada asked her what prayer she chanted. She said, "My prayer is, 'My dear Lord Jesus Christ, please have mercy on me.' I say this with all sincerity on every bead before I do my work." Prabhupada said, "This is a very good prayer. You can go on praying like this, and certainly Lord Jesus Christ will bestow his mercy on you."

Tribhuvanath: We went to see the Indian Ambassador with Prabhupada. The temple was so poor at the time that we did not have a car. I asked the guests if anyone had a car we could use. A hippie said, "I have one Swami can use." It was a ridiculous-looking Beetle with flowers painted on it. I thought, "How could we put Prabhupada in this?" But we had no choice. Srila Prabhupada, Shyamasundar, and I got in, and this hippie drove to the Indian embassy. When we saw the Indian Ambassador, Prabhupada was relaxed and transcendental. He spoke about Rupa Goswami and gave the Ambassador *The Nectar of Devotion*. For about a half an hour, Prabhupada talked, and at the end of it that gentleman was purified. Prabhupada addressed the Ambassador by his first name, saying "Last time I was here you said 'Swamiji, whatever you want, I will do if I can.' Now I have one request." By that time they had such a nice relationship that the Ambassador could not refuse. Prabhupada had completely melted him. Prabhupada asked the Ambassador to contact Indira Gandhi and arrange for five-year missionary visas for his disciples in India. It fascinated and amazed me how Prabhupada softened him by talking about the Goswamis and the philosophy. There was no businesslike talk. Prabhupada was an ambassador from the Goswamis, and when he met the Indian Ambassador he did it on his grounds. He didn't do it on the Indian Ambassador's grounds. Prabhupada didn't behave like a diplomat or in anyway try to conform to a mundane idea of negotiations.

Bhajahari: One time in '73 or '74 Prabhupada was not well but still wanted to visit Radha-London Ishvara. I drove Prabhupada from the Manor to Bury Place, where many devotees were waiting for him. After greeting the Deities, Prabhupada sat on his *vyasasana* while Yogeshvar tried to sing a song about Radharani, "*Radhe jaya jaya madhava dayite.*" He got that far, and it was obvious that he didn't know any more words. Prabhupada took over and began to sing, "*Radhe jaya jaya madhava dayite,*" and we all tried to follow, but we didn't know it very well. Then Prabhupada chanted Hare Krishna. Afterwards he rose from the *vyasasana* to leave the temple, and the devotees cleared a path for him while I ducked out through the door first to put his slippers on. As I got out the small door, Prabhupada came into the door and playfully stood in the doorway. All the devotees were behind him chanting, dancing, and leaping in ecstasy in a blissful *kirtan*. Yogeshvar shouted, "Srila Prabhupada, you are Radharani's mercy personified." The devotees went "*Jaya!*" At that moment I was putting Srila Prabhupada's slippers on, and I looked up to see his reaction. As I looked up, Prabhupada looked down at me and said, "Radharani's mercy contaminated." I was the only one who heard that. I have spent the last twenty years meditating on Prabhupada's humility in saying that. But I also wonder if he was talking about me, since I was touching his feet and now, "I am Radharani's mercy contaminated." There are different ways to look at everything.

Dhananjaya: I was with Prabhupada when he spoke with a cardinal in Rome who was the bishop of Bombay and who had met the devotees in Bombay. The cardinal said to Prabhupada, "What you're doing and what we're doing is the same." Prabhupada said, "Yes, but we have our book, *Bhagavad-gita*," and he presented a copy to the cardinal. "You should read this because it will give you more understanding about how to surrender oneself to God." Once Srila Prabhupada commented to me, "The Italians are religious by nature, and they want the blessings of God, but they don't know how to get those blessings. We should teach them how to become qualified for the blessings of God. This is the most important ingredient that is missing within the Catholic teachings. It is hard to become qualified to receive God's blessings."

Tribhuvanath: That morning Prabhupada had a bit of breakfast and left about noontime by train for the program in Glasgow, but no one had provided lunch for him. From breakfast until the evening he didn't eat, but he didn't complain even once. Anyway, we got to the hall, which was packed with 400 to 500 people, and had a massive, ecstatic *kirtan*. We let anyone come in, and street kids were there, dancing like anything. Prabhupada encouraged them, as there was some rapport between them and Prabhupada. Most of the time we were trying to get these kids out, but Prabhupada didn't like us doing that. After the *kirtan* Prabhupada gave an amazing lecture from the *Bhagavad-gita* and then said, "Are there any questions?" An impersonalist stood up and in so many words said, "I am God, we're all God, it's all one." Prabhupada didn't speak. This guy was in the front of the audience, looking straight up at Prabhupada, and Prabhupada was looking straight at him. He carried on for some time and then finally ran out of words. Prabhupada looked very grave, but like a lion. There was complete silence. Prabhupada said, "You are not God, you are dog." He said it in such an amazing way that the guy practically fell back in shock. The audience stood up, clapped, cheered, and whistled as if someone had just scored a goal in the World Cup. It was an amazing reaction. Prabhupada was surprised at the reaction. The people completely backed him up.

After the program, Prabhupada and the devotees went to the back and, because we were so poor, had a feast of oranges. Prabhupada ate about ten oranges. When Prabhupada was leaving, he was intoxicated with ecstasy. He was staggering down the hall with a beam that was incredible. I had never seen Prabhupada like that before. I was holding the door, and there was only Prabhupada and me. His servant was behind. When Prabhupada got to the door he put both his hands on my head and started rubbing it in a very gentle way. I couldn't believe it. He said, "I am very pleased with what you have done. Now you preach Krishna consciousness all over Scotland." It was so beautiful that it's hard to put into words. It was one of those moments that are never repeated.

Bhajahari: Another time, before I was asked to be in charge of the Manor, I was trying to organize Bury Place. At that time Shyamasundar was having spiritual difficulties, at least from the external point of view. He wasn't coming to *mangal arati* or chanting his rounds. He was out in the evenings. The devotees were struggling to maintain themselves, because there wasn't much money, but Shyamasundar rented a car. There was some agitation about his behavior. Devotees were talking, but nobody would directly bring it to Srila Prabhupada's attention. Revatinandan Swami, a senior devotee, wanted to complain to Prabhupada about Shyamasundar, and he approached me saying, "You come with me to tell Prabhupada," because I agreed that Prabhupada should at least know what was going on. We went in, paid our obeisances, and within a minute or two Srila Prabhupada had understood our purpose. He looked at me in disgust. He was not happy that I had come to him to complain. He said, "You should not criticize senior Vaishnavs." Then, without talking to me anymore, he looked at Revatinandan Swami and said, "You tell him to leave," he didn't even want to tell me to leave himself. I practically crawled out on my stomach. I had gone there to complain about the GBC and Shyamasundar and his inappropriate behavior. I didn't know anything about Prabhupada's relationship with Shyamasundar. By complaining about one of Prabhupada's dear disciples I was being impertinent.

Dhananjaya: Through Jayapataka Maharaj we had all been invited to Sridhar Maharaj's Math in Navadwip, where a big program was arranged with talks by Prabhupada's godbrother Sridhar Maharaj and other Gaudiya Math *sannyasi* godbrothers, as well as *prasadam*. We were there for a few hours and then returned. Prabhupada was waiting at the gate. He said to Jayapataka Maharaj, "Where have you all been?" Jayapataka Maharaj said, "We went over to Sridhar Maharaj's Math for a program." Prabhupada said, "You didn't tell me." No one had informed Prabhupada about this program. Prabhupada was upset. He called Jayapataka Maharaj up to his room and told him, "This is not right. All the local Bengalis in Navadwip think that you foreigners have come due to the preaching effort of Sridhar Maharaj, but he never preached in the West. I preached in the West. All of you have come because of me, but he is getting the publicity." He said, "You have to be very careful in your dealings with my godbrothers. They will take advantage. They will take all the credit, but they don't deserve that credit."

Tribhuvanath: I was in the room with Prabhupada when he was about to shave. He had gotten soaped up, and Nanda Kumar was standing behind him with a towel. Prabhupada was trying to use the razor and was disturbed. He looked at Nanda Kumar, pointed to the razor, because Prabhupada had a razor with an adjustment dial on it, and said, "No dial?" Nanda Kumar said, "No, that is not your regular razor, Prabhupada. It doesn't have a dial." Prabhupada said, "It is Gillette?" Nanda Kumar said, "No, it is not Gillette." In a wonderful, unbelievable way, Prabhupada said, "Simply bogus." He rejected that razor like he'd reject Mayavadi philosophy. The razor sort of floated to the shelf. I was fascinated by the way Prabhupada was so angelic.

Dhananjaya: Prabhupada looked at the Roman wall and some other Roman ruins and commented, "The Vedic civilization spread to Rome. This Roman style of architecture is found in the Vedic civilization."

It was also in Rome that Srila Prabhupada asked for a book to be written entitled *How Krishna Consciousness Can Solve All the Problems of the World.* Every morning he would ask us to bring all sorts of problems to him, and he would solve them through Krishna consciousness. In '74, there was an oil embargo going on. Prabhupada said that this could be solved very easily if people stopped using motorcars and instead went by foot, horse, or bullock-cart. He said, "In human society the normal way to travel is by foot, horse, bullock-cart, camel, or elephant. Those modes of transport have been around since time immemorial. Only in Kali-yuga do we have motorcars, and this motorcar society will not last very long. When the petrol dries up, what use are your motorcars?"

He also said, "I never intended the temples to be for household-ers. Temples are meant for *brahmacharis* and *sannyasis.* Household-ers are meant to live outside and work outside the temple." He told me, "I will give you a house to live in, and while you're there you should work." So, Srila Prabhupada had me and my family live in the Taporia house, which is now the Goshala, and with his personal attention the *mukut* business started in Vrindavan.

Prabhupada wanted me to manufacture not only Deity crowns and dresses but Gaura-Nitai Deities also. He even took me to Aligar because so much brass-making goes on there, especially the unfinished casting of Deities. He said, "The way we can spread the cultural aspect of Krishna consciousness is through Gaura-Nitai worship. Gaura-Nitai Deities should be sold as *sankirtan* paraphernalia, as Hare Krishna dolls, along with our books. People throughout the world keep many different kinds of dolls: Russian dolls, Spanish dolls, Mexican dolls, French dolls, Dutch dolls, and they can also keep Hare Krishna dolls."

Prabhupada said, "When a devotee sells a book he can say, 'By the way, we've got these Hare Krishna dolls. Why don't you take Them home as well?' The person in the street will say, 'What are these things?' 'Well, these are special dolls. If you look after Them nicely, They will fulfill all of your desires.' So the person takes Them, whatever the price, and puts Them in his display cabinet or on his shelf. He himself may not be particularly interested to know how to fulfill all his desires, but when his family members see these dolls they will ask, 'What are these little brass guys? Who are They?' 'Oh, these are Hare Krishna dolls, and I was told that if I look after Them nicely, They will fulfill all my desires.'"

Prabhupada continued, "Eventually at least one member of the family will want to know how to fulfill all their desires, 'What do I do?' The only place he can go is back to the devotees. The devotees will then teach him how to offer a little fruit, a flower, and some water with love and devotion. Later on, as they get more devotional, they can also be introduced to *arati* paraphernalia and then changing the dresses and so on. He said, "Gaura-Nitai are so merciful They can enter into the home of the meat eater and not take offense. We're distributing the book Bhagavat, and you can also distribute the person Bhagavat. We have 120 temples. If every temple takes a minimum ten pairs of these Hare Krishna dolls a month, that is 1,200 pairs of Gaura-Nitai Deities every month. That is good business. Learn how to do this. Push it like anything." Another one of

Srila Prabhupada's big visions was to distribute Gaura-Nitai Deities on a massive scale.

Bhajahari: Prabhupada was always trying to give Krishna to others, whether it was in the form of a sweet, some dialogue, his books, the Deities, or his disciples' association. He was always trying to create a situation where people would advance in Krishna consciousness. Even if people thought they were happy, he could see beyond that and was constantly aware of their suffering. He understood everything. He knew the only business in life was to give Krishna consciousness to others, and I like to think that he instilled a little of that in me. On that morning walk he said, "We are their good fortune," in other words, you and I can also give Krishna consciousness to people. After all, Prabhupada didn't say, "I am their good fortune. I have come from India to give this knowledge." No, "We are their good fortune." That is also Prabhupada's humility and compassion. His was the greatest compassion.

TAPE 10

Kanchanbala dasi
Nalini Kanta das
Sureshvar das
Adya das
Madhusudana das
Giriraj Swami
Tirtharti das
Vitthaleshvar das
Vamanajan das
Tamal Krishna Goswami
Madhudvisa das
Gohita das
Mulaprakriti dasi
Urvasi dasi
Ksudi dasi
Krishna Prema das
Chaitanya Chandra das

 **Kanchanbala:** When I first started going to the temple I had just turned 16 and was still in high school. I was interested right away and wanted to know more and more about Swamiji (that's how we addressed Srila Prabhupada in those days). I also wanted to tell Srila Prabhupada everything I did. I told him that I was living at home (far from the temple) and that my mother wouldn't let me

go to the temple. But I had an altar, and I offered *prasadam* and everything that I thought was beautiful to Krishna. I was into natural, earthy things, so I put cattails, moss, and bark on my altar. I wrote Srila Prabhupada a six-page letter telling him everything I was doing. I wanted to be totally honest, to lay it all out to him exactly: how I went out to school, did my homework, chanted on the subway, and so forth. He wrote back accepting everything I was doing, saying, "My sincere blessings for you for your nice prosecution of Krishna consciousness. Whatever you are doing at the present moment is approved by me, and I think on account of your becoming a sincere soul, Krishna is dictating from within and you are doing things so nicely." It was so encouraging, especially as the years went by and I gradually realized the standard of devotional service and Deity worship in the temples Prabhupada established. I remember one devotee asked Srila Prabhupada, "Have you told us all the rules and regulations?" Prabhupada said, "If I told you everything, you'd faint." He clearly gave us much room to toddle along.

 **Nalini Kanta:** My wife and I hitchhiked from the East Coast to Berkeley, because the devotees in Philadelphia had told us about the great Ratha-yatra Festival in San Francisco and that if we went we could meet His Divine Grace. At the time I was a guitar-carrying folk musician who wore a fringe leather jacket. I wrote to Prabhupada regularly, telling him who I was and sending him the lyrics to the songs I was writing. Every few months in Berkeley a letter would come with "His Divine Grace Tridandi Goswami A.C. Bhaktivedanta Swami" letterhead. One day such a letter came and all the devotees gathered around. Jayananda, the temple president, opened it while the devotees eagerly asked, "Who's it for, who's it for?" Jayananda read it and said, "Oh, it's for that guy Tom who lives up the block." I learned from this experience that His Divine Grace did not discriminate. He reciprocated with whoever came to him.

Sureshvar: I was initiated in Detroit in 1971. Being initiated by Srila Prabhupada was such an awesome experience that I was completely stunned at the initiation. The system was that strands of beads were draped on the microphone. Prabhupada chanted one round on each of those beads, and then the initiate would be called to come forward. So, Prabhupada chanted on the beads that were to become mine, and my name was called, "Richard Hall." I staggered up and knelt in front of him. Now, when you looked at Srila Prabhupada you were looking at a person who was unfathomable. It was like looking at the ocean, the ocean of truth. At the same time he was looking right through you. It was an incredible experience.

He asked me the four rules. I answered. He said, "Your name is Sureshvar das. It is a name for Lord Brahma. It means controller of the demigods. You are a servant of the controller." As he said this, I got more and more stupefied, and he saw that I was stunned. He had the beads in his hand, so he just held out the beads and said, "Come on, take your beads," and started rattling them in front of my nose.

Adya: My wife and I loved cooking all the time in the kitchen in the Manhattan temple. Once Prabhupada was due to arrive the next day, and we were told to make a skirt for Prabhupada's Tulasi devi, but my wife didn't know how to sew. We had an assignment we couldn't do, but we tried. My wife stayed up the whole night making that *tulasi* skirt. In the morning we brought the *tulasi* skirt, and the devotee said, "Oh, this is a terrible job. How could you do this? Don't you have any sense?" We were brokenhearted. My wife started crying, and I was hurt, but we put the skirt on Tulasi devi anyway. When Prabhupada finally walked into the room the first statement he made was, "What a beautiful *tulasi* skirt." We started crying again but this time out of great pleasure. Prabhupada's statement made

us realize that we just met a pure representative of the Supreme
Personality of Godhead.

Madhusudana: I had been involved in drug-taking,
and my parents thought the Hare Krishna movement
was another drug-taking cult. When they met Prabhupada he convinced them that wasn't the case. After
that, Prabhupada would often ask me how my parents
were, and once he said, "You are the father of your father. The father
means one who gives birth to life and you are giving birth to spiritual
life. So actually, you are the real father."

Giriraj Swami: Srila Prabhupada was on a morning
walk with many different types of people, including
many devotees. Svarup Damodar Prabhu was there,
and Srila Prabhupada discussed scientific matters
with him. By chance, my mother and father had come
to visit and were also there. Srila Prabhupada said to my mother,
who was approaching 60 at the time, "Oh, Mrs. Teton, you look so
young." She was really pleased.

At the end of the walk we came to the parked cars. At the time,
Srila Prabhupada was using a Rolls Royce, and he may have noticed
that my father was looking at his car. Very shyly and humbly Srila
Prabhupada looked down and said to my father, "My disciples have
gotten this for me." My father immediately said, "Oh, no, no, you
deserve it. You deserve it." Then again, dealing very expertly, Srila
Prabhupada said to my father, "So you can come with me. We can
ride back together in the car." My father said, "No, you go with the
other disciples." Afterwards, Hari Sauri, who was Srila Prabhupada's servant, said to Srila Prabhupada, "Srila Prabhupada, everyone loves you so much." Srila Prabhupada said, "Yes, because I love
everyone."

 **Tirtharti:** I was really hankering for Srila Prabhupada's personal association. I was desperate. It seemed that so many devotees were getting his personal association and that I was a nobody, a new devotee. Somehow I conned my way into a morning walk on Venice Beach. I was nervous and scared. I was walking on Srila Prabhupada's right, and he was talking about the waves and the ocean. One wave came up high and almost touched Srila Prabhupada's feet. I jumped up on the embankment and Prabhupada saw that the wave was going to wet his feet. He put his hand out to me and I helped him up the embankment. That was it for me. I actually touched Prabhupada and helped him up the embankment. But I started to feel my oats. I started getting puffed up, and I thought, "I'm gonna ask him a question. I am actually going to come right out and ask him a question." My heart's desire was to get Srila Prabhupada's recognition, not his answer to my question. I can't remember the exact question, but I asked something about Tulasi devi. Srila Prabhupada turned to me and said, "Why are you asking me this question?" I stuttered and said, "Well I am worshiping Tulasi devi, Srila Prabhupada . . ." He repeated, "Why are you asking me this question?" I lost it that time. I shut up and turned every color of the rainbow. Then he answered my question. In all his mercy, Prabhupada answered my question.

Sureshvar: It was in Miami Beach in 1975 that I got a chance to go on a morning walk with Prabhupada. There were about a dozen of us. As we walked along the shore, with Prabhupada leading the pack, I noticed how his cane put holes in the sand. When someone asked a question, he would stop and turn to answer. At one point in the walk I was right behind Prabhupada. Somebody asked a question. I don't know what the question was or how Prabhupada answered, because all I could think was "Wow! I am right in back of Prabhupada's head." I studied his head. It was golden with silver hairs and furrows in the back of his neck. Then Krishna gave me a wonderful realization. I was close to Prabhupada physically, but spiritually I was millions of miles away. That was too bad but true, and it was also enlivening because I realized that what the devotees had told me all these years was also true, that "real association is not physical, it's vibration, *vani*." I became happy that I had the opportunity to become intimate with Prabhupada through his vibration, through *vani*.

 **Vitthaleshvar:** The temple president, Rabindra Svarup prabhu, invited an Indian professor of Hinduism and philosophy to meet Prabhupada in Prabhupada's quarters. The professor came with several students. He and Prabhupada were introduced, and Prabhupada looked straight at him and said, "What is Hinduism?" The professor said, "I don't know, you tell me," perhaps thinking that he would be at an advantage if Prabhupada spoke first. His idea was to try to defeat Prabhupada and impress his students. Prabhupada looked at Bhakti Svarup Damodar Goswami and said, "He is teaching, but he does not know. What is that called?" Bhakti Svarup Damodar Goswami said, "He's a cheater, Prabhupada." Prabhupada pointed to Bhakti Svarup Damodar Goswami, looked at the professor and said, "He has called you a cheater. What do you have to say for yourself?" The professor tried to talk about something else, but Prabhupada stayed on that point. Somehow or other it went back and forth until the professor actually admitted that he was a cheater. He was so crazy he said, "But I am an honest cheater."

At one point in the conversation Prabhupada talked about surrendering to a spiritual master, "*tad viddhi pranipatena pariprasnena sevaya*." The professor didn't agree with Prabhupada's translation of the Sanskrit words. He said, "No, no, no. I don't accept that meaning. I want the—" Prabhupada said, "You don't know what the word 'surrender' means," and asked a devotee to read the dictionary definition for the professor. Prabhupada said, "He doesn't know what surrender means, and yet he is a professor."

The professor said, "I want the Sanskrit etymological meaning." Prabhupada pointed to the door and said, "Get out. You don't want a spiritual master. You want a Sanskrit teacher. Get out." The conversation went back and forth a little more, and finally Prabhupada smiled, put his head on his elbow, turned sideways, and, indicating the professor, said to all of us, "He's a madman." Everybody in the room cracked up in laughter, including the students who had come with the professor.

At one point in the conversation the professor got a little offensive. Brahmananda was in a room down the hall and could hear what was going on. All of a sudden, boom, boom, boom, the door flew open, and there was 300-and-some-pound Brahmananda with just a *lungi* on. "Excuse me, sir, you will have to come with me. Now!" The professor started trembling and saying, "I have said something? Have I offended you?" Brahmananda said, "Before you do, sir, come along." Afterwards Rabindra Svarup apologized to Prabhupada, "I had no idea he would act in such a horrible way. Please forgive me, Prabhupada." Prabhupada laughed and said, "That's okay, at least he was chastised."

Vamanajana: My wife and I ran a little store across the street called the Surabhi Store. We would arrange for Srila Prabhupada's afternoon refreshment of *dab* (fresh coconut). The last year that Prabhupada was here in Los Angeles, the GBC came to me and two others and asked if we would like to be Srila Prabhupada's bodyguards. He thought the three of us should split up the 24-hour watch. About the middle of the second week we were doing this, and my good friend Bhaskara, who was one of the other bogyguards, and I were having lunch, and he said, "Did you notice that Srila Prabhupada does the same thing at the same time every day?" I said, "Yeah, it's amazing. You can almost set your watch by him." Bhaskara said, "Someone gave him a brand new pair of slippers the other day, and he only wears them from his room to the curtains outside the temple room, and then he takes them off. After class, he puts them on, wears them to go upstairs, and takes them off at his door." I said, "Yeah?" He said, "They're new, and I looked at them last night and got the model number and the manufacturer's name and bought another pair exactly like them." "Well, what are you going to do with them? His feet are not the same size as your feet." Bhaskara said, "Tomorrow morning when he goes down for class, I am going to exchange them for my slippers, and then he will wear my slippers back upstairs. Then I will exchange them again, and I will have a pair of slippers that Srila Prabhupada wore. He will have only worn them one time, but Srila Prabhupada will have worn my slippers!"

I thought, "Wow, that's a good idea! Tomorrow I am going to go out and buy a pair of slippers and do the same thing the next day." The next day we got together at lunch again. I said, "Did you get your slippers?" He said, "Yeah." I said, "Where do I buy mine?" He said, "You shouldn't do it." I thought, "Yeah, you got your slippers." He said, "Let me tell you what happened. Srila Prabhupada put his slippers on in the morning, came downstairs, took them off by the curtain by the temple room, and I exchanged them. After class Srila Prabhupada came out, put on my slippers and wore them upstairs right into his room. He never took them off at the door." I said, "Really? What did you do?" He said, "I stood there chanting *japa* thinking, 'What am I gonna do now?' I was there about five minutes when a *sannyasi* came and asked, 'Is your name Bhaskara?' 'Yes.' The *sannyasi* said, 'Srila Prabhupada has a message for you. He thanks you very much for the new slippers. You may keep the old slippers. But most importantly, he said, it's not nice to play tricks on the spiritual master.'"

 **Tamal Krishna Goswami:** Prabhupada was in New Delhi when he heard from Tusta Krishna about what was to become Hare Krishna Land in Juhu. Tusta Krishna had made friends with one Mr. Nair, the owner of this land and the owner of *Free Press Journal*.

Prabhupada negotiated with Mr. Nair, and after a long time we signed a sales agreement. However, Mr. Nair had no plan to fulfill the agreement. We could not sign the conveyance, the final document to change the title of the property. A long, long period ensued during which Mr. Nair tried to remove the devotees from the land, and the devotees fought many heroic battles. Prabhupada had installed Radha-Rasa-Bihari at the Bombay *pandal* program, and those Deities were presiding at Hare Krishna Land. Prabhupada prayed to Them, "My dear Lord, I request You to sit down here." He promised Them, "I will arrange everything for You, but don't leave." Wherever Prabhupada was in the world, this battle with Mr. Nair was constantly on his mind. At one point, our temporary temple on the property was demolished. Prabhupada commented that our struggle was like the Kurukshetra battle.

Once we were staying at the house of the wealthiest man in Hyderabad, Mr. Panilal Piti, when Prabhupada arranged for Mr. Nair to meet him there. Mr. Nair felt that Prabhupada had some mystic power and would put some spell on him and take the land from him, so he brought his pseudo guru with him for protection. After a big dinner, Prabhupada was yawning. Mr. Nair and his guru immediately said, "Swamiji, I think that you must be getting tired. We should let you rest." Prabhupada said, "I am very tired," and he retired. Immediately Mr. Nair and his guru went to sleep in the next room. After about five minutes Prabhupada called me into his room. Although Prabhupada always slept after eating, Prabhupada wasn't sleeping at all. He said, "What are they doing?" I said, "They're sleeping." He said, "Go in there and wake up Mr. Nair, but don't wake up his guru." I went in, shook Mr. Nair's arm and told him, "Prabhupada wants to see you, *shhhhhhh,*" indicating that he shouldn't wake up his guru. Prabhupada preached to Mr. Nair, who sat listening and listening. Gradually Prabhupada got him to agree to sign the agreement all over again. He told Shyamasundar and me to immediately type the whole agreement. We typed it out on the old typewriter Prabhupada had, and Prabhupada got it signed. By that time, his guru got up and came in. Mr. Nair had signed away the land again. Mr. Nair kept hitting his head, asking, "What have I done? What have I done?" Prabhupada said, "It's okay." It was done.

Prabhupada had Shyamasundar and me to accompany Mr. Nair back to Bombay. As it turned out, our lawyers were working in cahoots with Mr. Nair and Mr. Nair's lawyers. Within a period of ten days, they convinced Shyamasundar and me that it was the greatest blunder to go ahead with this contract. We canceled the contract. We let it run out without fulfilling it. This was our fatal blunder.

Prabhupada was in Pune, and I called him up to tell him the good news, "Srila Prabhupada, I wanted to tell you." He said, "What has happened? Did everything go through?" I said, "No, Srila Prabhupada. We cancelled the contract." All I heard was "click." Prabhupada hung up the phone. Prabhupada came to Bombay, and for about the next two months, he would have one or another of us parade into his room, and he would say, "This foolish boy," showing his guest the contract, "he cancelled the contract." It was a huge blunder on our part.

There were many more such blunders, but Prabhupada's wonderful quality through them all was that he never gave up on his disciples. No matter how many mistakes a devotee might make, Prabhupada would see if that person wanted to continue to serve Krishna and to serve him; he would stand by that devotee. In the instance of the contract cancellation, Prabhupada did not reject me. He gave Giriraj Maharaj and me the opportunity to go through a hellish year and a half regularly going to Bombay, sitting in lawyers' chambers, trying to rectify the situation.

One of Srila Prabhupada's symptoms was that he never gave up on a devotee. He said about Krishna, "When you sincerely chant Hare Krishna, even one time, He will never leave you alone." I feel the same way about Prabhupada. He also never left you alone even if you made many mistakes in his service. He did not reject you, he accepted you just as the parent accepts the child. Prabhupada knew

that there would be mistakes, and he would chastise you like anything, but he never gave you the sense that he didn't love you.
Despite all of the grand mistakes that were made, I never got the
sense that Prabhupada loved me less because of them. I always felt
encouraged, not discouraged, despite our many mistakes.

 **Madhudvisa:** Prabhupada said, "Any questions?"
Immediately, many hands shot up. There were a lot of
questions. One man, who wanted to hear himself talk
more than he wanted to ask Prabhupada a question,
stood up and warmly said, "Your Divine Grace, how
are you enjoying your stay in Australia?" Prabhupada said, "I like it
very much." Everybody clapped. "Yeah!" Prabhupada said, "I like
every place very much." Everybody went, "Umm!" Prabhupada
said, "Because everything belongs to Krishna, therefore I like every
place."

The next person asked, "What do you think about Sai Baba?"
Prabhupada said, "Who is he?" Prabhupada's technique was to
diffuse a person like that. There were a couple of other questions,
and then a puffed-up young man, 22 or 23 years old, said, "Today,
I choose to be God. Today I choose to take the responsibility of the
whole universe upon myself; therefore I am God."

When Prabhupada got mad, his lower lip would quiver a little.
When he heard this young man, his lip began to quiver. Prabhupada
took a deep breath and said, "My God is powerful." The man said,
"I choose to be the all-powerful God." Prabhupada said, "I choose
to kick your face with shoes. Can you stop me?" The man said, "Give
me some time." Prabhupada said, "My God is powerful all the time.
Why should I accept you as God?" The whole auditorium burst
into laughter, and that man was mortified. Prabhupada said to him,
"Please, don't waste your time on this nonsense. Try to be god-
ly, don't try to be God." In this way Prabhupada immediately
changed from a ferocious lion to a soft, beautiful rose. This was
Srila Prabhupada's quality. He would use very harsh language. He

would deal very strongly when something was offensive to Krishna, but at the same time, he saw in everyone an opportunity for him to extend Krishna's loving, tender hand. Prabhupada's vision was that his spiritual master had sent everybody that he came in contact with, and his service was to bring them back to home, back to Godhead.

Sureshvar: In September of 1972, Srila Prabhupada flew to Dallas to install Sri Sri Radha Kalachandji. He arrived at Love Field via American Airlines. We ushered him into the VIP room, where he sat on a makeshift dais and immediately started talking about the three ways to fly. He said, "There are three ways to fly." Reporters were jotting down, "Three ways to fly." Prabhupada continued, "Pigeon." (He didn't say "Swan," he said "Pigeon.") "Pigeon, mantra, and machine. Formerly, people knew the art of training pigeons and could get on the pigeons and fly." I was standing next to a woman reporter and looking at her pad as she wrote, "Pigeon." Then he said, "Mantra. Simply by vibrating mantras, the yogi knew how to ride on the sound." She and the other reporters wrote down, "Mantra, machine." Then a lady asked, "Swami, if you know all these different ways to fly, why did you choose to fly American Airlines today?" Prabhupada said, "To be one with you." The lady turned to me and said, "I like that man!"

Giriraj Swami: Srila Prabhupada said that he was good friends with Doctor Mishra, who had a yoga camp in New York. When Doctor Mishra spoke Mayavad philosophy, Srila Prabhupada protested vehemently and argued, but on a personal level they were friends. Srila Prabhupada personally cooked for Doctor Mishra and nursed him back to life when he was sick. From this I understood that there's a difference between philosophy and one's personal dealings. On matters of philosophy, Srila Prabhupada strongly argued with him, but personally they were friends.

Gohita: Srila Prabhupada was in San Francisco for Ratha-yatra when a devotee who had an infamous *prasadam* distribution program in Laguna Beach gave Srila Prabhupada $30,000 cash. Srila Prabhupada knew how the person got the money, but he jokingly said, "Oh! So how did you get this money?" The devotee said, "Well Srila Prabhupada, I sell drugs." Srila Prabhupada said, "Oh! I used to sell drugs too. What pharmacy do you work for?"

Madhusudana: When I was 18 I was getting acne, and Srila Prabhupada asked me, "What is on your face?" I said, "They're pimples, Prabhupada." He said, "You should put a little *tilak* on them." So I put *tilak* spots on my face, but I was too embarrassed to walk on the streets with white dots on my face. The next time he saw me he asked me about my pimples again and why wasn't I using the *tilak*. I said, "I can't walk around like that, it's just too . . ." He said, "Take a little olive oil and boric acid and heat them in a spoon over the fire. Put that ointment on." Sure enough that combination produced a salve that looked just like any ointment. That was his personal, caring side.

Mulaprakriti: I was in Honolulu on my way to Japan to distribute books. Srila Prabhupada was also in Honolulu at that time, and he asked me to come to his quarters to talk about book distribution. I had the wonderful experience of being alone with Srila Prabhupada. He was sitting on his chair asking all sorts of questions about how people liked the books, what kind of people were taking the books, and what I told the people. He was so joyful that it seemed as if it were Srila Prabhupada's favorite topic. When he asked, "What kind of people take the books?" I strained my mind to answer and said, "Doctors, young people, and diplomats." Prabhupada said, "Diplomats? From what countries?" So I gave a list of the nationalities of anyone who had ever taken a book. Then I said,

"Someone from Albania took a book." Prabhupada said, "Albania. That's behind the iron curtain." I said, "Yes Prabhupada, they take them in their suitcase and because they have diplomatic immunity, no one can open the suitcase." He laughed, leaned back, and said, "Ahh! We cannot go, but Lord Chaitanya can go."

Nalini Kanta: When Srila Prabhupada was staying in his quarters in Los Angeles he was working very hard on his books. Every morning after *mangal arati,* announcements would be made, "Please don't bother Srila Prabhupada. Everyone wants to talk to him, but he is very busy. Only GBCs and *sannyasis* should have Srila Prabhupada's *darshan.*" I didn't accept that philosophy. I made an agreement with Raksana, Prabhupada's bodyguard, to let me upstairs one night at about 9:30, after all the big guns had met with Prabhupada and left. It was very late, and I was afraid. I was a small temple president with a $50 donation to give Prabhupada. Raksana made sure that everybody was gone. He talked to Srutakirti, and Srutakirti walked me upstairs and into Prabhupada's room.

At that time Prabhupada was standing, looking out the window with his back to the door, chanting *japa* softly. Srutakirti said, "Prabhupada, your disciple from Phoenix, Arizona has come here to see you." Srila Prabhupada turned around slowly. I was shaking in my boots because I was thinking, "Why are you bothering Prabhupada? He is busy, and you're a nobody in this Society." But Srila Prabhupada had a radiant smile on his face. The emanation of love from his heart was such that he made me feel like I was his long-lost son who had come back to see him. It was a personal, loving exchange that had nothing to do with fear or "What have you done for me?" or "You're a big devotee," or "You're a small devotee." It was the spiritual master showing his loving feeling for his disciple. I will never forget that.

Giriraj Swami: During the struggle to get Hare Krishna Land in Juhu, we did not have proper accommodations for Srila Prabhupada. Each time he came we arranged a different place for him to stay. Once he stayed with of one of our good friends and life members, Mr. Seti, who was building a house in the Juhu scheme. Although the house was not completed, Mr. Seti invited Srila Prabhupada to stay in an upstairs room. One day Srila Prabhupada was there talking with some respectable persons when suddenly a poor Indian laborer appeared at the doorway of the room. He was dark-complexioned and wearing only a little cloth around his waist. He walked right past the respectable persons and put some flowers on Srila Prabhupada's table. Then he put his head down in obeisances, stood up, and walked out. At first Srila Prabhupada was completely stunned and silent. He was so moved by this offering that he couldn't think about anything else for minutes. Finally he said, "Just see how he has come with devotion," and he quoted the verse, "*patram pushpam phalam toyam, yo me bhaktya prayacchati*. If one offers Me with love and devotion a leaf, a flower, fruit, or water, I will accept it." Srila Prabhupada said, "He offered some flowers with devotion, and how much I have been affected. Just imagine the greatness of Krishna. I am an ordinary living entity. Krishna's the Supreme Personality of Godhead, but even if Krishna is offered just a leaf or a flower with love and devotion, He will accept it. So how great is Krishna?"

Mulaprakriti: Srila Prabhupada gave me instructions about distributing books. First he asked, "What do you say?" I explained, "We tell the person, 'Oh you look like a spiritual person. This is a book from ancient India. It has so much knowledge.'" Srila Prabhupada pulled out the *Srimad-Bhagavatam* and slowly and carefully read the verse, "This *Bhagavat Purana* is as brilliant as the sun . . ." He said, "This verse is so wonderful, if you just tell people this verse how can they resist? You don't need to say anything. The *Srimad Bhagavatam* will sell itself."

He also talked about women. He said that in this age it was actually a benefit to be a woman. He said that, "In Kali-yuga, things are so degraded that people don't trust men. Hardly anybody will allow a man to come up to them or will open their door if a man knocks." He said that when he was a young man, a company was selling Brahmi Hair Oil and sent respectable young women door to door. Everybody opened their door and bought Brahmi Hair Oil. Prabhupada said, "It was never even proven that Brahmi Hair Oil had any medicinal properties." He explained that "Lord Chaitanya is sending nice young women to help the poor conditioned souls go back to Godhead. This is His plan."

 **Urvasi:** I was in the Chicago temple when Srila Pra- bhupada visited. That was the time of that very fa- mous, controversial press conference about the 64- ounce brain and the 32-ounce brain. When Prabhu- pada was at the airport about to leave, he saw one of the *mataji's* distributing big books, and with a huge smile he said, "My women disciples have a 64-ounce brain."

Tirtharti: I was with a devotee named Brahma Rupa, and both of us were hankering for Prabhupada's association. Once, Brahma Rupa had a bright idea. He got a pail full of flower petals to shower Srila Prabhupada when he came out the door. But Brahma Rupa was so nervous that he made the petals into a ball and hit Prabhupada on the head with that ball. I thought, "There goes Brahma Rupa's spiritual life. That's it for him." But Prabhupada just folded his hands. We said, "*Jaya*, Srila Prabhupada!" It was wonderful.

 **Ksudi:** On March 2, 1972, after Srila Prabhupada had laid the cornerstone for Mayapur, we went into his room, and I said, "Srila Prabhupada, I am going to Africa now. I hope this gives me an opportunity to increase my service to you." Srila Prabhupada said, "Service to Lord Chaitanya, service to Lord Chaitanya, service to Lord Chaitanya."

When I was in Africa alone because the other devotees had left, Srila Prabhupada wrote me, "I am very pleased at the responsibility you've taken to spread Krishna consciousness in South Africa at such a young age." It made me feel connected to Prabhupada and the Movement even though I was two miles from any neighbors and 2,000 miles from any devotees. Prabhupada also said, "I am praying that you will have the strength and enthusiasm to carry on this mission." Somehow or other I had that, even though I was nineteen years old and alone. Today my prayer is, "Please, Prabhupada, pray to Krishna that I may have the strength and enthusiasm to carry out whatever my mission is."

 **Krishna Prema:** I was born and raised in New Dwarka, and I remember my mother bringing me to the front of the temple during *gurupuja*. I remember seeing an old, wise man and feeling the awe and reverence that everybody treated him with. I was not quite scared, and I was not quite happy. My mother pushed me forward, so I went up to the *vyasasana* and said, "Can I have cookie?" Srila Prabhupada took a cookie off the plate and handed it down to me with a smile. All of a sudden I thought, "This guy is okay, he's given me a cookie."

Tamal Krishna Goswami: Prabhupada had a disciple named Chaita Guru, who was a Sikh by birth. Chaita Guru used to drive Giriraj Swami and me around Bombay to make Life Members and collect money to build the Vrindavan temple. After a while, this devotee thought that he should make his own way in spiritual life. He started canvassing Life Members and collecting donations on his own. I approached Prabhupada saying, "We have to write something to our Members to warn them about this person." Prabhupada hesitated. He was not ready to give up on this devotee. But when Chaita Guru started living with a *bhogi* yogi on Juhu beach to learn the art of passing a coin into one ear and out the other ear, I said, "Prabhupada, now it's reached the limit. It's the end. It's finished."

Prabhupada looked at me and said, "You do not know about Lord Nityananda's mercy." I said, "Why Srila Prabhupada?" He said, "Because there is no limit to Lord Nityananda's mercy and compassion, no end to His forgiveness." Later on, sure enough, that devotee came back, and Prabhupada tried to help him. He gave this person *sannyas*. Chaita Guru eventually left, but I met him a year ago and he is still on some type of spiritual path.

Srila Prabhupada is the manifest representative of Lord Nityananda Prabhu. His forgiveness is like Lord Nityananda's. In terms of dealing with our own shortcomings and in terms of dealing with each other, we have to always remember that there are very few instances in the history of ISKCON when Prabhupada rejected a devotee. It was very, very, very, very rare.

Giriraj Swami: One of Srila Prabhupada's first disciples was in Calcutta and had started to smoke *ganja* again. When Srila Prabhupada was told about this, he said, "Tell him that if he does not give up this bad habit of smoking, I will reject him." One of the devotees asked Srila Prabhupada, "Is that true, that if he doesn't give up smoking *ganja* you will reject him?" Srila Prabhupada said, "No. I cannot reject any disciple. I only said that to encourage him to stop smoking."

Chaitanya Chandra: I came to the L.A. temple in 1982 and was not fortunate enough to have Srila Prabhupada's association. My service was with ITV four days a week and book distribution on the weekends. One of my ITV responsibilities was duplicating tapes for distribution. Many times I duplicated *Your Ever Well-Wisher*, so I repeatedly saw Prabhupada, observed his nuances, and heard the tenor of his voice. At that time I'd read *Bhagavad-gita*, *Srimad-Bhagavatam*, and some of Prabhupada's biography. Once we were distributing copies of his biography on *sankirtan*, and I was explaining to someone what the book was about, how Prabhupada

came to America and many other things. The combination of having
seen Prabhupada many times on film, having read his books, and
having been exposed to his biography was so meaningful to me that
at one point this person interrupted me and said "So when did you
meet him?" And it hit me like a hammer that I never had. I forgot
that I had never met Prabhupada. To me, that speaks of his purity
and potency.

I am touched when I hear anyone's association with Srila
Prabhupada. For those of us who have never met him, but still feel
connected to him, these words are truly nectar because through
them we can experience him. No one should take this lightly. I think
that those who have met Srila Prabhupada have been very, very
blessed. For those of us who've not been so fortunate and who are
eternally envious of those who have met him, sharing those experiences with Prabhupada is a great responsibility. I hope everyone
will continue to share his or her mercy with us.

TAPE 11

Tamal Krishna Goswami
Kaushalya dasi
Revatinandan das

 **Tamal Krishna Goswami:** The devotees invited me to a *darshan* where I heard Prabhupada beautifully sing the Chintamani prayers. Afterwards he asked if anyone had any questions, and I raised my hand. At that time America was at war with Vietnam, and at our age the draft board was a problem. I was very concerned about whether or not I would be drafted, and so I asked Prabhupada to describe what the spiritual world was like. He looked at me and said, "In the spiritual world, there are no draft boards." Then he told a story. He said, "There was once a Christian minister who was preaching in England to coal miners. He said that the hell that awaited someone if they didn't accept the shelter of Jesus was a terrible place, dark, dank, cold, and wet. He said, "No one would want to go there," but all of the coal miners were thinking, "Well, if that's hell, where are we? We're already in hell. It doesn't sound very fearful to us. That's where we live now, we're coal miners." The minister was trying to think of a way to convince them to worship Jesus, and finally he said, "In hell, there are no newspapers and there is no tea." Then they all said, "Oh, then we must worship Jesus." Prabhupada said, "So in the spiritual world, there are no draft boards. Is that all right?" I said, "Yes," and everybody said, "*Jaya!*"

Kaushalya: The first time I met Prabhupada was in 1969. I was a sixteen year-old hippie living on the beach in Hawaii, meditating, reading the *Bhagavad-gita*, and trying to understand the meaning of life. One day as I was sitting meditating, a flyer flew by which said, "A.C. Bhaktivedanta Swami speaking on the *Bhagavad-gita* at Sunset Point." I thought, "This is amazing. I can hear an actual Indian swami talk about *Bhagavad-gita,* the book I have been studying for two years."

At the lecture Prabhupada sat on a slightly raised platform covered with a beautiful Indian rug, talking about how a bona fide spiritual master explains *Bhagavad-gita* as it is, without misinterpreting it, and how we must read such a *Bhagavad-gita*. There were only five or six devotees present. He finished talking and asked for questions. I said, "Swamiji, I've been reading this *Bhagavad-gita,*" and handed him mine. I said, "Is this one okay?" He said, "Come back to the temple and we'll talk." So I got in the back of an open, flatbed-type truck with a couple of devotees. Prabhupada was in the front with a couple of other people, and I was watching his head the whole time because it was a beautiful, bald head and it was bobbing with the motion of the truck. As he walked up the stairs to the temple, he said to me, "Come on in, and we'll talk." I went into the room, and he started talking to me about the *Bhagavad-gita*. I started talking to him about LSD, which I was very much into at the time, and how I had seen Krishna while I was on LSD. He said, "You don't need to take LSD. You can see Krishna because Krishna loves you and can show His favor to you." Then Govinda dasi brought in a tray of sugar cane. Prabhupada said, "Would you share this sugar cane with me?" I said, "No, no, I don't eat sugar." I was against any kind of sugar-eating. He said, "This is natural. It grows on the side of the road." He was reading my mind. He knew exactly where I was coming from. He showed me how to eat sugar cane, and we sat together chewing the pieces of sugar cane, putting our chewed pieces on the same plate. In retrospect it was amazing because it was so casual. He played me a tape of a record that he had done and showed me some other books. He said, "I would like you to stay at the temple," but he also told me that I would have to stop taking LSD. I said, "I can't do that. I'm getting so much spiritual insight from taking LSD." He said, "Well, I hope that you will reconsider." That was the first time I met him. He was pretty wonderful.

I went back to the forest to meditate some more and a short time later realized that the only way I could ever get spiritual enlightenment was to find Prabhupada. I called around because I didn't even know that there was a Hare Krishna movement, and I found out that Prabhupada was going to the La Cienega temple in Los Angeles in two weeks. When I saw him there I was dressed in a *sari*. He looked at me and said, "I remember you from Hawaii." He was very glad that I had come. He said, "Come to my apartment and we'll talk." So I went back to his apartment and he said to me, "Now do you understand the difference between your *Bhagavad-gita* and my *Bhagavad-gita?*"

 **Revatinandan:** In an evening class Prabhupada mentioned that he'd received a letter saying that a godbrother of his had passed away. Prabhupada said that when he was living in Vrindavan as a *vanaprastha*, this godbrother had kindly written him a letter, reminding him that Srila Bhaktisiddhanta Sarasvati had wanted him to take *sannyas* and preach in the West. Prabhupada said, "I did not want to take *sannyas*, because materially it is a very difficult position. But I received that letter from my godbrother, and around the same time my Guru Maharaj appeared before me three times in dream. Each time he walked away from me, turned around, and beckoned me to follow." These things prompted Prabhupada to take *sannyas*. He said, "In this way, my Guru Maharaj pulled me out of this material world." When he said "pulled", his voice got thick and two tears suddenly shot out of his eyes, as if they were squeezed out by a shudder of ecstasy, and went running down his

cheeks. Everybody in the room was speechless. I was impressed with the intense feeling he had when his Guru Maharaj called him to take *sannyas*.

Tamal Krishna Goswami: The first time Prabhupada saw me with a shaved head he said, "Ah, now you are an ideal *brahmachari*." He was pleased that I had shaved my head, because although I had been keeping my hair short, I wouldn't "shave up." I had joined with Vishnujana, and he had "shaved up", but I hadn't. When I finally did, Prabhupada appreciated it. On the first walk I went on, I asked Prabhupada, "How many pure devotees are there on the planet?" Srila Prabhupada asked, "How many devotees are there in ISKCON now? That is how many pure devotees there are."

Kaushalya: In Amritsar, he was training us in personal habits. "Because in India," he said, "everyone will watch all of your habits. Never touch your food with your left hand." He taught us how to peel a banana without touching it with our left hand. He taught us how to drink water from a glass without touching it to our lips. He was particular about our habits "because," he said, "everybody will be watching and making sure that I've taught you well."

Once Prabhupada asked me and Yamuna to lead *kirtan*. We were singing varieties of prayers, and when we finished somebody in the audience criticized our Sanskrit pronunciation. Prabhupada fired back at them, "You do not have one tenth of the devotion of these women. How dare you criticize their Sanskrit!" He was very angry. He had a transcendentally passionate personality and was very protective of us.

Tamal Krishna Goswami: Jayananda was supporting the temple single-handedly, and Prabhupada said that that wasn't fair. He said all of the *brahmacharis* should go out and get jobs. So we did, and everyone did what they knew best. I remember Vishnujana made bamboo flutes and stood on Haight Street playing Hare Krishna on a flute all day. Gurudas and I worked for Kodak, but I felt it was yoga because I gave my whole paycheck to the temple. Every day at lunch break I'd go out with Gurudas and take lunch, and we'd have *kirtan*. That lunch break was the only thing that saved me, but after a month or two the job was unbearable. Gargamuni went to Montreal and talked to Prabhupada, and Prabhupada said that if we didn't want to work like this then we should chant on the streets. So we had an *istagosti* and discussed the idea. I volunteered to organize the *sankirtan* because I wanted to get out of that Kodak job. I was ready to do anything to get out of that job. In the first letter that I wrote to Prabhupada, I told him the results of our street *sankirtan*.

Revatinandan: One time while we were walking side-by-side I asked, "Srila Prabhupada, this is not a judgmental question because whatever you eat, I'll eat and feel like it's what I should be eating. But I think that the food that we're getting here has not been offered to Krishna. They have a Krishna Deity, but you can't tell Him from the other Deities. They don't discriminate. How should we view eating this food?" Prabhupada looked at me and said, "Actually, a Vaishnav takes everything as the mercy of the Lord. We prefer to eat what is offered to Radha and Krishna, but we understand that everything is Krishna's mercy. But do not preach like this." I said, "Why is that?" He said, "Because the new devotees will take food simply as sense enjoyment unless they offer it first. We do not want to confuse them." As I thought about it, I was smiling because it was the first time I saw a clear example of Srila Prabhupada's priorities. He was an *uttama-adhikari* who came to the platform of a *madhyama-adhikari* to preach Krishna consciousness.

Tamal Krishna Goswami: We made about twelve dollars the first day. I went back to the temple and said, "Gargamuni, we did twelve dollars." He said, "Wow. I'm gonna give up my shop. This is big. This has huge potential." The next day I decided to take *Back to Godhead* magazines with us, and when people gave a donation I gave them a

Back to Godhead. By the end of five days the collections had gone up to forty dollars. I wrote Prabhupada day by day how it was increasing. Prabhupada wrote me, "Don't worry so much about money. If Krishna wants to, He can give you the whole U.S.A. The question is what will you do with it? Do you know what to do with it?" It was a sobering letter.

Kaushalya: We went to the Golden Temple, which is the Sikh's most holy temple. One of the temple people there showed us around. Prabhupada really liked it and was very impressed. They had a huge *chapati*-maker, like an upside down wok, with about ten men around it flipping *chapatis* with big, long spatulas. They were feeding poor people. We went to the inner sanctum of the Golden Temple and walked around. When we left they asked Prabhupada, "Would you sign our guest book, Swamiji?" He said, "Yes," and signed the guest book. In the place that said, "What are your impressions of the temple?" Prabhupada wrote, "Very spiritual," and he made sure that we all knew what he wrote, because he told us while he was writing it. Under religion he wrote, "Krishnite." It was very funny—not Hindu; Krishnite. That was a wonderful experience in Amritsar.

Tamal Krishna Goswami: Prabhupada was very pleased with this *harinam* party. When he left San Francisco to open the temple in Seattle, Prabhupada decided that the *sankirtan* party should go with him. At that point Jayananda went to Prabhupada and asked, "Swamiji, I'd like to travel with the *sankirtan* party." Prabhupada said, "But you are the Temple President." Jayananda said, "I think the *harinam* party is more important." Prabhupada said, "What will you do?" He said, "I'll be the driver." Prabhupada thought for a second and said, "Very good, you can go." *Sankirtan* was so important to Prabhupada that he was willing to let the person who was maintaining the whole temple, who was the temple president, become the driver of the *sankirtan* party. Jayananda joined our party in that way.

Revatinandan: Prabhupada was letting us ask questions. I said, "Prabhupada, it says in the *Srimad-Bhagavatam* that the fourteen different grades of planetary systems are arranged along the stem of the lotus flower. I always envisioned them as they are in the paintings, out in space around Brahmaloka. But here it says that they're along the stem of the lotus flower. How can that be? Visually they appear to be in all directions." Prabhupada looked at me, smiled, and said, "It may be a very big lotus flower," and shook his head a little bit. He said, "We cannot understand these things with our puppy brains," and smiled. It was immediately revealed to me that I have a very small scope for conceiving such things.

Tamal Krishna Goswami: Before the operation began, they gave me an anesthetic and said, "Count from ten, down." I got to about seven and that was it. I was meditating on Radha-Rasabihari in the *arati,* and then I had a very good dream. In my dream Srila Prabhupada had been called by the previous *acharyas* to make a report on his preaching mission on this planet. The previous *acharyas* asked Prabhupada, "What is your report?" Prabhupada said that he had studied the people of this planet and he had found that they had no capacity for any type of austerity. Nor were they very capable of studying, nor were they very pious. He said the only thing that they were able to do was "somehow take shelter at my feet."

After the operation they wheeled me to my assigned room. Prabhupada was sitting there. He said, "I came here as fast as I could. I wanted to stop the operation because I think you should have had this operation in America, but anyway it is done now." He had come all the way from Juhu in a Jeep in the middle of the rush hour to try to stop the operation. I told Prabhupada about the dream. Prabhupada listened very intently and said, "Actually, this is so."

Kaushalya: One time in New Delhi, somebody was talking about *maya,* saying, "This whole world is just an illusion." Prabhupada objected, "How dare you call it an illusion. It is beautiful. The mountains are beautiful, the oceans are beautiful, the rivers, the sky, the trees. This is a beautiful world. But it's temporary, and it's a perverted reflection of the spiritual world. If you see the beauty of this world, you'll see the beauty of the spiritual world, which is a million times more beautiful. If you said to me, 'Srila Prabhupada, look at the painting I have done for you,' and I said, 'It's an illusion,' that would hurt your feelings. In the same way it is offensive for you to call this world an illusion."

Tamal Krishna Goswami: When Prabhupada came to San Francisco, he wanted me to come back to India to take up my GBC service again because he couldn't find anyone to replace me. As soon as we picked him up, Prabhupada started talking about Hare Krishna Land and India. I could feel the pressure coming. Prabhupada and I went into his room, and he said, "What are you going to do? Are you prepared to come back to India?" I said, "Well, Prabhupada, I'm preaching now." Prabhupada was a little upset and said, "What is that preaching? Preaching means there must be results." I said, "There are results." He said, "What are those results? Let me see the results." So I had my ten new *bhaktas* come one by one, put a rose on Prabhupada's desk, offer their *dandavats*, and sit down. Prabhupada started to beam and said, "This is preaching." He was so happy to see this. He said, "So you stay here."

Revatinandan: One day on the way back from an engagement, our host wanted to show us a Durga temple that had just been constructed by the side of a river. As we went in Prabhupada told us to do what he did. He said, "I'm going to bow down with my right side toward the Durga Deity. When we bow to Radha Krishna, we bow with our left side toward the Deity."

Tamal Krishna Goswami: On the way to Madras, our train stopped in Bombay, but because I was a *sannyasi* and my wife was at the Bombay temple, I wouldn't go. I sent my party to give Prabhupada the report of my first preaching assignment as a *sannyasi,* while I sat in the train station waiting for them. Suddenly Yadubara came and said, "Prabhupada sent me here to bring you back. He said you can come to the temple." I said, "But I can't go. I'm a *sannyasi,* and my former wife is there." Yadubara told me, "No, Prabhupada said, 'It's okay.'" So I went with him to the temple. As soon as I came into Prabhupada's room I offered my obeisances, and Prabhupada said, "The temple is a neutral ground. You and your former wife can be here at the same time. There is no harm," and then he asked everyone to leave the room, which was quite unusual. Prabhupada generally didn't do that. He beckoned me over to the table, and he said, "Now give me your report." I gave him the report, and he was happy. He stood up, walked around the table, took me in his arms, and held me very tightly, embracing me on one side and then the other side. He said, "Take the *sannyas* mantra in your heart, go everywhere, and preach. Kirtananda's a *sannyasi,* Brahmananda's a *sannyasi,* and you're a *sannyasi.* Now I can retire peacefully and translate. Go and preach." My whole body was transformed. It was very rare that Prabhupada would use his body in that way, and I felt that his touch surcharged and empowered me. I went back to the train, and we went on to Madras.

Kaushalya: When we were first in India, the little Deities that we traveled with were in Prabhupada's room, and we would go into his room for *mangal arati.* Sometimes he would do the *puja.* After *mangal arati* he would speak on the *Bhagavatam* and the *Bhagavad-gita.* Then after that he would have *darshan.* Wherever we went throughout India, this would be the schedule. Once in Bombay, a man came in, prostrated himself in front of Prabhupada, and said, "Swamiji, you will save me. You can enlighten me." Prabhupada looked him squarely in the eye and said, "I cannot enlighten you. I can teach you how you can enlighten yourself. But you have to do the work yourself." Prabhupada was not one to say that just by his association you would be enlightened. You had to work at it. It would take effort.

Tamal Krishna Goswami: It was July of '70. Prabhupada had sent me to Europe to organize our temples in London, Paris, and Hamburg. At that time there was no GBC, but he put me in charge of coordinating those temples. I was in Paris when I got a telegram, "Come to Los Angeles immediately." I detached myself and got a plane to Los Angeles the same day. Prabhupada was very disturbed because he had detected that some poison had come from some of his godbrothers in India. Four *sannyasis* in our society had misunderstood how the movement was to be run and were confused about Prabhupada's position.

I arrived in Los Angeles in the evening, and the next morning Prabhupada called for me. He was very grave and looked almost shriveled. He said, "Have they told you?" I said, "Yes, Prabhupada." He said, "Can you take me out of here?" I said, "Yes, Prabhupada." He said, "Where will you take me?" I thought and said, "I could take you to Florida." He said, "It's not far enough." I said, "I could take you to Europe." He said, "The poison has spread there as well." I said, "Then, where do you want to go?" He said, "I want to go to India."

Prabhupada had the ability to accomplish many, many purposes by each one of his actions. In 1977 Prabhupada was lying in his bed in the Krishna-Balaram Temple, and we were reminiscing. He said, "Remember when you took me from Los Angeles?" I said, "Yes." He said, "At that time I went before Sri Sri Rukmini Dwarkadish, and I said, 'My dear Lord, You have called me all the way here, and You have given me this wonderful temple. Now why are You sending me away?'" Prabhupada said, "I couldn't understand why the Lord was sending me out. Now, I understand it was because He wanted to give me this Krishna-Balaram Temple. This is one hundred times every other temple in the world. But I didn't understand at that time."

Revatinandan: One evening Prabhupada said he wanted to have a feast for the Gita Press people. He said, "They have been sheltering us and feeding us, so we will cook for them." In the afternoon Prabhupada asked what chutney I was going to make, and I said, "apple." He said, "I do not think apple chutney is very nice. Make tomato or something like that." I said, "But, Prabhupada, we already purchased the apples." He said, "All right." So our cooks made *subji* and *puris,* and I made apple chutney and *halava* with milk.

A couple days earlier and throughout that week, Prabhupada had been teaching us *Jaya Radha Madhava* in the morning by having us repeat it after him. He took a special liking to that song, and that's when he started singing it before his morning class.

We were taking care of beautiful, metal Radha-Damodar Deities. The floor of the temple room was wooden, and Prabhupada mentioned that it hadn't been properly cleaned. Kaushalya volunteered to clean it, but the next time Prabhupada saw it he still thought it wasn't clean enough. Prabhupada said, "You're not doing it properly. Get two pots, one for dirty water and the other one for clean water, and do it like this." He pulled up his *dhoti,* got down on his hands and knees, put a rag in one pot of water, and scrubbed the floor. Then in the other pot of water he wrung the rag out and rinsed it. Again he put the rag in the fresh water and mopped up what he had done. He said, "In this way, you will keep one pot of water clean while the other one gets dirty. Always rinse the rag, and then soak up the dirt. That way you'll pick up the dirt, rather than just moving it around." He didn't hesitate to show Kaushalya exactly how he wanted it done and spent two or three minutes on his hands and knees scrubbing the floor in front of the Deities. That was a nice thing to see Prabhupada do.

Tamal Krishna Goswami: I asked, "Srila Prabhupada, can we celebrate Bhaktisiddhanta Sarasvati Thakur's Appearance Day in the evening? Then we will have a lot of guests." Prabhupada said, "No. It must be celebrated at noon." This was a Friday. I said, "Friday evening we can fill up the temple." He said, "No, it must be at noon." So we celebrated in Prabhupada's little room at the La Cienega

Boulevard temple in Los Angeles. Prabhupada did all of the prayers and spoke about his Guru Maharaj. He asked, "How is the feast going?" I said, "I'll take a look." It was about 10:30 AM, and nothing had been done. I said, "What is going on here?" and started screaming. They said, "You told us it was going to be Friday night." I said, "Prabhupada wanted it at noon." Maybe it was my mistake for not conveying the message. I went back to Prabhupada, and he said, "How is it going?" I said, "Nothing is done." Prabhupada didn't say a word. He looked at me, got up, walked out of his room, through the temple, through the *prasadam* hall, and into the kitchen. He immediately told the devotees, "Get this done, get that done, cut this vegetable." He was determined that the feast be offered by twelve. In one hour he personally cooked a twelve-course feast for at least seventy devotees. Prabhupada always said, "Deity worship is one hour's business. Cooking is one hour's business." One of the best things I remember about that feast was the way Prabhupada made the *puris*. He put each *puri* in the hot *ghee* and touched it. Every *puri* puffed up; perfect *puris*. The feast was offered, and then the whole *maha* plate was given to Prabhupada. Within three minutes it came out practically untouched. We were all eating this big feast, and we saw that Prabhupada didn't eat it. He was very upset.

Kaushalya: The whole town of Surat laid out a red carpet for Prabhupada. People strung *saris* from building to building to shade the path when we did *nagar sankirtan*. Everyone hung out of the windows and threw flowers and rice on us. Hundreds of people garlanded us, and the garlands piled up so high we had to take many of them off. Prabhupada tirelessly went to various programs, spoke for hours to hundreds of people, and gave them a little *prasadam*. Surat was magical. By that time Prabhupada knew that I had memorized the *Isopanisad* and was able to sing it. So once, when we went to a village outside of Surat, he asked me to sing the *Isopanisad*. I was only 18 and very nervous, but I stood up and sang all the verses. Prabhupada always treated us like his children, and when I finished he beamed like a proud father. He called me over and put my head in his lap. He patted my back and rubbed my head and said he was proud of me. It was one of those magical moments I'll never forget. He was very warm and affectionate.

Tamal Krishna Goswami: Our first meeting with all the members of Dai Nippon Printing Company, from the top chairman down, was like a tea ceremony, although we drank water while they drank tea. They were on one side of a big oak desk, and we were on the other. At the end of the meeting, each person formally presented his business card to Prabhupada and then left. Only the number seven man remained to show us out. Before we went to the limousine Prabhupada asked this man, "What is your goal?" The man took the business cards that had been stacked in front of Prabhupada, found his own, and placed it on top of the stack, indicating that he wanted to be the number one man. Prabhupada shook his head and laughed. Then he started to preach to this man about the nature of life, how temporary it was, and that to become "number one" was not the purpose of life.

Prabhupada was a transcendental negotiator. He had me be the heavy man. Dai Nippon would give a price, and I would say it's impossible. I would give a ridiculously low price and they would practically start crying. We would get into a big argument. Prabhupada would sit there in a neutral position, and finally he would act as if he was the arbitrator. He would say, "This is not good. There should not be quarreling like this. I will settle it. Neither side should argue like this. We must consider the needs of each side." He would pick the price that he wanted, which was still extremely low, but by that time they would think that Prabhupada was their savior. In this way we negotiated for each book, and Prabhupada got very low printing prices. He was proud that he had been able to get sixty thousand dollars worth of business with a down payment of five thousand dollars. He said, "They have so much trust and faith in my writing."

Revatinandan: That night all the people from the Gita Press showed up to hear a very philosophical lecture on the *Vedanta Sutra*. Prabhupada started speaking about *Vedanta Sutra* but after about fifteen minutes pointed out that the ultimate knowledge of *Vedanta* was knowledge of Radha and Krishna. He quoted the line, "*jaya radha madhava kunja bihari,*" which means that "Radha and Madhava are enjoying in the pleasure groves in Vrindavan." At that point he stopped talking and sat up very straight with his eyes closed. A little tremble went through his body. When we were traveling in those days, sometimes Prabhupada would be tired and would doze off while sitting in his seat or waiting on the *vyasasana*. But this time he was sitting up very straight, and there was a little tremor in his body. He sat quietly for several minutes, and both the Gita Press people and the devotees were spellbound watching him. We knew that he had drifted into a trance right there on the *vyasasana*. You could have heard a pin drop in the room. Nobody said anything, nobody moved. Everybody just watched him. Finally he opened his eyes and said, "So, this song is very nice. You should all learn to sing this song," got off the *vyasasana,* and went into his room. That was the end of the lecture.

Tamal Krishna Goswami: In London we had another interesting negotiation. By the time I got to London, in September of 1969, Prabhupada was about to get 7 Bury Place. But what is a temple without Deities? Prabhupada instructed us to install Radha Krishna Deities when the temple opened in December, but we didn't have any Deities, and he didn't ask for any Deities to be made in India. How are you supposed to find Radha and Krishna in London? We started to ask anyone and everyone. It was like a national alarm, "Anyone knowing the whereabouts of Radha and Krishna please phone such and such number," and that was the number of Mukunda's wife, Janaki. Week after week went by. Prabhupada would call us and say, "Where are the Deities?" We said, "We don't know where Radha and Krishna are." Prabhupada said, "You have to have

Deities." Finally, miraculously, when we were practically giving up, Janaki got a phone call. Someone said, "We have Radha-Krishna Deities." Immediately she informed Mukunda, and Mukunda and I went to this man's house.

The man took us into his study and said, "I have marble Radha-Krishna Deities. Would you like to look at Them?" 'Would we like to look at Them? Sure we wanted to look at Them.' He took off the cloth, and we offered our obeisances. That was Radha-London Isvara. We said, "They're beautiful, They're so beautiful." And They were beautiful. He said, "I'm considering giving Them to your temple." We said, "Can we bring our spiritual master to see Them?" He said, "Yes, you can do so." We raced out and immediately called Prabhupada's apartment near Regents Park. He was resting, so we decided to go there. We went in and told him, "Prabhupada, we found Radha and Krishna." Prabhupada immediately said, "Take me, I want to see Them." So, Prabhupada, Mukunda, Shyamasundar, myself, and maybe Gurudas went in the temple van. By that time it was the early evening. Prabhupada started to talk with this Indian gentleman in a very friendly way. The man said that these Deities were for some other society, but there was some difficulty, and they could not use the Deities. Prabhupada ignored that point and kept on asking the man, "Where are you from? How are you? How is your wife?" He had the man bring in his wife and children, and Prabhupada blessed everyone. He was talking and talking.

Finally, the man said, "Swamiji, don't you want to see the Deities?" Prabhupada said, "Yes, we can see the Deities." It was nonchalant, as if he was not even interested. The man said, "Please, I want to show Them to you." Prabhupada walked over to Them and said, "Hmm," turned around, walked back to the sofa and sat down again. The man said, "Swamiji, what do you think? Can you use the Deities?" Prabhupada said, "They look like They may be used." The man said, "Well, I'm thinking I can give Them to you." Prabhupada said, "Yes, we could accept Them." He told us, "Go and see how heavy the Deities are." Shyamasundar and I went over and I tilted

Radharani and said, "Not very heavy," although She was heavy. Shyamasundar had Krishna. Prabhupada said, "All right, we'll take Them now." He said, "Pick Them up." The man said, "Wait, wait, Swamiji, wait a moment." Maybe he had an idea of recovering some of the cost. Prabhupada said, "No, no, it's no problem. These are American boys, they're very strong." We carried the Deities out, and the man was protesting, "Swamiji, Swamiji, one minute." We walked to the van and put Them in. Prabhupada sat in the seat next to the driver's seat. He said to the man, "I'll take care of the Deities. We'll be in touch with you," and then he said, "OK, let's drive." We drove off and when we got around the corner, Prabhupada said, "Stop the car." We stopped, and Prabhupada said, "Take the cloth off the Deities." We took the cloth off and, with tears in his eyes, Prabhupada started to sing the prayers from *Brahma-Samhita*. He said, "Krishna has now appeared in London."

Kaushalya: I talked the *pujari* of Govindaji's temple into giving Prabhupada a house on the temple grounds. We cleaned this house, and Prabhupada came. He was very pleased. One day while the *pandal* program was going on, I said, "Prabhupada, it's kite-flying season. The sky is covered with kites." He said, "Are you going to fly kites today?" I said, "No, I wasn't thinking of it." He said, "I used to fly kites with my sister Pishima when I was young. Her kite always flew higher than mine and that made me angry. One day I decided to cheat and I flew my kite from the roof. My kite flew higher than my sister's, until she started chanting, "Govinda, Govinda, help me." Then her kite flew higher than mine. Even in our childhood we were always remembering Krishna." Finally he said, "So you go fly kites today."

Tamal Krishna Goswami: Pishima was adored and even worshiped, especially by the lady devotees. One time we were going in procession from Calcutta to Mayapur, and Pishima was in one of the rear cars. When she got out, all of the women rushed over to her.

Prabhupada said, "What are they doing?" I said, "Well, Srila Prabhupada, in a way they respect Pishima as they respect you." He said, "Why? What has she ever done? She's just an old lady."

Kaushalya: When he first arrived I showed him the flyers that I had made for the *pandal* program. They said, "A. C. Bhaktivedanta Swami and his foreign disciples will be behind Govindaji's temple . . ." Prabhupada looked at "foreign disciples," and said, "Why did you say 'foreign disciples'?" I said, "I thought it would be attractive to people." He said, "No. It should say 'American and European disciples,' that is the attraction." He made one of the men redo the whole thing, and then he said, "What can I expect? You're just an unintelligent woman." I was so upset that I walked out crying. I had worked so hard to put the program together. I found out later that after I left Prabhupada said, "I am very pleased with her but a guru's business is to discipline. If I don't discipline, how will you ever learn? Disciple means discipline. So, therefore I discipline." He was actually not mad at me.

Tamal Krishna Goswami: Whenever Prabhupada told me something, I would habitually, unconsciously, say "I know, I know, I know." One day Prabhupada said, "You know, you know. You think you know everything."

When Prabhupada did his construction projects in India he had a system of two signers on every check. Prabhupada was one signer, and I was the other, but there was a problem when Prabhupada traveled out of country. So one day I suggested to Prabhupada, "Why don't you sign some blank checks?" Prabhupada did not like that idea at all. He said, "This is my account. Is it all right with you if I decide how the money will be used?"

Revatinandan: One night we received an invitation from local politicians and businessmen to do a program at the Lion's Club in Indore. Prabhupada didn't want to go. He said to me, "I'm not going to this one. I do not like these men. They are snakes. You go and give the lecture." I said, "Oh, my gosh. What should I tell them?" He said, "Tell them that we are spreading their Hindu religion all over the world, so they're obliged to give us a donation. But before you talk, lead a big, good *kirtan*. The chanting is our mantra for charming snakes. Then they will be able to listen for a few minutes without arguing. Try to get them to give a donation and then go."

Tamal Krishna Goswami: Prabhupada would keep a key for his valuables under his wristwatch. He'd never part with that key. But as Prabhupada became very ill, he gradually took me into his confidence and one day gave me the ultimate vote of confidence by letting me hold that key, the key to his desk drawer. So I had the key, and naturally what would I do but lose it. Prabhupada asked for something that was locked up and I didn't tell him right away that I'd lost the key. I scoured Hare Krishna Land. I went everywhere looking for that key and I had people looking everywhere. We could not find it. Finally I went to Prabhupada and said, "Srila Prabhupada, I have to tell you something." Prabhupada was lying down because he was ill. He said, "Yes?" I said, "Prabhupada, I lost the key." Prabhupada said, "Call the GBC." I said, "Which one, Prabhupada?" He said, "Call the whole GBC here to decide what should be done." Oh, God. I thought, "Call the whole GBC?" There was nothing I could do. I thought, "Okay, I'm just gonna call the whole GBC body to Bombay, and when they come they could decide what to do with me." Suddenly I thought, "Let me try another key." Sure enough, it was an Indian lock, and somehow or other I opened it. I ran to Prabhupada and said, "Prabhupada, I opened it, I opened it." He said, "How did you open it?" I said, "I found another key." He thought and said, "That means the lock was not very good. It doesn't matter if you lost that key, because it's not a good lock. Now put the key on your *brahman* thread." Then he put the key on my thread. He said, "Don't ever lose this."

Prabhupada had a whole key system. One key led to another

key that led to another key. He had a key to the safe, and the safe had a key that opened up his Elmira, and in a special place in the Elmira was the key that opened up the safe in the Elmira.

Prabhupada had a lot of systems. Every key had to be labeled, and there had to be an index of all the keys and an index of every item in every Elmira. He wanted everything systematized. Prabhupada also told me, "You have to keep all documents for seven years." Sometimes he would quote the motto of Indian railways, "Keep the wheels moving." He said that was also a good motto for ISKCON.

Kaushalya: We were in New Delhi during the Bangladesh war. Every night Prabhupada wanted to work, talk to us, have meetings and *darshan* with different people, but we had to keep the lights off due to mandatory black outs. Prabhupada was unhappy about that and I decided to black out the windows. I put black cloth over the windows and that night surprised him by flipping on the lights. He said, "Oh, Kaushalya, you have blacked out the windows. That is first-class intelligence. First-class intelligence is you do what needs to be done without anyone telling you to. Second class intelligence is I say to you, 'Do this and that,' and you do it. Third-class intelligence is I say, 'Go do this or that,' you run out the door and then come back and say, 'What was I supposed to do?'"

Tamal Krishna Goswami: In the early days I was the temple commander in the La Cienega temple in Los Angeles. Prabhupada called me one day and asked me to get the *Bhagavatam*. He had his original *Bhagavatam* with the spiritual sky on the cover. He said, "Do you see this spiritual sky? It's very big. You cannot fathom how big this is. Three-quarters of Krishna's creation is the spiritual sky, and one-quarter is the material creation. That material creation has innumerable universes. One universe is so big the scientists can't measure it. We're on one planet in one of those universes out of innumerable universes, which constitute one-quarter of the creation. This one planet, Earth, is one of the smaller planets in this universe. On this planet there are seven continents, and on one of the continents, North America, there is a great city called Los Angeles. In that Los Angeles city, there's a long boulevard called La Cienega. On that La Cienega Boulevard, there is one church building that is now a Hare Krishna temple. In that one Hare Krishna temple, there is one Tamal Krishna, and he thinks that he is very important." (Laughs) I felt so small.

Revatinandan: Prabhupada walked in the room, looked at the preparations, and stopped. He said, "Where are the fruits? Where are the flowers? This initiation ceremony is a farce. I cannot bring the Lord of the Universe to a place like this. What is this?" The devotees had gotten rectangular stainless steel hotel pans for bathing the Deities, and Prabhupada was totally dissatisfied. He stood there for a long time, chastising Nanda Kumar, Shyamasundar, Acuryananda, one after the other. He said, "I am not going to do it. You have not prepared for it nicely. There should be flowers and fruit everywhere. I'm leaving." Then he hesitated. He got on the *vyasasana* and said, "All right. I will do it, but I do not think this is very nice." All of this was on TV. He was shouting for perhaps ten minutes. It was incredible. I was shaking. I was thinking, "I'm lucky that I wasn't in charge of any of the arrangements."

There was a *kirtan,* and then he said, "All right, Revatinandan Maharaj, perform the fire sacrifice." Pradyumna was there, and I had assumed that he was going to do the fire sacrifice, but maybe since it was Acuryananda's *sannyas* initiation, I was called upon to do it. Every time I made a mistake Prabhupada interrupted me, saying, "No, it is not like that. It is like this," and the more he chastised me the more nervous and upset I got. All of a sudden I was on the firing line too. His mood was intense that afternoon. I'd never seen him that angry. Finally in my confusion, I skipped "*namomaha.*" Prabhupada said, "You have forgotten '*namo.*' All right, I will finish these mantras." Much to my relief, he concluded the mantra chanting. I started feeding sticks into the fire with my right hand and using the ladle in my left hand to pour ghee on the fire. As I held up the ladle I realized, "Oops, it's supposed to be in my right hand." Prabhupada was looking at me as I switched hands, and he made a disgusted face and shook his head.

Then Prabhupada gave Acuryananda *sannyas*. Besides taking *sannyas*, which is serious enough, Acuryananda had also just been chastised very heavily. He was standing there shaking, holding a *danda* with his teeth clenched. When the ceremony was over, Prabhupada said, "All right," pointed at me and said, "Begin *kirtan*." I started leading *kirtan*. Prabhupada looked over at Acuryananda, and for the first time that afternoon he smiled a little and indicated that Acuryananda should dance. Prabhupada was pleased with his seriousness, but he also wanted him to get into the swing of the *kirtan*. It wasn't that serious. He should enjoy Krishna consciousness also.

Afterwards he got up and went to the back door to leave, but the car hadn't gotten there yet, and he had to stand in a drizzle of rain for a few minutes. The crowd was so packed in behind him that he couldn't go back inside. He got into the car and asked Nanda Kumar, "So, you have brought my *prasadam?*" Nanda Kumar said, "Well, Prabhupada, I thought that you would take your usual *prasadam,* since it's not as rich." Prabhupada said, "No, this is a Deity installation. I want *maha prasadam*. Go and get me a plate." Nanda Kumar went back in, came out with a plate of *maha,* and drove Prabhupada off. Nanda Kumar told me later that when they arrived at Prabhupada's apartment, Prabhupada's plate of *prasadam* fell off the back seat and landed face down on the floor of the car. Nanda Kumar went, "Oh no," to himself. Prabhupada went upstairs, and Nanda Kumar thought, "I hope Prabhupada forgets about his *prasadam*." But the first thing Prabhupada said was "Where is my *prasadam?* Bring me my *prasadam*." Nanda Kumar said, "Prabhupada, it fell on the floor." Prabhupada said, "Bring it." Nanda Kumar picked it off the floor, put it back on the plate, and brought it to him. Prabhupada ate the whole plate. It probably had dirt and whatnot in it, but Prabhupada ate it anyway because it was *prasadam*.

Tamal Krishna Goswami: I don't remember what, but I had foolishly forgotten something. Prabhupada looked at me. I said, "Prabhupada, I just can't remember." He said, "Yes, you cannot remember because there is nothing inside there to be able to remember with; simply zero, just zero." I thought, "After all these years, there's nothing in there." Oh boy, heavy chastisement.

Kaushalya: I went through a difficult bout of illnesses. Then I got better, traveled some more and ended up in Calcutta with hepatitis. I was taking Ayurvedic medicine, but I wasn't getting well. Prabhupada said to me, "You are not getting any better. What are you doing?" I said, "I am taking Ayurvedic medicine." He said, "Do not take Ayurvedic medicine. Ayurveda is preventative medicine. You are now very sick. You should go to a regular doctor and take regular medicine." So he thought Ayurveda was preventative, not curative. After all, he was a pharmacist prior to becoming a *sannyasi*.

Tamal Krishna Goswami: When we got to Rishikesh, Prabhupada was ill. We were staying in a very nice house, Gange *darshan*, overlooking the Ganga. Prabhupada had been lured there by Navayogendra Swami, who told him, "If you drink water there, you'll get your health back." As soon as we got there, Prabhupada started having his massage and told me, "Bring Ganga *jal*." I immediately put on my *gumsha,* got a *lota* and dove into the Ganga from the second floor. I swam back with the *lota,* and brought it to Prabhupada, who immediately took a full glass of Ganga water and then belched. Prabhupada said, "Ah, accepted," smiled, and was very pleased. Then he immediately ordered, "Go out and get *kachoris* and *jalebis*." One shop in Rishikesh was famous for its *jalebis* and *kachoris*. Prabhupada said, "Hot *jalebis* is a cure for soar throat. Now it is a little cold, so we must get hot *jalebis*." We ate hot *jalebis,* and he said, "Whenever you have a sore throat, eat fresh, hot *jalebis*." Another time Prabhupada gave me the cure for dysentery, namely eating hot *puris* cooked in *ghee* right off the fire with salt. Sure enough, when I had dysentery, I took hot *puris* and salt, and I was immediately cured. Like a cork.

Kaushalya: When we were in Calcutta Prabhupada showed us his childhood home. He talked about how his father showed him how to do a Ratha-yatra and how he used to have a small, childhood Ratha-yatra festival. I think his father was a very important influence on him. He loved his father and talked about him with reverence and respect. Seeing where he grew up was wonderful.

Tamal Krishna Goswami: Prabhupada's son, Vrindavan Chandra, and I were with Prabhupada. Prabhupada started to remember his *grihastha* life. He told his son, "Actually, your mother was a very good wife, chaste and devoted. One could not ask for a better wife. It was me. I was not very easy." He started to cry and said, "She was so good." He said, "I should not say this, I should not say it." I could see it was a way of healing any possible ill feeling that his son might have had towards him for leaving the family and taking *sannyas*. Prabhupada wasn't acting, but his heart was soft. This was one of those extraordinary moments when Prabhupada showed a mood very different from his official position. Such moments were special and charming.

Revatinandan: One of my godbrothers said, "Revatinandan, you know what Prabhupada said the other day?" I said, "What?" He said, "Prabhupada said that sometimes, even after going back to Godhead, a soul can fall again." I said, "Are you sure?" (I knew that in the *Gita* Krishna says, "Having returned to My transcendental abode, one never again returns to this world of miseries.") He said, "You can ask Prabhupada yourself, but that's what he said." When I got a chance, I asked Prabhupada, "Is it true that even after going back to Godhead, a soul sometimes falls again into the material energy?" Prabhupada said, "Yes." I said, "How does that relate with the *Gita's* statement?" With a wise, meditative smile Prabhupada said, "'Never' means 'practically never.' The soul is Krishna's marginal energy, which means that the soul eternally has the capacity to turn away or to turn toward Krishna. Generally a soul does not fall, but if he did, he probably wouldn't do it again. However, it is not inconceivable."

People say that souls never fall from the spiritual world in the first place, that they fall from somewhere besides Krishna's association. But Prabhupada was definitely speaking about being in Krishna's abode as described in the *Bhagavad-gita*.

Tamal Krishna Goswami: Prabhupada said about book distribution, "Hardback books are more important than soft back." He was very firm on this point. "Give out big books." He wanted more big books distributed. He liked the Radha-Damodar Party. He said, "You have understood a very important point, that in the Kali Yuga people don't come to the temple. You have to bring the temple to the people." That is also the whole idea behind book distribution, to go out to the people.

Kaushalya: After almost four years of living in India, I finally went back to America, partly because of my health, and partly because of my husband. Krishna consciousness in India was different from Krishna consciousness in the United States, at least at that time. When I saw the devotees wearing wigs and heard about them "changing people up" at the airports, I thought it was un-Krishna conscious. I was frustrated and unhappy and wanted to get back to Prabhupada as quickly as I could. So I went back to Bombay, walked into his room, and said, "Prabhupada, you wouldn't believe what they're doing in the United States. They're wearing wigs, they're "changing people up", they're doing this, and they're doing that." I was tattling on my godbrothers and godsisters. He said, "Are you perfect?" I said, "No." He said, "They are doing the best they can. They're trying. Don't criticize. Just stay here and cook for me, and don't worry about it."

Tamal Krishna Goswami: Prabhupada very clearly said that devotional life begins for people when they contact his books in any way. He said, "Even if they just touch a book, even if they look at the pictures in it." Therefore he told the book distributors, "Put the book in their hands. Never mind reading it, if they just touch the book, it will have so much power."

Revatinandan: I was alone with Prabhupada in his room one time, and I asked him, "Many times when we're out traveling, we stay up until midnight or two in the morning answering the student's questions." Prabhupada asked if we were distributing his books properly. I said, "We use the Krishna Books as altar pieces because Radha-Krishna is on the front and your picture is on the back. We also have a Pancha-tattva painting. We have *kirtan,* I give a lecture, we have more *kirtan,* then we give out *prasadam,* and we invite the students to look at the books and talk with us." Prabhupada smiled and said, "Oh, that is very nice, continue to do that. As long as you're presenting the books nicely, it does not matter how many you distribute, because your program is different. Your program will attract devotees." He was pleased. I said, "I'm a little worried because sometimes we're not up for *mangal arati.* We're not really following the *sadhana.*" Prabhupada was still smiling. He said, "That is all right. Because you are doing *sankirtan* that will be fine."

He said, "Our movement runs on two tracks, the *pancharatriki vidhi* and the *bhagavat vidhi. Pancharatriki vidhi* refers to the rules and regulations of Deity worship. Our temple *sadhana* is centered around *pancharatriki vidhi* because devotees become strong by being regulated.

"The *bhagavat vidhi* process of chanting, dancing, feasting, and philosophy was propagated by Lord Chaitanya. However, the *smarta brahman* community in India criticized Lord Chaitanya saying, "We do not find Your process in the *Vedas.*" So, when Lord Chaitanya instructed the Goswamis to write, in order to make the process appear more Vedic, they added some modes of Deity worship from the previous age, and that is the *pancharatriki vidhi.*

"Even though I say in my books that our movement runs on two tracks and they are both equally important, I will tell you that in this age you can get along without the *pancharatriki vidhi* if necessary. But you cannot get along without the *bhagavat vidhi.* This is why your *sankirtan* activity is sustaining you, even without the regulation of Deity worship." He said, "If a devotee needs to be strengthened, then send him to the temple. But otherwise *sankirtan* will be all you need."

Then he told me, "Do not preach this." I said, "Why?" I was ready to run out and start singing, I thought what he explained to me was wonderful. "Many devotees are attached to the Deities, and that helps them to be attached to Krishna consciousness. If you explain this, they may think that you are criticizing Deity worship or that the Deity is less important or unimportant. Therefore, do not preach this. I'm explaining this to you for your own understanding." That was very nice of him.

Kaushalya: Once he said, "The rules and regulations are because you have no self-control."

Tamal Krishna Goswami: Prabhupada also didn't like it when I fell asleep in the car. Once I was sitting next to Prabhupada in the back seat, and I appeared to be dozing. Prabhupada said, "You are sleeping." I said, "No, Srila Prabhupada, I am not sleeping." He said, "You are sleeping." I said, "I don't think I was sleeping." He said, "I said you are sleeping. Chant Hare Krishna." Prabhupada was chanting *japa* very quietly, and I started to chant, "Hare Krishna, Hare Krishna, Krishna Krishna, Hare Hare . . ." and dozed off again.

Another time Upendra was in the front seat, and his head was bobbing as he slept. Prabhupada leaned over and gently caught Upendra's *sikha* from behind. When Upendra bobbed forward, the *sikha* yanked. Upendra turned around angrily. He thought I had done it, but it was Prabhupada. Prabhupada had caught his *sikha.*

Kaushalya: A lady had prepared a huge and delicious vegetarian feast for us, but there were onions throughout the vegetables. One of the men leaned over to Prabhupada and whispered, "Prabhupada, there're onions in the vegetables." Prabhupada looked at him angrily and said, "Quiet. Eat. It doesn't matter, just eat" He didn't want to offend her. Being an appreciative guest was more of a concern to him than the fact that there were onions in the vegetables. He ate it and complimented her on her cooking.

Another time we were served chocolate. We all thought, "Oh, you're not supposed to eat chocolate, because it's got caffeine in it." Prabhupada said, "Eat it." He was casual in some ways and strict in other ways. I think his principle was that he didn't want to offend our hosts by being a stickler for the rules and regulations. It was a great example.

Tamal Krishna Goswami: Prabhupada had a big appetite and would take at least forty-five minutes to relish *prasadam*. He often ate alone, chewing with his eyes closed. When we went to India we got to eat with Prabhupada regularly because we would be invited to the homes of interested Indians. Then all the devotees would sit together, with Prabhupada at the head, and take *prasadam*. Prabhupada said, "This is preaching. We make members by eating." When we went to Surat in Gujarat he made a condition that he would only take *prasadam* at someone's home if that person became a Life Member. In thirty days we made thirty members. It was very nice. Prabhupada trained us how to take *prasadam*.

Kaushalya: The Maharaj of Jaipur decided to give us property behind Govindaji's temple. Prabhupada thought that, being a woman, I couldn't manage things on my own, so he left Devananda and an Indian *brahmachari* there to work with me. To make a long story short, the Maharaj backed out on his offer after Prabhupada left, which is why we don't have a temple in Jaipur. The three of us returned to Mayapur, where the rumor mill had been running hot and heavy that Devananda and I had had an affair. I was very upset about it. I told Prabhupada, "Prabhupada, I can't take it. I want to shave my head and live in an ashram in the forest. I don't want to suffer by hearing criticism and rumors." He said, "Why are you complaining? Look what I have to take. You think you have to take so much? Kaushalya, you are looking for a calm sea and you will not find it in this material world. You will only find it in Goloka Vrindavan with Krishna." He said, "If you shaved your head and lived in an ashram, I would worry about you, so you cannot go. You must stay with me." I said, "Fine, as long as I can stay with you." So that was that.

Tamal Krishna Goswami: During Prabhupada's final days in Vrindavan, someone brought him ice cream from New Vrindavan. (They had packed it in dry ice to keep it cold.) Prabhupada ate a teaspoon of the New Vrindavan ice cream. Then they gave him a ring they had made, and as soon as Prabhupada saw it he said, "So, where is the bride?"

Kaushalya: In Jaipur, Malati was cooking for Prabhupada. There were a lot of rascally, funny, black-faced monkeys in and around the Jaipur temple, and they kept stealing food. Malati went into Prabhupada's room in a panic, "The monkeys keep stealing your food, Srila Prabhupada." Prabhupada said, "I'll tell you what we'll do. We'll take a bow and arrow, shoot one monkey, and hang it over the kitchen. That will scare them all away." Everybody's jaw dropped because he said this very seriously. Then he laughed and said, "I'm just kidding." It was funny. He always said funny things like that.

Revatinandan: When the *sannyas* initiation was over I said, "Maybe I should go over to Prabhupada's apartment and apologize on behalf of the devotees." We all thought that it was the worst disaster we'd ever had, as far as our service was concerned. I got a ride over and asked Nanda Kumar, "Is Prabhupada still up?" He said, "Yes." I said,

"Can I see him?" He said, "Put your head in and see if he'll see you."
I did that and asked Prabhupada, "Can I come in?" He said, "Yes,
come." I came in, offered obeisances and sat down at his feet. I said,
"Srila Prabhupada, on behalf of all the devotees I want to apologize.
We did it badly and we're sorry to have displeased you." Prabhupada
smiled a little and said, "Do not pay it any mind." I was amazed,
because he was as cool as a cucumber.

I knew from experience that I should never, to Prabhupada's
face, use him as an example of a pure devotee. When I did this once
in India, he said with great vehemence, "I am not a pure devotee. I
am a rascal." So this time I said, "Prabhupada can you answer a
question about the consciousness of a pure devotee?" He said, "Yes.
Ask." I said, "Sometimes, it appears that a pure devotee may be very
angry or happy, but how does that really affect him?" I was thinking
that Prabhupada didn't seem even slightly upset. Prabhupada said,
"The consciousness of a pure devotee is very deep. It is like the
ocean. Near the surface there maybe many waves, but as you go
down into the ocean, you will find that it is still." I immediately
understood what he was saying. He continued, "In this way, the
consciousness of a pure devotee is so deep that nothing really
disturbs it. There maybe some ripples on the surface, but underneath remains very deep and still." I said, "Is it like that even at
death?" He said, "Yes."

TAPE 12

Radhanath Swami
Bhaktadas
Uttamasloka das

Radhanath Swami: When I first arrived in India, I went to the Himalayas and adopted the life of a *sadhu*. I wore *sadhu* robes, had a little bag and pot, traveled through jungles and mountains, and learned from many great *rishis*, yogis, and sages. Sometimes I lived in jungle caves with yogis, and sometimes I lived in caves alone, practicing meditation. At other times I studied Buddhism in Buddhist monasteries. In this way I traveled around India, searching for God-realization.

Everyone wanted to initiate me, because to have a foreign disciple was very prestigious for yogis, gurus, and all other spiritual personalities. But I felt that until I found a guru whom I would never leave, I could not accept initiation. At one point I went to Bombay to renew my visa, and as I was walking down the street I saw a big sign saying, HARE KRISHNA FESTIVAL AT CROSS MAIDAN. I went there and met many devotees at a big *pandal* program. Srila Prabhupada was going to speak later that day, so I stayed, talked with the devotees, and read Prabhupada's books. That night Srila Prabhupada came, sat on his *vyasasana* in the middle of the stage, and had *kirtan* with all of the devotees. There must have been more than 15,000 people in the audience.

I was an insignificant *sadhu* with matted hair, a bag, and a pot, standing in the back of this massive crowd. One devotee, Gurudas, went all the way through the crowd and came to me. He took me by the hand and said, "Srila Prabhupada wants you to sit beside him." I said, "How does Srila Prabhupada know me?" Gurudas repeated, "He wants you to sit beside him." We walked through the thousands and thousands of people, and I went on the stage. Srila Prabhupada looked at me, smiled, and indicated that I should sit near him. I sat a few feet away from his *vyasasana*. Madhudvisa Swami led a beautiful *kirtan*. All of the devotees had clean, shaven heads and beautiful, clean *dhotis* and *saris*. I had river-stained *sadhu* clothes with holes in them and matted hair down practically to my waist. I was trying to be a *sadhu*. I thought, "Why has Srila Prabhupada called me here? I am not a good example compared to his devotees." But he smiled upon me graciously and encouraged me.

 **Bhaktadas:** After we had purchased the temple on Watseka, I was transferred from Laguna to Los Angeles. My first service was with Bhavananda, painting, hammering, and sanding to prepare Srila Prabhupada's quarters. When Prabhupada moved into his apartment the work crew was there to greet him. He sat behind his desk, pulled out a bag of cookies, and handed one to each of us. We ate the cookies, and he said, "Now wash your hands and feet. You must always do this after eating."

Shortly after that, there was an incident that I remember fondly. The Sunday feast was still at La Cienega Boulevard temple, but after the feast I went back to Watseka to paint the ceiling of the temple room. I was on a scaffold singing the Hare Krishna mantra quite loudly. I thought I was the only one in the temple and wasn't paying much attention to anything else, just chanting and painting. I glanced down, and Srila Prabhupada was standing on the floor along with the temple president, Gargamuni, Karandhar, and perhaps Brahmananda. I was stunned. I scampered down the scaffold and offered my obeisances to Srila Prabhupada. Then I knelt on the floor in front of him with my hands folded. He looked at me, folded his hands and said, "Thank you very much." Afterwards the devotees told me that when they drove up they could hear me singing. Srila Prabhupada asked them to be quiet, and they listened to my chanting as they walked into the temple. Srila Prabhupada appreciated the loud chanting.

 **Uttamasloka:** I went to see Prabhupada at Rathayatra in San Francisco. Hundreds of us were waiting anxiously in the airport waiting room to meet him. The plane was twenty minutes late, so it intensified our anxiety and anticipation. Many of us hadn't seen Prabhupada and were wondering what it was going to be like when we finally saw him. We were chanting and chanting. Finally Prabhupada came around the divider. As soon as I saw him, tears poured from my eyes like a water faucet. It was unbelievable; it was so good. I paid my obeisances and cried. I was so happy; it was wonderful.

Radhanath Swami: After Prabhupada had lectured, he got up and started to walk off the stage. As he walked by me, I reached out to touch his feet, because I was taught you're supposed to touch a holy man's feet and place the dust upon your head. But one of his senior disciples yelled at me, "No one is allowed to touch Srila Prabhupada's feet." Very embarrassed, I pulled my hand back. Prabhupada looked at me, smiled, and gave me my first instruction. He said, "You can touch my feet." I touched his lotus feet and placed the dust on my head. He smiled very mercifully and told me, "You come and sit here every night."

Bhaktadas: In those days he would lecture on Monday evenings at the La Cienega temple. All the devotees would line the sidewalks waiting for him to arrive. When he drove up we all bowed down, and Srila Prabhupada walked down the line of devotees, sometimes patting a devotee on the head. We were always trying to understand whether or not he was accepting our service. If he patted you, you felt that, "I'm not worthy. He's just giving me some encouragement." And if he didn't, you felt the same thing.

After we'd moved into the new temple on Watseka Avenue, Srila Prabhupada gave *Sri Isopanisad* classes every day. One day after class he asked, "Is everyone chanting sixteen rounds?" I raised my hand and said, "Srila Prabhupada, I'm not chanting sixteen rounds." Srila Prabhupada said, "Why aren't you chanting sixteen rounds?" I said, "Srila Prabhupada, I am working twenty hours a day. The temple president doesn't give me sufficient time to chant." He said, "Then sleep two hours. Chant sixteen rounds." In other words, Srila Prabhupada strongly told me, "Don't diminish your work for the chanting. Diminish your sleep." I took it seriously and would spend late nights standing in the hot water closet trying to finish my rounds. Later I found out that hardly anyone chanted sixteen rounds, because the leaders thought that work was more important than chanting.

Uttamasloka: Our temple president, Dharmaraj, was artificially austere. To make us austere he didn't give us enough to eat, so we were always in anxiety and would pig out at the feast. We were addicted to *halava*. There was something about *halava* that was irresistible.

Once, on yet another day that we hadn't eaten enough, we were going to Detroit. Dharmaraj was bringing a huge vat of *halava,* but he wouldn't let us have any. All the way there I was in total anxiety, trying to steal some *halava* and eat it. Then I thought, "Here I am going to see the spiritual master, a pure devotee, but I'm thinking of *halava,*" and I was ashamed. Finally we got there, and we were told, "We need some volunteers to clean the house where Prabhupada will be staying." Nobody volunteered. I told myself, "Volunteer, you stupid idiot, don't be a sourpuss." My service at the temple had been cleaning the bathroom. I surrendered, got into it, and did it well. I accepted that I was a toilet cleaner. I thought about the *Gita* when

I cleaned, so I made a lot of spiritual advancement in the bathroom. When I went to the house that day, they said, "We need somebody to clean the bathroom." I said, "Me." I was in ecstasy cleaning the bathroom. I felt as if I had been trained for this.

When Prabhupada finally came he was offered a huge plate of fruit. We sat down with Prabhupada, and he said, "Have some." We were picking at it, and Prabhupada said, "Never be shy in business or in accepting *prasadam*." So we ate. I never forgot that instruction, and from that time on I have never been shy in business or *prasadam*.

Radhanath Swami: I knew many of the residents of Vrindavan, and some of them told me that Swami Bhaktivedanta and his disciples were living in Sharaf Bhavan, a wealthy man's house. When I went there early one morning, Srila Prabhupada was chanting *Jaya Radha Madhava.* I appreciated his chanting more than I had appreciated anything else in my whole life. Never before had I seen such gravity and intensity of devotion as I saw in Srila Prabhupada as he chanted Krishna's names. I had met many of the greatest yogis and gurus of the Himalayas, as well as many great Christian and Muslim saints. For six months I had traveled in Vrindavan, meeting *babajis,* many of his godbrothers, many famous Brijabasi saints. But I had never seen such a depth of love and compassion as I saw in Srila Prabhupada while he chanted *Radha Madhava.* My heart completely transformed. Then he gave a lecture, and every question I ever had was answered in that one lecture. Everything I had ever learned in every religion was included within his message, plus something far more sublime. It was at that time, sitting at his feet in Vrindavan, that I had accepted, "This is my spiritual master, and I must surrender my life to him."

Bhaktadas: I distinctly remember my initiation, because it was something you dream of and pray for and wait for innumerable lifetimes. But in particular, I remember when Prabhupada said, "Bill prabhu, come forward. Your name is Bhaktadas," He handed me my beads and said, "This name means that you are the servant of the devotees. The more you think of yourself as a servant, the more you will advance in spiritual life. The more you think you're becoming a master, the faster you will go to hell." In that one sentence he summarized the essence of the Krishna consciousness philosophy. Over the years I meditate on those words over and over and over again. I've attempted to serve the devotees in whatever way I can, and I've found that it is, without any doubt, the mercy of the devotees that helps one to advance in spiritual life. Our philosophy is that by the mercy of Krishna one gets a bona fide guru. And by the mercy of the devotees, one gets Krishna. In the neophyte stage, the *kanistha* level, we worship the Deity and neglect the devotees. Or we give the respect to the "big" devotees, swamis, and gurus, but we neglect the ordinary devotees. I know I'm guilty of every variety of offense, but I keep hearing Srila Prabhupada's words again and again echoing in my mind, "Become the servant of the devotees." I finally concluded that the highest service is to serve the newest devotee, the youngest devotee, because he's taking the bold step to try to leave the material world. If you help him, then you're really helping the Krishna consciousness movement. The people who are already mature in devotional service don't need so much help.

Uttamasloka: Normally, Prabhupada would give a name that started with the first letter of your Western name. Since my name was Ron, I thought I would be Rama or something like that. But instead Prabhupada gave me the name Uttamasloka. He said, "Your name is Uttamasloka, Krishna, who is praised with transcendental songs." I had enjoyed some local notoriety as a musician and in the beginning wanted to use my musical abilities to serve Krishna, writing songs and so forth. When Prabhupada gave me that name and said, "Krishna, who is praised with transcendental songs," I was in ecstasy. I thought it was wonderful and very special. I got *gayatri* at the same time, and Prabhupada personally spoke the mantra into my ear. That was also auspicious.

Radhanath Swami: Srila Prabhupada took us on *parikram* to many holy places. He took us to Govardhan, Varsana, and Nandagram. He took us to various places in Vrindavan like the Radha-Damodar Temple and the Radha-Govindaji Temple. One day he took us to Madhuban-Gokula and Brahmanda Ghat, where Krishna was accused of eating dirt and then revealed the universe within His mouth to Mother Yasoda. Srila Prabhupada animatedly told that story, right at the place where it happened. Wherever he took us he told us the story of that place. Then he told us to take bath in the Yamuna. All the devotees invited Prabhupada to take bath also. Srila Prabhupada said, "Today I am very sick and I cannot take bath. You all go in and enjoy a nice bath in Yamuna." All the devotees were in the Yamuna, and Prabhupada was sitting on the steps high over the river, watching the devotees enjoy the ambrosial water. He was smiling and became so ecstatic that he quickly got up, took off his clothes, put on a *gumsha,* and took bath with us. The devotees were ecstatic. Everyone gathered around him and bathed him with Yamuna water like an *abhisek.* Srila Prabhupada was happy to be bathing in the Yamuna along with his disciples in the holy land of Vrindavan.

Bhaktadas: When I became temple president in San Diego, I started writing to Srila Prabhupada once a month to give him a report on the temple activities. My first letter was in January of 1971. I was so nervous I agonized over every word, every comma, wanting to try and make it perfect. It probably took me weeks to write that letter. Srila Prabhupada wrote back, "It appears Krishna has blessed you. Now make sure all of our principles are followed, and then there will never be any scarcity." I found that to be an invaluable instruction, and I still try to live by that. We should have faith that Krishna will maintain and protect us if we are obedient to our spiritual master.

Uttamasloka: I found a big church on Avenue Road, which is a very good location in Toronto. It was a huge, wonderful building, perfect for us. The Christian group that had used it was moving to a new place, and it was for sale for a half a million. This was the best place we had found after years of looking. I went to Prabhupada and I told him about the building, "Prabhupada, we found a huge, amazing building. It was a church and has forty-foot-high ceilings. There's space for *brahmachari* quarters." I described everything to him. He said, "It sounds great. How much do they want?" I said, "They want $500,000." We had never paid that much for a building. He said, "That's a lot of money. What's the use of buying anxiety? All you'll be thinking about is collecting money. We don't need to purchase anxiety. That's not our business. Our business is to remember Krishna. That's all. It's a good location?" I said, "Oh, yes, Prabhupada." He said, "In good condition?" I said, "Oh, beautiful. Prabhupada, it's on a main road." He said, "Oh, but what's the use of purchasing anxiety. We don't need that. We don't want to purchase anxiety." I said, "Yeah, okay." He said, "Big temple room?" I said, "Yes, Prabhupada, nice temple room, wonderful. Maybe you can come to Toronto and see it." He said, "Maybe we'll come." I said, "Okay." About three weeks later he came to Toronto. We picked him up at the airport, and as we drove to the temple he said, "Can we go see the building?" I said, "Sure." We took him on a tour and there was one Christian still there. I told Prabhupada, "Here's the temple room, and here's the *prasadam* room, and we'll do this here and that there . . ." We were walking by a table where some Christian books had been left behind, and one title was, "What Does God Look Like?" Prabhupada picked it up and said, "Ask him if we can buy this." I said, "Can we buy this book?" He said, "You can have it." I said, "Okay." We got in the car and Prabhupada said, "Read something to me, read the book." I started reading the book, and it was going nowhere. He said, "They don't know what God looks like, it's just a bluff."

About 10:00 that night I got a phone call, "Prabhupada wants to see you. Come over to the apartment right away." I went over to the apartment and Prabhupada said, "Do you have all the plans, the blueprints of how you want to lay out the temple?" I said, "Yes, Prabhupada, I have everything." He said, "I think it would be an ideal temple." I said, "Yes, Prabhupada, it would be wonderful." He said, "How much do they want?" I said, "Five hundred thousand." He said, "Well, why don't we go there and ask if they'll take three hundred thousand dollars. How much do you have?" I said, "We have about forty thousand." He said, "Can you get another sixty?" I said, "We can try." He said, "Brahmananda, how much do we have in the BBT?" He said, "We have two hundred and something." Prabhupada said, "Give them two hundred thousand." Brahmananda said, "Prabhupada, we've never given that much to anybody." Prabhupada said, "That's all right, give it to them and see if they'll take three hundred thousand cash, and tell them that we'll worship Lord Jesus next to Lord Krishna on the altar." In other words, we'd preserve the Christian element. Prabhupada said, "Do you think they'll do that?" I said, "We can try." He said, "Can you handle the payments on three hundred thousand?" I said, "Prabhupada that's an awful lot of money. We don't want to purchase anxiety." Prabhupada slammed his fist on the table and said, "No, there must be anxiety! Otherwise we'll just be sitting around, eating *prasadam* and getting fat. There must be anxiety!" (Laughs). I thought, "Okay." He completely reversed what he had said before, "Well, we don't want to purchase anxiety," to, "There must be anxiety!" Everybody was shocked.

Radhanath Swami: Every day after the *parikram* devotees would take *prasadam*. Then Srila Prabhupada would have *darshan* in his room and meet his old friends from Vrindavan, his godbrothers and many others. There was a rule that devotees were not supposed to be there, because in the afternoon they were supposed to do *seva*, *harinam sankirtan*, and other services. But I used to sit there all afternoon, listening to him talk with his old Brijabasi friends. One day the regional manager of ISKCON for India saw me sitting with Srila Prabhupada. He told me that no devotees were allowed to be with

Prabhupada during his *darshan* time. I looked at Prabhupada, Prabhupada looked at me, and I said to this devotee, "I'm not a devotee." I pointed to my matted hair, he looked at Prabhupada, and Prabhupada smiled. Then he left, and I got to stay with Prabhupada.

It was beautiful seeing Prabhupada with his old friends, especially Krishnadas Babaji. When Krishnadas Babaji Maharaj came into the room, Prabhupada's eyes became filled with tears, and Krishnadas Babaji Maharaj's eyes became full of tears. Prabhupada stood up, and Babaji Maharaj called out, "Hare Krishna, Hare Krishna!" Prabhupada practically ran to him and embraced him. I had never seen such affection and love between two people as there was between Prabhupada and his godbrother Krishnadas Babaji. Prabhupada, with his arms around Krishnadas Babaji, took him to his own seat behind a little table. They sat together with their arms around each other, talking in Bengali. I couldn't understand, but Prabhupada was laughing and laughing. Every now and then they would slap each other on the legs. They were practically sitting on top of each other, and there were tears in their eyes. They were so happy to be together, discussing transcendental subject matters. It was amazing, because there must have been fifteen other people in the room, but Krishnadas Babaji Maharaj and Srila Prabhupada were completely oblivious of everyone. They were in their own world, hearing and chanting the glories of the Lord.

Bhaktadas: I was determined to remain a *brahmachari*. I felt that Krishna had protected me because I never had a girlfriend before I joined the movement, and I thought I could continue. But some of our senior men in Los Angeles told me that I should marry, and this destroyed my mental equilibrium. I started thinking about marriage, and I asked Prabhupada, "Should I get married?" He said, "It is better if you can remain a *brahmachari*." But he didn't say "no" or "yes." It wasn't specific. After this visit to San Diego in 1972, there was some talk that I should take *sannyas*. I searched my heart and concluded that every time a pretty girl walked in the temple my mind would be attracted to her. I said, "I don't want to take *sannyas* now. When I take *sannyas,* I want to be free of this." So I got married instead. Over the years I've come to appreciate the mercy of the *grihastha* ashram. Krishna's so kind to allow us that. Think of the poor Mayavadis who must take *sannyas* even though their hearts are full of desires.

Uttamasloka: On a morning walk in Toronto, perhaps in 1976, Vishvakarma, the temple president, said, "Prabhupada, lately the *brahmacharis* are agitated and are having difficulty maintaining their *brahmachari* mood. How should we deal with this?" Prabhupada said, "If they're agitated, tell them to get married. What's the problem?" Vishvakarma said, "But Prabhupada all of the big devotees, the *sannyasis,* tell them that it's a fall-down to get married." Prabhupada said, "Fall down from where? How can you fall, when you're already fallen?" In other words, what do they think they're falling from, that they're so exalted? He said, "Besides, the *sannyasis* are not the big devotees. A big devotee is someone who is humbly and sincerely serving Krishna. That's a big devotee. Not necessarily a *sannyasi.*" He said, "I give some devotees *sannyas* because they're so anxious for it that they keep bothering me about it. I give them *sannyas* so that they'll leave me alone."

Radhanath Swami: The devotees thought that I should join the movement. They told me that Srila Prabhupada was going to be taking them to different places in India, and that I could be Srila Prabhupada's personal servant because they were always getting sick in India, but since I was accustomed to living there, I didn't. I said, "Thank you very much for this wonderful offer, but I will serve Srila Prabhupada when he does something in Vrindavan." I had decided to stay in Vrindavan for the rest of my life. So the devotees criticized and harassed me, saying that I was a *sahajiya,* a bogus *smarta brahman.* They said that Lord Chaitanya's movement is to preach Krishna consciousness. I thought, "These Western people do not understand Vrindavan."

One day, as Srila Prabhupada was walking to his car after giving a lecture, I, along with crowds of other people, bowed down to him. When I got up Srila Prabhupada was in front of me. I was on my knees looking up at Srila Prabhupada, who had a serious, concerned expression and was looking right at me. I felt that he was looking into my soul and that it was touched by Srila Prabhupada's glance. Never before in my life had I had a sensation like that.

Srila Prabhupada asked, "How long have you been living in Vrindavan?" I thought, "Oh no, all the devotees have been chastising me and now Srila Prabhupada's going to chastise me." Shyly I said, "Srila Prabhupada, I've been here about six months." Prabhupada stood silently looking at me, penetrating me with his glance. It seemed like hours. Perhaps it was about thirty seconds. Then his face blossomed into a beautiful, ecstatic smile, and he said, "Very nice. Vrindavan is the most wonderful place," rubbed me on the head and walked on. I thought, "Everyone is chastising me for being in Vrindavan, but Prabhupada knows what I need to hear to become attached to him." After that I was ready to go anywhere and do anything for him, because I felt he understood and loved me. His encouragement made me attached to him and to devotional service.

Bhaktadas: In the middle of 1972 there was no plainclothes *sankirtan.* Everything was straight *saris, dhotis, tilak,* and "Here, we're from Hare Krishna, please read a book about Krishna." Around that time Srila Prabhupada wrote me a letter saying, "Make sure that you sell books by preaching, not by cheating." I was taken aback by this. I said, "What does he mean? He's written 'cheating.' What are we doing?" I wrote and asked, "Srila Prabhupada you mentioned, 'Sell books by preaching, not by cheating.' What do you mean?" He replied that if you act with the consciousness that Krishna is the Supreme Proprietor, the only Enjoyer, and the dear most Friend of all living beings, then you are not cheating. But if you act in any other consciousness, you are cheating. He didn't specifically say that we were lying on *sankirtan* to collect money and distribute books. But my understanding was that as Supersoul, Krishna is within us and within all others, and when we're on *sankirtan* we should be trying to please Him.

Uttamasloka: Prabhupada asked me, "Are you distributing books? Is that going well?" I said, "Yes, Prabhupada. We're distributing a lot of books." I gave him the figures, which were impressive. He said, "You're distributing books, but are you reading them too?" I said, "Oh yes, Prabhupada. Every day we have four classes." I explained that we daily alternated *Nectar of Devotion* and *Nectar of Instruction* classes. We also had *Srimad-Bhagavatam* classes, and at night Krishna Book, *Caitanya-caritamrta, and Bhagavad-gita.* He was very happy to hear that. A big smile came over his face, and, almost surprised, he said, "Oh, thank you very much." I had pleased him, and I was washed with an incredible feeling of satisfaction. He said, "The devotees, they're coming?" I said, "Well, not really. Maybe every six months a few people join." He said, "That's all right. *Manushyanam sahasreshu kaschid yatati siddhaye.* Out of many thousands among men, maybe one is interested. And out of thousands of those, maybe one becomes a devotee. So that's all right."

Radhanath Swami: One day he was giving *Srimad-Bhagatavam* class, and he said, "You are distributing my books. But are you reading my books? If you try to convince someone to buy the books, what happens if the person asks, 'Do you read these books? What are they about?' If you tell them, 'I don't read these books. I only sell these books,' then how will you convince them? Unless you are convinced of the subject matter of these books by reading them carefully, how will you convince others to buy and read them?" He strongly told all the book distributors that they have to carefully read his books.

Bhaktadas: Once I had the idea to try and sell the books through

bookstores. I invested some *laksmi* in radio advertising, produced a
radio ad for the Krishna Book, and placed Krishna Books in all the
bookstores in San Diego County. I wrote to Srila Prabhupada about
that and he wrote back, "This is very nice. Please let me know if it
is successful. If it is, we're prepared to spend millions and millions
of dollars to advertise our books." Of course, I didn't have enough
finances to do it the way it should have been done. But it was effective
inasmuch as the books were displayed in all the stores. Some of them
sold, but not enough to justify the amount that we'd spent. But I
think Srila Prabhupada liked the attempt to do something boldly.

When Srila Prabhupada was asked, "What is humility?" he
said, "Humility is to act boldly for Krishna." We may think that
humility is to be meek, quiet, or submissive. But no, Prabhupada
said, "Be bold for Krishna."

Radhanath Swami: After Srila Prabhupada left, I heard that he
would be going to the mountains of New Vrindavan in August to
give special *Bhagavat-dharma* discourses. Also, he was going to
celebrate Janmastami and Vyasa-puja in New Vrindavan, and people
were needed to help prepare. I thought that I would go to New
Vrindavan and then return to Vrindavan, India.

In New Vrindavan there was great enthusiasm to prepare
everything for Prabhupada's coming. I was helping with the painting
and renovations of an old, beaten-up house called Madhuban. The
night before Srila Prabhupada was to arrive, someone discovered
that the toilet didn't work. Everyone wanted to take rest, and I was
told to fix the toilet. I had never fixed a toilet in my life. I didn't know
what I was doing, but I was doing anything to try to get it to flush.
I was up all night, and just as Srila Prabhupada arrived I pushed the
lever and it flushed. I thought, "Prabhupada is going to be so happy,
he has a toilet that flushes." Srila Prabhupada went in the Madhuban
house, and I was feeling proud that I had made his toilet flush. When
it was time for Srila Prabhupada to use the toilet, the devotees said,
"This toilet works very nicely." Prabhupada took his *lota*, went out

into the field, and responded to nature in the field. Then he took his bath in the field. He said, "I enjoy responding to nature in the grass with the fresh breezes." The whole time Srila Prabhupada was there, he went out to the field to respond to nature. He never once used the toilet. So Srila Prabhupada gave me a lesson in detachment. We should be willing to give anything and everything to please our guru. But we cannot be attached to the results.

Bhaktadas: Once Srila Prabhupada lectured in a lecture hall at a Catholic school at the University of San Diego. Most of the persons who attended were priests, nuns, bishops, perhaps a cardinal, and Catholic lay preachers of Southern California. There was a big crowd, and my father also came. We put Srila Prabhupada's *vyasasana* on top of a desk, and he climbed up a chair, onto the desk and onto his *vyasasana*. He began his lecture by quoting a Sanskrit *sloka* that I have never been able to find. Then he said, "This means you are what you eat. In this age, most people are eating hogs." I will never forget that. I was sitting on the floor at his feet, and my jaw dropped. I thought, "Prabhupada how can you say this?" I couldn't believe he would speak like this to this particular audience. I could understand if he was calling the hippies, the drug addicts, hogs, but here he was saying the same thing to this highly, so-called cultured, religious, scholarly audience. I was dumbfounded. I looked at the faces of the other devotees, and they were dumbfounded too. If I had been speaking to this audience, it was the last thing I would have said. But Srila Prabhupada, having no false ego, could say anything and get away with it. If I had said that same thing they probably would have stoned me. I don't remember the rest of the lecture, and I've looked for it over and over again and never been able to find it.

On another occasion during the same visit, Srila Prabhupada went to the home of Dr. Duvari, an Indian gentleman. We ate there (I don't know if it was *prasadam*), and then Srila Prabhupada and Dr. Duvari had a philosophical discussion. Dr. Duvari presented every variety of Western atheistic philosophy, and Srila Prabhupada countered him. The conversation began at 7:30 or 8:00 in the evening, and it went on and on and on. At about 11:30 it was still going on. Three or four of us were sitting there silently watching Srila Prabhupada and listening. Srila Prabhupada became exasperated with this man and said, "You're a fool. I have never met such a complete fool such as you before." Finally Dr. Duvari put his head on Srila Prabhupada's feet and submitted. Since then his entire family have become Vaishnavs, and they're still the biggest supporters of the San Diego temple.

Uttamasloka: Prabhupada, along with devotees and people from the Indian community, attended a function at an Indian family's home. During the *kirtan,* Prabhupada sat on the couch and chanted while I played the *mridanga.* My four year-old son was there with his little wooden drum, but he was standing, gawking at Prabhupada. Prabhupada indicated that he should play his drum, and so Radha Gopinath started playing. The *kirtan* ended, and everybody thought that Prabhupada would speak, but he said to Brahmananda, "You speak." Brahmananda was shocked. After all, who wants to speak in front of the spiritual master? It's unnerving. Brahmananda stood up, stuttered, fumbled, and said something philosophical. I was thinking, "Ha ha. It's a good thing I'm not a *sannyasi,* because if I were, I'd be in trouble. He'd probably ask me to speak." Brahmananda sat down, and Prabhupada looked at me and said, "Now you speak." I almost froze to death. I was in shock. I sat there and thought, "Oh, my God," and he said, "Stand up." I stood up. I was in some kind of vacuum. I spoke and hoped it was transcendental. Nobody laughed, which might not have been good because usually people laugh when I speak.

Later on we were having *prasadam,* and I said, "Prabhupada, do you mind if we chant *bhajans* while you eat?" He said, "No, not at all." I said, "Prabhupada, do you have any favorite melodies for Hare Krishna?" He said, "Oh, yes." I said, "Which one?" He said, "All of them."

Radhanath Swami: Every day Srila Prabhupada went to the top of a mountain, where there was a beautiful pavilion. Devotees had worked very hard to make this pavilion, with a wonderful stage and a *vyasasana*, where Prabhupada could deliver his discourses. Hundreds of devotees and guests from all over America had come to hear these *Bhagavat-dharma* discourses. The devotees had also spent weeks making a palanquin for Prabhupada, but when it was time to use it they couldn't find it. Finally they found the palanquin and took him up the mountain to the pavilion with a *kirtan* procession. But the palanquin was so uncomfortable that when they got to the top, he said, "Isn't there a car that can drive me up here?" After that, Hayagriva drove him up in a Volkswagen.

Uttamasloka: I introduced Ayodhyapati to Prabhupada. I said, "Prabhupada, this is our cook. Every morning we have Basmati rice, *dahl, chapatis,* and a nice *subji.*" I described the whole dinner to him and said, "We eat one main meal a day, and in the evening we have a light snack, because we find that that's practical." Prabhupada said, "That's perfect." He had told us that we should have one main meal a day, either in the morning, afternoon, or evening. We chose the morning.

The next day we were sitting in the airport, waiting for Prabhupada's plane to Montreal, when Shivaram said, "Prabhupada, is there an ideal diet for *sankirtan* devotees?" Prabhupada said, "Oh, yes." Shivaram said, "What is it?" Prabhupada looked at me and said, "You tell him." So I described our *prasadam* program. Prabhupada said, "This is ideal."

Before that we had been in the garden, and Prabhupada had said, "Let's read from the *Gita.*" Jagadish read some verses from Chapter Eight about quitting the body at a certain time. Prabhupada said to him, "Say something." I thought, "Here we go again." Jagadish spoke, and then Prabhupada said, "Now you read and speak," gave me the book, and had me read and speak again. After that Prabhupada left.

When the next festival came in the summer of '76, many devotees were there and everybody was looking at Prabhupada, waiting for some small acknowledgement. Prabhupada was walking through the devotees, down the stairs, and down the pathway. I was at the end of the pathway. Prabhupada looked at me and smiled. Then he walked over to me and stopped. Everybody was shocked. He said, "Everything's going all right in Toronto and Chicago?" I said, "Yes, Prabhupada, everything is going wonderfully." "Good, that's good." Then he looked at Amarendra and he said, "And is everything going well in Detroit?" Amarendra said, "Oh, Prabhupada, I'm Amarendra, I'm not Govardhan." Prabhupada said, "Oh, okay, I'm sorry."

Bhaktadas: During the preparations for the Berkeley Ratha-yatra in 1970, devotees were cutting fruit for a huge fruit salad. We didn't get much sleep, maybe an hour or an hour and a half. We had a small morning program, and, one morning when we were sitting in the temple room reciting the Guruvastak prayers in English, Srila Prabhupada suddenly came in. We had no idea that he was coming. It was spontaneous. He sat down on his *vyasasana* and said, "Continue doing what you're doing." We continued, "The spiritual master is very satisfied when he sees the devotees eating *bhagavat prasada*." Srila Prabhupada said, "Yes! This is the best part!" (Laughs) We responded, "*Jaya*, Prabhupada!"

Radhanath Swami: On Janmastami night Sri Sri Radha-Vrindavan Chandra were being moved into a new temple, which the devotees had just completed. There was about a month's worth of work to be done, and the devotees were working frantically because at a certain hour Prabhupada was scheduled to see Radha-Vrindavan Chandra in Their new temple. So, just as Prabhupada was walking in one door, ladders and buckets were running out the door to the *pujari* room. When Prabhupada was inside, everything was perfect and complete. But the walls had just been painted. We were praying that Prabhupada wouldn't touch the walls. Prabhupada looked at the beautiful Deities, Radha-Vrindavan Chandra, with tears in his eyes. He said, "Your Radha-Vrindavan Chandra are most beautiful. They have appeared before you, like the most beautiful American boy and girl, just to attract your hearts. Your worship is very beautiful. But be careful. There are two paths of *bhakti*, the *pancharatriki vidhi*, and the *bhagavata vidhi*. *Pancharatriki vidhi* means worshiping the Deity with great devotion and performing all services for the pleasure of the Deity. And *bhagavata vidhi* means hearing and chanting the glories of the Lord." He said, "They are like two rails on the same train track, they must go together. If you are not attentively hearing *Srimad-Bhagavatam* and chanting the holy names every day, one day you will look at Radha-Vrindavan Chandra and think, 'Why has my Guru Maharaj left me with this burden?'" His words seared into our hearts. From that day on, the *sadhana* of the New Vrindavan devotees was incredibly strict. Devotees were getting up at two in the morning to chant their rounds. Everyone attended *Srimad-Bhagavatam* class. Prabhupada inspired that.

Uttamasloka: Professor Joseph O'Connell had done his Ph.D. dissertation on Chaitanya Vaishnavism and was teaching in the Department of Religious Studies at the University of Toronto. Professor O'Connell was favorably disposed to us, and I became friends with him.

One time Professor O'Connell sponsored Prabhupada's godbrother, Bon Maharaj, to come to Canada, and we met Bon Maharaj at the professor's house. We invited Bon Maharaj to the temple and he came for a *kirtan* and gave an erudite and articulate lecture. Then Professor O'Connell arranged for Bon Maharaj to meet with the Toronto ecumenical council, including leaders from the Jewish community, the Baptists, the Christians, and the Catholics. Bon Maharaj had written a translation and commentary on *Bhakti-rasamrita-sindhu, The Nectar of Devotion* and he gave an elevated talk about Radha and Krishna and how Radharani is the pleasure potency of Krishna. But he spoke in a language similar to Srila Bhaktisiddhanta

Saraswati Thakur. It was difficult to understand his points, and if one didn't know the basic principles, one wouldn't really get it. After he spoke, each council member took a turn to say something, trying to be nice. Then it came to me. I said, "We've heard Bon Maharaj speak about God, but I don't hear anyone else speaking about God. If that's what we have in common, why is it that we can't talk about that? Why can't we explore one another's realizations or concepts or understandings of what and who God is?" I agitated everybody.

Later on Prabhupada heard about this and asked me, "What did Bon Maharaj say?" I told him what I remembered. One of the things that Bon Maharaj said after I spoke was, "Lord Chaitanya never preached. He chanted and loved God, but He didn't really preach any philosophy." I had told Bon Maharaj, "That's not what my spiritual master says," but out of respect I didn't want to get too uppity with him, because he was Prabhupada's godbrother. When I related this exchange to Prabhupada, he gave many references from the *Caitanya-caritamrta* proving that Lord Chaitanya did preach the philosophy of Krishna consciousness and did explain who Krishna is, how we should understand Him, and how that fits into our devotional realization and progress. Prabhupada was happy that I had created a disturbance with the ecumenical council and had challenged Bon Maharaj.

Radhanath Swami: After the *kirtan* and *arati,* Srila Prabhupada told the devotees to read Krishna Book. It was a small temple, and it was completely overcrowded with devotees. The Deities were in the front, Prabhupada was in the back, and there was an aisle between Prabhupada and the Deities that was left open. Along the two sides of the aisle were all the *sannyasis* of North America, sitting facing each other with their *dandas* in hand. Behind them the devotees were crowded tightly together. A *sannyasi* started to read. By this time it was late at night, and it was so hot you could hardly breathe. Everyone was falling asleep. People were falling down and being caught by another. You would see the *sannyasis' dandas* bobbing back and forth as they fell asleep. Nobody could stay awake in the whole temple room, but Prabhupada was sitting on the *vyasasana* with his back straight, attentively hearing the glories of Lord Krishna. When the devotee finally read, "Thus ends the First Chapter of the Krishna Book, entitled, 'The Advent of Lord Krishna,'" everyone was so happy that they chanted, "*Jaya*, Srila Prabhupada!" Not because of the book, but because it was over (Laughs). With complete gravity Srila Prabhupada said, "Next chapter." Someone started reading the next chapter while the devotees were still falling asleep. We had fasted all day, and everyone was struggling and straining, because besides being tired, we were also very hungry. By this time it was after midnight. The second chapter is long. It seemed to go on for hours. Finally the devotee read, "Thus ends the Second Chapter of Krishna Book, entitled, 'The Prayers By the Demigods to Krishna in the Womb.'" Everyone was happy that it was over, thinking in terms of *prasadam* and sleep. They chanted, "*Jaya*, Prabhupada!" Prabhupada said, "Next chapter." They started reading the next chapter. Looking at Srila Prabhupada, I thought of how Maharaj Pariksit sat for seven days and seven nights hearing the glories of the Lord with rapt attention and tasting the sweetness of the ambrosia. *Srimad-Bhagavatam* states that the sign of a great soul is that he has a taste for hearing Krishna's glories. While we were struggling and straining, falling asleep, falling down, and praying that the reading would end, Prabhupada was completely immersed in the ecstasy of hearing Krishna's *lila*.

Finally the next chapter ended, and by that time the devotees were hardly able to say, "*Jaya*, Prabhupada" (Laughs). Srila Prabhupada looked at the pathetic group of us. He smiled, still sitting erect, completely immersed in Krishna's *lila,* and said, "I think that you are all very tired and hungry, so we will end here." Then as loud as you could imagine, everybody chanted, "*Jaya*, Prabhupada!" Srila Prabhupada was happy to see all of us together at New Vrindavan.

Bhaktadas: In 1972 there was a devotee named Devarishi in San

Francisco who had become famous as an expert *Back to Godhead* magazine distributor. But he had had a fall down of some sort, and the temple president in San Francisco had kicked him out. This temple president called me and said, "Don't let Devarishi in, he had a fall down." Then Devarishi showed up at the San Diego temple. I had a hard time keeping anyone out. Srila Prabhupada was there, and Devarishi was sitting on the front lawn wanting to come in. I said, "Why don't you come in and see Srila Prabhupada?" He came in and explained to Srila Prabhupada what had happened and how he wasn't welcome in the temples anymore. Prabhupada said, "You come and travel with me." This is an example of Prabhupada's compassion. Nobody wanted Devarishi, but Prabhupada said, "Come and travel with me. I want you." Prabhupada didn't reject anyone.

Radhanath Swami: When Srila Prabhupada came to New Vrindavan I was to garland him, which was a very special service. The plan was that Srila Prabhupada was going to be escorted into the temple, and when he sat on his *vyasasana,* I was to garland him. So when Prabhupada came out of his Lincoln Continental, I was right there with a tray with Prabhupada's garland on it. Everybody was pushing to be with Prabhupada, but because I had his garland, I was allowed to walk right behind him. We entered the temple, and Srila Prabhupada bowed down before Sri Sri Radha-Vrindavan Chandra. With great emotion he stared at the Deities for a minute or two, and then he sat on the *vyasasana.* By that time all of the devotees had crowded into the temple room and begun *kirtan.* I approached Srila Prabhupada with the garland. Srila Prabhupada looked at me, smiled, and then bent his head down for me to put the garland on. But I felt so shy that I didn't put the garland on him. Prabhupada was looking at me with his head bowed, indicating, "Go ahead and put it on." But I just stood there. Prabhupada didn't say anything, but with his eyes, he said many things. At that time I was a *brahmachari.* One of my *sannyasi* godbrothers was standing next to me, and I gave him the garland and he put it on Srila Prabhupada. Srila Prabhupada didn't look at my godbrother. He just looked at me, and he was pleased. He nodded his head as if to say, "Yes, this is correct, you have understood." He didn't say anything, but through his gesture and through his eyes he spoke in such a way that I could understand, "Yes. To be the servant of my servant is the best way to please me." That was one of the most wonderful instructions Srila Prabhupada ever gave me. With my life and soul I am endeavoring to try to follow that instruction.

Uttamasloka: The next year we were in Toronto when Prabhupada came again. By this time we had the new temple building, and Prabhupada came there. I was president of Chicago, and Madhavananda had taken over from Govardhan in Detroit. At one point there was some discussion about how the Indian community wasn't happy in Detroit, and Prabhupada said, "Can't Govardhan—" I said, "Govardhan isn't president there anymore, Prabhupada." He said, "Who is?" I said, "Madhavananda's president." He said, "Why is he president?" I said, "Well, Govardhan was having trouble, he wasn't chanting his rounds." He said, "How do you know he wasn't chanting his rounds?" I said, "Well, Prabhupada, he said he wasn't." Prabhupada said, "At least he is honest enough to admit it. You say you are. How do I know you are? Maybe you're lying." I said, "But Prabhupada, he wasn't coming to the morning program." He said, "You have to encourage him. Put him back as president. He did such good work there. He should be temple president." So Govardhan got reinstated as temple president.

As it happens, I had taken over Sri Govinda's position as temple president of Chicago. Sri Govinda met Prabhupada in New York hoping that, like Govardhan, he would be reinstated. But Prabhupada said, "Sometimes change is good. Let's leave things the way they are."

Radhanath Swami: Advaita Acharya, one of my godbrothers, asked Prabhupada about *siddha deha*. As soon as he said "*siddha deha,*" Prabhupada cut him off. He said, "What is this nonsense, '*siddha* *deha?*' You are filled with so many bad qualities. Don't talk about *siddha deha*. First purify yourself through *hari nam,* through following the regulative principles, through the basic principles of Krishna consciousness. Until you're purified, don't talk about '*siddha deha.*'" He was as strong as a lion.

Another devotee asked, "What if one falls down after taking initiation?" Again Srila Prabhupada was like a lion. He said, "What is this, 'fall down'? There is no question of fall down. You have taken a vow in front of your spiritual master, in front of the Deities, in front of the sacred fire, in front of the assembly of Vaishnavs. You have made your promise. How can you break your promise? No gentleman will break such a promise. There is no question of falling down."

Another devotee named Janardan asked Srila Prabhupada, "Sometimes people say that, 'I don't need a guru because God speaks to me within my heart.' What do we say to such a person?" Prabhupada became very grave and heavy. He said, "You don't know how to answer this question? You don't read my books? Why can't you answer this question, you rascal?" He chastised Janardan severely and then explained that in the *Bhagavad-gita,* Krishna says that He speaks only to the person who constantly serves Him with love, who worships Him with complete devotion, and who does not fall down under any circumstance. "Why don't you answer this? Why don't you know these verses?" He went on and on, chastising Janardan. It was so heavy that everyone was paralyzed. We couldn't cope with Prabhupada's anger. A devotee named Kulashekar asked Prabhupada a simple question to change the subject, but Prabhupada just went back to Janardan and continued to chastise him. He said, "You are a rascal. You have simply come to disturb me." In this way Srila Prabhupada stressed that we should know his books and be able to preach accordingly. He had given so much of his life and energy to write these books for us. He speaks through his books. We don't have to ask him these things personally. That was the lesson he taught us that day.

Uttamasloka: On a morning walk in Mayapur, Satsvarupa Maharaj asked Prabhupada, "How can we accelerate our advancement in Krishna consciousness?" Prabhupada said, "Just think that, 'I'm going to die in one minute.' If you knew that you were going to die in one minute, your consciousness would be focused on Krishna." That kind of mind set will give us the intensity of focus that we need.

Radhanath Swami: I was the *pujari* at the old Vrindavan farm, which was on the other side of the mountain. To see Srila Prabhupada each evening, I had to climb down one mountain, cross a small river, and then climb up another mountain. Every day I passed a rose bush that had one beautiful, fully blossomed rose. It was a miracle. I would pick that rose and offer that rose at Srila Prabhupada's lotus feet when he was sitting on his *vyasasana*. Often when he was lecturing he would pick up that rose and hold it in his hand. One day he had a garland of marigolds, and he was holding and smelling the rose I had offered him. As he looked at the rose he said, "Just like this rose is a flower and these marigolds are also flowers. Although they are both flowers, still the rose is the best of flowers. Similarly, we are all simultaneously one with and different from Krishna. Although we are one with Krishna, still Krishna is Krishna. Krishna is the rose." He used the different flowers as an example of *achintya bheda bheda tattva*, simultaneously one and different.

Bhaktadas: On July 1, 1970 we had organized a festival in the Starlight Opera Theater at Balboa Park. We tried to advertise and promote it, and although we had a reasonable crowd, not a lot of people came. Sitting on the stage on his *vyasasana*, Srila Prabhupada had begun lecturing about Lord Chaitanya, when some drunk hippie in the audience started screaming, "We want sex! We love sex! Sex, sex, we want sex!" Srila Prabhupada leaned over and asked, "What is he saying?" I said, "Srila Prabhupada, he says he wants sex." Srila Prabhupada stopped his lecture and spoke about the real purpose of sex. That was quite amazing. That lecture is in the archives and you can read it.

Uttamasloka: One time I asked, "Prabhupada, if somebody's having trouble with sex desire, what should he do?" He said, "Chant Hare Krishna more, that's all."

Radhanath Swami: During one evening *darshan* I was feeling a little guilty because I had lost my counting beads. In New Vrindavan in those days it was not easy to get counting beads. I was chanting sixteen rounds daily, but on that particular evening I wasn't sure whether I had finished my rounds or not. I was sitting a few feet from Srila Prabhupada's *vyasasana* when I thought, "I'm not sure whether I finished my rounds today." At that moment Srila Prabhupada looked at me very sincerely. During the *darshan,* when he wasn't talking to people, he'd chant *japa.* He held up his bead bag, took one of his counting beads, and very meticulously, slowly and deliberately pulled it down. Then he let go of the counting bead and opened his palm, still looking at me. I thought, "Srila Prabhupada wants me to get counting beads. He wants to make sure that I don't compromise, that I chant sixteen rounds properly every day."

Uttamasloka: Once, before I was initiated in Los Angeles, Srila Prabhupada was speaking about the verse in the *Gita* where Krishna says, "I am the taste in water" (Bg.7.8). Prabhupada said, "Even if a wino, a drunkard, drinks wine and thinks that, 'Krishna is the taste in this,' he can make some advancement. That consciousness will purify him." Of course, wine drinking is not purifying, but that consciousness is progressive. The drunkard should think like that.

Radhanath Swami: One evening, it was raining and very cold when the devotees gathered for *darshan* at the front door of Srila Prabhupada's house. Srila Prabhupada's secretary, Pusta Krishna Maharaj, came out and told us that Srila Prabhupada would not be giving *darshan* that night. We were very sad that we wouldn't have Srila Prabhupada's precious association, and we started walking away. Then through a window, Srila Prabhupada saw us and told Pusta Krishna, "Call them in." Usually *darshan* was outside, but on this night, Pusta Krishna Maharaj said, "Srila Prabhupada wants you to come in for *darshan*." We all crowded into his living room and sat down. Srila Prabhupada was very ill, and it was announced that he would not speak. With his head on his hand, Prabhupada sat with us while Pradyumna read about the symptoms of Kali-yuga from the Twelfth Canto of *Srimad-Bhagavatam*. Prabhupada was enlivened to hear Vedavyasa's descriptions of what will come in Kali-yuga. Every time Pradyumna read a symptom, Srila Prabhupada suddenly became free of his sickness. He became dynamic and joyful and began to speak. He said, "People will travel long distances just to go to a place of pilgrimage. This is a symptom of Kali. For example, today people living on the bank of the Ganges in Calcutta take much trouble to go to Hardwar to bathe in the Ganges. Similarly, you are in New Vrindavan. New Vrindavan is nondifferent than Vrindavan. You have no need to go anywhere. Vrindavan is here, and Krishna is here." Hearing this, all of the devotees became very happy.

Then Pradyumna read about how, in Kali-yuga, beauty will be judged by how long one grows his hair. Prabhupada said, "Yes, Vedavyas could see past, present, and future. At the time he wrote *Srimad-Bhagavatam,* there was no hippie movement, but he knew that the hippie movement would come." Then he began to explain how *Srimad-Bhagavatam* was the perfect scripture because it was compiled by Vedavyas. He had perfect realization, perfect vision of past, present, and future and perfect vision of Krishna. In this way, what originally appeared to be a despondent night of not hearing from Prabhupada became a most wonderful *darshan*.

Bhaktadas: Mr. Joshi was a retired Punjabi magistrate who lived in the Berkeley area across the San Francisco Bay. Every time Srila Prabhupada came to San Francisco he would go to Mr. Joshi's for lunch. Mr. Joshi would greet him with a garland of one-dollar bills. We'd all criticize Mr. Joshi, "Why aren't you giving one hundred-dollar bills?" (Laughs) Mr. Joshi would wash Prabhupada's feet, he would wash all the devotee's feet, and he'd have us sit down.

On this particular occasion, I was wiped out because I had been working hard for Ratha-yatra for a number of weeks. I was sitting down for *prasadam* feeling horrible, but I hadn't said anything to anyone. I was determined to grit it out. Srila Prabhupada looked at me and said, "Bhaktadas, you're not feeling well?" I said, "Srila Prabhupada, I'm a little sick." He said, "Go and take rest. You have worked hard, now take rest." I said, "Yes, Srila Prabhupada," paid my obeisances, walked into a back bedroom, layed down and passed out. After some time, I heard some noise and looked up to see Srila Prabhupada coming in. I jumped out of the bed and fell down at his feet in *dandavats*. I started to walk out of the room, when Prabhupada said to me, "Take rest! You've worked hard, take rest!" I said, "Yes, Srila Prabhupada," and got back into bed. There were two twin beds right next to each other. I was in the one on the right, and Mr. Joshi came and pulled back the covers of the other one. Srila Prabhupada crawled in, and Mr. Joshi tucked him in as if he were a child. It was very sweet. The two beds were only a foot and a half apart. Prabhupada's head and my head were quite close while we napped. Of course, for me it wasn't an ordinary nap. It was a Goloka nap, a *yoga nidra* nap. It was very extraordinary. It showed how Srila Prabhupada was compassionate, sensitive and caring. He didn't have an air that, "Hey, I'm the guru and you're a nobody and you get out, I'm taking the bed." He was equal to everyone. Of course, he was as good as God to me. But his kindness was overwhelming. Every time Srila Prabhupada saw me, the first thing he would say was, "Bhaktadas, are you happy?" He was always concerned. I was always happy when I was with Srila Prabhupada. Sometimes, before I went to see him I was angry, but when I saw him, everything disappeared. All problems evaporated. There weren't any problems in his presence.

Radhanath Swami: Toward the beginning of his visit in New Vrindavan, the weather became cold and rainy. Srila Prabhupada's secretary said that Srila Prabhupada was going to cut his trip short because the weather was not good for his health. Kirtanananda Swami became sad and told Srila Prabhupada, "If you cannot live here happily, then we will sell this place and start New Vrindavan somewhere else." I'll never forget Srila Prabhupada's reply. He said, "No. Because you are protecting Krishna's cows here, your mission is perfect. It is a success." Then he said, "I will stay until the end of my scheduled visit."

Uttamasloka: Prabhupada went to Portland, Oregon for a few days, and while he was there he spoke at a "New Age" meeting. A lady in the audience was with a child who was crying. Prabhupada said to her, "Can you please take the child out?" The lady said, "Is the child disturbing you?" Prabhupada said, "No, the child's not disturbing me. He's disturbing you and everyone else."

In Portland, I asked Prabhupada's servant, "What do you do with Prabhupada's old bead bags?" He said, "I give them away." I said, "Can I have one?" He said, "Sure," and he later sent one to Montreal for me.

Radhanath Swami: I was the *pujari* at Radha-Vrindavannath's temple, which was the *brahmacharis'* temple. Srila Prabhupada was very merciful to me. Every day I used to make *sandesh*. Whenever anyone from New Vrindavan visited Prabhupada, they would bring him a box of *sandesh* that I had made, and out of his great kindness Prabhupada always appreciated it. When he came to New Vrindavan, he told me that he wanted my *sandesh* with every meal, three times a day.

One particular night I came with a picture of Radha-Vrindavannath. Kirtanananda Swami had decided that Srila Prabhupada should not go to Their temple because the road was too treacherous and because the ashram was primitive. He thought it would be an inconvenience for Prabhupada. As the *pujari*, I thought, "If he's not going to come to see the Deities, the Deities can come to see him." So I brought a photo. Pusta Krishna was not allowing anyone in his room, but I said, "I have a gift for Prabhupada." So he said, "All right, come in." I offered Srila Prabhupada the picture of Radha-Vrindavannath, the only photo we had of Them. Prabhupada looked at it and was happy. He asked Kirtanananda Swami, "Is this Radha-Vrindavan Chandra?" Kirtanananda Swami said, "No, this is Radha-Vrindavannath, and this is the boy who always makes *sandesh* for you."

Srila Prabhupada began to talk about Vrindavan, and then he said, "You will take me to Radha-Vrindavanath?" Kirtanananda Swami said, "No, Prabhupada. The road is very bad. It is very difficult to go there." Prabhupada said, "Do you have a Jeep? We will go. I want to go." He insisted. They took him by Jeep part of the way, and then he walked the rest of the way. On the way he passed cows grazing, and one of them was the first cow of ISKCON, who Prabhupada had named Kaliya. She was a small, old, black Jersey. When she saw Srila Prabhupada, she ran to him. Prabhupada had not seen her since 1968, when he first came to New Vrindavan, and this was eight years later. One devotee said, "Prabhupada, this is a very special cow." Prabhupada said, "Yes, I know, this is Kaliya." Kaliya walked beside Prabhupada to Radha-Vrindavannath's temple.

Bhaktadas: Most of the devotees in San Francisco had never seen Srila Prabhupada and wanted to have his *darshan*. They had worked hard, so I gathered most of them and brought them to Srila Prabhupada's room. I wanted to bring Jayananda, but Jayananda kept saying, "I'm too busy, I don't have time. I have to work." I grabbed him: "You're coming. You're going to go see your spiritual master." Prabhupada was staying in Keshava Bharati's apartment. We went in and paid our obeisances. Jayananda sat down against the far back wall and instantly fell asleep. He didn't say a word to Srila Prabhupada, and Prabhupada didn't say a word to him. We had *darshan* for thirty or forty minutes, and when it was time to go I said, "Jayananda, it's time to go." He said, "Okay," paid his obeisances, and walked out. It was obvious that the relationship between Srila Prabhupada and Jayananda extended far beyond the range of the voice or body. It wasn't at all dependent upon bodily conditions.

Uttamasloka: Prabhupada was on a morning walk in New York when he stopped and looked up at some birds that were singing in a tree. He said, "Oh, they're chanting Hare Krishna." The devotees looked at each other stunned, thinking, "Wow, Prabhupada understands the language of the birds." They said, "Prabhupada, are they really chanting Hare Krishna?" He said, "It sounds like it to me."

Radhanath Swami: Prabhupada encouraged us and tried to increase our enthusiasm for devotional service. Once when he was eating the *sandesh* I prepared for him, he said, "This is the best *sandesh* that I ever tasted in my entire life." On another occasion somebody from some other place brought him *sandesh* and asked, "Do you like this *sandesh*?" He said, "It is very good, but it is not as good as Radhanath's." In this way he would enliven us and invoke our desire to serve him and Krishna. Another time, a devotee named Taru made sweet rice. Prabhupada said, "In forty years I have not tasted such good sweet rice." Still another time, Chandramali Swami made *pera* for Srila Prabhupada. Prabhupada said, "I have not tasted *pera* like this for many years. Please give this to me with all my meals."

Bhaktadas: At the end of a Christmas Marathon in '73 or '74, Rameshvar sent Prabhupada enormous book distribution scores. Srila Prabhupada wrote back, "Congratulations on selling so many books. This is very nice, and I'm very pleased." But in the final sentence, he wrote, "The highest realization is to save your self." That sentence was like a sledgehammer in my heart, because most of us were thinking, "We're saved, and we're saving others." But here he was telling us that the highest thing is to save ourselves. I felt that we had become like Christians, thinking "I'm saved by the blood of Jesus, and these people are all heathens. We're going to save them." I felt that we'd become puffed up and intoxicated by ourselves. The words in that letter always stayed with me.

Radhanath Swami: It was wonderful when Srila Prabhupada gave cookies to the children during *guru puja*. I thought, "This is a real preacher." The children couldn't understand philosophy, and they weren't able to follow the *Srimad-Bhagavatam* class. But Srila Prabhupada knew that if they became attached to him, they would go back to Godhead. So, with a beautiful, loving smile, like a father he would give each child a cookie. The children loved him.

Everything Srila Prabhupada did was to induce our love for him, because he knew that our love for him was carried to the lotus feet of Sri Sri Radha and Krishna.

Bhaktadas: Regarding the question of the origin of the *jiva*, Srila Prabhupada was asked, "Where did we come from? Were we originally with Krishna?" and so forth. I was with him several times when this question came up, and invariably he gave the same answer. He said, "You're sick, you have a disease. Do you care how you got the disease, or do you care about getting better? First get better, then you will understand." He made that point over and over again. Now there's so much discussion, people are studying different scriptures and saying, "We were originally with Krishna." or "We came from the *brahmajyoti* and that we've never been with Krishna." What is the point of speculating about it? Why not get healthy? To me the discussion is a waste of time, and that's how Srila Prabhupada always dealt with it. His instruction was "Just get healthy." He didn't want us to think that we're big scholars and that by studying books we were going to understand. This is not something we can understand by study. We can understand it when it's revealed to us due to our pure devotional service.

Uttamasloka: At the Mayapur festival in 1977 Prabhupada was so sick that he wasn't speaking or participating in any functions. Everybody was disturbed. We didn't know what to make of it all.

At one point the devotees from all the different temples had a *kirtan* contest. I was the president of Chicago, and we were really into *kirtan*. I had imbibed the Bengali style and introduced it in Chicago. (Later on it became popular all over the movement.) We chanted at a preliminary round, won, and were one of the few groups that went to the finals. But unfortunately, people started criticizing us. I told the men in my group to ignore it because it wasn't the mood that we were in. But it got out of hand and started to bother me too. At one point, Tamal Krishna Maharaj said, "Uttama, it looks like your group may win." I said, "No, I don't think so." He said, "Why not?" I said, "I'm not even going to chant, because people think that we're into it for nondevotional reasons, which is completely wrong. Nobody appreciates it." He said, "That's not true. Prabhupada appreciates it." I said, "How do you know?" He said, "Because when you first chanted, we were sitting with Prabhupada. We had been with him for days. Prabhupada wasn't looking at us, he wasn't speaking or moving. But when your *kirtan* group chanted, Prabhupada tapped his hand in time. When your *kirtan* reached a crescendo and the Bengali women responded with their yodeling, Prabhupada said, 'Just see, this is ecstasy.'" Tamal Krishna Maharaj said, "We were taken aback because before that Prabhupada hadn't said anything. Prabhupada appreciated your *kirtan*." I said, "OK, I'll stay."

Radhanath Swami: The depth of Srila Prabhupada's compassion was something that invoked a mood of surrender from my hard heart. He was willing to extend himself and sacrifice himself to give us Krishna consciousness. The compassion and the concern and the love he had for conditioned souls was something that I had never seen before. I lived with several of Srila Prabhupada's godbrothers who were, like Srila Prabhupada, extremely learned in the *sastra*. But Srila Prabhupada's deep, deep merciful nature to give his life for us was something that I had never experienced before anywhere in anyone.

TAPE 13

Jadurani dasi
Tripurari Swami
Bhagavat das

 **Jadurani:** My first conversation with Prabhupada was after he and the devotees left the park. At that time Hare Krishna wasn't well known, as it is now, and I had never heard of it. Some stranger came over to me and asked me if I'd like to go to the temple to see the Swami. I didn't know what that was, but intuitively I felt there was something there. I went to the temple and I saw the devotees chanting in front of Prabhupada's dais (*vyasasana*). A devotee came over and gave me a *chapati*, which I immediately started eating, and while I was eating it, I overheard two other devotees talking between themselves. One of them was saying, "The Swami just said, 'Whenever devotees fight, it should be taken like clouds passing by, because when clouds pass by, you hardly even notice it. So it should be taken as insignificant.'" I thought that was amazing.

 **Tripurari Swami:** Sometime in 1972 I got to go on one of Prabhupada's famous morning walks. At that time I had become a little bit known for distributing his books. Someone said, "Prabhupada, Tripurari das is here and he's distributing books." Prabhupada turned to me and opened his eyes quite wide and quoted the verse from *Bhagavad-gita,* "No one will ever be more dear to Me than one

who preaches the message of *Bhagavad-gita*." He encouraged me along those lines, and by his grace, I was already enthusiastic. His words further catapulted me into the service that I did for a long time in his manifest presence, namely distributing his literature and inspiring others to do so.

 **Bhagavat:** At the end of the talk, Prabhupada asked if anybody had questions. I said, "How does one become sincere?" because I thought that sincerity was the key quality in achieving self-realization. He said, "You become sincere by being sincere. You have to want Krishna consciousness. You have to sincerely want to surrender to a spiritual master and to Krishna," and he talked a little about those things.

Later on, once in Africa and once in India, I came into Srila Prabhupada's room to see him when some Life Members were present. He introduced me by saying, "This is my disciple, Bhagavat das, and he is very sincere." That struck me. It touched my heart that Prabhupada remembered that I wanted to be sincere.

Jadurani: Somebody invited me to see the Swami in his apartment. I went in, and ten or fifteen devotees were there chanting *japa,* although I didn't know what they were chanting. Prabhupada was sitting in front of his little altar that was surrounded by tall gladiola plants. He offered his obeisances to one of the pictures of Krishna on the altar. I was an impersonalist, and I thought he was offering his obeisances to the floor because everything is God. Then he went into his back room, which was called the sitting room, and somebody asked me to go back there. I didn't know anything, I just followed the requests. I noticed that Prabhupada reciprocated with everybody as they reciprocated with him. Whoever shook his hand, he shook their hand. When someone offered *pranams,* he did similarly. As they did with him, he did with them.

He sat back on his mat and said, "We are eternal, and everything

around us is temporary." Because Prabhupada is the external manifestation of Supersoul, you felt the power of the Supersoul speaking
when he spoke. Just that statement had a tremendous influence on
me. He asked me if I lived nearby, and I said, "Oh, yes, I live very
near," because I thought I was all-pervading, but actually I lived an
hour-and-a-half away. He said, "Oh, very good. Then you can come
for morning classes." Although it was very difficult to take an hour-
and-a-half train ride from the Bronx to downtown Manhattan, by the
power of his invitation I felt obligated to do it. I began taking the
train in the mornings. That was my first experience with him.

Tripurari Swami: On morning walks Srila Prabhupada used to ask
me, "So, Tripurari Maharaj, what are they saying?" That was his
standard kind of question to me, because he knew I was always in
the field preaching to people, distributing literature and so forth.
He knew that I would need arguments to counteract the people's
arguments, and he was curious what their arguments were. Each
time Prabhupada asked me I would give one or two of their arguments, and Prabhupada would defeat it in an enlightening way.

Once in Mayapur I told Prabhupada, "They're saying that we
should use our intelligence to understand absolute knowledge and
the truth of life and we should apply ourselves with all of our God-
given reasoning," as if to say Krishna consciousness was deviating
from reasoning. It does go beyond reasoning, but it picks up where
reasoning leaves off.

Prabhupada immediately replied, "Okay, use your intelligence.
Read and study the *Bhagavad-gita*." He usually responded in short
bursts like that. One time in Vrindavan he asked me what they were
saying. I said, "Prabhupada, they're saying that we're parasites; that
we are simply leeching off the society without contributing anything." He said, "So stop giving." Everyone was silent. He said, "But
you can't." That's all he said, but it was profound. I appreciated the
point that, "You say we're only parasites. Then we say 'Stop giving,'" because in fact someone else is supplying us. This *sankirtan*

movement is going on not because you're supporting us, but you are benefited by participating. The support is coming from above. Krishna's in the background supplying and supporting.

Bhagavat: Srila Prabhupada was looking at all of us sitting before him. He picked up a set of beads and said, "Whose beads?" I recognized them and said, "They're mine, Srila Prabhupada." He turned and said, "What is his name?" (They had the list of names in a book.) Aravinda said, "His name is Bhagavat das." Prabhupada looked at me and laughed. He said, "Oh, Bhagavat das." It was almost as if he knew me or was waiting for me to come. He said, "There are two things. There is the book Bhagavat, meaning scriptures like *Srimad-Bhagavatam* and *Bhagavad-gita,* and there is the person Bhagavat, meaning those persons who follow the *Srimad-Bhagavatam* and *Bhagavad-gita.* You are Bhagavat das, and you shall serve them both."

He had my beads in his hand, and he said, "What are the four rules?" I said the four rules. He said, "How many rounds a day must you chant?" At the time, as an austerity, I had been chanting twenty rounds a day. I said, "We are supposed to chant sixteen rounds a day, but I am chanting twenty." Prabhupada looked at me and frowned, as if to say, "Don't be so egotistical." Then he gave me my beads, and I started chanting in front of him. Prabhupada picked up the next beads and said, "Whose beads?" Subrata said, "Mine." Prabhupada initiated him and was about to give him his beads when he noticed that Subrata didn't have neck beads on. Just as Subrata reached for his beads, Prabhupada took them back. He said, "Where are your neck beads?" Then he looked at me and saw that I didn't have neck beads on either. Prabhupada said, "He has no beads either." He turned to Hridayananda, Aravinda, and Sridam and said, "You are the senior disciples. You know that they can't get initiated without neck beads. Why don't they have neck beads?" Everyone said, "We're sorry, we're sorry. We were busy with the lecture and TV show. We'll make sure that they have neck beads before the fire *yajna* tomorrow." Prabhupada said, "All right, all right. But before the fire *yajna* they must have neck beads."

Jadurani: When I went into the temple I noticed that lots of pots were there. Usually somebody brought the pots back to Prabhupada's quarters to wash them, but this time, because there was an engagement right after lunch, they had been left there. So I brought the pots to Prabhupada's apartment. When I got to the kitchen, Achyutananda said, "You're not supposed to be here unless you're initiated." I was so embarrassed and flustered that I didn't know what to do. Out of the corner of my eye I noticed that Prabhupada was sitting in his greeting room. I turned to Prabhupada and said, "Oh, yes, that's what I came to talk to you about, initiation." Prabhupada was calm and serene. He said, "Can you follow the principles?" I said, "Yes," although at that time I had only given up smoking. He said, "All right, in two weeks you can be initiated with Bob."

The day before initiation, I still didn't have any beads. In those days we didn't have *tulasi*, so we bought red beads at Tandi's Hobby Store and strung them ourselves. I asked some of the devotees what initiation meant. They said, "It means that we agree to serve the spiritual master. We accept him as God and we agree to serve him for the rest of this life and eternally thereafter." I thought, "Oh, okay."

For the special occasion of my initiation I wore tight black jeans and a black turtleneck shirt. I didn't know Prabhupada's *pranam* mantra yet, so when he handed me my beads and told me to bow down, I didn't know what to say. He said, "*Nama.*" I said, "*Nama.*" He said, "*Om.*" I said, "*Om.*" He said, "*Vishnupadaya.*" In that way we went through the mantra. Then he said, "Your name is Jadurani. Jadurani is the original queen in the Yadu dynasty. Although Krishna is eternal, He appears in a particular family of devotees to glorify that family. He appears just like the sun. As the sun is always there but it appears in the day and disappears at night, so Krishna's appearance is like that." I was honored to get the name Jadurani.

Tripurari Swami: During 1974 I traveled as a *brahmachari*, organizing book distribution and preaching throughout America. Then I came to Mayapur, but I had no GBC because the fellow who was my GBC in Los Angeles had left. The GBC called me in and asked me, "Who is your GBC?" I thought, "I don't know, I don't have a GBC." I didn't really understand what the GBC was. I didn't realize that you had to have one.

At any rate, after their meetings the GBC would read their resolutions to Prabhupada, and he would say, "Yes, this one is all right. Adjust that one. That one is not good." They brought up my name, and Prabhupada said, "What has Tripurari done?" With a quiver in their voice they said, "Well, Prabhupada, he doesn't have any GBC, and he's traveling around and raising so much—" Prabhupada cut them off and said, "He's distributing my books, he doesn't need a GBC." That was the end of the story. Three GBCs came to me afterwards and apologized. In that way, in my mind and in the minds of a number of leading men, I came directly under Prabhupada. Therefore they didn't really complain when I forced my way into the morning walks, because at the time I was Prabhupada's main instrument for distributing books.

Prabhupada gave me encouraging words about preaching. In 1977, when he had fallen ill and the festival was ending in Mayapur, he decided not to go to Vrindavan. I went to him with Panchadravida Maharaj and said, "Prabhupada, I'm not interested in going to Vrindavan for the rest of the festival." He said, "Why not?" I said, "Because you are the festival. Without you, there is no meaning to Vrindavan and the festival there. I would like to stay here with you." I felt that he deeply appreciated my sentiment, but he said, "No, you are a preacher. You should go."

Shortly thereafter many of us were sitting with Prabhupada when Ramesvara gave him a report that to date sixty-four million books in many different languages had been distributed. Prabhupada heard the report and said to me, "This sixty-four million is all your credit." I thought, "Prabhupada, this is all your credit. You are so encouraging to us."

I got some deep realizations when Prabhupada opened the Krishna-Balaram temple in Vrindavan. We had all worked hard selling books and directly raising money to build that temple. It was a great struggle for Prabhupada, and when I saw him offering *arati* to Krishna-Balaram, I was deeply touched. The temple was wonderful, and Prabhupada had wanted it so much. Now it was done, and somehow we'd been instruments in it. Watching him offer the *arati* to Krishna and Balaram was glorious. Visakha, the photographer, was behind me, and there was quite a push and a shove to get close to Prabhupada to witness the first *arati*. She said to me, "Maharaj, I want to photograph this for preaching." Preaching was so important that she wanted me to let her in front. I thought, "The hell with preaching. I'm not moving from here. I'm going to watch Srila Prabhupada offering *arati* to Krishna and Balaram."

Anyway, I got so much inspiration at that time. Hamsadutta was standing next to me, and tears were flowing from his eyes. I was also choked up and crying.

Later I went to Prabhupada, and his secretary didn't want to let me in, but I got in anyway. I said, "Prabhupada, I think I'd like to take *sannyas*." But I was submissive. I was known as an independent, rebellious maverick, but I have both sides, and before Prabhupada I was submissive. I was afraid to ask anything of him. I tried to say, "If you don't want me to take *sannyas,* then I don't want to. But maybe you'll want it. I want it only because that kind of commitment will draw me closer to you."

I tried to explain all this to Prabhupada when he asked me, "Why you should take?" Prabhupada played with me. He knew me, but he said, "So, you are *brahmachari?*" I said, "Prabhupada, it's me, Tripurari." I had a wife when I joined, but she had left. He said, "Oh, you are a *vanaprastha?*" Then he said, "What if you give up *sannyas* after you take it?" I said, "Prabhupada, I would never do that." I thought, "Out of love I want to do this for you." He said, "Others have said that 'I will never give it up,' and they have gone." I thought,

"Well, maybe he doesn't want me to do it. Gosh, I don't want to force my idea on him. This is not *bhakti; bhakti* is to take his idea and do his bidding. Not to impose my idea." I said, "I want to be as closely connected with you as possible. I want all three initiations." Then I backed off, I said, "Anyway, Prabhupada, I don't want to push it."

He didn't say "no" and he didn't say "yes." He was amused by it. I went to every GBC member there and told them, "I'm thinking of taking *sannyas*." They had just passed a rule that you couldn't do that, but they had also just been told that "Tripurari doesn't need a GBC." None of them opposed me except Brahmananda. Maybe I took it that the majority rules. When Tamal Krishna Maharaj heard that I was talking about taking *sannyas*, he told me, "Yes, you should do it immediately. Let's go to Prabhupada," and he dragged me back to Srila Prabhupada. He said, "Prabhupada, Tripurari wants to take *sannyas*, and all of us think it's a wonderful idea." Prabhupada said, "Tomorrow he will take *sannyas*." In a sense, my *sannyas* was in violation of the GBC resolution.

Prabhupada was present when Satsvarupa Maharaj performed a fire sacrifice for my *sannyas* initiation in the courtyard of the Krishna-Balaram temple. Afterwards, in Prabhupada's quarters, Prabhupada gave me the mantras, the *danda* and some instructions to preach.

Bhagavat: Srila Prabhupada asked if we had any questions. I was an avid reader, and by that time I had read the little blue *Bhagavad-gita* twelve or fourteen times. One of my favorite parts was "The Modes of Material Nature." Being philosophical by nature, I wanted to understand some of the more refined and subtle points. So I said to Prabhupada, "I'm confused because throughout your books and in your lectures, you say that when you become a devotee you're on the transcendental platform. But at the same time, you talk about being affected by the modes of material nature. Although I'm a devotee practicing the principles of devotional service and experiencing a certain amount of transcendental pleasure, at the same time I feel affected by the modes of material nature. How is it that I can be on the transcendental platform and still be affected by the modes of material nature?"

Prabhupada smiled. He saw that it was a thoughtful and introspective question and said, "That is a very good question." He answered, "It is just like being on a boat. When you're on the boat, no one can say you're not on the boat. You are on the boat. But sometimes big waves will come and rock that boat, so your position on the boat may not be steady. Those waves are the modes of material nature, and the boat is the transcendental platform. You're on the transcendental platform, but sometimes the waves of material nature rock the boat, and therefore your position is not steady."

Then he asked, "How will you become steady? For that you have to learn from the captain of the boat, the spiritual master, how to steer the boat. If you learn expertly, then your position in the boat will be steady even in the greatest storm. Similarly, on the transcendental platform, if you learn from the spiritual master how to steer the boat of transcendence through the ocean of material life, then you will become steady even in the greatest storm of the modes of material nature." I was extremely impressed at how Prabhupada explained complex philosophy with a simple analogy.

Jadurani: In 1966 or '67, Prabhupada began his Prahlad Maharaj series. Prabhupada explained how Prahlad would speak to his classmates when his teachers were out, and Prabhupada gave an analogy. He said that in an airplane there's a driver and a motor. Without the motor the plane doesn't run, and with the motor but without the driver, the plane also doesn't run. Similarly, even if you have all of the mechanical bodily arrangements, without the soul in the body, the body doesn't work. Prabhupada said, "Even though the body is so big and complicated if you take a small drop of poison, life is finished. In the same way, if the tiny soul, one ten-thousandth the size of the tip of the hair, is in the body, it brings the whole body to life."

Tripurari Swami: I asked him a question about sickness, because many of the devotees in my party were getting worn out and sick. A notion was going around that, because we were having intimate exchanges with many secular people with bad habits in an overtly nondevotional context, maybe we were taking some karma from the people. We were dressed in secular clothing, and in the context of preaching we would meet people on the street, shake their hands or pat them on the back, and they'd blow smoke in our faces.

Prabhupada answered strongly. He said, "By performing *sankirtan* you can never become infected by anything. The infection that others have will be counteracted, but you cannot become implicated." This is a principle of accepting service. Their reactions shouldn't show up on us, but instead they should become purified of those reactions.

Jadurani: After a couple of paintings in which the proportions were wrong, Prabhupada taught me a grid system to make the paintings more accurate. The pictures he gave me to paint from were in a frame with glass, so with some kind of marker or paintbrush he had me divide the picture in half and then in half again and then in half again to make sixteen lines across and sixteen lines down. Instead of trying to do the whole picture at once, I would paint one box at a time, and it would be more accurate. The first painting I did with that system was of his Guru Maharaj with long hair and a beard. I was surprised at how he looked, because Prabhupada was clean-shaven. Prabhupada told me that for four months of the year, called *chaturmasya*, devotees perform austerities, and at that time his Guru Maharaj didn't shave.

Bhagavat: When he was in Vrindavan, Prabhupada heard that the municipality wouldn't give us a permit to build the Bombay temple. Prabhupada asked Balavanta what we should do, and Balavanta said that we should engage in civil disobedience following Lord Chaitanya's example. Prabhupada said, "Good." He asked all the devotees who were there from all over the world to go to Bombay to preach, go on *sankirtan,* and engage in civil disobedience. Prabhupada appreciated Balavanta's spiritual solution. He said, "Just see this man's intelligence. Just see how intelligent he is. He has understood."

All the Australian, European, American, and African devotees went to Bombay right after the Vrindavan festival. I was given the responsibility of speaking with ministers. We were getting food from America to distribute to the people, and I spoke with different government officials to arrange for permits. I also collected donations of food and money for *prasadam* distribution to the public. Every day I went all the way downtown on the train and then came all the way back. In the evenings Prabhupada awaited my report, "What is the news today?" I said, "I collected 1,500 *rupees* from this man and sacks of grain from that person." He would say, "Very good." He was pleased to see any progress.

He would also ask me about the ministers I had spoken with. One day I spoke to the Chief Minister of the State of Maharastra. Prabhupada was pleased. He beamed. Here his American disciples were speaking with the highest government officials and arranging for so many things. He appreciated how resourceful, adamant, and tenacious we were about serving our spiritual master. He would praise me for my accomplishments, and I always felt good. I was doing my spiritual master's work.

Once he gave me a bank form and money to put in the bank. I took the money and the bank form and put them in either my pocket or my bag. He said, "Don't you count it?" I said, "Well, you gave me the money, Srila Prabhupada." He said, "No. Whenever giving or taking money, always count." I was thinking that in one sense this was a mundane affair but in another sense it was Krishna's money, which was very important to Srila Prabhupada. His point was that you never know what could happen. He wasn't just training us in spiritual matters, but he was training us in mundane matters as well. He saw that we were educated on one level, but on another level we

were totally uneducated about the practicalities of the material
world.

Jadurani: The picture he gave me to paint from was very old, as you
can imagine, since it was a picture of his Guru Maharaj. The details
weren't clear, so in my painting I didn't paint fingernails. He brought
that to my attention, and I said, "Well, I didn't see them." He said,
"All right," as if I had said something intelligent. He was tolerant and
patient with my lack of any kind of consciousness, what to speak of
Krishna consciousness. Everybody knows what fingernails look
like, and I realized that I should paint them in. I painted white *tilak*,
because the picture was black-and-white and our *tilak* was also
white because there was no *gopi chandana* at that time. We used
Fuller's Earth, which one of the devotees bought at a hardware store.
Prabhupada told me to make the *tilak* yellowish and also to make
a bright garland. He told me not to put a halo around his Guru
Maharaj (perhaps I had already put one). Then on a narrow, long
piece of paper, which subsequently he did for many paintings after
that, he wrote the mantra of that particular painting, in this case his
Guru Maharaj's *pranam* mantra, and he told me to write that at the
bottom of the painting. When it was complete he made a big
announcement. There were about ten devotees in the room, and he
said, "You have brought me Vaikuntha." Although he had brought
us Vaikuntha, he said that.

Tripurari Swami: Once Gopavrindapal wanted to ask Prabhupada
about organizing book distribution in a systematic way and about
training the devotees to conduct themselves in a particular way.
Gopavrindapal and I were in Vrindavan and he was pushing me,
"Let's go and see Prabhupada and talk to him about it." I was a little
reluctant.

    One day I heard that Prabhupada was going to cook, so I de-
cided, "I'm going to go there, invited or not, to witness Prabhupada
cooking." I shaved up, got clean, and went in. Prabhupada was tak-

ing massage and said to me, "Why have you come? Do you have some questions?" I said, "Prabhupada, I heard that you were going to cook. I wanted to come and watch or help you cook." I thought that would be a very enlivening experience. He said, "No, I am not cooking. I am a *sannyasi*," and he preached to me about what it meant to be a *sannyasi*, to be independent and so forth. He said, "I could live in the forest and be independent of all of this. They are making nice arrangements, and I'm accepting it."

Gopavrindapal came in and brought up his question, and, while Prabhupada very much appreciated the devotees' sincerity and concern for making preaching nice, he said, "It is a little artificial." Then Gopavrindapal mentioned how Tamal Krishna Maharaj had organized a quota system, i.e. that a certain amount of books should be sold or a certain amount of money collected. Prabhupada said, "That is Tamal Krishna Maharaj's concoction." He said that there may be some place for that to inspire the devotees, but Prabhupada's main point was that preaching was a spontaneous affair.

Prabhupada used me as an example. He said, "Just like our Tripurari Maharaj. Within his heart Krishna's giving him many things to say. He's saying them, and books are selling. So from within their heart each devotee will get inspiration. In this way Krishna consciousness will spread."

That's the way Prabhupada spread Krishna consciousness. He went in the direction that he saw Krishna manifesting. If devotees were chanting sincerely and practicing, something Krishna conscious must be coming. When a disciple was inspired and had an idea to do something, he would often say "Yes, do it," and the disciple would start a temple or whatever. It's not that it was planned out and Prabhupada had a notebook that he was referring to. Krishna was leading and sometimes even leading in the hearts of his disciples. Prabhupada was attentive to that. A *mahabhagavata* sees Krishna everywhere and in everything. Beginning devotees think, "I'm a devotee, everyone else is a demon." The higher devotee thinks, "I'm a demon, everyone else is a devotee."

Jadurani: Sometimes Prabhupada would give me instructions while I painted. He would squat in that typical Indian way and say, "Make the ponds pink," or make something else some other way. Sometimes he would come by and look, and I would ask him philosophical questions. For example, he was lecturing about how the Goddess of Fortune was born from the churning of the Milk Ocean. So, when he was standing behind me as I painted, I turned around and said, "How could that have happened?" Prabhupada said, "You should think, 'All right, I don't understand now but later on the understanding will come.'" He explained it a little bit, but still it's beyond the mind.

Bhagavat: On another occasion, Prabhupada asked Satsvarupa Maharaj to get Tamal Krishna to come to the room. It was in the evening, and I was just coming back from downtown to give my report. As I was going to Prabhupada's room, I saw Satsvarupa Maharaj, and he said, "Have you seen Tamal Krishna Goswami?" I said, "No, I just came back from downtown." He said, "Okay." I went to Prabhupada's room. There were about four Life Members in the room with Prabhupada. Prabhupada said to me, "Come in and sit down." I said, "You're busy now, Prabhupada. I'll come back later." He said, "No. Come in and sit down." I sat down in the corner. Then Tamal Krishna opened the door, and Prabhupada said, "Come in, sit down." He sat down. The two of us were sitting there for a half-hour or so while Prabhupada spoke to these Indian gentlemen. He didn't say a word to us. He was preaching. They all thanked Prabhupada, offered their obeisances, and walked out. Prabhupada said to us, "If you do not listen to me preach, then how will you learn to preach? You must listen to me preach so that you learn the art of explaining this philosophy to important and wealthy men." Prabhupada was training us. It was a constant education. He saw that we were going to be his leaders on some level or another, and therefore he wanted us to learn.

Jadurani: Prabhupada spoke every morning and on Monday, Wednesday, and Friday evenings. We would also meet him on many other occasions. As soon as anyone heard an instruction from Prabhupada they would repeat it to the other devotees, so we were hearing not only from Prabhupada directly, but from the devotees as well. Since we were dull, even though we heard so many things, they registered in their own time.

Under Prabhupada's instructions Govinda dasi and Gaurasundar introduced an *arati* ceremony which was simply a large tray with a small Jewish votive candle (Hebrew letters were still on the glass). There was a line of devotees in front of the Pancha-tattva, and they took turns offering the candle, each devotee offering it and then passing it on to the next one in line. Afterwards, somebody brought the *arati* paraphernalia to me for cleaning. One day, although I tried everything, the candle wouldn't go out. Prabhupada was standing nearby, and he said, "Why don't you blow on it?" I said, "I thought we're not supposed to blow on anything." He said, "When there's no other alternative, then that's all right." A little later my leg brushed against the tall gladiola plants that were around his oval altar. I said, "I just touched the plant with my leg. Should I offer my obeisances because the plants were on the altar?" He said, "Yes."

Tripurari Swami: Prabhupada never gave me any kind of advice or instruction on what to say to sell his books. Once I told Prabhupada, "The devotees are asking me how to sell the books. What is the technique?" He said, "What do you tell them?" I said, "Prabhupada, I tell them that you have to strictly follow all of the principles and read and chant." He said, "Yes, this is our only technique." In other words, preaching is really the overflow of the culture. When your culture overflows, you feel inspired and have something to say. Then you preach effectively. I think Prabhupada used me in his service for preaching and book distribution from internal inspiration, from wanting to please him.

Bhagavat: Prabhupada said, "Can you quote this verse?" The two of us looked at each other, and I thought, "Tamal Krishna Goswami will quote the verse," but Tamal Krishna Goswami thought I was going to do it. Neither of us knew the verse. Prabhupada said, "Just see. You are not reading my books. Every day you have to read, study, and learn my books just like a lawyer learns the law books. You must know everything, chapter and verse. If you do not know, how will you preach? Unless you know my books how will you teach these men? Do you know that every day even I read my own books? Do you know why I read my books?" We didn't want to venture any answer. Prabhupada said, "I read my books every day because even I learn something new when I read my books. These are not my books. I do not write these books." It seemed as if something mystical came over him at this point. He said, "Every morning, when I sit here to write my books, Krishna comes personally and dictates to me what to write. I simply take dictation from Krishna to write these books. Therefore, when I read them, even I learn something." The way he said it was so dramatic that we felt the weight of his words. I was thinking, "I'm speaking with a person who's speaking with God, who's right next to God. I'm only one person removed from God. He's so close." Yet I knew, because of the state of my own consciousness, how far away I actually was. But by some grace, I was being placed right next to God by being with Prabhupada. It was amazing.

Jadurani: Once in New York in 1967, Prabhupada called me into his room after his *darshan*. I was one of the devotees from Boston who had come to see him. He handed me a print of Radha and Krishna and the eight *gopis* and asked me to make a four-foot by five-foot painting of that. We didn't have the *Brahma-samhita* at that time, but he began explaining from the *Brahma-samhita* how in the spiritual world the palaces are made of touchstones and the cows give nectar that can fulfill anyone's desire and the ground is muddy with the milk of the cows. The trees are wish-fulfilling trees that supply all eatables upon demand, and the *gopis,* the associates of Radharani, serve Radharani and Krishna by fanning Them, singing and dancing for Them, and offering Them food.

I couldn't relate to the exalted description. As I looked at the print, my response to those beautiful words was "How come the gopis aren't looking at Radha and Krishna? Shouldn't they be looking at Them?" (They were holding their paraphernalia and looking in different directions.) Prabhupada said, "When you're dancing, you don't always have to look." Then he told me to make Krishna a little smaller. He said, "Krishna looks a little fatty there and He's too tall. Make Him a little thinner and shorter." I said, "Those flowers there, they're all blobs," because the artist hadn't made details. "What flowers should I put there?" He said, "You can transport any flower to Vrindavan." I said, "I heard that Krishna's eyes are red." He said, "Reddish, reddish-black." I asked him, "You say that Krishna's the color of a fresh rain cloud, but what color is that?" Prabhupada lowered his head and put his hand on it. Then he gradually brought his head up and his hand down. In great humility he said, "They say Krishna is the color of a fresh rain cloud, but I do not know what color that is."

One amazing thing about Prabhupada was that even an ordinary person could see him make simple gestures and hear him say simple things and get great realizations about the nature of a pure devotee. He emanated those truths by his glance and his words. You felt that he could see Krishna.

Tripurari Swami: Prabhupada taught us about Krishna-*lila* when we ventured a question about *rasa-tattva*. More often than not, he would answer to the effect of, "Why don't you go there and find out? What can I say about that? What will you know by my speaking about it? What can you grasp intellectually? This shouldn't be talked about."

Of course, it is in his books, and he does talk about it within certain parameters. But one will really know it by going there, by service and sacrifice. We hope that devotees and newcomers will be inspired by that, as well by serving his message. Then one can know him. Prabhupada is a big subject.

Some knew him as "Swamiji," and when he said, "Now there will be initiations," some didn't want to know him any further. Gradually he explained his mission, and some people stayed on while others decided, "That's enough for me."

We should try to go the limit. He personally exemplified unlimited service and sacrifice in relation to Siddhanta Sarasvati Thakur. He took the suggestion of his Guru as an order. Prabhupada said, "My Guru Maharaj ordered me, 'If you ever get money, print books.'" Actually his Guru Maharaj suggested it to him at Radha Kunda, but Prabhupada took it as an order.

In his commentary on verse 2.41 from *Bhagavad-gita*, Prabhupada writes how one-mindedness, fixed intelligence, is required for spiritual life. He quotes Srila Vishvanath Chakravati Thakur's prayer to the spiritual master, *yasyaprasada bhagavata prasado yasaprasadan na gatih kuto 'pi*. Prabhupada's idea of one-mindedness was service to the order of the Guru. His Guru's order was a suggestion, but he took it as an order and as his life and soul. So he's very extreme on this point, and if we can follow that example of faith in the Guru, then I think we can know Prabhupada as he is.

Yadurani: If Prabhupada just casually or even quickly looked at us, it had tremendous significance. Like many devotees, I felt that he wasn't just seeing my dress, this body, but he was seeing the soul. He saw me, although I couldn't see me. It was almost embarrassing, but at the same time it was not embarrassing because you knew that not only was he seeing beyond the body, but he was seeing beyond the faults and beyond the interactions of the modes of nature. He was seeing the soul, which is so full of wonderful qualities. It was embarrassing, and then it went beyond embarrassing; it was blissful when he would glance at you.

We hear that when Krishna took lunch with His cowherd

boyfriends, everyone would think, "He's just looking at me, it's just me and Him." That's how it was with many of us and Prabhupada. If ten people were in the room with him, each had a personal story of the same moments.

There were a few experiences that I had with Prabhupada's glance. He called me into his greeting room because some young Indian gentleman had come to speak with him. Prabhupada offered them some *maha* sweet, and before they ate it, they put it to their head. We had never done that. He glanced at me and indicated that we should be that respectful to *prasadam*.

Bhagavat: One day I was sitting in the room when Satsvarupa Maharaj said, "I won't be able to give you your massage today, Srila Prabhupada," and the substitute devotee also wasn't available. I said, "I have big hands and I am strong. I can give you a good massage." Prabhupada said, "Okay, you give me a massage." Everyone told me, "You have to massage Prabhupada strongly," so I was massaging his head, and in a deep voice which shook me to the core of my being, he said. "You are doing it too hard." I was shocked. I tried to lighten up a little bit. During the course of the massage, ants gathered to climb on his feet. I stopped massaging him and tried to move the ants. Prabhupada said, "What are you doing? Why have you stopped the massage?" I said, "Some ants are coming on your feet, Srila Prabhupada." He said, "They will not bother me. They will go away by themselves," and he waved his hand over the ants. There must have been about twenty disorganized ants ready to go onto his mat and his feet, but when he waved his hand, I swear those ants immediately formed a single file and marched in the opposite direction. It was as if he had complete control over nature, as if whatever he willed would happen.

I finished the massage, but I could tell that Prabhupada felt I did it a little too hard. On the morning walk a couple days later we were reading from the Krishna Book about Krishna fighting with the wrestlers. Two wrestlers, both fully grown men with bodies like solid slabs of stone, were to fight with two children, Krishna and Balaram. At that point Prabhupada stopped, picked up his cane, pointed it at me and said, "You are like those wrestlers." Everyone laughed. I never massaged Prabhupada again, suffice to say.

Jadurani: Prabhupada said, "Just keep hearing. Your material qualification or disqualification doesn't matter. Just keep hearing submissively, and everything will come. You will fully realize God." We had that faith.

Prabhupada gave many arguments to defeat Mayavadis which helped me tremendously. For example, Mayavadis say, "When you become self-realized, you become God and you become silent just like a water jug. When you're filling a water jug, it goes gurgle, gurgle, gurgle, but when it's full, it's silent." Prabhupada said, "The Mayavadis give this kind of argument, but an analogy must have many similar points. This analogy has no similar points. Is the living entity like a water jug? Can I become compared to a water jug? And this analogy contradicts the scriptures. In the scriptures it says that, 'Now that we've passed through all the lower species and come to the human form of life, it's time to talk about human subjects.'"

A Mayavadi also says, "I'm God." Prabhupada would counter, "Oh, you are God? How have you become a dog?" The Mayavadi responds, "I'm God, but I've forgotten." Prabhupada, "Okay, you may be God, but you're not that God who doesn't forget." In this way he would play both sides.

Purusottama cleaned in Prabhupada's quarters, and I painted there. Achyutananda worked in the kitchen. After class and breakfast, Prabhupada would come into the room where we were and say, "What did I say in class?" I would say, "God is everything, but everything is not God. Or is it that everything is God but God is not . . ." Then Prabhupada would continue teaching us. He would say, "The greatest illusion is to think that 'I'm God,' and LSD is the greatest illusion because it puts you in that foolish frame of mind."

We got to hear his lectures and his personal discussions, and we also heard from all the devotees. One little instruction he gave me was "Don't use washing machines. They're not nice." In those days Prabhupada washed his laundry in his bathtub, and the devotees who lived downstairs also washed their clothes this way. So besides everything else, we received little instructions here and there.

Bhagavat: In Bombay two Swami Narayan *sannyasis* came to see Prabhupada. In the Swami Narayan's camp, a *sannyasi* is never allowed to look at the face of a woman. If they do, they have to fast the next day. In the Swami Narayan temples, women listen from the other side of a curtain.

Prabhupada was in his room talking with Yasomatinandan and Yasomatinandan's seventy year-old mother, an old wrinkled Indian woman. We opened the door, and when these two *sannyasis* saw this old woman they became disturbed and covered their faces. We said, "Let's wait. Prabhupada will finish soon, and then you can go in." They went downstairs and waited. When the woman came out I went upstairs and told Prabhupada, "These Swami Narayan *sannyasis* wouldn't come in before when they saw Yasomatinandan's mother." He said, "Bring them now. I will talk with them." Prabhupada was very respectful toward them. He said, "I am so sorry, but one of my leading student's elderly mother came to see me. I saw her while her son was present in the room. My *sannyasi* servant was also here." They said, "Oh, but we do not see a woman under any circumstances." Prabhupada said, "Yes, I understand, Lord Chaitanya was also very strict."

Then Prabhupada started to ask them questions about their religion, and immediately a confrontation began. They said that Swami Narayan was God. Prabhupada said, "Where in the *Srimad-Bhagavatam* does it say that Swami Narayan is God? I have not seen. I have seen Rama, Nrsimha, Varaha, Chaitanya Mahaprabhu mentioned in *Bhagavatam,* but where is Swami Narayan?" They said, "It is in this book." Prabhupada said, "Who has written that book?

Is it the *Vedas?* Is it written by Vyas?" They said, "No, such and such Swami wrote it." Prabhupada said, "Oh, that Swami? Who is he and what *parampara* is he from?" Prabhupada was going on and on, hammering. He wouldn't let them go for a second. They tried to embarrass him by making him feel like he was less than them because he was talking to an elderly woman. He showed them that he was transcendental to talking to an elderly woman. They didn't understand the philosophy, and Prabhupada cut them to rivulets. He completely worked them over. They said, "Oh, okay, we're going to leave, Swamiji. We've had enough now." When they walked out, it was as if their heads had been in a ping-pong game. I said, "Srila Prabhupada, you are the greatest," and I started going on and on, praising Prabhupada. Prabhupada said, "You appreciated?" I said, "Yes. You had an answer and a verse for everything that they said." He said, "Yes, this is the way to preach. So, you like this preaching?" I said, "Oh yes, no one can defeat you, you are the best." Prabhupada said, "Oh, so you think so?" I said, "Not just me." Everyone in the room confirmed, "Yes, Prabhupada is the best. Prabhupada is the greatest." He said, "Oh, maybe, maybe." He was humble and he enjoyed the whole thing.

Jadurani: In the early '70s we were not only painting Krishna, but we were also painting for the *Srimad-Bhagavatam*. Of course, Krishna is very distinctive. He's blue, He wears a peacock feather, and He has a yellow dhoti, so even if it's a bad painting, you know that it is Krishna. But there are many people mentioned who are not so distinctive. Prabhupada told us how to paint them. For example, kings do not have a beard but have a small moustache. We couldn't imagine that a king could be a Vaishnav, because we thought that you're only a Vaishnav if you wore a *dhoti*. But Prabhupada said kings with helmets could also be Vaishnavs. So we had general descriptions of kings like Prithu, or *brahminical* ladies like Mother Saci.

I wrote to Prabhupada and asked, "It's easy to understand that

Krishna is in His picture. But how is somebody like King Prithu or Saci Mata in their picture?" Prabhupada wrote back, "They are present by your consciousness." That is, if we're thinking that it's them and we're painting not by concoction, but from Prabhupada's authorized instructions and especially from his books, then these people are actually present.

Sometimes we'd learn in a positive way, and sometimes we'd learn in a negative way; that is by the school of hard knocks. For example, in the early '70s, I did a painting for the cover of Adi-lila Volume Three of Lord Chaitanya's *sankirtan* party going to the Chand Kazi's house. Lord Nityananda was playing the *mridanga*. I asked Prabhupada "Is that all right?" He said, "Lord Nityananda doesn't play *mridanga*." Because we had to do many details, and not all the details were in the manuscript, we had to ask many questions a normal reader of his books, even a normal devotee reader, wouldn't have thought to ask. What did Ramananda Raya look like? How old was he? Did he have hair? Was he a *sannyasi?* Prabhupada patiently answered hundreds and hundreds of such questions. Sarvabhauma Bhattacharya is such-and-such years old. Ramananda Raya is in his forties. One question was about Lord Nityananda's *sannyas,* and Prabhupada said, "He never took *sannyas.*" Then we knew not to paint Him the same way we painted Lord Chaitanya as a *sannyasi.*

In the original Krishna Book, Prabhupada used Devahuti prabhu's painting of *rasa-lila,* based on an Indian print that Prabhupada had copied. Devahuti's painting was a little stylistic but dignified and very nice. When we were doing another description of the *rasa-lila* from the Third Canto, I thought, "I'll make a more realistic one than Devahuti's. With proper lighting and realistic folds of the cloth, this one will be much better than hers." We went through a great endeavor. Murlivadana, the BBT photographer, took about ten or fifteen devotees in a van to some big park in New York where they posed for the *rasa* dance, the girls with their hair long and Krishna with His long hair. They were moving around and things were flowing as you would imagine they would if they were dancing. Murlivadana took pictures, I painted from the pictures, and the painting went in the book. When Prabhupada saw it, he said, "This has ruined my whole book. You have made it like a hippie plaything. Jadurani is a hippie rascal. Devahuti's was much more dignified. The *rasa-lila* is Krishna's smiling face," (the different Cantos are like different parts of His body) "and you have made it like a plaything." So in that case also we got instructions in a negative way.

Tripurari Swami: In Los Angeles we couldn't go to the airport to distribute literature dressed in devotional attire, so we reasoned that we should put on secular clothing and go in a covert way. The first time we went, the devotees with me were told to cease and desist or be arrested, but I managed to get through the day without being apprehended. At the time I thought, "Oh, what a wonderful facility this is. By standing in one place you can send Prabhupada's litera- ture all over the world." I prayed to Prabhupada that we could distribute his books widely, and my prayer came true. Even unwill- ingly, many airports facilitated our distribution.

Then a debate started. Kirtanananda Swami was with Prabhu- pada in India, and he complained, "Many devotees are wearing secular clothing." He thought that it was a compromise of our prin- ciples. Prabhupada was quite concerned. We responded, "It's not that we're regressing. We have no interest whatsoever in wearing these clothes." I would never go before Prabhupada with secular clothing on, but for the service of Krishna, to increase book dis- tribution, we accepted it. Prabhupada could perceive our mood through our letter, and he sanctioned it. Ultimately he found prece- dents for this principle based on scripture. For example in *Caitanya- caritamrta*, Prataparudra Maharaj changed from secular to devo- tional dress in order to get the association of Mahaprabhu.

When I was first recommended for *sannyas*, Prabhupada wrote, "Actually he doesn't need to take *sannyas*. He is already doing more than any *sannyasi*." (Laughs.) That made many *sannyasis* wonder

"What is he doing?" They asked me, "How are you pleasing Prabhupada by selling books?" But that statement was just Prabhupada's
generous way of encouraging me. He also wrote, "Anyway, it is
against the etiquette for a *sannyasi* to wear secular clothing as Tripurari must sometimes do so." But later he explained that the real
principle is for the *sannyasis* to do the needful for preaching. So,
there was a controversy about that, and Prabhupada sided with the
dynamic idea of making adjustments for preaching, rather than
sticking to the form. He was not a man of form but a man of
substance. Not a man, but a great devotee.

Bhagavat: In the evening I was sitting with Srila Prabhupada on the
roof above his apartment in Bombay. Just the two of us were there
talking until 10:00 or 11:00 at night. He was telling me about Indian
history, about Gandhi. He said that Gandhi had the proper plan for
revitalizing India. He said, "Gandhi never wanted big cities. He
never wanted factories to open up. He never liked that. Gandhi was
concerned that people in the villages have the basic necessities of
life. His plan was to first arrange for everyone to have food, clothing, education, a good water supply, religious training, and some
occupation, a craft of making cloth or jewelry or something of that
nature. These were the basic principles that Gandhi lived by. He
felt that if, in every village, the basic needs of the people were met
through simple, self-sufficient principles that later they could
develop some factories here and there."

Prabhupada's vision was that, "Sadhu Patel and Nehru be-
trayed Gandhi. They thought that India's future was through developing factories to create jobs. Now look what has happened. Young
men have left the land. Instead of growing food, they have come to
the cities to live in squalor in shantytowns. They work in the factory
for only a few *rupees,* not even enough money for a decent living."

Prabhupada said, "India has become spoiled by the Western
civilization. Gandhi and Chitaranjana das wanted simple life, self-
sufficient life. Gandhi and Chitaranjana das wanted to save India.

But their attempt was spoiled by politicians."

On the morning walk the next morning, I was at Srila Prabhu-pada's side as we walked down the beach. We seemed to walk an extraordinarily long distance. Prabhupada usually never walked that far down the beach. At a certain point, he turned and seemed to offer respects to a statue of Gandhi that was in the distance. Then we walked back, and some people joined us. By divine arrangement, one of them started talking about Gandhi. Prabhupada turned to him and said, "What is this I hear? This is all nonsense." He went on saying, Gandhi is this and Gandhi is that. Then he looked at me and smiled. I thought, "This is a little secret that he had shared with me." I felt honored. But at the same time he was letting me know, "You have to know what to say, when to say it, and how to say it in order to preach this philosophy." He was making me aware of how to preach.

Jadurani: For the paintings for *Caitanya-caritamrta,* Narottam asked Prabhupada about a thousand questions, sometimes in letters and sometimes by phone. Prabhupada was traveling around the world, and we were on a marathon because each book had to come out in a week. We couldn't wait for letters to come back from India, so sometimes Ramesvara would call in questions to Paramahamsa Swami, Prabhupada's secretary. Paramahamsa Swami would call Ramesvara back with Prabhupada's answers, and then Ramesvara would bring the messages back to us. Sometimes I would write the questions and give them to somebody going to India. Prabhupada would write a one or two line answer between my written lines and another devotee, who was returning from India, would bring that back. Everything was going very fast.

In '69, we asked some questions for each painting, and Prabhu-pada encouraged us by writing, "If you discuss it amongst your-selves and use your discretion that will be better than asking me." In the same letter, he answered one of our questions and showed us that asking him was better than using our own discretion. We were doing the painting of Krishna fighting with Jambavan. In the Krishna Book, Jambavan is addressed as the "king of the gorillas" and also as *riksha-raja,* which means, "king of the bears." The question was, "Was Jambavan a gorilla or a bear?" Prabhupada answered, "He is neither a gorilla nor a bear. Just like somebody may be named, Krishna das or Krishna, but that doesn't mean that he's Krishna. So Jambavan may be called 'the king of the bears' or 'king of the gorillas,' but that doesn't mean he's a bear or gorilla. Otherwise how could his beautiful daughter, Jambavati, become Krishna's wife?" Prabhupada said, "Jambavan was like a big, strong man of your country." In this way, we got further instructions about Krishna consciousness. To know anything we were fully dependent on Srila Prabhupada.

Bhagavat: There were three or four African disciples living in the house with Srila Prabhupada. One day Prabhupada called for Brahmananda and said, "Where are my clothes? Yesterday the African servant took my clothes to wash them, and he hasn't returned them." The servant came in, and Prabhupada said, "Where are my clothes?" The servant said, "I don't know. I washed them and put them on the line, but now they're gone." Prabhupada said, "Someone has stolen my clothes?" Brahmananda said, "We didn't lock the back door, so maybe some thieves stole the clothes." Prabhupada laughed and said, "They are stealing pieces of silk from a *sannyasi.*"

Prabhupada had two shoulder pieces of cloth left. He put one over his top and the other around his bottom. It was uncomfortable and his legs were sticking out. The next morning the African disciples came to hear Srila Prabhupada's lecture on *Srimad-Bhagavatam.* When Prabhupada saw the devotees he said, "You are wearing my shirt. You are wearing my *dhoti.* You are wearing my top." Brahmananda got furious. He started disrobing them in front of Prabhupada, taking off the shirt, taking off the *dhoti,* saying, "You took your spiritual master's clothes, what's the matter with you?"

Prabhupada laughed. He thought it was humorous that they were wearing his clothes.

Jadurani: Twice I wrote to Prabhupada asking if I could be a *sankirtan* devotee. Twice he wrote back, "No, your specific talent is painting. You should do that. But even in spiritual life variety makes one more fit for work, so you can go on *sankirtan* sometimes."

In 1974, when Prabhupada wrote many letters glorifying the book distributors, I started feeling left out. In a letter to the Chicago temple, he wrote that only two devotees should stay back to take care of the Deities, and everyone else (that meant one hundred and fifty devotees), should go out all day on book distribution. He always stressed book distribution, and I was glum because I wasn't doing that. I wrote to him again and asked if I could distribute books. He said, "Just because I write something to one person, it doesn't mean that it's the same for everybody. Making pictures for the books is the same as distributing them." He rejected my proposals.

Bhagavat: Communists had taken over Tanzania, the country next to us. They held a midnight session of Congress, and the next day passed a law that no one could own property in the State of Tanzania anymore. All the property was now owned by the State, and everyone had to pay rent to the State. Prabhupada was furious. He said, "This is thievery. The people worked hard, earned money, bought property, developed it, and now the government rogues are stealing it from them. They are the worst rascals." At that time Prabhupada was interviewed by the BBC and asked, "What is your message?" He said, "My message is that I want to kick out these rogues, rascals, thieves, and no-good politicians. The whole world is filled with such rogues and thieves. They are stealing the people's hard-earned money. They are stealing their land. They are stealing their lifeblood! They are bloodsuckers." Prabhupada was vehement. He said, "A real king is the protector of the people. A real king will see that everyone is living nicely, that all people have food, clothing, care, attention, and medical needs. The king takes so much responsibility that if anyone dies young, he feels responsible. If the son dies before the father, the king feels personally responsible. But these men are stealing. There are no qualified people to be king in this world. We need a king who has honesty, decency, and integrity." Prabhupada talked about the qualities of kings like Maharaj Yudhisthir and Rama. The BBC man said, "Is there anybody in the world who is qualified to be king of the world?" Just when he said that the videotape ran out, but the interviewer didn't know it. Prabhupada looked at him, put his cane on the ground and said, "Yes, me." Just like that. He was qualified to be king of the world. The interviewer looked completely shocked. But Prabhupada realized that nobody else in the world had the qualifications, and that only a pure devotee could do this.

Tripurari Swami: Akinchana Krishnadas Babaji came to see Prabhupada in Vrindavan when I was there, a month or so before Prabhupada departed. Prabhupada said, "Please forgive me for all my offenses. Now the war is over. Please try to help them." Akinchana Krishnadas Babaji was quick to say, "No, no, you have not offended anyone. With all that you have done in the name of Guru Maharaj in preaching, you cannot make offense." It was very charming, very endearing. Prabhupada would speak harshly about his godbrothers, and you have to understand why and for what reason; circumstance, time, and some of his godbrothers were inimical.

In Prabhupada's estimation, one of his godbrothers was inimical at one time, but after that godbrother departed, his Vyasa-puja was being celebrated, and Prabhupada sent me with some other *sannyasis* to go and observe it. I had thought that Prabhupada didn't like the fellow, but such feelings don't run very deep. What runs deep in the heart of Prabhupada or any *param* Vaishnav is love; what to speak of love for the people in general, love for the devotees and devotees of the same banner, godbrothers, certainly.

We should understand this because we have our own experience now with differences amongst godbrothers. They speak strongly about one another. But if they carry on the mission nicely, we also must have some deep appreciation. And we must have a tear for those who are not carrying it on. We're not against them.

I think that Prabhupada very much demonstrated this, and if we didn't see it, we didn't see Prabhupada. As much as he criticized some of them, he loved them deeply, and it came out at different times. He was not a politician, patronizing them, saying something nice about this one or that one. When Prabhupada was in Seattle and he got telegram of the disappearance of Keshava Maharaj from the world, he glorified Keshava Maharaj with a tear in his eye. He had deep feelings for him, deep love.

Jadurani: Once in Boston, I was sitting in his *darshan* room, and he was telling me something brilliant. I said, "Gee, Swamiji, you know everything." He said, "Unless one knows everything, how can one be a teacher?" Another time he was saying something brilliant, and I said the same thing, "You know everything." He put his head down and said, "I have done nothing extraordinary, I simply canvass on behalf of the disciplic succession."

Bhagavat: One morning he was talking with us about the future of the ISKCON movement. He said that he wanted to buy all the land in Mayapur and establish a self-sufficient community. Once that was established, he would then declare independence from India, secede from the country and make his own country, the Country of Mayapur. Then his temples around the world would become embassies for the Country of Mayapur and the temple presidents would be ambassadors. We would print our own money, called Chaitanyas. There would be one Chaitanya, five Chaitanyas, and ten Chaitanyas. For our export, we would make devotional items and sell them all over the world. Prabhupada had a vision of his own country, his own embassies, his own ambassadors, his own monetary system, his own economic system, and his own export production. Sometimes we don't realize how big Prabhupada was actually thinking, how grand he wanted this mission to be. When I remember this discussion I think, "Whew! We're so far away from where he wanted to take this movement. How much harder we need to work."

Jadurani: Based on a two-inch-by-three-inch picture without details, I was painting Lord Nrsimhadev. At the bottom of the picture there was an Indian rug that Lord Nrsimhadev and Ananta were on. I needed a reference for an Indian rug. I remembered that there was an India rug in a print of Sita Rama and Hanuman on the wall directly behind Prabhupada's sitting place. Prabhupada was working in the next room, so I tiptoed in to look at the print, but it was a little far away unless I stepped on Prabhupada's mat. I didn't want to step on the mat, so I stood in front of it, but to see the picture I had to jump up and down. Prabhupada looked at me and asked, "What are you doing?" I said, "I'm trying to see this picture as a reference for my painting, but I don't want to step on your bed." In the daytime he used the mat for sitting, and at night he slept on it. He said, "In Krishna's service, you can step on my head." That was his whole frame of being. He was willing to sacrifice anything to help others come to Krishna.

Tripurari Swami: In terms of Gaudiya Vaishnavism, there was no more-widespread campaign than Srila Prabhupada's. He was practically on every continent, conducting it like a great general but in an unassuming, humble way. Upon arriving in America he wrote a prayer and signed it, "the most insignificant beggar."

It always amazed me. Usually a humble person gets nowhere. Usually you have to get out there and assert yourself. But Prabhupada was humble in that he was not at all self-asserting but always asserting on behalf of his Guru Maharaj and Chaitanya Mahaprabhu. His was a dynamic kind of humility, the kind that would allow him to sit on the elevated seat and to chastise and give orders. But he was truly humble to the order of his spiritual master, humble to the call of Chaitanya Mahaprabhu.

How Prabhupada tolerated me and all of us, crude stock that we were? Chaitanya Mahaprabhu teaches us to respect everyone, and Prabhupada did. Even while saying, "I'll kick on your head with shoes," Prabhupada showed respect for people, and he brought Krishna's attention to them by doing so. When a devotee speaks strongly about someone, then Krishna goes to that person and says, "My devotee has paid attention to you, so please forgive him." The pure devotee's words draw Krishna's attention to that person. So even when Prabhupada spoke strongly and harshly, even when he called someone a "dog" or a "nonsense," more often than not the person was charmed. Prabhupada was the epitome of Mahaprabhu's sloka, "One should chant the holy name of the Lord in a humble state of mind, without false prestige, and be ready to offer all respects to others, expecting none for himself."

TAPE 14

Prahladananda Swami
Balavanta das
Sureshvar das
Dayananda das

Prahladananda Swami: I was looking at a little cartoon about Prahlad Maharaj and thinking, "Prahlad, what a nice name." When I got my initiation letter from Srila Prabhupada saying that my name was "Prahladananda," I thought, "Wow, that's amazing!" Afterwards I heard from Srila Prabhupada's secretary, Devananda, that when Prabhupada received my letter requesting initiation he said, "How can I initiate this boy? There's no letter of recommendation." Devananda said to Prabhupada, "Well, I just talked to him on the telephone, and he seems like a nice devotee." Prabhupada said, "Oh, you recommend him?" Devananda said, "No, I don't even know him, how can I recommend him? I just talked to him." Prabhupada said, "If you think he's a nice boy, then I'll give him initiation."

Balavanta: Once Srila Prabhupada was glancing around the Boston temple room when it was so filled with devotees that there was literally standing room only. I was in the back of the room, and my eyes and his eyes locked. It was only for a fraction of a second, but I felt that there was a personal connection between us. At such

339

a time one may think, "Oh, I'm special," but I didn't think that, because I realized that Srila Prabhupada had the capacity to relate to and connect with every person in that room. Srila Prabhupada was the external manifestation of the Supersoul, God in the heart of every living entity. Srila Prabhupada is not the Supersoul, he's a perfected *jiva* soul, and because he's perfected he has a transparent, direct connection to the Supersoul. Your connection and my connection to the Supersoul may be covered due to our false ego and conditioning. But in Srila Prabhupada's case, there was no false ego and no conditioning. The spirit soul and the Supersoul were in perfect harmony. He could know my heart perfectly, because the Supersoul knew.

After that, in other meetings with him, I sensed even more how much he knew because, after all, the Supersoul is closer to us than we are to ourselves. There couldn't be anyone closer, and Srila Prabhupada was directly connected to Him. When Srila Prabhupada spoke, I understood that Supersoul was speaking. Srila Prabhupada himself explained that once when he was in New York. In an interview a reporter asked him, "Can you speak to God?" Srila Prabhupada said, "Yes." Rameshvara began to explain to the reporter that what Prabhupada meant was that God within is the intelligence, and when one takes help from the intelligence, one's taking help from God. Perhaps that was to make it more palatable to the Western mind. Prabhupada stopped Rameshvara emphatically and said, "No, directly." Anyway, my experience in Boston was astounding to me.

 **Sureshvar:** Before the lecture and initiation, Srila Prabhupada sent Silavati's sons, Girish and Virabhadra, out of the room because they didn't have *tilak* on. The boys were living in New Vrindavan with us and were eight and ten years old. Even though they were just boys, Prabhupada motioned them out of the room saying, "Go put on *tilak*." While they were out of the room, anointing their bodies with *tilak*, Prabhupada starting talking about *tilak* and how it was

our trademark. Srila Prabhupada said, "We are selling Krishna for free, and still no one will take," and he started laughing. Then Srila Prabhupada started giving an intricate lecture, or maybe I was tired, but I couldn't follow what he was talking about. When I finally started to catch on, Bhagavan das' baby son interrupted his lecture by clanging *kartals*. When the child did that, Prabhupada expertly used it in his lecture. He said, "Just like this child, he has had practice." Prabhupada had been talking about transmigration of the soul, and when Prabhupada said, "He has had practice," he started beaming at this little boy, and the boy started beaming at Srila Prabhupada. We were looking at the boy looking at Prabhupada. There was a dramatic pause, as if there was something going on between Prabhupada and this little boy.

 **Dayananda:** One time we were riding in the car. I was driving, Prabhupada was on the passenger side, and somebody else was in the back seat. Prabhupada said, "So, how old is Chandramukhi?" I said, "She's two." He said, "So you can send her to *gurukula*." There was a *gurukula* in New Vrindavan at that time, but only Sila-vati's kids and Dwarkadish were enrolled there. I said, "When she's five, Prabhupada?" He said, "No, you can send her now." I thought, "I'm not going to do it." (Laughs)

Balavanta: I visited New Vrindavan in March of 1970. At that time the devotees had obtained a plate of Srila Prabhupada's *prasadam* from Los Angeles where Prabhupada was staying. As they passed it out the devotees were making a big production out of this *prasadam*. I was skeptical, but I happened to get a golden raisin from the plate, and I popped it in my mouth. That was an experience. It tasted like a golden raisin, but the intensity of the taste was magnified thousands of times. I began to realize what the devotees were talking about. This was something extraordinary. This personality was very different from anyone else we'd experienced before or since.

Prahladananda Swami: Once I asked, "Srila Prabhupada, should I control my desire to eat *prasadam?*" Prabhupada chuckled and said, "No, you can eat as much as you want, but don't fill yourself up to here." (points to his neck). Everyone laughed.

Another time I asked Srila Prabhupada, "Swamiji, how will I know whether or not Krishna wants me to do something?" Prabhupada chuckled and said, "You won't know." He said, "You'll do the wrong thing." Everyone started to chuckle and laugh also. When Prabhupada saw that the others were chuckling and laughing, he looked at me compassionately so I wouldn't feel offended. Prabhupada was sensitive toward everyone he dealt with.

Sureshvar: Srila Prabhupada was in New Vrindavan for his Vyasa-puja in 1972, and he gave what became a famous Vyasa-puja address. He very intelligently started talking about the meaning of Vyasa-puja and how the spiritual master considers himself a humble servant of the previous *acharyas* and of Krishna. The spiritual master doesn't think he's God almighty, which is what one may have thought by seeing all of the worship being offered to Srila Prabhupada while he was seated on the *vyasasana.*

There were many guests, journalists, scholars, and all kinds of people present, and Prabhupada talked about how he considered himself "the dog of God." He said, "If you want to please a big man in this world, it's difficult to meet him, what to speak of pleasing him, because he's so big. But if you simply give his dog a two-cent lozenge, then the master is easily pleased. So I am the dog of God. It is very difficult to please Krishna, but it's easy to please me. Just chant Hare Krishna." Afterwards we had a roaring *kirtan,* but before the *kirtan,* Srila Prabhupada took questions. In his lecture Prabhupada had talked about how strong *maya,* is and the first question was from a longhaired fellow in the back. He said, "If the purpose of life is to know God, Krishna, then why is *maya* so strong?" Without a blink and with great power Prabhupada said, "Your purpose is not strong!" We all went *"Ahhh!"* We were stunned by Prabhupada's rapid and profound reply to that question. He wasn't just speaking to that guy, but he was speaking to everybody.

Dayananda: Once I took Prabhupada to a park in Los Angeles when it was raining. I didn't want Prabhupada to get wet while he walked, so I tried to put the umbrella over his head. Prabhupada said, "It doesn't matter, I like the rain. It rains like this in Calcutta. This reminds me of Calcutta." On a couple of occasions he said that Los Angeles somehow reminded him a little of Calcutta.

Balavanta: My wife and I were in the Boston airport, and my wife gave Prabhupada a garland—some say that women should not be allowed to give garlands to Prabhupada, but she gave him one then and again at *gurupuja* time. When she garlanded him, Prabhupada smiled. Then he went to New York, and we also went. I was temple president at that time, and one advantage of being temple president was that you could write to Srila Prabhupada. Previously anyone could write to Srila Prabhupada, but he started getting too much mail. Then only the temple presidents wrote to him on behalf of all of the devotees in the temple. Also, temple presidents could visit Srila Prabhupada when he came to the United States. Once a number of us temple presidents went into Prabhupada's room, and Prabhupada said, "Where are your wives? The wife is protection for husband. When the husband goes traveling, the wife should also go."

Prahladananda Swami: Dr. Rao was an Indian and a Mayavadi who had asked the devotees to open a center. Rupanuga had done that, but Dr. Rao had never surrendered. Prabhupada preached to Dr. Rao very simply. Prabhupada said, "To know who your father is, who do you ask? You have to find out from your mother. Your mother is the authority on the identity of your father." Dr. Rao wouldn't accept that. So Prabhupada repeated the same analogy three times. "If you want to know who your father is, you have to find out from your mother, the *Vedas*." Since Dr. Rao didn't accept that simple analogy, Prabhupada didn't go any further. He stopped right there. Then Dr. Rao said, "Swamiji, I wrote one article for *Back to Godhead* magazine, but it's never been published." Prabhupada took his little bell and rang it. Pradyumna came in, and Srila Prabhupada said, "Dr. Rao has written an article for our *Back to Godhead,* and it has not been published. It must be published." I thought, "It must be published; his article? What kind of article could it be?" Then Prabhupada said, "It is very important to write for *Back to Godhead.* I want all of my disciples to write for *Back to Godhead.*" So I realized the importance of writing for *Back to Godhead,* and I realized that Dr. Rao's article would never be published. Prabhupada was very kind to Dr. Rao.

Balavanta: Prabhupada gave a nice lecture, and then he began to banter with the Indians, especially one Dr. Mahanti who was about forty, young enough to be Prabhupada's son. Prabhupada smiled and was cordial, friendly, and loving with this man. He said, "What part of India are you from?" Dr. Mahanti said, "From Orissa." Dr. Mahanti was a little proud because he had a Ph.D. in biology. Prabhupada said, "Why have you come to America?" Dr. Mahanti said, "I am a biologist," as if to say, "I'm your countryman, and I've succeeded in the material world. I'm an important man, a professor, so be proud of me." Prabhupada said, "Oh, poor frogs," and the room exploded in laughter. Dr. Mahanti wasn't hurt—if it would have hurt him, Srila Prabhupada wouldn't have said it. However, he protested. He said, "No, no it is for science." Prabhupada laughed and said, "Oh? We'll take your body for science." Amid the laughter, Dr. Mahanti said, "Yes, yes, I'll do it, I'll do it." Prabhupada laughed and said, "No, no. This inquiry of science is not very important. It is better to study the *Vedas.* Study the *Srimad-Bhagavatam.*"

Dayananda: While on a walk in Dallas, Prabhupada was told that H. L. Hunt lived right across the river from where they were walking and that he was one of the richest men in the United States. Prabhupada said, "If you see him, what will you tell him?" Someone said, "We'll tell him that we have a school here and we're producing first class citizens." That was in context with what Prabhupada was saying at the time. Prabhupada said, "No, tell him he's a thief and that he's stealing from Krishna."

I heard this story, and later, when I was Prabhupada's secretary for a month in the beginning of 1976 in Mayapur, we were walking on the roof of the Mayapur building, when Jayapataka Swami came with a Life Member. He introduced the Life Member, an industrialist from Calcutta, to Prabhupada. This man was very respectful. Prabhupada said, "What is your business?" The man said, "I manufacture glass. I have a glass factory." Prabhupada said, "Oh, very good. How do you manufacture glass?" The man said, "Well, glass is made from silicon, which is in sand." Prabhupada said, "Who owns the sand?" The man was pious and bright. He said, "Oh, Swamiji, Bhagavan owns the sand." In other words, God owns the sand. Prabhupada said, "Oh, you are stealing from Bhagavan?" Prabhupada put this man on the spot, and the devotees laughed and the man laughed as well. Then he faded back a little bit, and the topic changed until he came back a few minutes later and said, "Prabhupada, I give in charity." Prabhupada said, "Oh, you are just a little thief then." Prabhupada wasn't going to let him off the hook. I love to think about how Prabhupada called a big man a thief but did it in such a way that it was effective. It's like precept and practice. Prabhupada was able to do it in such a skilled way that the man was laughing.

Sureshvar: Prabhupada spent most of the lecture blasting and hammering away at modern, materialistic, industrial civilization. During the questions and answers one fellow from Jamaica, who was an industrialist, raised his hand and said, "Prabhupada, what about the wheels of industry?" Without hesitating Prabhupada said, "Stop those wheels." At other times Prabhupada encouraged us to use technology for Krishna's service, but in this case Srila Prabhupada came down heavily by saying, "Stop those wheels." He must have known the man could hear that in the right spirit. Of course Prabhupada also used those wheels, but he turned them in a spiritual direction.

Balavanta: We were in the Bible Belt, and many Christian guests attended the Sunday feast lecture. Prabhupada talked about Christianity. In his lecture Prabhupada explained very nicely that Christ was our guru. Then a man in the back said, "What happens to followers of Guru Nanak?" Prabhupada said, "The followers of Guru Nanak are fortunate." Another guest named Peter, now being emboldened, said, "Prabhupada?" "Yes?" "Who is Sai Baba?" Prabhupada said, "I do not know, there are so many bogus Babas. Just know who is Krishna. That is sufficient." It was wonderful. Peter had been resisting our preaching, but at that moment he surrendered and became a devotee of Prabhupada. He is now Parampara das.

Prahladananda Swami: Once Prabhupada came to the University of Buffalo and lectured to many students in one of the university rooms. Afterwards he asked for questions. One boy stood up and said, "Swamiji, tell us truthfully, are you really happy?" Prabhupada became grave. He said, "If I told you, would you believe me?" The boy said, "Swamiji, come on, tell us. Are you really happy?" Srila Prabhupada looked at him even more gravely and said, "If I told you would you believe me?" The boy repeated, "Oh, come on Swamiji, just tell us. Are you really happy?" Then Prabhupada smiled beautifully and said, "Yes, I am very happy." The devotees said, "*Jaya*, Prabhupada!" This boy's grin turned into a big frown, and he sat down. Just by his smile Prabhupada could defeat someone.

Sureshvar: I went in the temple room in time to hear some questions and answers that Srila Prabhupada was fielding after his arrival talk. Jay, Mother Jahnava's younger brother, had been associating with some born-again Christians, and he asked a question in a challenging mood. He said, "So, what is this love of God you're feeling?" When Prabhupada answered questions, he would answer the mode or the intent of the questioner. He would answer the spirit of the questioner. In this case Srila Prabhupada said, "What is this love of God that I am feeling? It is that I am not afraid of anything." Because the questioner was challenging, that's how Prabhupada chose to answer.

Balavanta: A boy who had been one of the top men with Maharishi Mahesh Yogi came to Srila Prabhupada and announced that Maharishi had sent him to Prabhupada. He had told Maharishi that he wanted to go higher, and Maharishi had responded, "If you want to go higher you must go to Swami Prabhupada." The devotees thought, "This is wonderful, what a breakthrough." The boy was introduced to Prabhupada, and the boy said to him, "Maharishi recognizes you are the real thing, and Maharishi's program is to make people a little more qualified to follow your path. Maharishi is helping them get started. After that they can come to you." Prabhupada listened to his presentation with his eyes closed, sitting behind a table in his typical fashion. Everyone was waiting to see what Prabhupada would do. Being passionate, we were thinking "This is our opportunity to make all these people devotees." When the boy finally finished, Prabhupada opened his eyes and said, "This is bogus. Just chant Hare Krishna; there is no need for anything else."

Prahladananda Swami: We had an engagement at the University of Buffalo, where a priest in the audience said that he had practiced silent meditation. Prabhupada said that silent meditation is not for this age.

Before the lecture Prabhupada introduced Brahmananda by saying, "This is Brahmananda das. He is one of the senior members of our movement, one of my advanced disciples." This was my introduction to praising the devotees. At that time a senior devotee meant that one was in the movement for two or three years. But I saw that Prabhupada praised his disciple in front of the audience and all the devotees. That impressed me.

On the way back from this engagement, Prabhupada was riding in the back of a car, and I was riding in the front of another car. Every time the car I was in pulled up to Prabhupada's car, I saw him and offered my obeisances. I don't know how many hundreds of time I offered my obeisances to Srila Prabhupada on the way back. Later, when I saw Brahmananda prabhu he said, "Yes, Prabhupada saw you offering your obeisances, and he was chuckling." Prabhupada thought it was amusing.

Dayananda: Tamal Krishna was in charge of a traveling *sankirtan* party, and he was a much more effective leader and manager than I was. I was the temple president of what had been a small Los Angeles temple but, with Tamal's presence, it became a much larger entity, with many more *brahmacharis* and *brahmacharinis*. Besides being temple president, I was also working all day. So Tamal Krishna went to Prabhupada for clarification. He asked, "What's my position, and what's the position of Dayananda, the temple president?" Prabhupada answered, "Dayananda remains the temple president." Then Prabhupada suggested we have elections, and he personally nominated some people for different posts. He nominated me for temple president, Tamal Krishna for secretary, Jayananda for vice president, and Silavati for head *pujari*—I don't know if head *pujari* was an elected position. Prabhupada also nominated Virabhadra for temple commander. The devotees voted for everyone Prabhupada nominated, except that we didn't want Virabhadra as the temple commander because he was only twelve years old. So we nominated and elected Vishnujana as the temple commander instead. Madhudvisa was the treasurer, nominated by Prabhupada and elected by us.

When Tamal became the secretary there was a question, "What does the secretary do?" Prabhupada said, "The secretary is the person who deals directly with the spiritual master." It was a predefinition of the GBC secretary. Later on I realized that Prabhupada was incredibly skilled in the way he managed the whole situation. The temple was in a major transition, and yet I remained the president. I've thought about it a lot since then, and I've seen that sometimes a temple president is not very effective, and another guy comes in who's much more effective. One idea is, "Let's get rid of this old one and put in the new one." But the way Prabhupada did it was so skillful—he created a new position and kept the temple president so that there was consistency in the management.

Balavanta: The GBC would make resolutions, and then Srila Prabhupada would approve them. In fact, sometimes he would attend our meetings. He used to chastise us by saying, "Why are your meetings taking so long? You should finish up your business in two or three days, and in the remaining time you should discuss how we can become Krishna conscious and give Krishna consciousness to others." But we would meet for weeks. When Prabhupada attended the meetings he said, "First you should make a proposal, then it should become resolution. Not simply discussing."

There was one time when we were sitting with him on the veranda. He was sitting in the sun on an *asana* at one end. We were in Mayapur, and his heart was obviously absorbed in Chaitanya *lila* and various ecstasies. Meanwhile, externally, his young disciples were holding their GBC meeting. Someone made a proposal, it was debated back and forth, and then it became time for a vote, yea or nay. The first vote was, "All those in favor, raise your hand," and on this occasion the majority was in favor of the resolution. Once that became clear, Prabhupada raised his hand too and said, "Yes, I will vote for it." He wanted to see what the majority was before he voted. And then he laughed.

But sometimes he was much more serious about our resolutions. The first time I attended a GBC meeting, a resolution was passed that women with children and no husband could not live in the temple. The idea was that this was a tremendous drain on the temple finances. The woman couldn't go on *sankirtan,* and the temple had to give money for the child and so on. We thought that the husband who fathered the child should take responsibility and that there was no real place for these women in the temple. How can you put a woman with a child in the *brahmacharini ashram?* It's disruptive. And you can't give an apartment to every woman with a child. It's not practical. So we drew a line. Women with children and no husband cannot live in the temple. Once all the resolutions were fixed, they would then be read to Srila Prabhupada for approval, and typically he would approve them. But after he heard that resolution, "A woman with a child but without a husband may not live in the temple," there was silence. We could feel that this resolution was worse than the others. Finally Satsvarupa Maharaj said, "Srila Prabhupada, should we change that one?" Prabhupada said, "Hmm." He didn't open his eyes, and he said, "As far as I am concerned, my only desire is that they become Krishna conscious. It does not matter if they are women with children or without children. I only want to give them the opportunity to be Krishna conscious." He still didn't open his eyes, and we could feel his compassion, his ocean of compassion. And here we were, the foolish manipulative management. Satsvarupa Maharaj said, "We'll withdraw that one, Prabhupada." Prabhupada said, "Hmm." That whole day's worth of resolutions were scrapped, and we went back, started over again, and changed them. He never actually said that we had to, but by his response it was clear that we were on the wrong path.

Sureshvar: There were initiations going on at the time, before the actual inaugural *arati,* and Srila Prabhupada was sitting on the *vyasasana.* I was sitting to the left of His Divine Grace. While the initiation ceremony was going on he was moving his lips. I wanted to hear what he was saying, so I snuck up behind the *vyasasana* and put my ear behind Srila Prabhupada. He was chanting the *Brahma-samhita* in deep, soft, resonant tones. *Premanjana-cchurita-bhakti-*

vilocanena . . . On and on, it was just wonderful. Then I went back to my place. During the initiation, all of a sudden Srila Prabhupada wanted something, but neither Shyamasundar nor Pradyumna could understand what he wanted. Srila Prabhupada was looking all over the room to see if anybody could understand what he wanted. Finally his eyes fell on me. It's the only time I remember Srila Prabhupada looking directly at me, except for my initiation. He looked at me with such compassion while I was sitting there with a stupid grin on my face. His look said to me that I was an idiot but he still loved me. I thought, "That's right, Srila Prabhupada, I'm an idiot. You love me, and I'm an idiot." I was blissful. Anyway, finally somebody understood what he wanted, and the ceremony continued. Then at some point Srila Prabhupada got off the *vyasasana* and left the room. But the ceremony still went on. Finally it was time for the inaugural *arati* of Radha-Kalachandji, and when the curtains opened, there was Srila Prabhupada on the stage doing *achaman,* with Sri Sri Radha-Kalachandji in front of a very spartan background. I thought, "What a treat. I've never seen Srila Prabhupada do *arati*." I watched him perform this *arati,* and it made a strong impression on me. It was deliberate and meditative, with deep *bhakti*. It wasn't quick circles. After Srila Prabhupada offered the water in the conch to the Deities, he turned to us, put the water in his hand, and started flinging drops of water out at the congregation. I was leaping up in the air to catch these droplets of water and thinking how the spiritual master extinguishes the blazing fire of material existence. That was wonderful.

Balavanta: When Prabhupada offered the *arati* to Srila Bhaktisiddhanta, it was a gorgeous sight to behold. The way he offered the paraphernalia was astounding. Every movement was perfectly coordinated and the circles that he made were like an orbit. But somehow or other, in setting up the *arati* tray, the devotees hadn't put a bowl for the conch shell water. As temple president, I was standing next to Prabhupada, holding the *arati* tray. He offered the water in the conch, and it was time to put a little bit into a container, but there was no container. He looked at me, and I looked around into the sea of devotees, motioning for someone to get a container from the kitchen or the *pujari* room. But everyone's attention was on Prabhupada. Conceivably, Prabhupada could have gone on and done another offering, but he wouldn't. He was standing there waiting. It became a crisis, and it became apparent that I wasn't going to be able to solve the crisis quickly and easily. Finally, with a flip of his wrist, Prabhupada shot the water from the conch shell into *tulasi's* pot on the *vyasasana*. When he did that the *kirtan* stopped just long enough for everyone to go, "Haribol! Haribol!"

Prahladananda Swami: One time my mind was wandering while I was absorbed in some type of yoga meditation. Prabhupada looked at me and said, "Our process is *bhakti*, not meditation." I was surprised and impressed by Prabhupada's sensitivity. Another time Prabhupada was giving a lecture at the university when he said, "Brahmananda told us that young boys and girls take off their clothes and go in with the pigs." Some of the other devotees and I became a little disturbed by hearing this. Prabhupada saw that we were disturbed and immediately changed the subject. He was sensitive when he spoke and noted people's reaction to his words.

Dayananda: In Iran, Prabhupada was talking to Mrs. Patel, a wealthy, aristocratic, Indian woman from Gujarat. She and her husband were wonderful Vaishnavs and were supportive of and gave money to the movement in Iran. When she was talking with Prabhupada in his room, a young British or American hippie type came in and sat for a while. The guy finally said, "Swamiji, what about doing good for other people? Can't we just do good for other people?" Prabhupada looked at him and said, "What good can you do? You cannot even take care of yourself." By this time, 1976, the movement had progressed to such an extent that Prabhupada could say it like it was to these young people. In the beginning, Prabhupada had to cultivate young, irresponsible hippie types, but in fact, what good can down-and-out people do for others? The only good that they can do for the world or for anyone, including themselves, is to take up Krishna consciousness.

Prahladananda Swami: At the end of the lecture, when Srila Prabhupada was leaving, a girl approached him and said, "What is the difference between Taoism and Krishna consciousness?" Prabhupada said, "Krishna consciousness means we chant Hare Krishna Hare Krishna, Krishna Krishna Hare Hare, Hare Rama Hare Rama, Rama Rama Hare Hare." That's all he said. I realized that preaching didn't necessarily mean that one had to do a complete analysis of the person's personality or attack anyone. One could preach simply and be effective at the same time.

Balavanta: Once we were in the room with Prabhupada discussing the "In God We Trust" party. Someone said, "Prabhupada, if we take over the government, will we finish all of these nonsense religions?" Prabhupada said, "Oh, why? We have no quarrel with these religions. We would only like to see that they actually practice their religion. That is what we would like to see."

Dayananda: Once a few of us were in Prabhupada's garden when Nanda Kumar was his servant. After some time, Prabhupada wanted to go inside, and we walked with him behind the temple into his quarters. Downstairs from Prabhupada's quarters there was a room with some cupboards, and some of the Krishna Book paintings were sticking out from one of the cupboards. Other paintings were on the floor, leaning against the wall. Prabhupada noticed that the Krishna Book paintings were not nicely protected and said, "Why are these here? What are these doing here?" Nanda Kumar said, "I don't know Prabhupada. It's not my responsibility." Prabhupada shot back, "It is too your responsibility." That was a clear indication that Prabhupada expected his disciples to take responsibility for things that they saw in his Movement.

Sureshvar: At some point during one of those lectures, Srila Prabhupada told us frankly that we had all come to Krishna because of *prasadam*. He told us that we were all *prasadam bhaktas*. When Prabhupada said that, he was being fanned by Abhirama prabhu, who was the temple president. Abhirama is reserved. He doesn't open his mind, he's a cool customer. But, when Prabhupada said that we were all *prasadam* devotees, he looked at Abhirama and said, "You too, Abhirama?" Abhirama became sheepish, out of character completely, and said, "Yes, Srila Prabhupada, me too." Srila Prabhupada said, "*Jaya,*" his head wheeled slowly, like the sun rising, and his smile got bigger until it was ear to ear. It was so funny.

Prahladananda Swami: Once Satsvarupa Maharaj was mentioning some of the devotees who lived at the temple and explaining their qualities to Prabhupada. Prabhupada said, "Devotee? A devotee means they're first class. If they're a devotee, they're first class." In other words, rather than analyzing the different personalities, Prabhupada said, "If they're a devotee, then they're first class."

Balavanta: On a whim I wrote to Srila Prabhupada, "Maybe I'll also run for mayor." Amarendra had run for mayor, so on one line of my letter I mentioned running in relation to myself. Most of Prabhupada's reply letter was encouraging me to do this. He responded to other points I had made, but not very much. Instead he went on about how we must set the perfect example in all fields of life, so why not politics? I was stuck. Srila Prabhupada wanted me to do this. We corresponded a number of times and he told me what to say. I ran for office as Amarendra had done, and I was able to debate these fellows in public. It was a wonderful experience. Prabhupada told me to concentrate on the spiritual side of the issues and not get into all their details. He wanted us to give the public Krishna consciousness, and that's what we did.

Prabhupada said, "They've come here thinking that they will solve all their problems but this place is like a prison house. The people are like a wealthy man's sons who have come to the prison house by misfortune. Somehow they've gotten the idea that they will solve all their problems in the prison house. But they will never find happiness there. They've forgotten that they are the sons of a wealthy man. So they should be reminded. This is the sum and substance of the purpose of human life. You speak like this." And basically we did that, but we didn't get many votes. After the election I wrote to him and said, "We didn't get many votes." He wrote back, "It doesn't matter that you have not gotten many votes. I have seen that you have not compromised our philosophy. My spiritual master also never compromised. So Krishna will note what you have done to try to make them Krishna conscious. I am proud of you. Go on in this. There is no failure for the devotee." I was a little discouraged from not getting as good a response as I had hoped, but Prabhupada encouraged us.

Dayananda: For years Prabhupada treated me a little differently than the *brahmacharis* and *sannyasis* because I was a householder. He was not so strict but a little bit more lenient with me. But that changed when I came to Mayapur in 1976 to learn Sanskrit. I had already learned a little bit and was teaching Sanskrit in the *gurukula*, but I wanted to advance further. So an Indian devotee was teaching me to read a Sanskrit commentary on the *Gita*. I thought, "This is bona fide. It's a commentary by Baladeva Vidyabhusana, which is in our line. Prabhupada bases his commentary on that commentary." During a morning walk Prabhupada asked me what I was doing, and I told him that I was reading Baladeva's commentary and studying a *Gita* grammar. Prabhupada said, "We'll talk about it in the evening." At 4:00 that evening I came for Prabhupada's *darshan*. Several people were there in the room, and Prabhupada was talking with somebody. Then the conversation stopped. He turned, looked at me, and said, "Why are you going over the head of the spiritual master?" He was very strong. At that time the few people who were into Sanskrit tended to deviate. One of them was into Goswami writing and *lilas*. Prabhupada wasn't pleased with our direction, and he pulled me down to earth, saying, "Look, this is a deviation." After that, I became Prabhupada's secretary for a month, and he treated me strictly. I'd been temple president and I thought I'd achieved a certain level of responsibility, but when I made a couple of little mistakes he took me to task. So this was also his compassion. It shows relationship, it shows different kinds of treatment according to different people and circumstances. Prabhupada was incredibly flexible in the way he would train and relate to people.

Sureshvar: Srila Prabhupada stayed in New Dvaraka for more than a week in June '76. It was at this time that some devotees had formed a "Gopi Bhava" club, and Prabhupada corrected the *sahajiya* tendency that they had developed. I went to one of their Gopi Bhava meetings, and I knew something was wrong, because they minimized *Bhagavad-gita*. Prabhupada came down heavily on these Gopi Bhava devotees, and it's what they needed, what we all needed to hear. They were the first full-blown *sahajiya* group in the West. It was a weed growing around our creeper of devotion, *bhakti lata,* so Prabhupada pulled it out strongly. There were many famous quotes that came out of their meeting. The devotees asked him, "But Prabhupada, you say that everything is in your books, and the pastimes of the *gopis* are there too." He said, "Yes, my books are like a drug store but when you walk in the drug store, you can't just buy any medicine. You have to get the medicine that's appropriate for you. First Kurukshetra *lila,* then *rasa lila*." Another answer Prabhupada gave to one of their challenges was, "First deserve, then desire." So Srila Prabhupada was so sweet but so heavy. He was as hard as a thunderbolt and as soft as a rose.

At that time I was indexing the Eighth Canto at the BBT in Los Angeles, and I had mixed feelings. On the one hand I thought, "Boy,

Srila Prabhupada's been here a week. This is great." On the other
hand I thought, "I wonder when he's going to leave," because he was
so heavy. I wasn't even his personal servant. I was just living in the
same neighborhood where he stayed. He was in his quarters in
Rukmini-Dwarakadish *dham,* and I was thinking, "This is intense.
I don't know how long I can go on being in the same neighborhood
as Prabhupada." So that was another indication that I had a long
way to go before I could be intimate with Srila Prabhupada.

Prahladananda Swami: Once I wrote Prabhupada a letter and
asked him, "How does *bhava* turn into *prema?*" I had been reading
the *Bhakti-rasamrita-sindu* by Bon Maharaj. Srila Prabhupada had
told Rupanuga prabhu that we should only read the purports but not
the translations in that book. The purports were by Srila Jiva Goswami or Vishvanath Chakravarti Thakur. Rupanuga didn't like me
reading that book, but I'd stay up at night and read it secretly. I
thought that it would give me some special realizations. After a while
I was convinced that I was on the stage of *bhava,* and it was just a
question of time before it turned into *prema.* That's why I asked Srila
Prabhupada about how *bhava* turns into *prema.* He wrote me a one-
page response on preaching, which surprised me. Srila Prabhupada
wrote, "I've heard that you're all going out in Buffalo. This is very
good. You should all go out, chant Hare Krishna all around Buffalo,
distribute *Bhagavad-gita,* and preach about *Bhagavad-gita* as much
as possible. The boys and girls in your country generally are good
souls—that's why they've taken birth in such a nice country. Just
like here, in San Francisco, we've had Ratha-yatra, and ten thousand
boys and girls were dancing and chanting in full transcendental
ecstasy. I've heard that in just two weeks in New York they've
distributed three thousand *Back to Godheads,* and that in Buffalo,
you're also distributing *Back to Godheads* very nicely. Please continue in this way and your success in life is assured. As Krishna sees
that you are working seriously to bring His other children back to
the spiritual kingdom, then He will bestow all of His blessings upon

you. Krishna is never ungrateful for our efforts to serve Him, rest assured. Regarding your question, 'how does *bhava* turn into *prema*?' there is no need to trouble yourself over such advanced questions at the present time. Shortly I will be publishing *The Nectar of Devotion*, and that will be explained there. As far as the fifty dollars you sent me, I find no enclosed money in your letter. Do you know where it is?"

So at once I realized that Prabhupada was quite sensitive. Instead of answering my question directly, he answered it in another way. It was not the answer that I expected, but if I actually wanted these advanced stages of Krishna consciousness, the method was going out and distributing Prabhupada's books and chanting Hare Krishna in the street. That would gradually give me what I was looking for.

Balavanta: Rupanuga wrote to Prabhupada to ask if he could go to law school. Although I had not asked Rupanuga, he also asked Prabhupada if I could go, as well as other people like Amarendra. Srila Prabhupada wrote back, "Yes, you may go, but not that all of our men should become lawyers. But, in Balavanta's case, I can understand that he wants to use this for political preaching, so in that way it is all right. But not that everyone should become lawyers." Then he said, "I have always wanted a lawyer on the GBC." So on that basis he gave us permission.

Dayananda: In 1969 Gargamuni started the incense business and convinced me to quit my job and work in the incense business full time. I shaved up, and when Prabhupada saw me he said, "Oh, you have become *brahmachari*?" He was surprised that I shaved. Much later he mentioned to Jayatirtha that he didn't think it was a good idea that I had quit my job. He thought I should have remained as a professional rather than going into the incense business. Once he told me a story about sticking to your guns. He said that in British India, there was an office with a couple of British overseers and a lot of clerks. One day these overseers announced that no one should wear *tilak* in the office. The next day only two men wore *tilak*. The British overseers called these two men in front of everyone and said, "Okay, these men are the real devotees, the real Vaishnavs. You others are all imitations." Prabhupada told this story to illustrate that we have to stick to our guns.

Prahladananda Swami: The devotees went to the airport to greet Srila Prabhupada when he arrived and created more or less a riot. They ran through the airport chanting and screaming and were disrespectful to the people. Prabhupada was disappointed by this behavior. In any case, afterward we all went to Keshava prabhu's home. Prabhupada went upstairs, and we performed an *abhishek*. I was fanning Srila Prabhupada, and I remember how he became compassionate. He said, "These people are unhappy. We simply want them to become happy." Prabhupada's compassion and those words summed up the whole mission of Krishna consciousness for me. We are trying to help unhappy people become happy.

After the ceremony Tamal Krishna Maharaj and Vishnujana Maharaj related some stories about preaching to the students in Berkeley. They said to Srila Prabhupada, "We had a problem with the vendors in Berkeley because we were giving out free *prasadam*. They became envious and filed a petition with the police chief saying that we were creating a disturbance by giving out food without a license. Then we got a petition from thousands and thousands of students asking for our food, and we presented that to the police chief. We asked him, 'Which is better, thousands of signatures from the students, or a few signatures from the vendors?' The police chief understood that a few signatures were not as good as thousands and thousands of signatures, so he said, 'All right.'" Then the vendors attacked the devotees, and Vishnujana Maharaj and Tamal Krishna Maharaj defended them. Prabhupada thought for a few minutes and said, "Yes, wherever there is Chaitanya Mahaprabhu's movement there will be victory." The devotees said, "*Jaya*, Srila Prabhupada!"

By this time Jayananda prabhu, who had been working on the Ratha-yatra carts, had fallen asleep in the back. The devotees were going to wake him up, but Prabhupada said, "No, don't, he is doing more work than all of you." Then when we were leaving someone brought in a huge bowl of fruit for Srila Prabhupada. I thought, "Wow, we're going to have a feast now." Srila Prabhupada took a little *prasadam* and offered some to the devotees. He gave me a strawberry and said, "Don't eat very much at night."

Balavanta: In the airport, literally everyone's consciousness was on Srila Prabhupada. He commanded that much attention. This was a busy metropolitan airport, but he was so regal, with his head held high, that people deferred to him. It was obvious that he was a very important person. It was like other animals making way for a lion as it goes through a jungle. Similarly, people made way for Srila Prabhupada and didn't mind doing so. The airport people provided a VIP room for him, and we put a simple *vyasasana* in it—it was a cushion with some wooden legs. We put this *asana* on top of a table. Remember, we were all young, and we were coming out of a most unregulated lifestyle, so everything was a daze for us. There wasn't an older person amongst us. We figured Srila Prabhupada's seat had to be high, and there were chairs for everyone else. Srila Prabhupada was old enough to be our grandfather, and yet we were the people that Krishna had sent to him somehow. So we directed Srila Prabhupada to this room and up to the table. That was the stopping point. We said to him "This is your seat." He looked at us questioningly and we said, "Oh, it's sturdy, Srila Prabhupada." Perhaps it was against his better judgment, but in any case he climbed up a little step, went on this table and sat on the *asana*. He was very charitable to us. Rather than hurt our feelings, he would do something which is unbecoming for a gentleman of his age—to walk on top of a table and sit on a wooden *asana* with a cushion on it. But because we had done it for him and because we were trying in our immature way to honor him, he accepted it. A materialistic gentleman would have said, "This is not right, take this out of here. I'll sit on the chair with the others. Don't be so foolish." But there was nothing of that nature in him. It was a loving exchange.

Dayananda: At the end of 1970, Srila Prabhupada was considering going back to India. Rupanuga, Karandhar, some others, and I were sitting with Prabhupada in his garden in Los Angeles when he said, "Shall I go to India? I'm thinking to go to India and to take a group of devotees with me." It turned out that he took quite a few devotees. Our Los Angeles temple was practically cut in half. We also gave him several thousand dollars to take with him. But we managed somehow. Karandhar and I were amazed. It was like a cell splitting in half and then growing again. It was incredible to experience that kind of growth. In the garden that day, we were all feeling a lot of pressure and changes. These things affected me particularly. On the other hand, Rupanuga always had a mature presence with Prabhupada and seemed able to communicate easily with him. When Prabhupada asked Rupanuga, "Should I go to India?" Rupanuga said that he was not much in favor of the idea. Another devotee, maybe Karandhar, supported Rupanuga. Then Prabhupada asked me, "Dayananda, what do you think I should do?" I had never given advice on such a monumental thing. This was completely beyond my realm, so I said something diplomatic. I said, "Prabhupada, I think you should do whatever is your desire." Prabhupada shot back at me, "My desire is to spread this *sankirtan* movement all over the world." His words entered my heart. How could I not be grounded in that idea? For me it was the right time and the right place to be influenced by Prabhupada in that way. It's something that I think about regularly.

Prahladananda Swami: One of the *matajis* stripped the paint off the Deities and was going to repaint them. Prabhupada said, "Who told you to do this?" She said, "Baradraj." Prabhupada said, "Baradraj? Who is Baradraj?" She was shaking. Prabhupada said, "I'm your spiritual master, and I'm right here. Why didn't you ask me?" She ran out of the room crying, and it was doubtful whether we could install Radha-Kalachandji. Then the devotees discovered some quick-drying paint, so they painted the Deities, and Srila Prabhupada installed Them. I was amazed at how expertly Prabhupada directed everyone. After he personally performed the sacrifice, Prabhupada did the first *arati*, and the whole room was blissful. Sri Sri Radha-Kalachandji and Srila Prabhupada were giving so much mercy that the whole room became like Vaikuntha.

Dayananda: Vishnujana and the other devotees who did puppet shows were practicing one that depicted Narada Muni asking Krishna, "What's *maya?*" Then all of a sudden Narada Muni is in the desert, gets married, has a family, and the family gets washed away in a flood. Narada Muni calls out, "Oh, Krishna, my family!" and then once again he's back with Krishna. But this is not a bona fide story. The devotees were practicing this show in a parking lot outside of Prabhupada's quarters, and Prabhupada saw them. He didn't like it. He said, "What story is that? What story are they doing?" They told him, "You know Prabhupada, that one about Narada Muni falling into *maya.*" Prabhupada said, "Narada Muni doesn't fall into *maya.*" Prabhupada checked it. He was always supervising to see that things were done in a bona fide way.

Balavanta: When devotees did a play on Chaitanya *lila,* Prabhupada made it clear how much pleasure it gave him. He told us that when he was young he had been in a Chaitanya *lila* play. He and the other actors rehearsed for a long time, and when they finally performed it by the end of the play everyone in the audience was crying. Prabhupada said, "I did not know why they were crying."

We put on the play of Lord Chaitanya and the Kazi. Prabhupada laughed and even interrupted the play to make statements. When one of the *brahmans* said, "If we give the holy name to the common people, it will be expanded." Prabhupada said, "It is already expanded. It cannot be stopped." We had a clay *mridanga* that was broken beyond repair, so we covered it with plaster of paris, and when the Kazi's men came to stop the *kirtan,* one of them picked up this *mridanga* and threw it on the ground. Prabhupada's eyes got big. It was a great offense. I was near the *vyasasana,* and I whispered to Prabhupada, "It was already broken, Prabhupada." I don't think that placated him too much. He didn't get angry, but we would never do that again.

Dayananda: After the program we went to a separate room, the *brahmachari* room, and had a puppet show about Prahlad. Vishnujana had made the puppets. Behind the puppets' screen, Silavati was Prahlad's mother, while Vishnujana and one or two other devotees took other roles. At one point Hiranyakashipu was about to give Prahlad some poisoned food, and there was a plate of sweets on the puppet stage. Prahlad was offering these sweets to his spiritual master, when someone told one of the *brahmacharis* to bring the plate of sweets to Prabhupada. When Prabhupada received these sweets he said, "Oh, you're trying to poison me?" It was so funny. Prabhupada made this joke, and everybody got a kick out of it.

Balavanta: I had the opportunity to talk with him a little about the play. He said, "Yes, this play is so nice. There should be more plays of this standard." I said, "The devotees worked hard for this, Srila Prabhupada. They had many rehearsals." He said, "Yes, whatever you do sincerely for Krishna will be a success."

Sureshvar: When Srila Prabhupada first came to Chicago for Rathayatra, he arrived around 6:30 in the morning. We had *gurupuja* for him with ecstatic chanting and dancing. One devotee, perhaps Mahabuddhi prabhu, was dancing like he was doing the twist or boogeying. Srila Prabhupada stopped this ecstatic *kirtan* and pointed to a picture of Lord Chaitanya with his arms upraised. He said, "Dance like Sri Chaitanya Mahaprabhu." Sometimes he would encourage anybody, however they were dancing, but in this case he wanted the devotees to come to a high platform. "Dance like Sri Chaitanya Mahaprabhu."

Prahladananda Swami: Once the *gurukula* students were reciting verses from *Bhagavad-gita*. One of them, Krishna Smaranam, had a good memory. Although I wasn't living in the temple, I was also memorizing *Bhagavad-gita* verses, because if you knew a whole chapter then you'd get a whole plate of *maha-prasadam*. I was trying to keep up with the *gurukula* students so I could get a *maha* plate also. When this little boy recited many verses I thought, "Wow, this is fantastic! He's expert!" Prabhupada asked him, "So what is the translation?" Krishna Smaranam said, "I don't know." Prabhupada said, "This is useless. They must know the translation." Then I realized that I also have to know what the verses mean. It's not enough to simply parrot the words.

Balavanta: Prabhupada was there Friday, Saturday, Sunday, and left on Monday. On Sunday morning I was very tired because we had been up twenty-four hours, so I missed *mangal arati*. Usually I went, but not that morning. That afternoon there was a small group of devotees in Prabhupada's room, and he said, "One thing is, the devotees here do not go to *mangal arati?*" It had been a huge *mangal arati*. I said, "Oh, yes, Prabhupada, they go to *mangal arati*." He said, "Hmm."

Dayananda: When the realtor came, we toured that building, then we toured the other building, and we decided that we wanted the Watseka building. Prabhupada said to the minister, who was the representative of the church that owned the Watseka building, "You are serving God, and we are serving God. We're both servants of God. We are just as poor as church mice, and so in some sense we can ask you to give the building to us for the service of God. However, we won't ask you that. But you give us your best price." Prabhupada obviously wanted the building and was negotiating with the minister like anything, practically pushing him.

Balavanta: We went for a morning walk in a park in Atlanta. At that time, Atlanta was up-and-coming, urbanized, and trying to become the next great city. The city planners were totally immersed in that consciousness. Since I was the temple president, Prabhupada spoke to me. He pointed to the skyscrapers and said, "Do not be impressed. Krishna will finish it in a moment."

Prahladananda Swami: Once he said, "People are so foolish that they don't know that sometimes there's a chemical—potassium phosphate—in margarine, that's from stool. Yet they think that margarine is better that butter. People are so foolish."

Dayananda: When we were in his garden in Los Angeles in 1970, Prabhupada started talking about Russia. He said that his first impression of the Russian men was how strong they were. They had picked up the luggage effortlessly. He was a little critical of such physical strength because after all, our intention is not to be muscle-bound, but to be spiritually inclined. Then he commented on the women. He said the women in Russia were also big, and he said that the gopis were tribhangalalita, meaning that the gopis had an attractive figure, unlike the Russian women. Those first impressions of Russia made it seem a little formidable at the time.

Balavanta: There was an era when the book distributors and the devotees who did temple services had some tension. The book distributors would exaggerate their position to some degree, and this caused anxiety, but there were quotes where Prabhupada said, "One of the best things is to go distribute my books." Many book distributors were at the temple for Prabhupada's visit, and after the Sunday Feast lecture, one book distributor raised his hand with the idea to resolve this dispute once and for all. He asked, "Srila Prabhupada, what pleases you the most?" Everybody was in great anticipation. Prabhupada's immediate response was, "When you love Krishna." We all said, "*Haribol!*" It was a very pleasing answer.

Sureshvar: The last time I saw Srila Prabhupada was in Los Angeles when I worked at the BBT indexing his books—at that time, Canto Eight. In that canto, Srila Prabhupada writes about the days of the week and how they relate to the planets. In one morning lecture in Los Angeles, Srila Prabhupada said, "I am traveling all over the world, and I'm asking this question, 'Why are the days of the week in that order?'" He was asking us, too. "Why is Sunday the first day?" Some devotee piped up and said, "Because it is the Lord's day." Srila Prabhupada said, "Don't bring in religion." He wanted to establish this information on a scientific basis, as many people view religion as sectarian and sentimental. He said that the order of days of the week relates directly to the order of the planets. Sunday is first because the Sun is closest. Then Monday as the next planet is the Moon, Tuesday—Mars, Wednesday—Mercury, Thursday—Jupiter, Friday—Venus and Saturday—Saturn.

Another memory I have was when the sun was just peeking through the trees on a morning walk in a park in Santa Monica, and a little old lady in the park saw our squadron of saffron moving toward her. I was wondering what Srila Prabhupada was going to say. He didn't say "Hare Krishna," but he said, "Good morning," with very long, gracious tones. The lady gave a nice return greeting and a look as if to say, "This is the most wonderful thing I've ever seen." Srila Prabhupada knew just what to say and when to say it.

Balavanta: Srila Prabhupada came into the temple room and sat on the *vyasasana*. Everything was fresh. The devotees had worked literally twenty-four hours a day for a week. In fact, when he got to his room later, Prabhupada commented, "Wherever I go, there is always the smell of fresh paint," and then he laughed. So, in the temple room it was hushed. Most of the devotees were in the temple, but not all could fit so they were also spilling out in the hallways and porch. Prabhupada chanted Parama Karuna. In fact, during that visit he chanted that song every time he came in the temple. Afterwards he gave his opening address, and he made everybody ecstatic by saying, "On my tour I have been in Los Angeles, Mexico City, Caracas, and Miami, and now I have come to Atlanta, and I see your temple is the best." Then, more importantly, Srila Prabhupada said, "Krishna came and demanded surrender. Lord Chaitanya does not make such a demand. He simply distributes love of God to everyone." As he began this address, all of us settled down to hear him speak. Everyone was hanging on every word, but we didn't expect what was about to happen. He was speaking in a normal voice, and then he stopped. There was silence. You could see his tears. His eyes were closed, and tears were coming from his eyes. It was like trying to hold your hand to stop the water flowing from an open faucet. The pressure is such that you can't, and the water leaks out. That was like the pressure from his eyes—almost as though, if his eyes were open, the water would shoot out, just as it's described in the *Caitanya-caritamrta*. When he opened his mouth to go on speaking, the words wouldn't come out. The emotion within him was like a volcano. He was almost shaking as his body filled with emotion. He tried three or four times to go on speaking, and he couldn't. No one knew what to do. What was the etiquette? Should we get up? Begin chanting? Or just be quiet? It was an intimate thing, and yet we were in a public room. He was struggling within to go on, and finally he was able to speak, but his voice barely came out, and when it did it was very high. He said, "Just take shelter of Lord Chaitanya and be happy. Chant Hare Krishna."

Prahladananda Swami: That night we all watched Prabhupada's arrival because it was on television. Television cameras had recorded Prabhupada's airport arrival. Then Purushottama came back and said that before Prabhupada went to sleep he said, "I pray to Krishna every night to please protect me from *maya*."

Dayananda: To the end, Prabhupada was a warrior. I was in Iran during Prabhupada's disappearance *lila,* and one by one we all went to visit Prabhupada. When I got to Vrindavan, I immediately went to his room. I had a suit on, and some devotee said, "Go get changed," but Jayadvaita said, "No, no, those are his preaching clothes. Let him come in." I went in. Prabhupada was lying on his bed, and when I went next to him he asked me what I was doing. I said, "I'm still in Iran with Atreyarishi." He said, "What are you doing with your money?" Fortunately I was giving fifty percent of my income to Atreya for the preaching project. I told him that, and he said, "Good." He liked that. He put his hand on my head, and that was a very emotional time for me. Prabhupada was lying there in such an emaciated state, yet he put his hand on my head. I felt that my hair was impure, yet Prabhupada touched it.

Then Prabhupada wanted to continue translating the *Srimad-Bhagavatam.* Pradyumna came in to read verses from the *Bhagavatam,* and Prabhupada gave his purports. I was always impressed by Prabhupada's determination. In general, from his schedule and lifestyle, he was like a warrior, constantly preaching, leading *kirtans,* administrating his book distribution and book publishing, managing his movement and his personal spiritual life, sometimes chanting his rounds late at night. He was such a fighter, such a warrior, and he was so determined to accomplish his spiritual goals.

TAPE 15

Mukunda Goswami
Brahmananda das
Jayadvaita Swami
Dayananda das
Arundhati dasi
Jayapataka Swami
Mangala Nitai Maharaj
Dina Bandhu das
Babhru das
Rambhoru dasi
Hridayananda das Goswami
Yogeshvara das
Badrinarayan das
Brajendranandana das
Prithu das
Rabindra Svarup das
Srutakirti das
Bhagavat das
Malati dasi
Romapada Swami
Nara Narayan das
Madhusudana das
Manjari dasi
Madhudvisa das
Ekanath das
Urvasi dasi
Rasjna dasi

 **Mukunda Goswami:** Sometime in June 1966, Prabhu-
pada needed a better place in the Bowery, and there
was pressure on me to help him find one. I didn't know
exactly what to do, but I got a *Village Voice* and started
looking for some kind of rental that might be suitable.
Prabhupada's loft in the Bowery had been difficult to access,
and I thought, "A ground floor place would be good." I was going
down the rental column, and the first or second place that I called
was the storefront at 26 2nd Avenue. I met the agent, Mr. Gardner,
a sprightly-looking, youngish, good-natured man who was wearing
tennis shoes, denims and a T-shirt, and I told him about Prabhupada—how he was a scholar, an author, and a spiritual leader, and
that the Prime Minister of India appreciated his work. Mr. Gardner
was quite impressed. He liked the idea of somebody like that renting the storefront. Then Srila Prabhupada and Karlapati, Carl Yer-
gens, arrived and were introduced. We went into the storefront,
sat on a ledge just inside the window, and discussed whether or not
we could pay the $100 per month rent. Prabhupada had some very
interesting things to say, but we did most of the talking. In the
course of the conversation, we found out that there was also an
apartment available on the other side of the courtyard for $80 a
month. Prabhupada thought the storefront and apartment were
suitable for his needs. In front of Prabhupada and Mr. Gardner, Carl
and I had a little powwow as to how we could pay the rent, and we
decided that between us it wouldn't be a problem. Mr. Gardner said
that he would repaint the apartment, which would take a few days,
and then we could move in and Prabhupada could start giving
classes. We didn't tell Mr. Gardner about *harinam* and *mridangas*
and *kartals* but about yoga classes. At some point during the conversation, Prabhupada said that Mr. Carl (he used to call us by our
first names with a "Mr." appellation) and Mr. Michael were trustees
of our Society. We talked a little more, and Prabhupada presented
a set of three *Bhagavatams,* First Canto–Parts 1, 2, and 3, to Mr.
Gardner. Mr. Gardner was a little reluctant to take them, but

Prabhupada insisted and then signed them. Mr. Gardner was humbled and honored by getting these books and said, "Oh, thank you, it is very kind of you." That was a substantial gift. Prabhupada, with his distinguished, transcendental presence, began to talk about how we were going to create a Society. He said to Mr. Gardner, "We would also like you to be a trustee of our Society." Mr. Gardner thought for a minute, looked at the books, and said, "Okay."

We talked a bit more about what Prabhupada was doing, how the Movement was expanding, and how Prabhupada liked America. Then Prabhupada said that Mr. Carl and Mr. Michael were trustees, and, as all the trustees do, they pay a subscription of $20 dollars a month. He said, "We would like you to participate in this way too." Mr. Gardner hesitated for a moment, but then agreed. Prabhupada said, "Of course, it will be easier for you if you just deduct it from the rent. So we immediately got a $20 discount on the rent. Mr. Gardner was a little taken aback, but he agreed. When all was said and done, Mr. Gardner was in good spirits.

 **Brahmananda:** Here at 26 2nd Avenue there used to be a sink. That sink was important. After the *kirtan,* while Prabhupada was sitting on the platform, he would slice an apple without coring or skinning it, and then pass it around. He would also take one slice. He would chew it, somehow separate the core and the skin, and then lean back and spit the core and skin into the sink. Everyone would say, "Wow." No one else did that. But now that sink is missing. That sink should be there with a sign: "Prabhupada used this sink like a spittoon."

Mukunda Goswami: Before Prabhupada moved in, he asked me to go to Con-Edison and see if we could get the deposit, which was substantial for us, waived because we were a charitable organization, not a commercial venture. So I toddled to the Con-Edison office and explained Prabhupada's desire and the reason for it. But I was talking to a brick wall. Con-Edison doesn't make those kinds of arrangements. We would have to pay like everybody else. I wasn't a daring and active devotee, and so I said, "Okay, that's the system, that's the way it is." When I reported this back to Prabhupada, he wasn't happy at all, and eventually Prabhupada went to Con-Edison himself and convinced them to waive the deposits on the utilities for these two places.

Then, over a period of one or two weeks, things started happening at 26 2nd Avenue. This dingy place was transformed by the addition of carpets, tapestries, paintings, and many guests. One of the guests was Allen Ginsberg, which inspired everybody to come and take part in the *kirtans* more. This was the beginning of Krishna consciousness spreading outside India.

Brahmananda: Every day I would go to New York City to work at the Board of Education. One day I saw a *New York Times* newspaper lying in the subway with a picture of Dr. Radhakrishnan, the President of India. I ran back to the temple with it to show Prabhupada, because he had been telling us about Dr. Radhakrishnan. Prabhupada had asked him to join in this movement, but Dr. Radhakrishnan was a Mayavadi, a deluded scholar, who said that one should not think of Krishna but one should think of the unborn within Krishna. Prabhupada had invited Dr. Radhakrishnan to preach Krishna consciousness, and Dr. Radhakrishnan told Prabhupada, "When I retire, then I will do it." The newspaper article stated, "Dr. Radhakrishnan Retires." After Prabhupada saw it, he wrote Dr. Radhakrishnan a letter inviting him to take up Krishna consciousness. Nothing came of that.

Later, when Prabhupada toured South India, he visited Dr. Radhakrishnan. By that time he had gotten a stroke and couldn't speak. He was paralyzed. Prabhupada said, "He spoke so much nonsense, and now he cannot speak at all."

Jayadvaita Swami: A standard Sunday feast menu included a few different kinds of rice—*pushpanna,* white rice, and maybe one other. There would be a wet subji like Prabhupada's cauliflower and potatoes and a dry *subji* and sometimes some other *subji* also. There were always spicy cauliflower and pea *samosas,* cooked dry, and a couple different kinds of *pakoras.* There were white *puris,* different kinds of noodles, a few different chutneys—plum, apple, raisin, pineapple; and a variety of sweets like simply wonderfuls, *halava,* sweet rice, and *gulabjamans.* People were jolly. No wonder people joined; you'd have to be nuts not to join. The Sunday feast was not a small thing.

Many years later, book distribution was a big thing, and Prabhupada said one person could remain at the temple. Everyone else could go distribute his books. In some places the managers got the idea that the feast should be cut down, and they started having four or five preparations so that one person could cook everything and everybody else could distribute books. Prabhupada wrote a letter about that and said, "No, it should be opulent. The feast program should go on full strength."

Dayananda: At that time I was living with someone, and after we saw the wedding ceremony of Subal and Krishna devi, we decided that we wanted to join the community. I thought there must be some formality for joining, so I went to the devotees and said, "We would like to go and speak to Swamiji. What should we do?" They said, "Oh just go up, he is on the 5th floor." I said, "But is there some formality? Should I make an application?" "No, no," I was told. "Ranchor, Swamiji's servant, will answer the door, and you tell him that you want see Swamiji." I said, "That's all I have to do?" He said, "Yeah. Go ahead."

So we went up, and sure enough, Ranchor answered the door. We said, "We would like to see Swamiji." He said, "Yes, come in."

I was shocked. I thought, "There must be more." We walked in, and although we knew better, Prabhupada had to tell us, "Please take your shoes off." We ran back to the door, took our shoes off, then came back and sat down. Prabhupada said, "Yes, you want something?" I said, "Swamiji, we would like to join your community and be married." Prabhupada said, "First you have to be initiated." I said, "Oh, yes, I want to be initiated." I had an idea that this was the procedure. I had been attending the classes regularly, and he said, "You like our philosophy?" I said, "Yes!" He said, "Do you have a job?" Many people were coming who weren't working, but I had a job, so I said, "Yes, Swamiji," and I explained that I did electrical lineman work. I said, "I climb those electrical poles." Prabhupada said, "Very good," and he agreed to our proposal.

Some devotees say that the philosophy or the *prasadam* or this or that attracted them, but my decision to join Krishna consciousness was because I wanted to be part of Swamiji's group. I wanted to be part of his Society, his family.

Brahmananda: I was living on 6th Street, and my college roommate came and said to me, "I just went to an unusual Swami. They were into singing and dancing." We were into meditation and yoga, so singing and dancing seemed odd. My roommate said that this Swami had a big tape recorder. We refused to wear a wristwatch because we didn't want to know what time it was. Time was mundane, what to speak of a tape recorder. My roommate said, "Allen Ginsberg was there." Allen Ginsberg was our hero, so I said, "Oh, we have to go." I went to 26 2nd Avenue and sat at the door. Prabhupada came in. He was to get up on the platform, but instead he stopped, turned, and looked at me. I'll never forget that. It's burnt into my memory.

Many years later Prabhupada asked me, "How did you join?" I said, "My friend told me about you, and I came, but my friend didn't join." Prabhupada said, "Oh, the same with me." He said that his friend, Narendranath Mullik, brought him to Srila Bhaktisiddhanta, but Narendranath did not join.

**Arundhati:** Srila Prabhupada had some little Radha-Krishna Deities that traveled with him. We were in his apartment one day when he said, "I would like somebody to bathe my Deities. Is there anyone that would like to do that?" I said, "I will, Srila Prabhupada." I wasn't *brahman* initiated, but that didn't matter at the time. The next morning Srila Prabhupada and I sat down in front of his Deities. He took his little brass Radharani and showed me how to polish Her by doing it himself, using tamarind and fuller's earth. Then he handed Krishna to me, saying, "Now you do Krishna." So I polished Krishna. Then he showed me how to bathe the Deities, and he asked me to come every morning to do that. So while he was in New York I did that. Sometimes he was in the room with me, and other times he would go on his morning walk.

Then I returned to Boston with the other devotees and when Prabhupada came there I took care of his Deities again. During that time, Satsvarupa said to Prabhupada that he was concerned about the women in the temple because they were fighting with each other. Prabhupada said, "Well, they should be married. Immediately arrange for them to get married." There were four of us, Saradiya, Rukmini, Jahnava, and me.

So, Saradiya and Vaikunthanath were arranged to be married, Jahnava and Nanda Kishor, Rukmini and Baradraj, and Prabhupada said that I should marry a young man named Dayal Nitai. But I didn't want to marry Dayal Nitai. He didn't seem right, and I was very upset, going up on a hill, praying to Krishna and crying. Satsvarupa told Prabhupada, and Prabhupada said, "Nothing is by force in Krishna consciousness. She can get married at a later date." So everybody got married except me.

When everybody was married, the whole Boston temple suddenly changed, and I started feeling out of place. I prayed to Krishna to send me a husband. Prabhupada continued his travels, and one day about two months later, Purushottam, Prabhupada's servant, called the Boston temple from Columbus, Ohio and said, "Srila

Prabhupada wants to know if you want to come here and marry Pradyumna." I said, "Okay," and I went to Columbus. I had met Pradyumna once.

When I got there, it turned out that Prabhupada's Deities had been lost while he was traveling. They had been missing for some weeks, but on the day that I arrived in Columbus, the Deities came back too. Prabhupada said to me, "The Deities like the way you serve Them, so now that you are here, They have come back also." So I got to bathe his Deities again.

 **Jayapataka Swami:** Once, at a disappearance festival for Srila Bhaktisiddhanta Saraswati Thakur, Prabhupada was explaining how the disciple tries to carry out the order of his guru and the previous guru, the grandfather guru, as well as the order of the previous *acharyas*. He gave us the example of Srila Bhaktivinoda Thakur, how he had begged door-to-door to build the first temple at Mayapur Dham, and he explained how the different *acharyas* had contributed to the development of Mayapur Dham. Prabhupada said, "To please my spiritual master and the previous *acharyas*, I am also trying to do something in Mayapur Dham. I am very grateful to everyone who is helping me." Then he couldn't speak any further. He choked up and started crying. There was a long silence. We didn't know what to do. Prabhupada finally said, "The secret of success is to satisfy the desires of the previous *acharyas*."

 **Mangala Nitai Maharaj:** We bow down to the lotus feet of A. C. Bhaktivedenta Swami Prabhupada because he preached Krishna consciousness all over the world. He's stimulating and inspiring us. While I was preaching in Kashmir, I wrote to him, "This Kashmir is full of Muslims, yet I'm preaching over here." In reply he wrote, "Oh, Mangala, are you afraid to preach amongst the Muslims? I am preaching amongst the *mlecchas*. Don't be disheartened."

Dina Bandhu: Prabhupada would take *charanamrita,* pay his obeisances to Radha and Krishna, and then go to Lord Jagannath. Somehow I always managed to be at the *charanamrita* bowl. One day I was standing behind Prabhupada when he took the *charanamrita,* and he looked at me with a heavy, horrible look. My heart stopped. He said, "It is salt." He looked around at all the devotees and said, "It is salt." He was upset. He paid his obeisances, sat down, and immediately said, "Who has done this?" Some poor *brahmacharini* in the kitchen came in shaking, and Prabhupada said, "Why have you done this?" She giggled and said, "It's Krishna's mercy." Prabhupada said, "It's not Krishna's mercy; it's your stupidity."

When Prabhupada was personally doing the installation for the large Gaura-Nitai Deities that Govinda dasi had made for our temple, everybody was in the temple room. I thought, "If we are installing Deities there should be a feast," so I went into the kitchen and cooked everything I could think of, like *rasagullas, sandesh, halava,* and *puris* while I listened to the ceremony over the speakers. Finally there was a fire sacrifice and then an offering. After that, Nanda Kumar, Prabhupada's servant, came in, loaded up Prabhupada's plate with *mahaprasad* and went upstairs. When he came back he said, "Prabhupada usually eats a little sweet, but today he ate every single sweet." He said that Prabhupada smiled at him and said, "Sweets means *rasagulla* and *sandesh.*" At that point I knew that my whole life was perfect. That was the only time I ever got to cook for Prabhupada.

Babhru: In 1972, Srila Prabhupada came to Honolulu to install our Deities, Sri Sri Pancha-tattva and to give *sannyas* initiation to one of his disciples, Siddhasvarupa, who became Siddhasvarupananda Goswami. Prabhupada was in Hawaii for ten days, and every day he commented on the beautiful *tulasi* plants. At the time, taking care of Tulasi devi was my life's work. I started taking care of her at the beginning of 1970 when Hawaii had the first *tulasi* plants in ISKCON. Prabhupada told Govinda dasi how pleased he was with our big *tulasis*. We had a bunch of them in front of the temple and lining the sidewalk up to the temple. Prabhupada also said that Tulasi was crowding the sidewalk a little, and he said, "It's an offense to brush against Tulasi." Another time he teased us by saying that it was an offense to step on her shadow. The next night the *brahmacharis* were trying to leap over her shadows, which was hard to do because a street lamp cast her shadow across the whole sidewalk. Govinda dasi asked Prabhupada, "What should we do?" Prabhupada laughed and said, "Don't live. Don't die."

Every day Govinda dasi gave me reports about how pleased Srila Prabhupada was with Tulasi devi's care, and I got a little impatient since I had been doing this work for two and a half years. One night I said, "Govinda dasi, I would like to hear these things firsthand." Gaurasundar, Govinda dasi's husband, was protective of Srila Prabhupada when he was in Hawaii, and we weren't allowed to get very close to Prabhupada. But Govinda dasi grabbed me by the arm, dragged me out to the car, and shoved me in the back. Gaurasundar had an old Buick just for this visit. Gaurasundar was in the driver's seat, and Prabhupada was in the passenger seat. Govinda dasi said, "This is Babhru, he does all the work for Tulasi devi." Prabhupada gave me a great big smile and said, "That is very nice. We should always engage our body and our mind in Krishna's service." And I knew at that minute that to him I was transparent.

 **Rambhoru:** When Prabhupada entered the airport, he walked along a big, red carpet with devotees on either side, and I got close so I could size up this person. My first impressions were that he was short, that his feet didn't touch the ground, and that I couldn't understand him. That embarrassed me because I thought I was spiritually enlightened, but I knew that Prabhupada could understand

me a lot better than I could understand myself.

Some devotees guided Srila Prabhupada onto a large *vyasasana* in the VIP room. Devotees flanked him, fanning him with a *chamara* and a peacock fan while someone washed his feet and another person offered *arati*. Other devotees were laughing, chanting, singing, and crying. I thought, "If Prabhupada were to look at me, he'd see what an idiot I am and how puffed up I am."

The devotees formed a semicircle around Prabhupada while I hid behind a large couch some distance away so that I could look at Prabhupada without him seeing me. Prabhupada was looking at his disciples from England, Paris, Spain, and other places, but he kept noticing that there was a peculiar thing happening behind the couch as I was crouched there. Prabhupada repeatedly looked around and then looked back at me. Although I had tried to hide myself, I had made myself more obvious. Every time Srila Prabhupada looked at me, my heart broke. I felt humiliated by his glance, and I started to cry. I sobbed and sobbed, and after about ten minutes I felt purified. I felt clean and rejuvenated. It was my first experience of the glory of being humiliated by a pure devotee.

Hridayananda Goswami: A GBC man had let his hair grow out a little bit. When he walked to Prabhupada's room in Vrindavan, Prabhupada immediately said, "Oh, the hippie seeds are sprouting again."

Yogeshvara: In Geneva, a famous Mayavadi Sanskrit scholar came to see Prabhupada. He had written a book about Krishna in which he said that the dust raised by the hooves of the cows refers to this, and the *gopis* are symbolic of that. Srila Prabhupada said, "I have been looking at your book." The man said, "It took me twelve years to write that book." Prabhupada said, "Yes, and there are still mistakes in it. The proof of whether one truly understands Krishna is whether or not one engages in devotional service. Just like these young boys and girls. Their's is the age for enjoying, but they have given that up to engage in devotional service to Lord Krishna." The Sanskrit scholar started chuckling. He said, "I smoke, I drink; I could give up these things if I wanted to, but I don't want to." Srila Prabhupada, said, "Yes, therefore you have many, many births to go on the spiritual path." The scholar said, "It's time for me to leave now," but before he left, Srila Prabhupada presented him with a copy of *The Nectar of Devotion* and said, "I request you to look through this book. I think you will find it of great interest." Afterwards, myself, Satsvarupa Maharaj, Hansadutta, and Guru Gauranga gathered around Prabhupada to make sure that we had understood what had happened. Prabhupada was quiet. Guru Gauranga said, "He was a big demon, wasn't he Prabhupada?" Prabhupada said, "He has been influenced by association with Mayavadis, but I noticed that in his book he has said the name 'Krishna' many times. This will greatly benefit him." Prabhupada was so compassionate, so kind, so concerned even for this Mayavadi scholar who had done much damage through his writing.

The next person to see Srila Prabhupada was a very humble man. Srila Prabhupada said, "Do you have any questions?" The man said, "No, I was happy to hear that you are in Geneva, and I was honored by this opportunity to meet you." Srila Prabhupada thought for a second and said, "Yogeshvara, bring my harmonium. Satsvarupa, you play *kartals*. Hansadutta play *mridanga*." Prabhupada sang "Hari hari bi phale." Afterwards the man stood up, thanked Srila Prabhupada, and left. Srila Prabhupada looked at us and said, "He was a simple soul. Therefore I sang for him because I knew he would appreciate it."

Prabhupada had a wonderful facility for reciprocating with people according to their needs and disposition. His was an inspiring example of giving Krishna at every moment, in every situation.

Badrinarayan: Prabhupada asked for questions, and a professor from Cal Tech stood up and said, "You are talking about *kirtan,* but this is sentimental." He rambled on, quoting verses from *Vedanta Sutra.* Prabhupada didn't even look at the professor. He was looking at Lord Jagannath, chanting on his *japa* beads, and seemed like a lion getting ready to pounce. The professor stopped speaking. Prabhupada said, "Are you finished?" Then Prabhupada quoted the *Puranas,* the *Upanisads,* and other scriptures and hammered away at this professor. The professor had been standing proudly, but he became a little deflated, then he was on his knees, and then he sat down. Prabhupada finished in a crescendo, made his last point, and said, "Do you have any question?" The professor said, "Can we have *kirtan?*"

Brajendranandana: About 1972 or '73, before they sent us out on the traveling party, I was allowed to go into Prabhupada's quarters. I was in great awe because Srila Prabhupada was much more relaxed in his quarters than in the *Bhagavatam* class. It was a different mood. I watched him take his Ayurvedic medicine so elegantly and gracefully. Then one devotee said, "Prabhupada, they are going out on the subways every day, and even before they make an announcement, people give a donation." Prabhupada said, "Oh, that is love. Just like a little boy brings his father's shoes without being asked." Prabhupada had an amazing look of compassion. He said, "You should tell them that they are suffering because they have forgotten to bring their love to Krishna." The next time I had an opportunity to distribute on the trains, I said that, and I collected more than anyone else.

On that same occasion, Bali Mardan prabhu asked, "Prabhupada, they are saying that they are from Apple Records. Is that okay?" Prabhupada said, "Do not sell records. Sell books." "But Prabhupada, they are saying they are from Apple Records, and they are selling books." Prabhupada laughed and said, "Rupa Goswami said, 'Make them Krishna conscious first, and then give them the rules and regulations.' Somehow or other get them to take a book and utter the name Krishna."

Prithu: In Sweden, Prabhupada was lecturing on the four classes of men—the *brahman*, or first-class man; *ksatriya*, second-class; *vaishya*, third-class; and *sudra*, fourth-class—to a university crowd of rowdy students. As soon as he finished, a student in the front stood up and said, "Of course you think you are a first-class man. That's why your followers offer you flowers and you sit on a high seat." I was boiling with anger. If Prabhupada had made a little sign, I would have pounced on this student and ripped him to shreds.

It was dead silent in the room. Prabhupada practically pleaded with this student, saying, "No, no, no. I am not a first-class man. I am a fifth-class man." Everybody was shocked. It was dead silent again. In this deafening silence Prabhupada said, "Because I am the servant of everyone." We were astounded when he said this, and I saw that his lip was quivering and two big tears came behind his spectacles. It was clear that he was really the servant of the whole world, that he didn't think much of himself. On one side, he had so much power, and on the other side, he was so humble that he considered himself fifth-class, the servant of everyone, the person who was supporting and giving to everybody and not expecting anything in return. This was such a sublime moment for Krishna's pure devotee. I will never forget it.

Rabindra Svarup: Once, at the temple on Henry Street, Pradyumna brought a teaching assistant from Columbia University to see Srila Prabhupada. Prabhupada asked him, "What do you teach?" He said he taught religion. Prabhupada said, "What is religion?"

The man said, "Religion is a search after the divine." Prabhupada said, "Yes, that's very good, but there must also be finding." Then there was an incredible discussion, because Prabhupada began making statements and then saying, "Do you agree or do you disagree?" The man would say, "Well, that's true." Then Prabhupada asked the next question, and said, "Do you agree or disagree?" If the man kept agreeing, he was going to have to surrender. It was amazing. The man figured out what was happening one step before the final step. Prabhupada again asked him, "Do you agree or disagree?" The man was silent. He said, "Well, I think it is very nice." Prabhupada laughed, "Partial agreement is better than none," and then he changed the subject.

There was a bunch of reporters there, and they started asking Prabhupada questions. One reporter said, "Do you consider yourself the savior of the American youth?" Prabhupada's eyes got big, and he said, "Yes, but not just in the future, it is already a fact. Just see my students and how they are bright-faced. Formerly they were morose because they were hippies, but now everyone knows them as bright-faced. So it is already done. Your government is trying to stop this drug-taking, but their attempts are unsuccessful. If they gave me money, then I would be able to stop this drug problem." That was his appeal. It was amazing the way he did things.

 **Srutakirti:** Before I was his servant, I read Krishna Book to him every evening in his garden in Los Angeles. Prabhupada was happy listening to Krishna's pastimes. As the days went by, I would speculate on which stories he liked. He seemed to enjoy hearing about the pastimes of Krishna killing the demons. So one night I read about Dvivida the gorilla urinating on the sacrifice, and Prabhupada was laughing. He had so much fun listening to this pastime. The next day I was looking for another pastime that Prabhupada would enjoy and perhaps laugh about. But when he saw me looking through the book he said, "Anywhere, anywhere. Krishna is like a sweetball.

Wherever you bite it, it's sweet. So just read." I immediately started reading.

Bhagavat: One of the things that struck me about Srila Prabhupada was how concerned he was about the welfare of his disciples. That especially struck me in Bombay. I had cut my foot, and Prabhupada noticed it during *gurupuja*. At that time he was receiving worship from a hundred devotees, and *arati* was going on. He called me to the *vyasasana,* completely ignoring everyone in the room for that moment, and said, "What happened to your foot?" I said, "I cut myself." He said, "Are you all right? Is it very bad? Have you gone to the doctor? Do you need medicine?" I assured him that I had taken care of it. Then he said, "Remember, if you need anything, come and see me, and I will help."

Srila Prabhupada displayed deep care and affection. Nothing was as important to him as the welfare of his disciples.

Malati: Once we were getting ready for the first Radhastami at Bury Place. There was a big pot of the famous chutney, Radha Red, on the kitchen floor. My daughter ran into the kitchen and fell into this chutney which was hot off the stove. Some of the devotees were upset because they thought that we couldn't offer the chutney. They thought that the whole pot was destroyed. Prabhupada heard about it, immediately called me, and said, "Take her to the doctor." Prabhupada was immediately concerned and practical. Others were thinking, "What do we do about the chutney?" But Prabhupada's thought was, "What do we do about the child?" To this day my daughter has scars from that chutney.

Prithu: We had a gorgeous temple that was the ISKCON headquarters in Germany. But at that time, Krishna consciousness in Germany was in shambles. We had had some trouble with the German government. Jayatirtha went to Srila Prabhupada and said, "I think we won't be able to maintain this temple. It would be better to split up into smaller centers." But Prabhupada liked this temple. He appreciated the Deities there and the location. When he heard Jayatirtha's idea he said, "Even if your child has been born deaf and blind, does it mean you kill it?" We were shocked that he said that. Then he became angry. He said, "Does it mean you kill it?" Jayatirtha said, "No, no, no." Prabhupada said, "Don't be a rolling stone. Become determined."

Hridayananda Goswami: Another time we were walking with Prabhupada in Waikiki, Hawaii. Gurukripa said, "Prabhupada, you won our hearts. Your personality is so attractive that we couldn't help but love you." Prabhupada smiled and said, "Yes, that was my trick."

Rambhoru: I went to Vrindavan about a year and a half after I joined. At that time, 1975 and '76, there was a surge of *sannyas* hype. Everybody was taking *sannyas*. Gargamuni Swami had said to my husband, who was twenty-nine and had been married for a year and a half, "Oh, you are too old. You should take *sannyas* immediately." Then I was shipped off to India to assist Himavati, whose husband took *sannyas* shortly thereafter. I was so new in the movement that I didn't know what all this meant.

Hansadutta, Himavati's husband, was determined to take *sannyas*. Prabhupada said, "You cannot take *sannyas* unless your wife agrees." Srila Prabhupada said to Himavati, "So you agree that your husband takes *sannyas*?" Himavati said, "I don't agree. I don't agree that my husband and I are advanced enough for that step. But if you give my husband *sannyas,* Srila Prabhupada, I will accept it." Prabhupada said, "No, no, no. You have to agree, otherwise I will not do it." She replied, "No, Srila Prabhupada, I don't agree that my husband is advanced enough, nor am I advanced enough, but if you give him *sannyas,* I will accept it." This went on for four days, discussing back and forth. She never agreed. Yet at the Mayapur festival in 1976, although there was no arrangement in the *sannyas* arena, Hansadutta jumped in all ready with his dyed clothes, and Prabhupada gave him *sannyas*.

I was in Vrindavan with Himavati, and we had no idea that Hansadutta had done this. The devotees trickled back from Mayapur to Vrindavan, and, as insensitively as can be, they said, "Do you know what happened at the Mayapur festival? Your husband took *sannyas*." Himavati was hysterical and astonished because she had not agreed and had not expected that. When Prabhupada came, she stormed in his room and said, "You know, Srila Prabhupada, now that my husband has taken *sannyas*, I hate everyone, and I hate everything in this material world." Prabhupada was silent for a few moments. Then he said, "Very good. Now you are making advancement."

 **Romapada Swami:** Prabhupada rang the bell on his desk, and his servant came in and offered obeisances. The servant was supposed to have done something but he had neglected to do it. Prabhupada's mood shifted from one of happily appreciating the devotees' artwork to being strong and firm with his servant. Everybody in the room became silent. As soon as the servant left, Prabhupada withdrew that anger and was again as before. Anger did not control him, but he used that mood to instruct a disciple and help that disciple stay properly situated in devotional service.

Another point is that as Prabhupada writes, he also does. When persons came for *darshan,* without fail, there was always some *prasadam* for them even if it was something simple like cut fruit or macadamia nuts. Prabhupada would have his servant stay at the door to distribute *prasadam* to the guests as they left. Prabhupada was conscious of cultural etiquette. As Western devotees, if we have the right philosophy but the wrong behavior, we still feel justified. But Prabhupada also taught us the culture of Krishna consciousness.

 **Nara Narayan:** I joined the Krishna consciousness movement in San Francisco, just after Ratha-yatra in 1968. Shortly after that, Srila Prabhupada came to San Francisco. I was immediately transferred to Seattle to build an altar and *vyasasana* for Prabhupada's visit, and in the fall or winter of 1968, Srila Prabhupada came to Seattle. The temple was a little house, which was full of devotees from the Los Angeles *sankirtan* party. When Srila Prabhupada came, we wanted to have guests come, but few came. However, once we were delighted when around twenty students came from the University of Washington. Prabhupada gave a lecture, and in the middle of the lecture he said, "Please do not misunderstand. Misunderstanding is already there." We were thunderstruck.

Also in Seattle, during the disappearance day celebration for Srila Bhaktisiddhanta's Sarasvati, Prabhupada described how his spiritual master told him to spread Krishna consciousness in the Western world. He had only been given a few words of instruction: "You should go and spread Krishna consciousness in the English language." Many years passed, and at some point, Prabhupada said, he began to see his spiritual master in dreams, and his spiritual master said to him, "It is time to go." Prabhupada said, "I was thinking, how I can leave my four children and do this?" It seemed as though tears shot from his eyes as he said this. He looked around at us, his eyes shining, and he said, "But now, I have so many children." From the way he spoke, it almost gave the impression that the whole world had gathered inside that tiny room in Seattle. We could envision that somehow there would be a huge world movement. Yet at that time there were less than seventy devotees.

Jayapataka Swami: Prabhupada invited all of his godbrothers from the Gaudiya Math to attend the Ananta Sesa inauguration to put the Ananta Sesa at the bottom of a twelve foot foundation hole for the new temple. Prabhupada said to his godbrothers, "For the pleasure of Srila Bhaktisiddhanta Sarasvati Prabhupada, let us all cooperate together and form a governing body. If we unite and preach together he will be pleased." Everyone was amazed. Prabhupada had already created forty temples, yet he was inviting everyone, "Let's work together." Prabhupada showed us what Krishna consciousness is. To please the guru he desired total cooperation. But nobody accepted. Maybe people had different attachments, but Prabhupada's vision was universal. He said, "Okay, they don't want to work together, but we will do it." Then he established the Governing Body, and he said, "I am doing everything simply as an offering to please my spiritual master. There may always be detractors, but I am simply trying to do this to please the previous *acharya*."

Dina Bandhu: Prabhupada was due to arrive at the L.A. Airport, and we went there and had a huge *kirtan*. We were jumping up and down, waiting for Prabhupada, and there was a big, black sweeper there, mopping the floor. He saw all this commotion, and, as he came over to see what was going on, Prabhupada came through the door. All the devotees hit the ground. When the sweeper saw Prabhupada he said, "Look at that man, he's shining, he's shining! Look at that man, he's shining!"

Prithu: I was sitting on a bench chanting my rounds near Hippie Hill in San Francisco, when an old, black man came by. He said to me, "That old man who started this thing, he was a cool cat. I was living in the Bowery and he was living in the Bowery too. But then again, Jesus was born in a barn." And he walked away.

Madhusudana: At one point early on, Prabhupada was recuperating from a stroke. We heard that if he spoke too much, he would get tired and it would be bad for his health. We were concerned, so I wrote him a letter asking him not to speak much. I didn't want him to get tired. He wrote back saying, "My dear boy, if I would not speak how would you come?" His mission was to preach. How ridiculous it was for an 18-year-old boy, who didn't know much, to instruct him that way. But he also wrote, "I am taking help and precaution from Gaurasundar and Govinda dasi." So he lightened the blow. He was being careful, but he didn't need my advice.

 **Manjari:** Prabhupada was in Iran for Lord Balaram's Appearance Day in the summer of 1976. It was a nice atmosphere. All the flowers were blooming in the summer heat. At one point, Prabhupada called Iran heaven on earth. At night he would sit on the balcony with the devotees and guests. Iran is a Muslim country, so three times a day, at *gayatri* times, over the loudspeakers they have a chant calling everybody to pray. It's beautiful. Prabhupada listened to these prayers going on and then turned to Atreya and asked, "What is this?" Atreya said, "This is the Muslim call to pray to God. They're saying the names of God." Prabhupada said, "That's very good. They're calling everyone to prayer." Atreya said, "But, Prabhupada, isn't it better to say the name of Krishna rather than Allah?" Prabhupada said, "You're asking me to be sectarian?"

Badrinarayan: Once Prabhupada was looking at a newspaper someone had given him. On the front page was hype about the moon shot, "One small step for man, one giant step for mankind." Prabhupada looked at that cursorily and then went to the fifth or sixth page where there was a small article that said, "Taxes are going up to pay for the moon shot." Prabhupada said, "This is their real business. The moon expedition is just a ploy to milk the people."

Bhagavat: As exalted and as glorious as he was, Srila Prabhupada was humble, unlike other gurus who'd say they were something wonderful. Once there was a dispute between senior devotees about Srila Prabhupada's position. A woman disciple wrote to Srila Prabhupada, "Some of the devotees say that you can see what's in the hearts of all your disciples, and other devotees say that you can't do that. What do you say? Please tell me." Prabhupada's secretary read this question and Prabhupada said, "For a greatly advanced pure devotee, this is not at all difficult. He can easily see what is going on in the hearts of all his disciples."

The secretary said, "Okay, I should tell her that you can do this?" Prabhupada said, "I didn't say that. I said, 'A greatly advanced pure devotee could see that.' I am not a greatly advanced pure devotee. I am not even a devotee. I am just trying to be a devotee." So in that statement, he simultaneously exhibited his humility and also showed us what our state of consciousness should be in trying to develop our Krishna consciousness: We are *trying* to be a devotee.

Prithu: We were walking with Srila Prabhupada under the Eiffel Tower in Paris, when Shivananda asked Srila Prabhupada, "What about your internal life, Srila Prabhupada?" Prabhupada was immediately strong. He said, "That you do not require." Shivananda asked again, "But, Srila Prabhupada, we would like to know, what about your internal life?" Prabhupada became furious. He said, "That you do not require." He turned away and walked on, disgusted. We could understand that what is going on between the pure devotee and Krishna is personal, private, and precious. It's not meant for public display. The sentiments and the exchanges between Krishna and His pure devotee are on the *raganuga* platform and are not subject to discussion. Srila Prabhupada said later, "First deserve, then desire." We were fools to try to enter into something that was dear to him.

Madhudvisa:
Under the shade of a jackfruit tree
About a hundred years ago;
In a little house near Calcutta,
A most unlikely place I know.

But 'twas there that Mahaprabhu
Would spread his nam far and wide.
Siddhanta Saraswati
Did preach there and reside.

A most important day it was
In the sorry, sad world of men,
Where millions had been killed in wars,
Been killed and born again.

Been born again to suffer
In the sea of pain and strife.
A most important day it was,
The dawn of new life.

Under the boughs of a jackfruit tree
About a hundred years ago;
In a little house near Calcutta,
A most unlikely place I know.

But it was from that history
Would spread our ISKCON far and wide.
A boy was born,
Not quite born with Krishna on his side.

It was he who brought
Krishna bhakti to the West.
To the Western world,
which was of true religion quite divest.

Receive this sacred knowledge
Of the soul and God from him.
Oh, Srila Prabhupada, you filled our hearts
With nectar to the brim.

Under the boughs of a jackfruit tree
About a hundred years ago;
In a little house near Calcutta
Where the Ganges waves did flow.

The day after Krishna's birthday
He came forth from his mother's womb:
The factual messiah
Who could save us all from doom.

Now our cup of life was empty
And our future hope was dark and dim.
Come Prabhupada to save us,
Bow to him, bow to him.

Under the boughs of a jackfruit tree
About a hundred years ago;
In a little house near Calcutta,
A most unlikely place I know.

But it was there that Mahaprabhu
Would spread his nam far and wide.
Siddhanta Sarasvati
Did preach there and reside.

Srila Prabhupada ki jaya!

Rabindra Svarup: We'd all come to greet Prabhupada in the airport, and there was a big press conference in the passenger lounge. A reporter asked Prabhupada, "Why have you come to America?" He said, "I've come to give you a brain. Your society is headless." He liked to provoke reporters. Then when the press conference was over, Prabhupada was walking back along the long concourse, and I was about twelve or fifteen feet behind him. Coming at us was a weird sight as a television reporter was running, and linked to him was was a guy with a mini-cam on his shoulder. In those days, the mini-cams were not so mini. They came up to Prabhupada. Prabhupada stopped, and they got themselves together while Prabhupada watched. Finally, one guy stuck a microphone into Prabhupada's face and said, "How does your group differ from other Buddhists?"

Prabhupada was so cool. He looked at this reporter, and without a moment's hesitation said, "We have nothing to do with Hinduism or Buddhism. We are teaching the truth, and if you are truthful, you will accept it." The guy was utterly speechless.

There were two things going on in that conversation. One, which always happened with reporters, was that the reporter was playing his little role as a reporter, and Prabhupada was supposed to play his little role as an interviewee. But Prabhupada didn't buy into that structure at all. He was talking to this jiva about his life and the meaning of it. That's what got to the reporter. Second, when Prabhupada answered like that, it destroyed the mental platform on which the question was asked. It got the guy right down to the truth. So when I think of Prabhupada's teachings and how he taught, this incident stays in mind as an example of how we should be and how we should preach. Prabhupada managed to do it in just a few words.

 **Ekanath:** During *gurupuja* in Bombay, the devotees were offering flowers and paying obeisances when I decided to act so-called humbly. When I circled my flowers before His Divine Grace, as is normally done, I deliberately avoided eye contact with Srila Prabhupada and within my mind I loudly declared myself to be a fool and rascal, not deserving to be there. After I paid my *dandavats* and walked back to my spot, a devotee elbowed me and said, "Did you see that?" I said, "See what?" "Srila Prabhupada gave you a gigantic smile." When I heard that, I became embarrassed, because I understood that Srila Prabhupada had read my mind. Even though I lacked seriousness, he had accepted my offering.

Hridayananda Goswami: Once, on Venice Beach, we just finished our walk and returned to the parking lot, where Prabhupada led us in a foot-stamping exercise to get the sand off our shoes. Just then some huge dogs came. Brahmananda and other physically large devotees were there, but everyone was bewildered. No one knew what to do because these dogs were so big. Prabhupada laughed, stepped forward fearlessly and chased the dogs away with his cane.

Prabhupada was fearless. He knew how to deal with every living being. Another time I was with Prabhupada in New Vrindavan in 1972 when he was on his mat, taking a massage outside. When the climate was nice he would take open-air massage every day. Somehow or other a few kittens were playing near Prabhupada, wrestling with each other and rolling around, and they actually rolled onto Prabhupada's lap. I thought, "Oh my God, these embodiments of pollution have rolled onto Prabhupada's lap." (Laughs) But Prabhupada was very kind and affectionate and began to pet the little kittens. He looked up at me and said, "Look, even here there is love." Then I understood that our original love for Krishna becomes perverted in the form of material desires and lust. When Prabhupada saw these little kittens affectionately embracing and rolling around, he could see their original love for Krishna. So he said, "Even here there is love."

The kittens were innocently lying in Prabhupada's lap, and he was petting them when he made another statement that I think is important for any devotee that has responsibility, either as a so-called leader or as a mother or father. Prabhupada said, "If I put my head on your lap and you cut my throat, that is the greatest sin." In other words, if we exploit or abuse the person who's taken shelter of us, that is the greatest sin.

Malati: Just before our departure to London, we went to Srila Prabhupada's apartment and requested his blessings. He was sitting on a low *asana* and had a big garland on. We were allowed to put our head to his feet, and he put his hands on our head. Then, laughing, he put out his arms and asked me to give him my child, Saraswati. Prabhupada held her by his chest, with his face and her face both facing forward. He encircled Saraswati with his garland while he was still wearing it, and then he smiled largely and said, "They will say, 'What kind of *sannyasi* is he?'" He was referring to his godbrothers. He had just spoken to us about how his godbrothers had been sent to London and how they could not get anything done. He said, "The *sannyasis* have gone. I now am sending *grihasthas*."

Brajendranandana: I had the late shift for guarding Prabhupada's quarters in Mayapur, and I wanted to be noticed by Prabhupada. So, when Prabhupada went to the restroom, I thought, "Here's my chance," and I ran down the corridor to wait outside the bathroom with a stick in my hand. When Prabhupada came out he looked at me and said, "What is this? You are guarding?" I said, "Yes, Prabhupada." He said, "What is he guarding?"

Urvasi: I was in the Montreal temple in 1975, and we were going to go to the Mayapur festival and the opening of the Krishna Balaram temple. Before we left for India, I went to Los Angeles to visit my parents, who were favorable to Krishna consciousness. My mother had made garlands for Srila Prabhupada and helped cook. When I was leaving to go back to Montreal, my mother said, "Is there anything I can give your spiritual master? I would like to send something along with you." I said, "Whatever you want." She had guava trees, and she said, "I've made some guava jam. Do you think he would like that?" I said, "I am sure he would." I took her jam with me to India, and in Vrindavan I gave it to Prabhupada's servant to give to him. Later the servant told me that Srila Prabhupada wrote my mother a letter appreciating the jam. It was so sweet. He appreciated that little service so much and wrote quite a long letter to my mother and talked about me, "Your daughter is nicely engaged in devotional service. She is happy, and she is being well cared for."

My mother appreciated that very much.

My mother left her body recently, and I was with her for a couple weeks leading up to her death. I sat by her bedside and read *Bhagavad-gita* to her every day. She had on headphones with Prabhupada chanting *japa,* and just moments before she passed on, she was listening to the Krishna Meditation tape. Her little bit of service and her appreciation for a pure devotee is Srila Prabhupada's mercy.

Rasajna: When I moved into the Brooklyn temple, we gradually started doing a little theater. We helped direct the plays in a more so-called professional manner. I hadn't met Srila Prabhupada yet, but when he was about to come, we prepared the play, "Krishna Kidnaps Rukmini." I played the part of Rukmini, and my husband, Loitaksha, played Krishna. When it was time for the performance, the curtains opened, and there was a big empty space in front of Prabhupada, who was in his rocking chair. Everyone else was behind him. The play opens with Rukmini sitting on the stage writing a letter to Krishna. All of a sudden I got nervous. Even after all my years of doing theater, I thought, "Prabhupada, oh my God, how can I do this?" This was way beyond the fear of going to an audition. I thought, "Here's Prabhupada, the spiritual master of the universe, and I am performing Rukmini. Me. He's going to see this as ridiculous." My knee started shaking. I tried to press it into the floor, and then I took a deep breath. At that point, Prabhupada's presence calmed me down instead of making me nervous, and we had a wonderful performance. Towards the end of the play, when Rukmi's hair gets shaved in a strange way, all the devotees laughed. Prabhupada stopped them from laughing, saying, "Why are you laughing? This isn't funny." After all, it was humiliating for Rukmi. Prabhupada trained us in so many ways.

After the play we were taking our makeup off, when Mohanananda, Prabhupada's servant, came and told us what Prabhupada had said about the performance. Prabhupada had said, "This is better than reading my books," and "I want to take this whole troupe with me to Africa." Unfortunately that wasn't possible because we were the main event of the Brooklyn temple's Sunday feast program. But the fact is that Prabhupada put great importance on theatrical performances. He wanted Krishna consciousness to be presented as a cultural movement. Once in the *Bhagavatam* class he said, "All my disciples should act in plays because when you play the part of any of these characters, you get the feeling of what it's all about. It becomes more real." We tend to forget about our feelings because we get caught up in the process. But when you perform a part, you have to use your feelings to portray the character. For the period of the performance you're transformed. Prabhupada also complimented me. He said, "Rukmini, she was the best."

Another time, we had an ecstatic performance in Mayapur at the Mayapur festival in 1977. Prabhupada was sick and not giving lectures, but he would come to see the play and then go back to his room. We were doing a portion of the *Ramayana,* and I was playing Surpanaka. Somehow we got trees on stage to create a forest effect, and I was coming up the stairs in the back, when Prabhupada saw me and started clapping and laughing. During the exchange between Surpanaka, Lord Ramachandra, and Laksman, he was laughing hard and slapping his legs with both hands. I looked out for just a moment, and all the devotees were watching him. He was the only one who was watching the play. Then he stood up and gave a standing ovation. It was ecstatic. The amazing thing is that Prabhupada did not judge. He was like a child when he watched plays. All our inhibitions as actors and actresses would go away. His personality was amazing in that he could be like a child and also be a wise, saintly person. It's an amazing combination.

Hridayananda Goswami: One *mataji* asked Prabhupada if he was present in his pictures. Prabhupada said, "Yes, therefore my disciples commit so many offenses."

Babhru: At the airport, most of the devotees kept a *kirtan* going on the sidewalk while a few of us sat inside with Srila Prabhupada. He was in a seat, and we were on the floor. Satsvarupa Maharaj was reading newspaper clippings from around the world about the Movement and about Srila Prabhupada. All of a sudden Srila Prabhupada stopped him and said, "I hear that Aniruddha is here in Hawaii, but he has not come to see me." Aniruddha had been staying aloof from the temple, perhaps not doing so well, but had come to the airport to see Srila Prabhupada off. He was in the back of the crowd. At Srila Prabhupada's insistence, the devotees convinced Aniruddha to come inside. Apparently Aniruddha was feeling a little shy. He came in with cut-offs, a T-shirt, and a little stud in his ear and offered his *pranams* to Srila Prabhupada. Prabhupada said, "So, Aniruddha, how are you?" Aniruddha smiled sheepishly and said, "Actually, Prabhupada, not so good." Then Prabhupada signaled to Aniruddha to sit next to him on a seat. Aniruddha said, "No, no, I can't do that." Prabhupada said, "No, no, there is no problem. There is no difficulty. You can sit down." So they sat together and exchanged pleasantries for a few minutes, and then Srila Prabhupada looked at us and said, "In the Los Angeles temple, he was the beginning."

It was clear that what was important to Srila Prabhapda was not a devotee's temporary situation but that the devotee had rendered some important service and that Srila Prabhupada had really appreciated it. That understanding created a revolution in my mind.

Srutakirti: As his servant, I tried to avoid politics. I was only nineteen or twenty years old, and I didn't understand much, so I stayed clear of it. I think I was saved from a lot, and I was always able to appreciate Srila Prabhupada through my personal service to him. Today's very special; it's Father's Day, and Srila Prabhupada was very much my father.

Madhudvisa: Separation.
Well, there is no separation.
As I speak this, now I know
That separation doth the strength
Of love connections show.

Now one who feels no separation
Did no connection get.
And one who feels deep separation
Has firm connection yet.

Now separation does not mean
To make a show of tears;
To make one's sorrow prominent
Just to win beginners' cheers.

Separation means to feel
Deep within your heart
That I depend on Prabhupada
And nothing shall us part.

Now we all depend on Prabhupada,
From neophyte to master.
And one who puts aside his grace
Is heading for disaster.

He is the first, he is the last,
The acharya, and the founder.
No one worked so hard as he
Or kept a standard sounder.

To the end of time he will be known
As ISKCON's suckling mother;

His books, the nourishment of us all—
Where comes such another?

So as we're struggling forward
We should hang upon his grace.
Brother side of brother,
Both in our humble place.

And as we are expanding
No one should forget
The heavy dues we owe to him—
Unrepayable the debt.

And then, if we're honest,
We'll know for sure he's here
And will always feel secure
And free from fear.

But if we think that now he's gone,
We will struggle on our own.
Ahhh. Dread fear and death surround—
Hey, what can you do alone?

A little karma, a little charisma,
It will all be finished in the end.
Punah mushika bhava: again become a mouse,
To ignominy condemned.

Do not think there's aught in you
That Prabhupada does not lend.
Know this truth, depend on him,
And you will see him once again.

Srila Prabhupada *ki jaya!*

GLOSSARY

abhishek—the ceremony of bathing the Deity of the Lord or the feet a great devotee.

arati—a ceremony of worship to the Deity form of the Lord or His pure devotee.

asana—seat

ashram—(1) one of the four spiritual orders of life; (2) a residence for those in spiritual practice.

atmarama verse—a verse from the *Srimad-Bhagavatam* (1.7.10), which explains that all types of spiritual seekers are attracted to Krishna.

babaji—a renounced devotee who practices chanting Hare Krishna in solitude.

Bhagavad-gita—"Song of God," the essential summary of spiritual knowledge spoken to Arjuna by the Supreme Lord, Sri Krishna.

Bhagavatam—See: *Srimad-Bhagavatam*.

bhakta—a devotee, one who practices devotion (to God).

bhakti—devotion and love, especially for the Supreme Lord.

bhava—ecstasy; the stage of *bhakti* just prior to pure love for God.

bhoga—unoffered foodstuff.

bhogi yogi—bogus yogi.

bidi—a cigarette.

brahmachari—a male celibate student of the spiritual master.

brahmacharini—a female celibate student of the spiritual master.

brahman—the intelligent class; a second spiritual initiation.

Brahma-samhita—a scriptural text, prayers by to Lord Krishna by Lord Brahma.

burfi—a sweet similar to a milk fudge.

chaddar—a shawl.

Chaitanya-caritamrita—the authoritative scripture by Krishnadas
    Kaviraj, which describes Lord Chaitanya's teachings and
    pastimes.

Chaitanya Mahaprabhu, Lord—the avatar of Lord Krishna in this
    age whose mission is to teach love of God through the chant-
    ing of His holy names.

chamara—a yak-tail fan.

chapati—a whole-wheat flatbread.

charanamrita—water remnants from bathing the Deity or a saintly
    person.

chelas—followers.

dahl—a spicy bean or pea soup.

danda—the staff of a sannyasi.

dandavats—prostrate obeisances.

darshan—audience with the Deity or a saintly person.

dham—a holy place.

dharmsala—an inexpensive residence set up especially for pilgrims.

dhoti—the standard Indian men's garment, a simple piece of cloth
    wrapped around the lower body.

diksa guru—the guru who gives formal initiation into devotional
    life.

gumsha—a short cloth wrapped around the lower body.

Gaudiya Math—the spiritual organization and missions founded
    by Srila Bhaktisiddhanta Sarasvati, the spiritual master of A.C.
    Bhaktivedanta Swami Prabhupada.

Gaudiya Vaishnav—a follower of Lord Krishna (Vishnu) in the
    line from Lord Chaitanya Mahaprabhu.

gayatri—a transcendental vibration chanted by *brahmans* for
    spiritual realization.

GBC—the Governing Body Commission of ISKCON, the International Society for Krishna Consciousness.

ghee—clarified butter.

Gita—See: *Bhagavad-gita.*

gopas—the cowherd boys and men of Vrindavan, who are among the most advanced devotees of Lord Krishna.

gopis—the cowherd girls and women of Vrindavan, who are the most advanced and intimate devotees of Lord Krishna.

gopi bhava—the state of love felt by the *gopis,* Krishna's most intimate devotees.

gopi chandana—a light-yellow clay found in India and used especially to apply the *tilak* mark.

grihastha—the stage, or one in that stage, of householder life according to the Vedic social system.

gur—a type of dark, natural sugar.

gurukula—the school of the spiritual master.

gurupuja—the ceremony of worship to the spiritual master.

halava—a dessert made from toasted grains, sugar, and butter.

harinam [sankirtan]—congregational, public chanting of the holy names of Hari, or Krishna.

Isopanishad—See: *Sri Isopanishad.*

japa—soft, measured chanting of the holy names of God, performed with the aid of 108 prayer beads.

jaya—an expression of acclaim.

jalebis—a dessert made by deep frying swirls of batter and then soaking them in a flavored syrup.

Janmastami—the day of celebration of the "birthday," or appearance day, of Lord Krishna.

kachori—a deep-fried stuffed savory pastry.

kanistha—neophyte.

kartals—small hand cymbals used to accompany
   chanting during *kirtans*.

karma—action; results of fruitive actions.

karmi—one engaged in karma (fruitive activity); a materialist.

kichari—a cooked preparation made from spiced rice and lentils.

ki jaya—an expression of acclaim.

kirtan—chanting of the Lord's names and glories.

kirtan mandap—a shelter for a *kirtan* party.

kopins—a men's undergarment.

Krishna—the all-attractive Supreme Lord, God, in his original,
   eternal form.

kurta—the long, loose-fitting, Indian men's shirt.

lila—transcendental pastimes of the Lord; a type of relationship
   with the Lord.

lota—a small pot for water used for personal cleaning.

madhyama-adhikari—one in the intermediate stage of God
   realization.

maha—See *maha prasadam*.

mahabhagavata—a great personality who sees all in relation to
   God.

maha prasadam—*prasadam* remnants directly from the plate or the
   person of the Deity or the pure devotee.

mandir—a temple.

mangalacharanam—the standard prayers of glorification to the
   spiritual master.

mangal arati—pre-dawn worship ceremony in temples of the Lord.

mataji—"mother," a respectful appellation for women; a
   respected woman.

maya—illusion, accepting as true what is not; forgetfulness of
   Krishna, or God, and our own spiritual nature.

mayavadi—impersonalist or voidist, who adheres to the mistaken belief that God is ultimately formless and without personality.

mleccha—a low-class person; meat-eater.

mridanga—a two-headed drum used to accompany chanting in *kirtan*.

muchi—dirty.

murti—a bona fide form of the Lord, wherein He appears to accept service.

nagar sankirtan—the congregational chanting of the Lord's names in moving line.

pakoras—vegetable pieces fried in a spiced chick-pea-flour batter.

Panchatattva—Lord Chaitanya with His associates.

pandal—a large tent covering.

parampara—the line of disciplic succession; also, that in accordance with their teachings.

paratha—griddle-fried whole-wheat bread.

parikram—circumambulation of a holy place.

pranams—obeisances with folded hands.

prasadam—"mercy," vegetarian foodstuffs and other items that are sanctified by being first offered to Lord Krishna for His enjoyment.

prema—pure, spontaneous devotional love for God.

puja—worship service.

pujari—the priest who cares for and performs worship service for the Lord.

Puranas—the eighteen historical, scriptural supplements to the *Vedas*.

puri—a fried, puffed, white-flour flatbread.

puspanjali—a flower-offering ceremony.

Radha, Radharani—the eternal consort of Lord Krishna, a manifestation of His internal pleasure potency.

rasa—the relationship between the Lord and the living entities, which is in different categories.

rasa lila—Krishna's pastime, or *lila,* of dancing with the *gopis.*

rasagulla—a milk sweet made from curd soaked in sweetened water.

rasa malai—a sweet consisting of flattened curd balls in sweetened, flavored condensed milk.

Rathayatra—a large *sankirtan* festival wherein Deities of the Lord ride in parade.

Rig Veda—the first of the four *Vedas,* the original scriptures spoken by the Lord Himself.

sadhana—disciplined spiritual practice.

sadhu—a saint, holy man, or Krishna conscious devotee.

sahajiya—a pretender who imitates the outward mood and ecstasies of the Lord's devotee, but who is without any real devotion or internal realization.

samadhi—(1) a spiritual trance, complete absorption in God consciousness; (2) a tomb memorial of a saintly person.

Samhitas—collections of Vedic scriptures.

samosa— a fried pastry, stuffed with spiced vegetables.

sandesh—a sweet prepared from milk curd.

sankirtan—congregational glorification of God, especially through chanting of His holy name, the recommended process of yoga for this age.

sannyasa—the renounced order of spiritual life.

sannyasi—one in the renounced order of spiritual life.

sari—the standard woman's garment in Indian society, a long piece of (usually decorative) cloth wrapped around the lower and upper body and often also covering the head.

shila—a small stone form of the Lord.

siddha deha—one's personal spiritual identity.

sikha—the tuft of hair a shaven-headed Vaishnava devotee leaves at the center back of the head.

siksa guru—the guru who gives spiritual guidance.

sloka—a verse.

Sri Isopanishad—an ancient, 19-verse, Upanishadic scripture providing insight into God's nature.

Srimad-Bhagavatam—the scriptural *Purana,* or history, written by Vyasadeva specifically to give an understanding of Lord Sri Krishna.

subji—a cooked vegetable preparation.

thali—a plate

tilak—sacred clay marking the body of a devotee as a temple of God.

tulasi—a great devotee of Krishna, in the form of a plant.

ugra-karma—horrible, or sinful, works that bring concomitant karmic reactions.

Upanishads—108 philosophical treatises that appear within the *Vedas.*

urad dahl—a soup made from the *urad* bean.

uttama-adhikari—one in the highest stage of God-realization.

Vaishnav—a devotee of the Supreme Lord Vishnu, or Krishna.

vanaprastha—one retired from householder life to cultivate greater renunciation, according to the Vedic social system.

vani—the order, or instructions, of the spiritual master.

varnashram—the four divisions of society and four divisions of spiritual life.

varnashram-dharma—*varnashram,* especially the rules and duties of *varnashram.*

Vedanta Sutra—the philosophical summary of all Vedic conclusions, written in short aphorisms by Srila Vyasadeva.

Vedas—the original four revealed scriptures, first spoken by the

Lord Himself, and their supplements.

Vishnu—the all-pervading Personality of Godhead, a plenary expansion of Krishna.

vyasasana—the seat of honor offered to the spiritual master.

Vyasa-puja—the observance of the appearance day of one's spiritual master, the representative of Vyasadeva.

wala—seller.

yajna—sacrifice; sacrificial ceremony.

yogi—one who practices spiritual discipline to link with the Supreme.

To order
more volumes of

MEMORIES

Anecdotes of a Modern-Day Saint

or

MEMORIES:
THE VIDEO SERIES

please
contact:

www.monsoonmedia.org

or

www.prabhupada.tv